SCHAUM'S OUTLINE OF

THEORY AND PROBLEMS

OF

INVESTMENTS

•

JACK CLARK FRANCIS, Ph.D.
Professor of Economics and Finance
Bernard M. Baruch College
City University of New York

RICHARD W. TAYLOR, Ph.D., C.F.A.
Professor of Finance
Arkansas State University

SCHAUM'S OUTLINE SERIES
McGRAW-HILL, INC.
New York St. Louis San Francisco Auckland Bogotá Caracas
Lisbon London Madrid Mexico Milan Montreal
New Delhi Paris San Juan Singapore
Sydney Tokyo Toronto

JACK CLARK FRANCIS, Ph.D., received his Bachelor's and M.B.A. degrees from Indiana University and obtained his Ph.D. from the University of Washington in Seattle. Dr. Francis has been a Professor of Economics and Finance at Bernard M. Baruch College in New York City since leaving the Federal Reserve. Before that he was at The Wharton School of Finance. He has authored five editions of *Investments: Analysis and Management* and two editions of *Management of Investments,* both published by McGraw-Hill, Inc. among other titles.

RICHARD W. TAYLOR, Ph.D., is currently Professor of Finance at Arkansas State University in Jonesboro. He received his Ph.D. from Louisiana Tech University and is a chartered financial analyst (C.F.A.). Dr. Taylor has published papers in such journals as *The Financial Review, Financial Analysts Journal,* and *The Journal of Portfolio Management*. In addition, he has served as a referee for several business and finance journals.

This book is printed on recycled paper containing a minimum of 50% total recycled fiber with 10% postconsumer de-inked fiber.

Schaum's Outline of Theory and Problems of
INVESTMENTS

2 3 4 5 6 7 8 9 10 11 12 13 14 15 16 17 18 19 20 SHP SHP 9 2

ISBN 0-07-021807-2

Sponsoring Editor: John Aliano
Production Supervisor: Annette Mayeski
Editing Supervisors: Meg Tobin, Maureen Walker
Cover design by Amy E. Becker.

Library of Congress Cataloging-in-Publication Data

Francis, Jack Clark.
Schaum's outline of investments/Jack Clark Francis, Richard W. Taylor.
p. cm.—(Schaum's outline series)
Includes index.
ISBN 0-07-021807-2
1. Investments—Outlines, syllabi, etc. 2. Investments—Problems, exercises, etc. I. Taylor, Richard W. II. Title.
HG4521.F695 1992
332.6—dc20 91-29019
CIP

Dedicated to the memory of my late father-in-law,
M. James Moss, M.D.

JACK CLARK FRANCIS

Dedicated to the memory of my grandparents,
Clyde and Ida Woodring.

RICHARD W. TAYLOR

Preface

This INVESTMENTS book is designed to aid investors, students of financial investing, and those studying for the Chartered Financial Analysts (CFA) exam. The book may be used as a textbook, a supplement to a textbook, a reference book, or a self-study tool.

In the Schaum's tradition, this book emphasizes solved problems. Many definitions, explanations, graphs, and realistic examples are provided too. But, question and answer sets and solved problems are the backbone of all Schaum's books. Oftentimes the answers to the solved problems cannot be determined from material covered in the preceding pages. The reader is expected to learn by reading the question and its solution.

This book has many numerical examples and problems that have quantitative answers. There are not as many essay questions and answers. This is in keeping with the Schaum's emphasis on solved problems. It is also appropriate because investment decision-making largely involves quantitative theories, financial planning that is denominated in dollars, and choices between quantitative alternatives.

We wrote INVESTMENTS to be a comprehensive monograph that does not favor any particular approach to investment analysis. At least one complete chapter is devoted to every major investments theory or school of thought.

We have labored to create a unique and valuable learning tool. But, we have not done it all ourselves. John Aliano, Schaum's Executive Editor; Meg Tobin, Schaum's Senior Editing Supervisor; Maureen Walker, Front Matter Editor, and some expert reviewers who read earlier drafts of the book and made valuable criticisms and suggestions contributed significantly to this final product.

JACK CLARK FRANCIS
RICHARD W. TAYLOR

Contents

Chapter 1

Money Market Securities

1.1 MONEY MARKETS

The *money market* is a large, wholesale market where billions of dollars of low-risk, unsecured, short-term, zero coupon debt instruments that are highly liquid are issued and actively traded every day. The money markets in the United States are large—larger than the New York Stock Exchange, for example.

Investors buy money market securities at *discount* from their face values and reap whatever income they may earn from price appreciation that typically occurs as the maturity date of the security draws near. At maturity the face value (or principal) is repaid to the investor owning the security on that date. If market interest rates rise, then the market prices of almost all debt securities fall in response, so investor losses that result from changes in the market interest rates are a possibility—this is called *interest-rate risk*. Most issues of money market securities have such high credit ratings that *risk of default* is almost nonexistent.

1.2 MARKETS ARE MADE BY DEALERS AND BROKERS

Brokers are salespeople who work for a commission, and they have no money of their own invested in the securities they sell. *Dealers* are market-makers who put their own money at risk by investing in an inventory of the security which they are marketing. Security dealers make markets by investing in an inventory of the securities being sold and hiring brokers to sell the securities. Money market dealers include big banks (like Citibank, Morgan-Guaranty, Bank of America, and Chase-Manhattan) and investment-banking-and-brokerage firms (like Merrill Lynch Pierce Fenner and Smith and Salomon Brothers). Most dealers will also act as brokers for their clients.

Money market commission rates are tiny, typically a small fraction of 1 percent of the value of the transaction. That is why money market securities are like money: There is zero commission charged for dealing in domestic money.

Multimillion dollar money market transactions are routinely done hurriedly over the telephone without the aid of lawyers or contracts. No deal is any better than the character of the individuals and the institutions behind it. Therefore, the existing money market participants will only deal with respectable individuals who are employed by stable organizations that are well-known for being trustworthy.

Money market dealers are financial *market-makers* who earn their livelihoods by (1) helping savers get good investments and (2) channeling the invested money to those who need to borrow funds.

1.3 UNITED STATES TREASURY BILLS

United States Treasury bills (T-bills) are the most riskless security in the world. T-bills are default-free. Investors can nevertheless suffer losses from changes in the market interest rates, because the market prices of all debt securities vary inversely with market interest rates. The Federal Reserve Bank of New York holds a sealed-bid auction at which millions of dollars worth of Treasury bills are issued every week. New T-bills with maturities of 13, 26, and 52 weeks (and occasionally tax anticipation bills) in denominations of $1,000, $5,000, $10,000, $100,000, and $1 million are issued to pay off previously issued Treasury securities that are maturing and/or to increase the federal debt. Roughly one-quarter of the outstanding federal debt is in the form of T-bills.

EXAMPLE 1.1 After making several phone calls, Mr. Tom Clark, the manager of the T-bill trading desk at Salomon Brothers, learns that most T-bill dealers around the world are offering to sell T-bills that mature in 1 month at a price that results in an *asked yield* of 6.10 percent. None of these dealers *hit* or accept Tom's offer to buy at a *bid yield* of 6.15 percent. (The bid yield of 6.15 percent results in a lower dollar price than the asked yield of 6.10 percent since bond prices and bond yields move inversely.)

Tom needs to buy some more T-bills because that particular money market security is currently selling so briskly that Salomon's brokers are about to sell out the firm's inventory of it. So, Tom calls back one of the dealers and drops his bid yield from 6.15 percent to 6.11 percent (a change that results in a higher bid price in dollar terms). Tom is relieved to hear the seller say that they are willing to raise their asked yield to 6.11 to meet Tom's bid yield of 6.11 percent if Tom will buy *size*. Tom asks how much size and is told $30 million worth at that price. Tom gladly agrees to the 6.11 percent yield; a $30 million trade is consummated in a routine 20-second phone call. The paperwork for the transaction is taken care of later by the operations (or back-room) personnel at the buyer's and seller's firms.

The *bid-asked spread* of two *basis-points* (6.11% − 6.09% = .02) is the dealer's reward for making a market in T-bills. A few basis-points on a multimillion T-bill transaction translates into a bid-asked spread worth several thousands of dollars to the dealer who gets it.

SOLVED PROBLEM 1.1

Lorraine Sabatini invested in a $10,000 T-bill that had 24 days until it matured. She paid a purchase price of $9,940.47, held the T-bill to maturity, and then redeemed it for its face value. What was Lorraine's rate of return?

SOLUTION

Lorraine earned a short-term capital gain of ($10,000 − $9,940.47 =) $59.53. Her 24-day rate of price appreciation was 598/100,000 of 1 percent.

$$\frac{\$10{,}000.00}{\$9{,}940.47} = 1.00598 = 1.0 + (598/100{,}000 \text{ of } 1\%)$$

Since there are 15.2 time periods of 24 days length in a 365-day year, we annualize Lorraine's 24-day rate of return to obtain her effective annualized rate of return of 9.48 percent per annum:

$$(1.00598)^{15.2} = 1.0948 = 1.0 + (9.48\% \text{ ann. rate of ret.})$$

In terms of simple (or noncompounded) rates of return Lorraine earned a slightly lower rate of return over the 24-day period:

$$\frac{\$59.53}{\$10{,}000} = .00593 = 593/100{,}000 \text{ of } 1\%$$

Annualizing the simple rate of 24-day interest reveals that Lorraine's annualized simple rate of interest was 9.01 percent per annum:

$$\left(\frac{\$10{,}000 - \$9{,}940.47}{\$10{,}000}\right) \times \left(\frac{365 \text{ days}}{24 \text{ days}}\right) = .0901 = 9.01\%$$

Simple rates of return are less than the true (or effective) rates of return (or interest rates) because they ignore compounding (and the interest on the interest).

1.4 BANKER'S ACCEPTANCES, BAs

A *banker's acceptance (BA)* is a document that starts out as a tentative loan agreement and later becomes a marketable money market security. BAs begin as a written order for a particular bank to pay some stipulated amount of money to the holder of the BA on a specified date. When a bank accepts a BA two things happen: (1) a loan agreement between the accepting bank and some borrower who has applied to that bank for a loan is finalized, and (2) that bank assumes the irrevocable legal responsibility to pay off that BA on its maturity date. After being accepted by a reputable bank BAs can be traded in active secondary markets. BAs are high-quality loan agreements backed by the legal obligations to pay of both the borrower and the accepting bank.

SOLVED PROBLEM 1.2

Describe how a BA can be created.

SOLUTION

Two banks are required to create one BA. The buyer's bank and the seller's bank insert themselves, for prepaid fees, as middlemen between the buyer and the seller to facilitate the transaction and ensure that the prearranged delivery and payment occurs. The exporter ships the goods to a warehouse in the city near where the importer is located and sends the accompanying paperwork to the importer's bank for acceptance. If the imported goods arrive on time and in good condition, the importer's bank accepts the BA by having one of its officers sign and return it to the exporter's bank.

BAs are essentially interest-bearing loan agreements stipulating that the importer pay the accepting bank weeks or months later. The importer's bank can either (1) sell the BA before its maturity date to another investor, or (2) hold the BA as an investment in its own portfolio. When the BA matures, the importer must pay whoever owns it at that time.

1.5 FEDERAL FUNDS

All banks that are members of the Federal Reserve system (or Fed) are required to maintain deposits at their district Federal Reserve Bank. The purpose of these deposits is to provide liquidity in case of a *run* on the bank's deposits. These required deposits must meet or exceed a stipulated minimum percentage of a bank's average deposits that are called *reserves on deposit at the Fed,* or more simply, *reserves.*

Some banks (in particular, big city banks) often have insufficient deposits to meet the reserves the Federal Reserve requires. In contrast with those banks that usually generate insufficient deposits to meet their required level of reserves, some other banks (typically, small- and medium-sized suburban and country banks) usually experience insufficient loan demand to utilize all their reserves. This latter group of banks has *excess reserves;* they enjoy deposit inflows that provide more reserves than the bank can lend out profitably. The *Fed funds market* is a money market that grew up to balance this disparity of required reserves between these two groups of banks.

Federal Reserve regulations require that every 2 weeks the banks of the nation tally up their loans and deposits to make sure that they meet the legal reserve requirements. In order to meet the Federal Reserve system's requirements those banks that have insufficient reserves may borrow reserves from those banks that have excess reserves. These bank reserves are typically borrowed for only 1 day (or overnight). The interest rate on these short-term interbank loans is called the *Fed funds rate.*

The *Fed funds market* is essentially an interbank money market where banks and Fed funds dealers buy and sell excess bank reserves. The Fed funds rate fluctuates minute-by-minute every day that banks are open. This so-called "funds rate" is thought by many to be the best measure of how tight the lending capacity of the U.S. banking system is stretched at any given moment. The Fed funds rate has fluctuated between 2 and 20 percent (stated at an annualized rate of interest) over the decades and has been more volatile than any other published rate of interest at times.

The Fed funds market is a communications network rather than a centralized marketplace. Many of the transactions are consummated when two banks deal directly with each other. Some middle- and large-sized banks operate as dealers, and there are several private firms that broker Fed funds. Most transactions are in the $1 million to $40 million range.

SOLVED PROBLEM 1.3

What are *term Fed funds?*

SOLUTION

Term Fed funds are Fed funds loans covering periods as short as a week or as long as 6 months, and, in a few cases, as much as 3 years. These longer-term arrangements develop when a bank that is perennially short of reserves makes a deal with a bank that consistently has excess reserves.

1.6 CERTIFICATES OF DEPOSIT, CDs

Thousands of small investors in the United States purchase certificates of deposit (CDs) at banks. For a small saver, buying a CD is like opening a savings account. Most banks and their branches sell CDs in denominations of $1,000, $5,000, and $10,000 with maturities as short as 14, 30, 60, 90, 180, and 360 days and as long as 2, 3, and 5 years. These CDs are governed by a deposit contract that stipulates a rate of interest on which the banker and the depositor settle before the agreement is signed. If savers withdraw the deposit before the CD matures, they receive a lower (penalty) interest rate. Money market CDs are similar to the CDs for small savers—except that the denominations are larger, they are traded in active secondary markets, they pay (20 to 50 basis points) higher rates of interest, and their terms are negotiable.

Aggressive big city banks send vice-presidents out to call on large corporations, municipalities, and foreign governments and sell the bank's CDs. This is called *buying deposits.* The bank vice-president negotiates with the financial officers of the corporations, municipalities, and foreign governments by tailoring the maturity, the dollar amount, and the interest rate on each CD to whatever terms the investment officer will accept (and, of course, from which the bank can expect to profit). These negotiable CDs are issued in $100,000 or more denominations. Maturities of 1 to 3 months are common. Bankers call the process of aggessively buying deposits when credit conditions warrant it *liability management.*

The level of interest rates paid on negotiable CDs follows T-bill rates closely. But, CD rates are always above T-bill rates because T-bills are less risky—they are default-free. In contrast, only the first $100,000 of each CD is insured by the FDIC and therefore the possibility of default exists for CDs.

SOLVED PROBLEM 1.4

What is the effective interest rate that banks pay to obtain deposits from a CD with a 7 percent rate of interest?

SOLUTION

Banks are required to meet reserve requirements and to pay for Federal Deposit Insurance Corporation (FDIC) insurance on CD deposits. As a result of these expenses CDs cost the banks that issue them more than merely the interest rate on the CD. Taking 3 percent out of every CD dollar of deposit to hold as non-earning required reserves at a Federal Reserve bank means that the effective interest expense costs the bank about 103 percent of the interest rate paid written on the CD's contract agreement. In addition, FDIC insurance adds another 8 basis points to the effective interest expense. Thus, if a bank has a 7 percent CD, The *all-in cost* of that CD is

7.0% × 1.03 = 7.21%	103 percent of 7% because of 3% required reserves
+ .08	eight basis points for FDIC insurance
7.29%	the all-in cost to a bank for a 7% CD

SOLVED PROBLEM 1.5

What is the yield on a CD with an 8 percent coupon rate, 90 days to maturity when initially issued, and 60 days remaining until its maturity, if it is selling at 1 percent above (or 101 percent of) its face value?

SOLUTION

We have $r = .08 = 8\% =$ coupon rate, $T = 90$ days to maturity at initial issue, $t = 60$ days remaining to maturity, $P = 1.01$ and we solve for the yield y. The multiplication factors used in the annualization are given first:

$$\frac{360}{t} = \frac{360}{60} = 6 \text{ times} \qquad \text{multiplication factor for the } T\text{-day yield}$$

$$\frac{T}{360} = \frac{90}{360} = \frac{1}{4} \qquad \text{multiplication factor for the annual interest rate } r$$

$$y = \frac{1.0 + r(T/360)}{P} - 1.0$$

$$= \frac{1.0 + .08\left(\frac{90}{360}\right)}{1.01} - 1.0$$

$$y = 1.00990099 - 1.0 = .00990099 = \tfrac{99}{1000} \text{ of } 1\%$$

The yield over the 60-day holding period is $.0099 = \frac{99}{1000}$ of 1%.

$$y = \left[\frac{1.0 + r(T/360)}{P} - 1.0\right]\left(\frac{360}{t}\right)$$

$$= \left[\frac{1.0 + .08\left(\frac{90}{360}\right)}{1.01} - 1.0\right]\left(\frac{360}{60}\right)$$

$$= (.00990099)(6 \text{ times}) = .0594 = 5.94\%$$

The annualized yield published in the newspapers would be 5.94 percent; this is not a true effective or compounded rate of return, cy:

$$\text{cy} = \left[\frac{1.0 + r(T/360)}{P}\right]^{360/t} - 1.0$$

$$= \left[\frac{1.0 + .08(\frac{90}{360})}{1.01}\right]^{360/60} - 1.0$$

$$= \left(\frac{1.02}{1.01}\right)^{6} - 1.0 = (1.00990099)^{6} - 1.0$$

$$= .06089 = 6.089\%$$

The compounded rate of return, cy, is 6.089 percent at an annual rate.

1.7 EURODOLLARS

A deposit that is made in either an American or foreign bank or branch bank located anywhere outside of the United States is called a *Eurodollar deposit* as long as it is denominated in dollars. Dollars deposited in the Singapore office of Chase-Manhattan Bank in a dollar-denominated account are called Eurodollars, for instance. In addition, dollars deposited in the New York City office of Barclay's Bank (headquartered in Great Britain) are Eurodeposits. The interest rate on Euros tracks the Fed funds rate; foreign banks from around the world can sell their excess reserves held in dollars in the Fed funds market in the United States. Such transactions are called *Europlacements*.

The Eurodollar market exists around the world; it is open 24 hours a day. New York City and Singapore are the world's major *Eurocenters*, where most big Eurodollar transactions occur. The major Eurodollar brokerages are international firms that have offices in New York City, London, Singapore, Paris, and other Eurocenters. They broker both Eurodeposits and foreign exchange, since the two are interrelated. These firms are essentially providing their client banks fast information processing networks that encircle the globe.

The market for Euros is like the Fed funds market, except that some lags are added. Some Eurodollars are sold in an active cash market where delivery is immediate, just like Fed funds. More often they are sold "tom next" (for tomorrow next delivery, that is, with a 2-day lag) to allow the foreign exchange forward market the time it needs to clear. The minimum sized Euro transaction is $1 million, with trades of $10 to $50 million being most common.

1.8 COMMERCIAL PAPER

Commercial paper is an unsecured promissory note for a stipulated amount that matures on a specific date and is issued by a corporation. Over 1,000 industrial firms (like GM), finance companies (like the General Motors Acceptance Corporation), commercial banks, bank holding companies, and municipalities that have high credit ratings issue these debt securities at a *discount* below their maturity value.

Commercial paper can be issued in bearer form or as a registered security; the bearer form is more popular. Denominations as low as $25,000 occur, but multimillion papers are most common. Corporations that are temporarily cash-rich and money market mutual funds are the main buyers. Most of it is held to maturity, but active secondary markets also exist for investors who need to liquidate their commercial paper before its maturity date.

There is a *tiered market* for commercial paper. Corporations with the highest ratings can borrow for 40 basis points above the rates paid on Treasury bills with similar maturities, while some issuers may have to pay as much as 200 basis points above the T-bill rate. Corporations with medium- and low-quality credit ratings are denied access to the commercial paper market.

Commercial paper dealers (like Goldman, Sachs & Company, for instance) charge a $\frac{1}{8}$ of 1% fee to find investors. The dealers also stand ready to make secondary markets in the paper they sell. The largest issuers (like GMAC) sell their own paper directly to buyers.

SOLVED PROBLEM 1.6

Fidelity's money market mutual fund bought \$5 million commercial paper directly from GMAC (to save the dealer's fee) for \$4,875,000. Fidelity earned what effective rate of return after holding the investment until its maturity 90 days later?

SOLUTION

$$\frac{\$5{,}000{,}000}{\$4{,}875{,}000} - 1.0 = .02564 = 2.564\% \text{ per quarter}$$

$$(1.02564)^4 - 1.0 = 1.10657 - 1.0 = 10.657\% \text{ per annum}$$

Fidelity earned 2.564% per quarter, or 10.657% at an annualized effective (compounded) rate of interest.

SOLVED PROBLEM 1.7

In addition to the interest expense, what other costs are involved for companies that raise money by selling commercial paper?

SOLUTION

Issuers pay the following costs, in addition to the interest on the loan:

(1) \$6,000 to \$30,000 charge to have the issuer's commercial paper rated by a service like Standard & Poors

(2) Agents fees to banks that do the necessary paperwork for the issuer

(3) $\frac{1}{2}$ of 1% of the value of the issue, the fee payable to a bank for a standby loan commitment to back the commercial paper issue

(4) $\frac{1}{8}$ of 1% dealers fee to sell the paper

1.9 REPURCHASE AGREEMENTS, REPOS

Repurchase agreements are collateralized loans. Dealers in Treasury securities, dealers in securities issued by federal agencies, and large banks are the primary borrowers that use repos. To a lesser extent dealers who make markets in BAs, CDs, and Euros also use repo financing. These security dealers use repos to help finance their inventories of securities. Securities in the dealers' inventory are used as collateral. Most commonly, the security dealer sells several million dollars worth of securities to a bank and simultaneously promises to buy back those same securities the following day at a slightly higher price. Such transactions are called *overnight repos*. Repos are sometimes called *sale-repurchase agreements,* a less popular name but descriptive of the transaction.

Repos are sold at discount so that the amount by which the loan repayment exceeds the amount of the collateralized loan equals the borrower's interest expense for that loan. This interest expense is normally stated as a percent of the loan and referred to as the *repo rate*. The repo rate is the interest rate that lenders charge borrowers for making repo agreements. The repo rate fluctuates from 10 to 200 basis points below the Fed funds rate. The repo rate is lower than the Fed funds rate because the repos are viewed as being less risky since they are collateralized loans and Fed funds are not.

Many billions of dollars of overnight repos are created every day. It is impossible to accurately measure the entire volume of repos, but it has been estimated that the *term repo* market is twice the size of the overnight repo market. Term repos are just like overnight repos, except that the collateralized loan lasts for a week, a month, a few months, or occasionally longer. The repo market is enormous and growing.

To summarize, a security dealer that obtains a repo gets a collateralized loan. The party that facilitates the creation of a repo by making the loan to finance the inventory creates a position for itself that is called a *reverse repo,* or, more frequently, simply a *reverse*. One firm's repo is another firm's reverse, they are simply opposite sides of the same transaction.

An *open repo* is a continuing contract for the lender to provide the dealer with a certain amount of funds for an extended time period. However, the agreement allows either party to terminate it at any time. The security dealer also typically has the *right of substitution* in a open repo. The dealer can substitute other securities of equal value for the collateral if desired. The rates on open repos are slightly above the overnight repo rate.

SOLVED PROBLEM 1.8

If Morgan-Guaranty Bank repos $20 million worth of Treasury securities overnight at 8 percent interest, what will be the interest expense the bank must pay to gain this temporary liquidity?

SOLUTION

Using a 360-day year and assuming a flat loan, the interest is

$$\begin{pmatrix}\text{Principal}\\ \text{amount}\end{pmatrix} \times \begin{pmatrix}\text{repo}\\ \text{rate}\end{pmatrix} \times \left(\frac{\text{days repo is outstanding}}{360 \text{ days}}\right) = \begin{pmatrix}\text{interest}\\ \text{due}\end{pmatrix}$$

$$(\$20 \text{ million}) \times (.08) \times (\tfrac{1}{360}) = \$4{,}444$$

Thus, Morgan Bank should pay the repo dealer ($20 million principal + $4,444 interest =) $20,004,444 when it buys back its securities.

With term repo transactions the interest income goes to the lender holding Morgan's securities as collateral. As a result of this additional interest income it receives from holding Morgan's securities, the lender must deduct that interest income from the price Morgan Bank would have to pay to repurchase its securities. To make matters more complicated, the lender may require that Morgan Bank post margin. This would involve a loan for slightly less than the securities $20 million value so that the lender held collateral that was worth more than the loan, to protect itself in case of losses of any kind. Thus, the lender might give the securities a $500,000 *haircut* (that is, require a margin of $500,000) and only loan $19.5 million on the $20 million of collateral.

True-False Questions

1.1 Eurodollar CDs are pound-denominated CD deposits that are made in foreign banks that are located in foreign countries.

1.2 If someone makes a dollar-denominated deposit in the Los Angeles branch of a Japanese bank that deposit is not a Eurodollar deposit.

1.3 When the yield that is bid for a Eurodollar deposit is raised the dollar value of that bid is thereby decreased.

1.4 Most money market securities are sold at a discount from their face value so that the only income their investors get is from possible price appreciation.

1.5 Most money market securities have maturities of 270 days or less in order to be exempt from the requirement of SEC registration.

1.6 Money market securities are issued by firms that sometimes have poor credit ratings.

1.7 Some Treasury bills have longer maturities than other money market securities.

1.8 A treasury bond that had 20 years until maturity when initially issued, but that had only 6 months left until its approaching maturity date would be categorized as a money market security.

1.9 Money market commissions are high compared to the commissions on other securities because they are not traded in organized exchanges.

1.10 Banks that are members of the Federal Reserve system are required to keep 11 percent of all their deposits on reserve at their Federal Reserve bank.

1.11 Banks that are members of the Federal Reserve system must calculate their reserve requirements every quarter and meet the requirement every quarter.

1.12 Yankee CDs are dollar-denominated CDs sold in the United States at the offices of foreign banks.

Multiple Choice Questions

1.1 The bid-asked spread is best described by which one of the following statements?
(*a*) It is the broker's commission.
(*b*) It is the dealer's gross income from a transaction.
(*c*) It is larger for illiquid securities than it is for liquid securities.
(*d*) All of the above are true.
(*e*) None of the above.

1.2 How do T-bills pay interest to their investors?
(*a*) Coupon interest.
(*b*) Possible price appreciation above their discounted price.
(*c*) T-bills pay no interest.
(*d*) Cash dividends.

1.3 Eurodollars are best described by which of the following statements?
(*a*) Eurodollars can be purchased by U.S. banks for immediate delivery to obtain overnight reserves, just like Fed funds.
(*b*) Eurodollar deposits are often not available for a couple of days after they are purchased because of delays in clearing the foreign exchange portion of the transaction.
(*c*) Eurodollar deposits are not traded as actively as other money market securities.
(*d*) Both *a* and *b*.
(*e*) None of the above.

1.4 When a broker is selling Eurodollars at what point is the identity of the borrower revealed to the potential lender?
(*a*) The borrower is revealed initially so the lender can decline the transaction if the borrower is deemed undesirable.
(*b*) If the borrower and lender want to haggle over the interest rate the broker puts them in direct contact with each other.
(*c*) The potential lender is informed of the potential borrower's identity only after all other arrangements have been completed so that the lender has an opportunity to reject the borrower.
(*d*) None of the above are true.

1.5 Bankers acceptances are best described by which one of the following statements?
(*a*) BAs are ancient documents that are usually used in international trade.
(*b*) BAs ensure payment to the seller, but they do not provide any assurances to the buyer of the goods.
(*c*) Two different banks must cooperate to create one BA.
(*d*) Both *c* and *a*.
(*e*) All of the above.
(*f*) None of the above.

1.6 Which of the following are characteristics of money market securities?
(*a*) They are issued by the U.S. Treasury, municipalities, foreign governments, and large corporations that have high-quality ratings.
(*b*) All have terms to maturity that are 270 days are less.
(*c*) All tend to have large amounts of purchasing power risk.
(*d*) Both *a* and *b*.
(*e*) Both *b* and *c*.

1.7 A basis point is which one of the following?
(*a*) One dollar, $1
(*b*) One percentage point, 1 percent
(*c*) One penny, $.01
(*d*) One one-hundredth of one percentage point, .01 of 1 percent

Answers

True-False

1.1. F 1.2. F 1.3. T 1.4. T 1.5. T 1.6. F 1.7. T 1.8. F 1.9. F
1.10. F 1.11. F 1.12. T

Multiple Choice

1.1. d 1.2. b 1.3. d 1.4. c 1.5. d 1.6. a 1.7. d

Chapter 2

Common and Preferred Stock

2.1 COMMON STOCK

Common stock certificates are legal documents that evidence ownership (or equity) in a company that is organized as a corporation; they are also marketable financial instruments. Sole proprietorships and partnerships are other popular forms of business organization, but only corporations can issue common stock.

2.2 THE CORPORATION

In 1819 Chief Justice Marshall of the U.S. Supreme Court formulated the following definition of a *corporation:*

> A corporation is an artificial being, invisible, intangible, and existing only in the contemplation of the law. Being a mere creature of the law, it possesses only those properties which the charter of its creation confers upon it either expressly or as incidental to its very existence....

The founders of a corporation obtain a corporate charter from the state, have shares of common stock printed, and sell the shares to different people in order to raise the capital to start the new business. Thus, common stock is always the first security issued by every corporation. Bonds and preferred stock may be sold later to raise additional capital.

2.3 CHARACTERISTICS OF COMMON STOCKS

Common stockholders have a *residual claim* on the earnings and assets of their corporation. This means that if the corporation goes bankrupt, the law says that all bills (such as employees' wages, suppliers' bills, and bondholders' interest) must be paid before common stockholders are entitled to divide up whatever assets remain from the bankrupt operation. There is virtually never anything left for the stockholder in a bankrupt corporation.

SOLVED PROBLEM 2.1

Common stock owners enjoy four main advantages from their investment. Name and discuss each one of these advantages.

SOLUTION

(1) *Limited liability.* If a corporation goes bankrupt and does not have enough assets to pay all it bills, the common stock owners cannot be forced to participate in the payment of unpaid bills. Stockholders cannot lose more than the cost of their investment.

(2) *Profit taking.* Stockholders enjoy an unlimited participation in the firm's earnings.

(3) *Marketability.* Shares of common stock are marketable securities designed to be bought and sold with ease.

(4) *Corporate control.* Only common stock owners are entitled to vote at the typical stockholders' meeting. Thus, common stock investors have a voice in management.

Voting

Common stock is voting stock (unless it is "classified common stock," as explained in the section on page 11). The power to vote for the board of directors and for or against major issues (such as mergers or an expansion into new product lines) belongs to the common shareholders because they are the owners of the corporation. As long as their stock is appreciating, most stockholders are not interested in the voting power they possess and will sign and return the proxies that are mailed to them by the company. A *proxy* allows a named person, usually a member of management, to vote the shares of the proxy signer at the stockholders' meeting. The use of proxies usually allows management to be able to vote its decisions into effect at stockholders' meetings.

Preemptive Right

The *preemptive right* allows stockholders to subscribe to any new issue of stock so that they can maintain their previous fraction of the total number of authorized and issued shares (or outstanding shares). Some states automatically make the preemptive right a part of every corporate charter; in others, its inclusion as a part of the charter is optional. The preemptive right, if exercised, can prevent the dilution of ownership control inherent in additional stock issues.

SOLVED PROBLEM 2.2

Mr. Forde owns 52 percent of the outstanding shares of the Forde Corporation and is Chairman of the Board. If the Forde Corporation sells a new stock issue that doubles the number of shares outstanding, Mr. Forde's share of ownership and control of the new larger number of outstanding shares diminishes to what percent if he does not exercise a preemptive right that allows him to buy 52 percent of the new issue?

SOLUTION

Assume that the company has 100 shares outstanding. If the number of shares double, then, 200 will exist. Mr. Forde owns 52 percent of the original shares or 52 shares. This is 26 percent of the total shares after the number of shares double ($\frac{52}{200}$ = .26 or 26%).

Par Value

Par value is the book value assigned to shares of stock when they are created. It was originally used to guarantee that the corporation received some minimum price for the stock. Unfortunately, the idea never worked well. Sometimes, shares were sold at par to friends, while outsiders were sold shares at higher prices. Thus, *watered stock* could be issued anyway.

SOLVED PROBLEM 2.3

The Gorman Manufacturing Corporation was founded with an initial offering of 100,000 shares of common stock that had a par value of $1 per share. These shares were sold for a price of $10 per share. (*a*) What did the net worth section of Gorman's balance sheet look like after this initial offering?

Gorman had after-tax earnings of $100,000 during its first year of operations. Half of these first-year earnings were paid out as cash dividends and the other half were retained in the firm. (*b*) What did Gorman's balance sheet look like after its first year of manufacturing was complete?

SOLUTION

(*a*) After the initial offering the equity (or net worth) section of Gorman's balance sheet was as follows:

Par value, $1 per share, 100,000 shares	$ 100,000
Paid-in surplus, $9 per share	900,000
Total net worth (or equity)	$1,000,000

(*b*) After 1 year of manufacturing operations the net worth section of Gorman's balance sheet was

Par value, $1 per share, 100,000 shares	$ 100,000
Paid-in surplus, $9 per share	900,000
Retained earnings	50,000
Total net worth	$1,050,000

Classified Common Stock

Traditionally, stock referred to as class A was nonvoting, dividend-paying stock issued to the public. Class B stock was voting stock and was held by management, which therefore had control of the firm. It paid no dividends; however, the owners could enjoy the benefits of owning stock in a growing company if their shares appreciated.

The issuance of classified common stock can be useful as a way for the management of a corporation to stop the so-called *corporate raiders* from tendering an unwanted offer to buy a controlling interest in their corporation with the intent of reorganizing it. Outside investors are sold a class of stock that receives cash dividends but has little or no voting power. In contrast to the outsiders, management members get a different class of common stock that receives no cash dividends but has voting power. This arrangement decreases the possibility of corporate takeovers that are unfriendly to management, but it may not be in the better interest of the majority of the shareholders if the management is incompetent.

Cash Dividends

According to their investment goals, stockholders may be very concerned about *cash dividends*. Generally, rapidly growing corporations pay little or no cash dividends in order to retain as much capital as possible to finance internal growth. Established firms tend to pay out a larger proportion of their earnings as cash dividends.

Some companies, public utilities in particular, take pride in paying regular, substantial cash dividends. A few other corporations announce publicly that they intend to pay zero cash dividends in order to finance rapid corporate expansion with retained earnings. At one time it was thought desirable to have a policy of paying stable dividends. Today most companies determine dividends according to the needs of financing and investor expectation about growth. Investors (such as retired people) who prefer regular income from large cash dividends will buy dividend-paying stock. In contrast, investors in high income tax brackets may prefer price appreciation because at various times in the United States capital gains have been taxed at a lower tax rate than cash dividend income.

2.4 PREFERRED STOCK

Preferred stock legally provides that preferred stockholders receive preferential treatment over common stockholders (but not over bondholders) in certain aspects. Preferred stockholders receive two primary advantages over common stockholders: (1) after-tax earnings in the form of cash dividends cannot be paid to common stockholders unless the preferred cash dividends have already been paid, and (2) preferred stockholders receive a prior claim on the corporation's assets in the event of a bankruptcy. Preferred stockholders generally receive a larger rate of return on their investment than bondholders in compensation for the slightly greater risk they assume. However, they generally receive a lesser rate of return than the common stockholders because they assume less risk.

Voting

Prior to 1930, preferred stockholders had few, if any, voting rights; it was felt that as long as holders of this class of stock received their dividends, they should have no voice in the company. More recently, there is a trend to give preferred shares increased voting rights. Moreover, nonvoting preferred may become voting stock if preferred dividend payments are missed for a stated length of time.

Preemptive Right

Common law gives common and preferred shareowners the right to subscribe to additional issues to maintain their proportionate share of ownership. However, the existence of the preemptive right depends on the law in the state where the corporation is chartered and on the provisions of the company's articles of incorporation.

Par Values for Preferred Stock

Most preferred stock has a par value. When it does, the shares' cash dividend rights are usually stated as a percentage of the par (or face) value. However, the amount of the preferred's cash dividends could be a specified dollar amount even if there were no par value. As with common stock, it seems that preferred that has a par value has no real advantage over preferred that has no par value.

Cash Dividends from Preferred Stock

Preferred stockholders should expect to get more income from dividends than from capital appreciation. The dividend paid is usually a stipulated dollar amount per year. Since cash dividends usually do not increase, the prices of preferred stocks usually do not increase much either.

Most of the preferred issues outstanding have a *cumulative cash dividend* clause. This means that the preferred stockholder is entitled to a dividend whether or not the firm earns it. If the corporation misses any part of a preferred dividend, it is not lost but must be made up in a later year before any cash dividends can be paid to the common stockholders. Not all preferred stock is cumulative.

Noncumulative preferred stock is entitled to cash dividends only if they are earned. If the corporation omits a cash dividend payment that dividend is lost to the preferred stockholders forever. To protect preferred investors, the corporation cannot legally pay dividends to its common stock during some dividend period if it has missed a preferred dividend during that period.

It should be noted that even with a cumulative dividend provision, preferred stock carries no obligation to pay cash dividends in any period in which the company does not have "sufficient current earnings." If the directors decide to apply profits to a capital improvement instead of paying a dividend, the preferred stockholders have no legal recourse (as do the bondholders). Both the common and preferred stockholders are stuck with the directors' cash dividend decisions.

SOLVED PROBLEM 2.4

The Baker Corporation was unable to meet its $6 per share preferred dividend one year because of cash shortages. As a result, the Baker Corporation's cumulative preferred stock is in *arrears* for $6 per share. At the end of its next year the Baker Corporation has $8 of earnings per share that it can disperse as cash dividends, and all $8 must go to the preferred stock (rather than $6 to preferred and $2 to common). After this $8 payment, how much will the firm still be in arrears to its cumulative preferred stockholders?

SOLUTION

The Baker Corporation must pay the $6 preferred dividend in arrears plus the current dividend of $6 for a total of $12. Therefore, after the $8 payment to preferred stockholders, it is still $4 in arrears.

Adjustable Rate Preferred Stock

Adjustable rate preferred stock (ARPS) has cash dividends that fluctuate from quarter to quarter in accordance with the current market interest rates. Each issue's prospectus specifies some formula tying that preferred stock issue's rate of cash dividends directly to some readily observable market interest rate. ARPS was created to make the cash dividend rates on preferred stock reflect current market conditions and thus be more competitive with bond investments. Furthermore, the fluctuating cash dividend rates were supposed to reduce the price fluctuations in ARPS.

Participating Preferred Stock

Participating preferred stock is uncommon; it is entitled to a stated rate of dividends and also a share of the earnings available to the common stock. Participating preferred stock is not very popular with common shareholders because they may feel that some of the earnings per share that would have gone to increase common stock cash dividends are siphoned off to pay larger participating preferred cash dividends. Financially troubled firms sometimes use participating preferred stock as a "sweetener" to help sell stock and thereby raise needed capital.

Money Market Preferred Stock

Money market preferred stock (MMPS) has a finite life that expires very soon after it is issued—some issues mature after as little as 7 weeks. MMPS is typically offered in large denominations, such as $100,000, because it is targeted at large corporate investors. These issues are sold at a *Dutch auction* in which potential buyers bid for the stock by offering to accept a certain rate of cash dividends for the short life of the MMPS. The entire issue is sold at the lowest dividend rate bid that is able to fill all the lower bids that were submitted.

2.5 COMMON STOCK DIVIDENDS AND SPLITS

The one-period rate of return from an equity share is defined as follows:

$$\begin{pmatrix}\text{One-period}\\ \text{rate of}\\ \text{return}\end{pmatrix} = \frac{(\text{price change}) + (\text{cash dividend, if any})}{\text{purchase price}} \tag{2.1}$$

When a corporation declares a stock dividend or stock split the one-period rate of return must be calculated so that it is not distorted by these *changes in the unit of account.*

Stock Dividends

Stock dividends are paid in shares of the issuing company's stock. When a stock dividend is paid, the Stock account is increased and the Capital Surplus account is decreased. Stock dividends and stock splits are economic equivalents except for these technical details in the accounting entries.

Stock Splits

When a company divides its shares, it is said to have "split its stock." If a corporation had 2 million shares outstanding and split them 2-for-1, it would end up with 4 million shares outstanding. In a stock split, the firm must correspondingly reduce the par value of the common stock, but it does not change its Capital Stock and Paid-in Surplus accounts. If the firm's stock had a par of $1 before the split, then the 2-for-1 split would give it a par of 50 cents per share.

A corporation's major reason for splitting its stock is to reduce the stock's market price. The split divides the market price per share in proportion to the split. For example, a $100 per share stock will sell at $50 after a 2-for-1 split, just as a $100 per share stock will sell at $50 after a 100 percent stock dividend. In both cases there will be twice as many shares outstanding so that the total market value of the firm is unchanged by the paper shuffling. In essence, stock splits and stock dividends do not affect the total value of the firm or the shareholders' returns (contrary to what some people think).

Most companies do not like the prices of their stock to rise too high because the high cost may decrease its popularity. The $30 to $60 range of per share prices seems to be most popular among investors. Thus, a stock split may be used to restore a popular market price to a high-priced stock.

Calculating Returns after Splits

To calculate a common stock's single-period return after a stock split or stock dividend, adjustments must be made to the stock's price and cash dividend data in order to keep from calculating a one-period rate of return that is distorted.

$$\begin{pmatrix}\text{One-period}\\ \text{rate of}\\ \text{return}\end{pmatrix} = \frac{(\text{adj. capital gain or loss}) + (\text{adj. cash div.})}{\text{adj. purchase price}}$$

Price adjustments are needed to ensure that only actual changes in the investor's wealth will be measured, rather than the meaningless price changes which are associated with a stock dividend or split. For example, if a 2-for-1 split or a 100 percent stock dividend occurred, the share prices would be halved before the stock dividend or split (or doubled afterward) so that no changes in the investor's wealth would be attributed to it in calculating rates of return.

SOLVED PROBLEM 2.5

If a share of stock that originally sold for $100 per share falls to $50 per share as the result of a 2-for-1 split or 100 percent stock dividend, what is the stock's one-period rate of return during the time periods before and after this change occurred?

SOLUTION

The stock's price and cash dividend must be adjusted so that its single-period rate of return can be calculated without naively distorting the stockholders' true rate of return. Table 2.1 traces the correct calculations for a change in the unit of account that occurred between periods 2 and 3. Since the investor owns twice as many shares after the stock split but each share has half of its previous market price, the investor's wealth is unchanged. The inves-

Table 2.1 A 2-for-1 Stock Split, or Equivalently, a 100 Percent Stock Dividend

		Split or Dividend		
Time Period (t)	$t = 1$	$t = 2$	$t = 3$	$t = 4$
Market price per share	$100	$100	$50	$50
Cash dividend per share	$5	$5	$2.50	$2.50
Earnings per share	$10	$10	$5	$5
Number of shares held per $100 original investment	1	1	2	2
One-period rate of return	5%	5%	5%	5%
Shares outstanding	100,000	100,000	200,000	200,000

tor's income in this example is $5 of cash dividends per period per $100 of investment both before and after the change in the unit of account. Stated differently, the stock prices and cash dividends must be adjusted so that the true 5 percent rate of return per period that was earned before and after the split can be calculated.

SOLVED PROBLEM 2.6

If an investor buys a share of stock for $100 per share and the stock pays a 50 percent stock dividend, what is the adjusted cost on which the investor should calculate his or her taxable gain when the stock is sold?

SOLUTION

The adjusted cost is $66.67 per share, as shown below.

$$\frac{\$100 \text{ original cost}}{1.0 + .50 \text{ dividend}} = \frac{\$100}{1.5} = \$66.67$$

Thus, if the stock is sold for $100 at some date after the investor received the 50 percent stock dividend the *taxable* price gain would be $33.33 per share ($100 purchase price − $66.67 adjusted cost).

True-False Questions

2.1 Treasury stock are shares of its own outstanding stock that a corporation purchased in the secondary market and holds in its vault.

2.2 Corporations frequently obtain permission from their shareholders to have more shares of stock authorized than the firm actually issues.

2.3 Par value stock must be paid for with either cash or tangible property that is worth as much or more than the par value of the stock.

2.4 The *book value* per share of common stock equals the difference between the corporation's total assets and its total liabilities divided by the number of shares outstanding.

2.5 The par value of a share of common stock has a significant influence on its market value.

2.6 Stockholders in a small corporation (with, say, six shareholders) cannot sell their shares without advance permission by a majority of the other shareholders.

2.7 Most common stockholders leave their shares in a safe at their broker's office.

2.8 It is the duty of the *registrar* to double-check the transfer agent and make sure that the old number of shares equals the new number shares after trades are completed.

2.9 The funds that a corporation receives from most issues of preferred stock may be viewed as being permanent capital that the issuing corporation need never pay back (unless it desires to buy back its own securities for some reason).

2.10 Partnerships can issue preferred stock.

2.11 Preferred stock is a fixed income investment like a bond that has few, if any, of the legal guarantees of interest payment that are inherent in a bond.

2.12 Since stock dividends and stock splits are identical except for some technical details of the accounting entries, the New York Stock Exchange has adopted a rule calling all distributions of stock under 25 percent per share *dividends* and distributions over 25 percent *splits* even if the corporation involved calls its action something different.

Multiple Choice Questions

2.1 Treasury stock is best described by which one of the following statements?
(*a*) It has no voting privileges.
(*b*) It receives no cash dividends.
(*c*) It may be resold at any time.
(*d*) All of the above.
(*e*) None of the above.

2.2 The advantage of leaving common stock shares on deposit at the client's security broker's office is best described by which one of the following statements?
(*a*) The shares are kept in a safe deposit box for free.
(*b*) Shares held at the broker's office can be liquidated in several day's less time than shares brought into the broker's office by the investor.
(*c*) The broker can collect cash dividends and either reinvest the funds or mail the funds to the owner of the shares.
(*d*) All of the above are true.
(*e*) None of the above are true.

2.3 The *transfer agent* for an issue of stock is best described by which one of the following statements?
(*a*) The transfer agent double-checks to make sure that the registrar performed their job correctly.
(*b*) Either the issuing corporation or a bank may be the transfer agent.
(*c*) The transfer agent issues new stock certificates and cancels old ones when a trade occurs.
(*d*) Both *b* and *c*.

2.4 Common stockholders have which of the following rights?
(*a*) They can legally demand information from a corporation in which they are a shareholder and thus gain access to its books.
(*b*) They can vote for the common stockholders' cash dividend.
(*c*) They can vote for the preferred stockholders' cash dividend.
(*d*) All of the above.

2.5 Preferred stockholders receive priority over common stockholders with respect to which of the following?
(*a*) Cash dividends cannot be paid to common stockholders unless the preferred stockholders receive their stated cash dividend.
(*b*) In the event of bankruptcy and liquidation, the preferred shareholders are paid before the common stockholders.
(*c*) Preferred shareholders (not common shareholders) get to elect the Chairman of the corporation's Board of Directors.
(*d*) Both *a* and *b* are true, but *c* is false.
(*e*) All of the above are true.

2.6 Common stockholders have the right to vote on which of the following?
(*a*) Dissolution or consolidation of the corporation
(*b*) Selection of the Board of Directors
(*c*) Amendments to the corporate charter or bylaws
(*d*) All of the above
(*e*) None of the above

2.7 Which one of the following equations correctly defines the *dividend yield* (y) from a share of common stock?
(*a*) $y = \dfrac{\text{(purchase price)} + \text{(cash dividend, if any)}}{\text{purchase price}}$
(*b*) $y = \dfrac{\text{(price change)} + \text{(cash dividend, if any)}}{\text{purchase price}}$
(*c*) $y = \dfrac{\text{price change}}{\text{purchase price}}$
(*d*) $y = \dfrac{\text{cash dividend (if any)}}{\text{purchase price}}$

2.8 A share of preferred stock is
(*a*) A legal claim to ownership
(*b*) A marketable security
(*c*) A debt security
(*d*) Both *a* and *b*
(*e*) All of the above

2.9 Which of the following statements best describes the convertibility of preferred stock?
(*a*) Some issues of preferred stock may be converted into common stock at the option of the investor any time and at a conversion ratio that never changes.
(*b*) Some issues of preferred stock may be converted into common stock at the option of the investor within a limited number of years after the preferred stock is issued.
(*c*) Some issues of preferred stock may be converted into common stock at the option of the investor only after a specified number of years have elapsed since the preferred stock was initially issued.
(*d*) All of the above are true.
(*e*) Preferred stock is never a convertible security.

2.10 In assessing the probability that an issue of preferred stock will pay its cash dividends, which of the following considerations is the most important?
(*a*) Whether or not the cash dividends are cumulative
(*b*) The level and trend of the issuing corporation's times-fixed-charges (including preferred cash dividends) ratio
(*c*) Whether or not the issue is redeemable (or callable)
(*d*) Whether or not there is a sinking fund attached to the preferred issue

Answers

True-False

2.1. T 2.2. T 2.3. T 2.4. T 2.5. F 2.6. F 2.7. T 2.8. T 2.9. T
2.10. F 2.11 T 2.12. T

Multiple Choice

2.1. d 2.2. d 2.3. d 2.4. a 2.5. d 2.6. d 2.7. d 2.8. d 2.9. d 2.10. b

Chapter 3

Corporate Bonds

3.1 CHARACTERISTICS OF CORPORATE BOND ISSUES

Entrepreneurial firms, partnerships, and corporations may issue bonds to raise capital. Bonds are debt securities that are similar to the money market securities discussed in Chapter 1. However, corporate bonds differ from money market securities because (1) on the date they are issued bonds have more than one year until maturity, (2) the federal law requires that every corporate bond issue be governed by a legal contract called an *indenture*, (3) most bonds pay coupon interest, and (4) corporate and municipal bonds involve more default risk than money market securities.

SOLVED PROBLEM 3.1

What are some of the main features of the *Trust Indenture Act of 1939?*

SOLUTION

The 1939 Act requires an indenture that specifies the terms governing every company's bond issue. An indenture is written by a bond issuer stipulating protective provisions the firm provides for its bond investors. The 1939 Act also requires that the indenture contract specify a *trustee* (which is usually a commercial bank) to monitor the issuing corporation on behalf of the bondholders and to make certain that the provisions of the indenture are not violated.

3.2 THE DETERMINANTS OF CORPORATE BONDS' DISCOUNT RATES

Default risk increases as a company moves closer toward bankruptcy. *Quality ratings* are published estimates of corporations' default risk. There is very little chance that a company with high-quality ratings will be declared bankrupt.

Moody's Investor Services, Standard & Poor's (S&P), and Fitch's are the major firms that evaluate the default risk of bond issues and publish quality ratings. One or more of these firms rates practically all nonbank corporate bond issues of any size, whether or not the issuer requests it. Or, for a fee, any of these firms will periodically reevaluate its rating for a given bond issue and continually republish it year after year. Continuing ratings make a bond issue easier to trade in the secondary bond markets.

The Corporate Bond Rating Process

Figure 3-1 depicts the 12-step process followed at S&P in the development and maintenance of a bond issue's quality rating. It usually takes weeks to complete the process, although the process can be hurried if necessary to get a new issue ready. After the background research is completed, the quality rating to be assigned to a given issue is finalized and then released to the public.

Corporate Bond Ratings Defined

Table 3.1 lists and defines the bond quality ratings. The bond rating procedures used at Moody's are similar to those used at S&P; the ratings of any given bond issue by the different rating firms are usually identical. There are two main factors that determine corporate bond ratings: (1) the issuer's financial condition and (2) the indenture contract that governs the issuing firm.

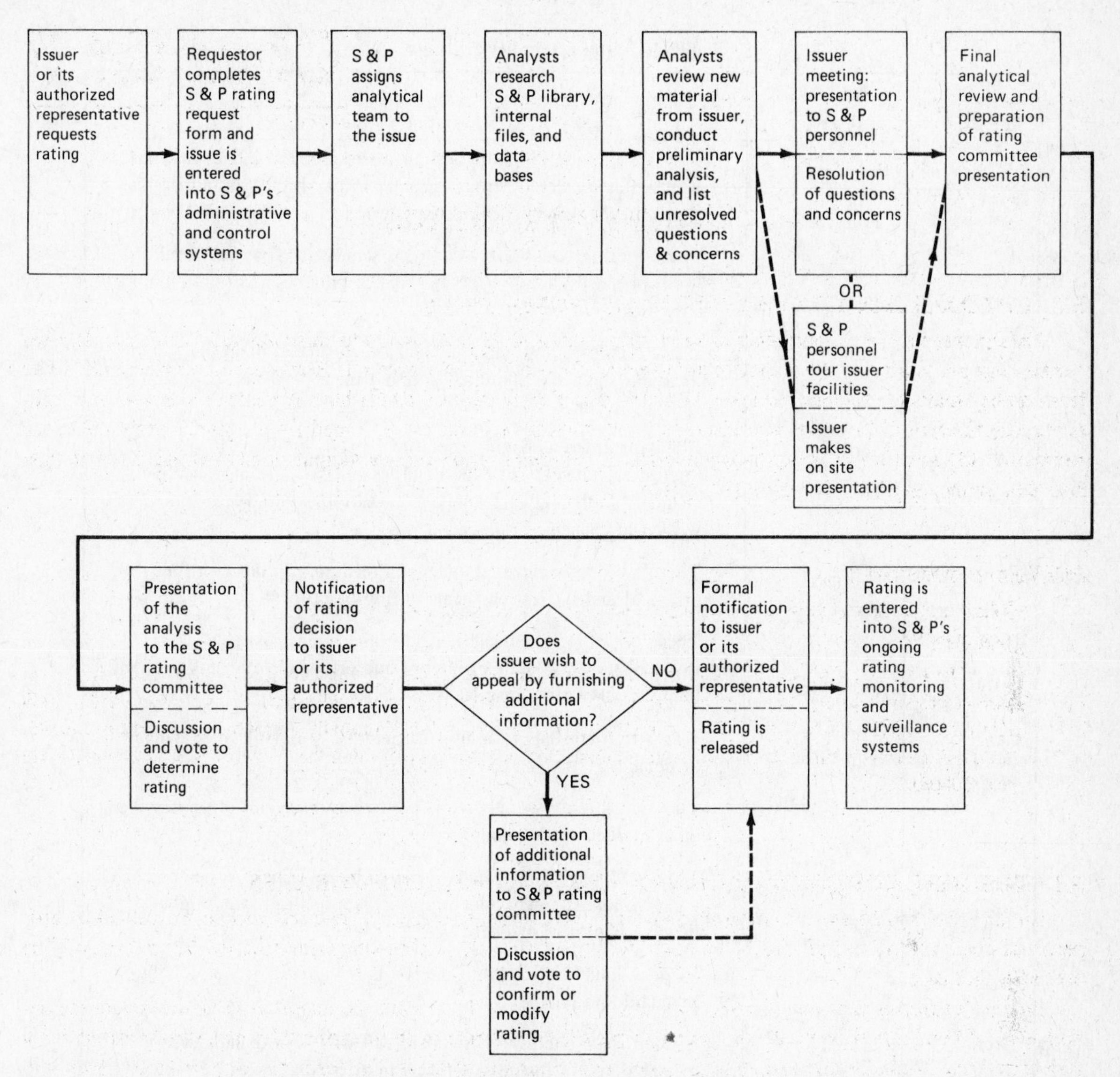

Fig. 3-1 The corporate bond rating process at Standard & Poors. (*Source: Standard & Poors Rating Guide*, McGraw-Hill, New York, 1979, fig. 3-1, p. 19.)

3.3 THE ISSUER'S FINANCIAL CONDITION

The most important pieces of financial information considered when a rating agency evaluates the financial strength of the bond issuer are (1) the level and trend of the issuer's financial ratios and (2) the issuer's significance and size.

Financial Ratio Analysis

The financial health of a bond issue depends on the underlying strength of the issuing company. Therefore, financial analysis of the issuer's financial statements is important.

(I) Financial Coverage Ratios

Most bond analysts and bond raters who sit on rating committees would probably agree that one of the main determinants of the quality rating of a bond issue is its *coverage ratio*. A coverage ratio is a measure of how many times the issuing company's earned income could pay the interest charges and other fixed costs

Table 3.1 Bond Quality Ratings

Moody's	Standard & Poors	Definition of Rating
Aaa	AAA	The AAA rating is the highest rating assigned to a debt instrument. It indicates extremely strong capacity to pay principal and interest. Bonds in this category are often referred to as "blue-chip" bonds.
Aa	AA	These are high-quality bonds by all standards. They are rated lower primarily because the margins of protection are not quite as strong as those of Aaa and AAA.
A	A	These bonds possess many favorable investment attributes, but there may be a susceptibility to impairment if adverse economic changes occur.
Baa	BBB	Bonds regarded as having adequate capacity to pay principal and interest are rated BBB if the bond issue lacks certain protective elements so that adverse economic conditions could lead to a weakened capacity for payment.
Ba	BB	These are bonds regarded as having minimum protection for principal and interest payments during bad times.
B	B	These bonds lack characteristics of other more desirable investments. Assurance of interest and principal payments over any long period of time may be very weak.
Caa	CCC	These are poor-quality issues that may be in default or in danger of default.
Ca	CC	These are highly speculative issues, often in default or possessing other marked shortcomings.
C		This is Moody's lowest-rated class of bonds. These issues can be regarded as extremely poor in investment quality; they might become bankrupt suddenly.
	C	Income bonds on which no interest is being paid are rated C by Standard and Poor's.
	D	A bond issue rated D by Standard & Poors is in default, with principal and/or interest payments in arrears.

related to the bond issue. The earnings available for the payment of bond charges are usually defined to be the total corporate income before taxes, with interest expenses included. Essentially, a coverage ratio greater than 1 indicates that the issuing firm has more than enough income to pay its interest expense. The value of the ratio is important because it has implications for the probability that the firm defaults.

The *trend* of financial ratios is important too. An upward trend suggests that better times lie ahead, assuming the ratios continue to rise. A flat trend portends little change. A downward trend causes bond analysts to warn potential investors that troubled times may lie ahead and to suggest lower quality ratings for the bond issuer.

A low times-interest-earned ratio or other coverage ratio may be the result of two causes. First, earnings may be too low. If so, the firm's poor profitability would also show up as low rates of return on assets and as rates of return on equity that are below those of other similar firms. Second, the firm may be too deeply in debt and thus incur too much interest expense. If so, this will also show up as high financial leverage ratios.

SOLVED PROBLEM 3.2

Discuss how the firm's financial coverage ratios can affect the market price of a firm's bond.

SOLUTION

If a firm's coverage ratios fall (or rise) indicating an increased chance that the firm will (or will not) default on its bonds, then, the bond quality rating agencies lower (or raise) the rating they publish. When a firm's quality rating falls (or rises), the appropriate risk-adjusted discount rate to use in calculating the bond's present value rises (or falls). Bond ratings and the appropriate discount rate move inversely. When the discount rate used in the present-value calculations changes, the bond's value moves inversely with this market interest rate.

SOLVED PROBLEM 3.3

What factors might a financial analyst consider when evaluating a corporation's financial ratios besides how the ratios compared with some relevant standard of comparison?

SOLUTION

Table 3.2 summarizes the method suggested by one analyst in evaluating coverage ratios to see what quality rating to assign to bond issues. Table 3.2 indicates bond analysts consider both the issuer's coverage ratios and the stability of the underlying earnings.

Table 3.2 Coverage Ratios and Quality Ratings

Coverage Ratio	Stability of Earnings	Quality
6 and over	Cyclical	Very high
4 and over	Stable	Very high
3 to 6	Cyclical	Medium to high
2 to 4	Stable	Medium to high
Under 3	Cyclical	Low
Under 2	Stable	Low

Source: Jerome B. Cohen, Edward D. Zinbarg, and Arthur Zeikel, *Investment Analysis and Portfolio Management,* 4th ed., R. D. Irwin Inc., Homewood, Ill., 1982, p. 481.

(II) Financial Leverage Ratios

Companies that use borrowed funds to expand (rather than retaining earnings to increase the owners' equity) are said to be using *financial leverage*. Ideally, money will be borrowed at a low interest rate and reinvested within the firm at a higher rate of return—the yield spread is profit. If a firm uses too much financial leverage, its fixed interest expense will grow to such a high level that, if profits fall even slightly, the firm will not be earning enough to pay its contractual interest expense. This can lead to bankruptcy; that is why bond investors evaluate the indebtedness of issuing firms.

(III) Liquidity Ratios

There are several *liquidity ratios* that financial analysts use to evaluate the solvency of a firm and thus to determine if the firm will be able to pay its bills on time. The two most common liquidity ratios are the *current ratio* and the *quick ratio.*

(IV) Turnover Ratios

Turnover ratios are used to measure the *activity* within a firm. Use of these ratios is based on the premise that assets not being actively employed must not be very useful and are therefore probably not liquid or profitable.

The *accounts-receivable-turnover ratio* and the *collection-period-in-days ratio* give some indication of the liquidity of the current asset called *accounts receivable*. The *inventory-turnover ratio* measures how rapidly a firm sells out and replaces its inventory. The *total-asset-turnover ratio* is designed to gauge whether all the assets owned by a firm are being used or if some are lying dormant. Bond rating agencies, bond investors, and others who have loaned the firm money can get different perspectives on the liquidity and quality of management by studying the turnover ratios.[1]

[1]For more details on how these ratios are calculated, refer to Chapter 12.

SOLVED PROBLEM 3.4

The Blough Corporation has an accounts-receivable-turnover ratio of 6 and an inventory-turnover ratio of 12. Since there are 12 months in 1 year, the turnover ratio of 6 means that Blough's accounts receivable turn over once every two months, averaged over the entire year. Blough's inventory turnover of 12 means that the inventory turned over once each month, on average. Stated differently, we can conclude that Blough allows its customers an average of 2 months to pay their bills and has an inventory that averages one month old. Are Blough's turnover ratios too high, about right, or too low?

SOLUTION

Financial ratios can be compared with their own historical values to determine their trend and also with the ratios of competitors to get a relevant perspective. Some standard of comparison is needed to assess the meanings of financial ratios; ratios vary from industry to industry.

The Blough Corporation's accounts receivable collection period of 2 months might be normal for a neighborhood grocery store that sells on credit or for a public utility that issues monthly bills to its customers. But a 2-month collection time would be absurdly fast for a savings and loan association's home mortgage department, because home mortgage loans have their payments spread out over 15 to 30 years. As far as Blough's inventory is concerned, a one-month-old inventory would simply be impossible for the products produced by whisky distilleries, construction companies that build skyscrapers, or shipyards that assemble ocean liners. However, a fresh-fish market or a vegetable dealer should never allow their inventory to become one month old or health inspectors would probably close the business for selling unfit food. Thus, each industry has it own normal turnover ratios. The Blough Corporation's turnover ratios cannot be evaluated because we do not know the firm's industry or Blough's own historical ratios.

(V) Cash Flow Ratios

A company's annual *cash flows* are usually defined to be its annual earnings before interest expense and income taxes plus its annual depreciation. (Other, more sophisticated, cash flow definitions are also used.) The cash flows generated by a firm can be put into a perspective that facilitates financial analysis by calculating cash flow ratios of various kinds. For example, the cash flows divided by the firm's total long-term debt measures *cash flows as a percentage of debt.* If this cash flow ratio is less than the firm's interest rate paid on total long-term debt, the firm may default on its interest payments.

(VI) Profitability Ratios

Since most bonds typically earn only their fixed interest rate, an increase in the issuer's profitability does not necessarily generate capital gains for bonds. Nevertheless, bond ratios and bond investment analysts are interested in the profitability of firms issuing bonds because profitability is an important indicator of a firm's financial health. One of the more useful profitability ratios is the *rate of return on total assets,* which measures the profitability of the firm's total assets. The rate of return on assets will be lowest for firms that have too many assets, high debt levels, low earnings, or some combination of these problems. Profitability ratios are considered by bond raters in assigning quality ratings.

SOLVED PROBLEM 3.5

How can all the different financial ratios possibly be employed simultaneously in the determination of bond quality ratings?

SOLUTION

Four financial ratios that are frequently considered in quality rating determinations are shown in Table 3.3. These average values were computed from a representative sample of industrial companies that have ratings in each of the rating categories. The patterns of ratio values in Table 3.3 conform to our economic intuition and can thus provide numerical guidelines for bond rating purposes.

When examining Table 3.3, remember that different ratio values are appropriate for each industry. Also, through the ups and downs of the normal business cycle the values of every firm's ratios vary in a cyclical fashion. Thus, bond rating is not quite as simple as Table 3.3 may suggest.

The Economic Significance and Size of the Issuer

Bond analysts should consider more than a company's financial ratios. The bond issuing firm's competition, its size, its importance in its industry, and related factors must also be considered before assigning a qual-

Table 3.3 Average Relationships between Four Financial Ratios and the Quality Ratings of Industrial Bonds

Rating Category	Pretax Fixed-Charge Coverage	Cash Flow to Long-Term Debt	Pretax Return on Long-Term Capital	Long-Term Debt to Capitalization
AAA	7.48 times	309.0%	25.6%	8.9%
AA	4.43 times	118.4%	22.0%	18.9%
A	2.93 times	75.4%	18.0%	24.5%
BBB	2.30 times	45.7%	12.1%	31.5%
BB	2.04 times	27.0%	13.8%	45.5%
B	1.51 times	18.9%	12.0%	52.0%
CCC	0.75 times	15.1%	2.7%	69.3%

Source: Standard & Poor, *Debt Rating Criteria,* 1986, p. 51.

lity rating or making an investment. The analysis of factors external to the bond issuing firm should start with the firm's competitors.

SOLVED PROBLEM 3.6

List and discuss some of the important industry factors considered by a bond analyst.

SOLUTION

Position in the economy: Is the firm in the capital-goods sector, the consumer-durables sector, or the consumer-nondurables sector?

Life cycle of industry: Is the industry in a growth, stable, or declining phase?

Competitive nature: What is the nature and intensity of the competition in the industry? Is it on a regional, national, or international basis? Is it on price, quality of product, distribution capabilities, image, or some other factors? Is the industry regulated, which provides some competitive protection?

Labor situation: Is the industry unionized? If so, are labor contracts negotiated on an industrywide basis, and what is the recent negotiating history?

Supply factors: Does the industry generally have good control of key raw materials, or is there a dependence upon questionable foreign sources?

Volatility: Is there an involvement with rapidly developing or changing technologies? Is there a dependence upon a relatively small number of major contracts (as is sometimes the case in the defense industry)?

Major vulnerabilities: Is the industry likely to be a prime target for some form of political pressure? Are substantial environmental expenditures likely to be mandated? Are near-term energy shortages possible? What is the ease of entry into the industry?

Answers to the questions above inform the bond analysts about the industry's potential.

SOLVED PROBLEM 3.7

What are some key questions that bond raters consider when evaluating an issuer's competition?

SOLUTION

Market share: Does a company have a large enough portion of the market share to significantly influence industry dynamics? This may be especially important in a market dominated by a few producers. Does the company have the opportunity to exercise price leadership? Does the company offer a full range of products or have proprietary products or a special niche in the market?

Technological leadership: Is the company usually among the first with new developments, or is it typically a follower? How do research and development expenditures compare with the industry average?

Production efficiency: Is the company a relatively low-cost producer? Are its facilities newer or more advanced than the average? Is it more or less vertically integrated than the average? If mandated expenditures are required, has the company already complied to a greater or lesser extent than its competitors? Does the company face a more onerous labor situation than its competitors?

Financial structure: How does a company's use of leverage and various types of financing vehicles compare with that of others in the industry?

SOLVED PROBLEM 3.8

List and explain the protective provisions provided by the bond issuer to ensure the safety of the bondholder's investment.

SOLUTION

The issuer can pledge specific assets as *collateral.* In addition, the issuer can *subordinate* other legal claims on its assets or income. The so-called *after-acquired property clause* is an example of a subordination clause. Such a clause states that if an issuer acquires additional assets after the first mortgage bond is outstanding, these new assets will become part of the first mortgage bond's collateral. The issuer can also provide for a *sinking fund* with which to pay off the bonds even if the issuer defaults on its other debts. An unlimited variety of provisions can be found in indentures. But, nothing is granted for free. Each protective provision bondholders obtain reduces the rate of return they can expect to earn from their bonds; the natural economic order requires a tradeoff of risk for return.

True-False Questions

3.1 If the Standard & Poors Corporation gives a Goodyear Tire & Rubber Corporation bond issue a quality rating that the Chief Financial Officer (CFO) of Goodyear thinks is too low, Goodyear's CFO can appeal to Standard & Poor's to get the rating revised.

3.2 The Trust Indenture Act of 1939 was designed to protect lenders that finance the inventories of bond dealers.

3.3 A *serial bond* issue has the maturities of different bonds in the issue scheduled to occur periodically at differing times.

3.4 *Income bonds* may be paid more than coupons, they can get a portion of the issuer's profits.

3.5 *Collateral trust bonds* are secured by securities left on deposit with a trustee.

3.6 The *marketability* of a bond issue generally increases with the size of the issue.

3.7 When a company sells a new issue of bonds to pay off an old issue that is expiring the new bonds are called *refunding bonds.*

3.8 If the Board of Directors of a corporation elects not to make a scheduled interest payment on an issue of subordinated debentures, the bondholders cannot take any legal action under the terms of their indenture contract to force the payment.

3.9 *Yield curve–adjusted notes,* called YCANs, pay a changing coupon rate that gets reset each year to some fixed rate (such as 15 percent) minus a fluctuating lower rate of interest (such as LIBOR, the London interbank overnight rate).

3.10 The assets pledged as collateral are important because these assets might be used to pay the interest in case of default.

Multiple Choice Questions

3.1 Which of the following bond quality ratings applies to default-free bonds?
(*a*) AAA.
(*b*) Aaa.
(*c*) Both *b* and *a* are default-free.
(*d*) None of the above are default-free.

3.2 Which one of the following companies is a bond rating service?
(*a*) Dun & Bradstreet
(*b*) Dow-Jones
(*c*) Moodys
(*d*) All of the above
(*e*) None of the above

3.3 If a $10,000 face value bond is selling for $10,212.50, its price will be quoted in the financial newspapers in which one of the following ways?
(*a*) $102\frac{1}{8}$
(*b*) 2.125 premium
(*c*) 102.125 × 100
(*d*) 102.2

3.4 Which one of the following statements best describes corporate bonds?
(*a*) Bond investors are creditors of the corporation.
(*b*) A bond is an engraved certificate evidencing corporate borrowing.
(*c*) The majority of bonds make coupon interest payments once per annum.
(*d*) Both *a* and *b* are true.
(*e*) None of the above are true.

3.5 An indenture is best described by which one of the following statements?
(*a*) *Deed of Trust* is a synonym for indenture.
(*b*) It is a legal contract describing the rights of specific bondholders.
(*c*) It describes the duties of the *Trustee*.
(*d*) Both *b* and *c* are true.
(*e*) All of the above are true.

3.6 An indenture may contain protective clauses dealing with which of the following topics?
(*a*) Collateral
(*b*) A sinking fund
(*c*) Subordination clauses
(*d*) All of the above
(*e*) None of the above

3.7 The quality ratings of a corporation's bond issue are primarily determined by which of the following?
(*a*) The level and trend of the issuer's financial ratios
(*b*) The level and structure of interest rates
(*c*) The issuer's financial condition and the indenture contract that governs the issuing firm
(*d*) All the above

3.8 Mortgage bond issues that are subordinated to the first mortgage bonds are called which of the following?
(*a*) Closed-end mortgage bonds
(*b*) Limited open-end bonds
(*c*) Open-end bonds
(*d*) Both *a* and *b*
(*e*) All the above

3.9 *Guaranteed bonds* are which of the following?
(*a*) Corporate bonds that are guaranteed by the U.S. government
(*b*) Corporate bonds of one company that are guaranteed by another company that acquired the first company
(*c*) May be guaranteed with respect to principal or interest or both
(*d*) Both *b* and *c*

3.10 One bond with an AAA-grade rating might pay a higher yield-to-maturity than another AAA-grade bond issued at a different time by the same corporation because of which of the following reasons?
(*a*) Bonds with longer maturities always pay higher rates of interest than similar bonds that have shorter maturities.

(*b*) The bond market is sometimes simply irrational and evaluates the riskiness of some bond issues erroneously.

(*c*) One of the bond issues may have protective provisions that makes it safer than other bond issues from the same issuer.

(*d*) All the above are true.

Answers

True-False

3.1. T 3.2. F 3.3. T 3.4. T 3.5. T 3.6. T 3.7. T 3.8. F 3.9. T
3.10. F

Multiple Choice

3.1. d 3.2. c 3.3. a 3.4. d 3.5. e 3.6. d 3.7. c 3.8. d 3.9. d 3.10 c

Chapter 4

The Time Value of Money

4.1 COMPOUND INTEREST

Money has *time value* because it earns interest. Furthermore, if left to compound the money earns interest on the principal and also on the previously earned interest. As a result, a dollar invested today can grow to a dollar plus *interest* and *interest-on-the-interest* at some future date. For example, consider putting $1 in a federally insured bank so that the risk of default can safely be ignored. The future value of the $1 saved at a 5 percent rate of interest is calculated to be $1.05, as shown below.

$$p_t = p_0(1 + i)^t \tag{4.1}$$

Assuming that $t = 1$ and $i = 5\%$ allows us to rewrite Eq. (*4.1*) as

$$p_1 = \$1.00(1 + .05)^1 \qquad \text{since } 5\% = .05$$
$$\$1.05 = \$1.00(1.05)$$

We will use the following notation in this chapter:

p_t = present value at the end of time period t.
p_0 = present value now, at time period $t = 0$.
p_1 = present value one time period from now (at $t = 1$), or, the future value after one period.
t = a time period counter (that usually tells the number of years).
i = rate of interest per year.[1]

Table 4.1 shows the future values p_t of a dollar saved now ($p_0 = \$1.00$) and invested at different interest rates ($i = .01, .05, .10,$ and $.15$) for various numbers of years ($t = 1, 2, 3, 4, 5, 6, 7, 8, 9, 10, 15, 20, 25,$ and 30).

Table 4.1 The Future Value of $1 Saved at Interest Rate *i* for *t* Years

Time Period, t	Rate of Interest, i			
	$i = 1\%$	$i = 5\%$	$i = 10\%$	$i = 15\%$
1	1.010	1.050	1.100	1.150
2	1.020	1.103	1.210	1.323
3	1.030	1.158	1.331	1.521
4	1.041	1.216	1.464	1.749
5	1.051	1.276	1.611	2.011
6	1.062	1.340	1.772	2.313
7	1.072	1.407	1.949	2.660
8	1.083	1.477	2.144	3.059
9	1.094	1.551	2.358	3.518
10	1.105	1.629	2.594	4.046
15	1.161	2.079	4.177	8.137
20	1.220	2.653	6.727	16.367
25	1.282	3.386	10.835	32.919
30	1.348	4.322	17.449	66.212

[1]All interest rates must be stated as decimal numbers for computational purposes. So, a 10 percent rate of interest must be stated as $i = .10$ instead of $i = 10\%$ in the computations. Likewise, $i = 25\%$ must be written as $i = .25$.

Note how \$1 earning 15 percent interest that is reinvested and compounded for $t = 5$ years will more than double ($p_5 = \$2.011$), as shown in the computations below.

$$\begin{aligned} p_5 &= p_0(1 + i)^5 = \$1.00(1.15)^5 \\ &= \$1.00(1.15)(1.15)(1.15)(1.15)(1.15) \\ &= \$1.00(2.011) = \$2.011 \end{aligned}$$

Figure 4-1 illustrates the *march of compounded interest income;* it summarizes the numerical examples from Table 4.1.

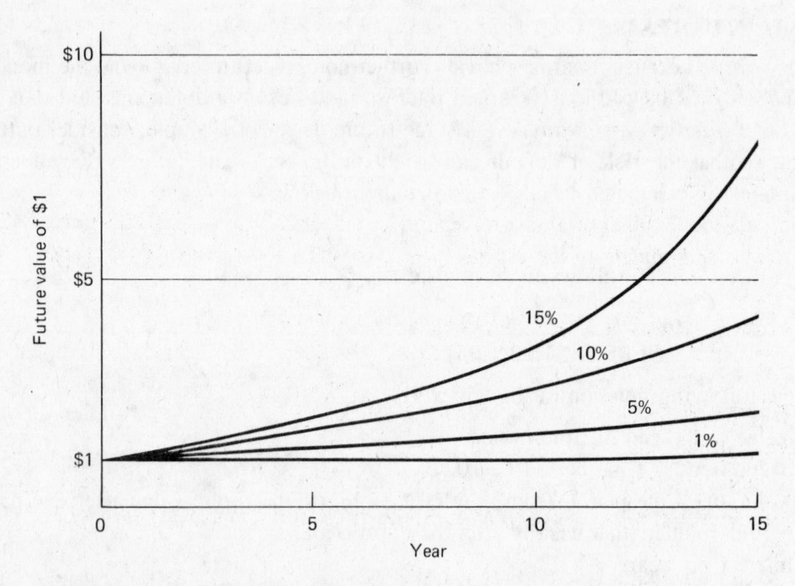

Fig. 4-1 The effects of time (t) and the rate of interest (i) on future values.

SOLVED PROBLEM 4.1

Find the future value of \$1.00 saved at an interest rate of 10 percent for (*a*) 1 year, (*b*) 2 years, and (*c*) one-half of 1 year.

SOLUTION

We have $p_0 = \$1.00$ and $i = 10\% = .10$.

(*a*) For 1 year, $t = 1$.

$$p_1 = p_0(1.10)^1 = \$1.00(1.10)^1 = \$1.10$$

(*b*) For 2 years, $t = 2$.

$$p_2 = p_0(1.10)^2 = \$1.00(1.10)^2 = \$1.21$$

(*c*) For one-half of 1 year, $t = \frac{1}{2}$.[2]

$$p_{1/2} = p_0(1.10)^{1/2} = \$1.00\sqrt{1.10} = \$1.00(1.049) = \$1.049$$

[2]If a calculator is not available to find the square root, the hand calculation can be carried out with the aid of logarithms, as shown below for one-half year, $t = \frac{1}{2}$:

$$\begin{aligned} p_t &= p_0(1 + i)^t \\ \log p_t &= \log p_0 + t[\log(1 + i)] \\ &= \log(\$1) + \tfrac{1}{2}(\log 1.10) \end{aligned}$$

You can find the value of p_t by using tables of logarithms and antilogarithms. If the natural or naperian base $e = 2.71828$ logarithms are used the logarithm of the price is

$$\begin{aligned} \log_e(p_t) &= \log_e(\$1) + \tfrac{1}{2}[\log_e(1.10)] \\ &= 0 + \tfrac{1}{2}(.09531) \\ &= (\tfrac{1}{2})(.09531) = .047655 \end{aligned}$$

The antilogarithm is

$$\begin{aligned} p_t &= \text{antilogarithm of } \log_e(p_t) \\ &= e^{.047655} = \$1.0488 \end{aligned}$$

SOLVED PROBLEM 4.2

Find the future value of \$1,500 saved at an interst rate of 5 percent for (*a*) 1 year, (*b*) 2 years, (*c*) one-half of 1 year.

SOLUTION

We have $p_0 = \$1{,}500.00$ and $i = .05$.

(*a*) For 1 year, $t = 1$.

$$p_1 = p_0(1.05) = \$1{,}500(1.05)^1 = \$1{,}575.00$$

(*b*) For 2 years, $t = 2$.

$$p_2 = p_0(1.05)^2 = \$1{,}500(1.05)^2 = \$1{,}653.75$$

(*c*) For one-half of 1 year, $t = \frac{1}{2}$.

$$p_{1/2} = p_0(1.05)^{1/2} = \$1{,}500\sqrt{1.05} = \$1{,}500(1.025) = \$1{,}537.04$$

SOLVED PROBLEM 4.3

If Charles deposits \$100 in a savings account at a federally insured bank now at 12 percent interest, how much will accumulate in the account in 7 years if no withdrawals are made?

SOLUTION

We have $p_0 = \$100$, $i = 12\% = .12$, and $t = 7$.

$$p_7 = p_0(1.12)^7 = \$100(2.2106) = \$221.06$$

SOLVED PROBLEM 4.4

For her thirteenth birthday, Sally's grandparents give her a \$5,000 savings account to help her pay for her college education. The account is earning 5 percent interest. If no withdrawals are made, how much will be in the account when Sally has her nineteenth birthday and is in college?

SOLUTION

We have $p_0 = \$5{,}000$, $i = 5\% = .05$, and $t = 19 - 13 = 6$ years.

$$p_6 = p_0(1.05)^6 = \$5{,}000(1.34) = \$6{,}700.00$$

SOLVED PROBLEM 4.5

When he is 30 years old, George saves \$1,000 in his Individual Retirement Account (IRA) at 6 percent interest. It can accumulate tax-free compound interest until he retires. How much will this \$1,000 grow to when George reaches age 65 and retires?

SOLUTION

We have $p_0 = \$1{,}000$, $i = 6\% = .06$, and $t = 65 - 30 = 35$ years.

$$p_{35} = p_0(1.06)^{35} = \$1{,}000(7.6861) = \$7{,}686.10$$

SOLVED PROBLEM 4.6

Freda deposits \$50 in a savings account at 5 percent interest for 3 months. At the end of the 3 months how much will be in the account if no withdrawals are made?

SOLUTION

We have $p_0 = \$50$, $i = 5\% = .05$, and $t = \frac{1}{4}$ = one-quarter of a year = 3 months.

$$p_{1/4} = p_0(1.05)^{1/4} = \$50\sqrt[4]{1.05} \qquad \text{since } x^{1/4} = \sqrt[4]{x}$$
$$= \$50(1.0123) = \$50.615$$

4.2 DISCOUNTED PRESENT VALUE

Divide both sides of Eq. (*4.1*) by the quantity $(1 + i)^t$ to obtain the *present-value formula* in Eq. (*4.2*):

$$p_0 = \frac{p_t}{(1 + i)^t} \tag{4.2}$$

The *present value* p_0 equals the discounted value of the *future value* p_t. When finding present values the following new names are assigned to the algebraic symbols defined in Section 4.1:

i = the rate of interest = the *discount rate*.

$1/(1 + i)^t = \text{PV}(i, t)$ = the *present-value factor* for a discount rate of i and a future value t periods in the future; also called the *discount factor*.

The discount rate that should be used to calculate the present value is what economists call the *opportunity cost* or the *appropriate time value of money*. If the present value of a savings account earning a 10 percent per year rate of interest is to be determined, then the 10 percent interest income is the opportunity cost of not saving the dollar.

Table 4.2 shows the present value of $1 received at different possible time periods t in the future for various discount rates.

Figure 4-2 illustrates how the present value of future amounts declines with the discount rate and the length of time until the benefit is received.

Table 4.2 The Present Value of $1 to Be Received *t* Periods in the Future Discounted at the Rate *i*

Time Period, t	Discount Rate or Interest Rate, i			
	$i = 1\%$	$i = 5\%$	$i = 10\%$	$i = 15\%$
1	.990	.952	.909	.870
2	.980	.907	.826	.756
3	.971	.864	.751	.658
4	.961	.823	.683	.572
5	.951	.784	.621	.497
6	.942	.746	.564	.432
7	.933	.711	.513	.376
8	.923	.677	.467	.327
9	.914	.645	.424	.284
10	.905	.614	.386	.247
15	.861	.481	.239	.123
20	.820	.377	.149	.061
25	.780	.295	.092	.030
30	.742	.231	.057	.015

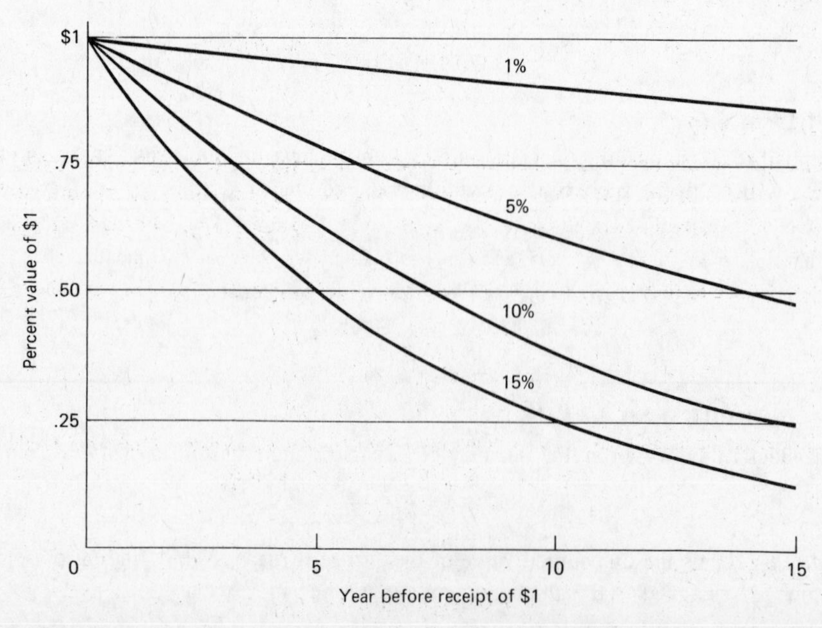

Fig. 4-2 The effects of time t and the discount rate i on the present value of $1.

SOLVED PROBLEM 4.7

Using a 10 percent discount rate, find the present value of a \$1 cash flow if \$1 is received (*a*) in 1 year, (*b*) in 2 years, and (*c*) in 6 months.

SOLUTION

We have $i = 10\% = .10$ and $p_t = \$1$.

(*a*) For 1 year $t = 1$.

$$p_0 = \frac{p_t}{(1.10)^1} = \frac{\$1}{1.10} = \$1(.9090) = 90.9¢$$

(*b*) For 2 years, $t = 2$.

$$p_0 = \frac{p_t}{(1.10)^2} = \frac{1}{(1.10)^2} = \frac{\$1}{1.21} = \$1(.8264) = 82.6¢$$

(*c*) For 6 months, $t = \frac{1}{2}$.[3]

$$p_0 = \frac{p_t}{(1.10)^{1/2}} = \frac{\$1}{\sqrt{1.10}} = \frac{\$1}{1.0488} = \$1(.95347) = 95.4¢$$

SOLVED PROBLEM 4.8

A professional football player signs a contract for \$100,000 per year salary plus a \$200,000 bonus after playing on the team for 3 years. Since the football player keeps all his investable funds in a savings account that earns 5 percent interest, we will use 5 percent as a discount rate.

(*a*) What is the present value of \$1 if we have $i = 5\% = .05$ and $t = 3$?

(*b*) What is the present value of the \$200,000 bonus?

SOLUTION

(*a*)
$$p_0 = \frac{p_3}{(1.05)^3} = \frac{\$1}{1.1576} = 86.39¢$$

(*b*)
$$p_0 = \frac{p_3}{(1.05)^3} = \frac{\$200{,}000}{1.1576} = \$172{,}771.25$$

SOLVED PROBLEM 4.9

The Reliable Corporation promised Fred a \$10,000 retirement at the end of 25 more years of service. Assume 10 percent is the best interest rate Fred can earn on his long-term savings. What is the present value of the retirement bonus?

SOLUTION

We have $i = 10\% = .10$, $t = 25$, and $p_{25} = \$10{,}000$.

$$p_0 = \frac{p_{25}}{(1.10)^{25}} = \frac{\$10{,}000}{10.8347} = \$922.96$$

SOLVED PROBLEM 4.10

The Apex Corporation adopts an accelerated depreciation strategy that delays its payment of \$36,000 of income taxes for 4 years. (*a*) What is the present value of postponing this income tax? Assume Apex can always buy back its own outstanding bonds and save 10 percent interest on the debt reduction.

[3] If a calculator is not available to find the square root, the computations can be done by hand using logarithms, as shown below:

$$p_0 = \frac{p_t}{(1+i)^t} = p_t(1+i)^{-t}$$
$$\log p_0 = \log p_t - t[\log(1+i)]$$
$$= \log \$1 - \tfrac{1}{2}(\log 1.10)$$

The value of p_0 can be found by using a table of logarithms and antilogarithms. Using base e logarithms yields

$$\log_e(p_0) = \log_e(\$1) - t[\log_e(1 + .10)]$$
$$= 0 - \tfrac{1}{2}(.095310)$$
$$= -.047655$$

The antilogarithm yields the price:

$$p_0 = \text{antilogarithm of } \log_e(p_t)$$
$$= e^{-0.047655} = \$.9534625$$

Based on Apex's opportunity to use its funds to save 10 percent interest expense, the opportunity cost for debt capital is assumed to be 10 percent. (*b*) What is the appropriate discount factor?

SOLUTION

We have $p_4 = \$36{,}000$, $i = 10\% = .10$, and $t = 4$.

(*a*)
$$p_0 = \frac{p_4}{(1.10)^4} = \frac{\$36{,}000}{1.4641} = \$24{,}588.48$$

(*b*) The discount factor is

$$\frac{1}{(1.10)^4} = .6830$$

SOLVED PROBLEM 4.11

Twenty-three-year-old Ira's parents paid in advance for a $1,000,000 trust fund that he will inherit on his thirty-fifth birthday. Ira does not want to wait for the money. So, Ira went to the bank where his trust fund is being held and asked how much that bank will pay him now for the $1,000,000 cash flow they are holding for him that is guaranteed to be forthcoming 12 years (35 − 23) in the future. The bank charges a prime rate of 10 percent on its least risky loans. What is a fair present value for the bank to pay Ira now for his future inheritance?

SOLUTION

We have $p_{12} = \$1{,}000{,}000$, $t = 12$, and $i = 10\% = .10$.

$$p_{12} = \frac{p_{12}}{(1.10)^{12}} = \frac{\$1{,}000{,}000}{3.1384} = \$318{,}630.82$$

Ira did what is called *factoring* an account receivable.

SOLVED PROBLEM 4.12

Joe is wondering whether he should pay $40 per share for a growth stock that pays no cash dividends but is appreciating rapidly. Joe estimates that he could sell the stock for $55 per share in 2 years. If Joe can borrow the money to buy the growth stock at 12 percent interest, (*a*) what is the present value of the anticipated stock sale? (*b*) Should Joe buy the stock?

SOLUTION

We have $p_2 = \$55$, $t = 2$, and $i = 12\% = .12$.

(*a*)
$$p_0 = \frac{p_2}{(1.12)^2} = \frac{\$55}{1.2544} = \$43.85$$

(*b*) Yes. The stock's present value of $43.85 exceeds its current price of $40.

4.3 ANNUITIES

An *annuity* is a series of periodic cash flows of equal size. The coupon payments from a bond, monthly social security payments, and other retirement plan payments are examples of annuity streams.

The Present Value of an Annuity Stream

The present value of one future cash flow can be calculated with Eq. (*4.2*). The *present value of an annuity* is the sum of a series of *T* equal-sized cash flows, as shown in Eq. (*4.3*):

$$p_0 = \sum_{t=1}^{T} \frac{A_t}{(1+i)^t} = A\left[\sum_{t=1}^{T} \frac{1}{(1+i)^t}\right]$$
$$= \frac{A_1}{(1+i)^1} + \frac{A_2}{(1+i)^2} + \cdots + \frac{A_T}{(1+i)^T} \tag{4.3}$$

The following additional notation is adapted to use with annuities:

T = the *terminal* time period, when the final payment is made.

A_t = the annuity payment made at the end of time period t. Note that $A_1 = A_2 = A_t = A$ for all t for any given annuity stream (by the definition of annuities).

$$\text{PVA}(i, T) = \sum_{t=1}^{T} \frac{1}{(1+i)^t}$$

where PVA(i, T) equals the present-value factor for an annuity stream with a discount rate of i that runs for T time periods.

Table 4.3 contains a numerical example illustrating how to determine that the present value of a 3-year $1 per year annuity with a discount rate of 5 percent equals $2.72 (rounded to the nearest cent).

Table 4.3 The Present Value of a 3-Year $1 per Year Annuity Stream at 5 Percent Discount Rate

Present Value in Period t	End of Year 1	End of Year 2	End of Year 3
	$\$1 = A_1$	$\$1 = A_2$	$\$1 = A_3$
$95.2¢ ←	times .952 = PV(.05, 1)		
$90.7¢ ←		times .907 = PV(.05, 2)	
$86.4¢ ←			times .864 = PV(.05, 3)
$2.723 = $1[PVA($i$, T)]			

The present-value factors for annuities, denoted PVA(i, T) can be tedious and error-prone to calculate by hand. Table 4.4 contains the present value of annuity factors for several discount rates and various numbers of years. Most finance textbooks contain annuity tables.

Table 4.4 The Present Value of a $1 Annuity for T Years, PVA(i, T), Calculated with Discount Rates i = 1%, 5%, 10%, and 15%

Number of Years, t	Discount Rate or Interest Rate, i			
	i = 1%	i = 5%	i = 10%	i = 15%
1	.990	.952	.909	.870
2	1.970	1.859	1.736	1.626
3	2.941	2.723	2.487	2.283
4	3.902	3.546	3.170	2.855
5	4.853	4.329	3.791	3.352
6	5.795	5.076	4.355	3.784
7	6.728	5.786	4.868	4.160
8	7.652	6.463	5.335	4.487
9	8.566	7.108	5.759	4.772
10	9.471	7.722	6.145	5.019
15	13.865	10.380	7.606	5.847
20	18.046	12.462	8.514	6.259
25	22.023	14.094	9.077	6.464
30	25.808	15.372	9.427	6.566

Some annuities (British Consols, for instance) that continue their payments to infinity are called *perpetuities*. The present value of a perpetuity is [a mathematical geometric progression of Eq. (*4.3*) that simplifies down to] Eq. (*4.3a*):

$$p_0 = A \sum_{t=1}^{T=\infty} \frac{1}{(1+i)^t} = A\left(\frac{1}{i}\right) \tag{4.3a}$$

The Future Value of an Annuity Stream

The future value of equal annual savings deposits made over a number of years is called the *future value of an annuity*. Equation (*4.1*) defined the future value of 1 year's savings deposit. Equation (*4.4*) shows how to sum up several years' equal-sized savings deposits to obtain the *future value of a T-year annuity,* denoted by p_T.

$$\begin{aligned} p_T &= \sum_{t=1}^{T} A_t(1+i)^{T-t} = A\left[\sum_{t=1}^{T}(1+i)^{T-t}\right] \\ &= A_1(1+i)^{T-1} + A_2(1+i)^{T-2} + \cdots + A_T(1+i)^0 \end{aligned} \tag{4.4}$$

Table 4.5 contains a numerical example illustrating how to determine that the future value of a \$100 per year stream of savings for 4 years equals \$464.10 if the interest rate is 10 percent.

Table 4.5 The Future Value of a 4-Year \$100 Annuity Stream with a 10 Percent Interest Rate

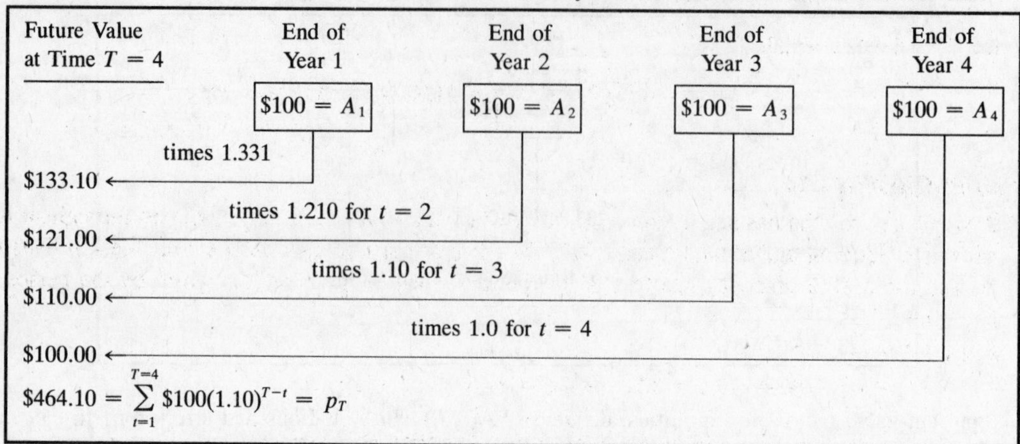

Calculating the future-value factors for an annuity stream can be expedited by using a calculator or a table. Table 4.6 contains the future values of \$1 annuities calculated with different rates of interest and various numbers of years.

Table 4.6 Future-Value Factors for a T-Year Annuity Accumulating at Rates of Interest i = 1%, 5%, 10%, and 15%*

Number of Years, t	Interest Rates, i			
	i = 1%	i = 5%	i = 10%	i = 15%
1	1.000	1.000	1.000	1.000
2	2.010	2.050	2.100	2.150
3	3.030	3.153	3.310	3.473
4	4.060	4.310	4.641	4.993
5	5.101	5.526	6.105	6.742
6	6.152	6.802	7.716	8.754
7	7.214	8.142	9.487	11.067
8	8.286	9.549	11.436	13.727
9	9.369	11.027	13.579	16.786
10	10.462	12.578	15.937	20.304
15	16.097	21.579	31.772	47.580
20	22.019	33.006	57.275	102.444
25	28.243	47.727	98.347	212.793
30	34.785	66.439	164.494	434.745

*It is assumed that \$1 is received or paid out at the end of each year. This is called an ordinary annuity.

SOLVED PROBLEM 4.13

Tom has been saving \$1,000 per year in a savings account at 5 percent per year interest since he was 62 years old.

(*a*) What should the future value of the \$1,000 per year stream of savings be when Tom reaches age 65 if he keeps making the deposits every year for 3 years?

(*b*) If Tom had started saving \$1,000 per year when he was 35 years old what would be the future value in the account when he reached 65 years old?

SOLUTION

We have $i = 5\% = .05$ and $A_t = \$1,000$.

(*a*) $T = 65 - 62 = 3$.

$$p_{t=3} = A\left[\sum_{t=1}^{3}(1.05)^{3-t}\right] = \$1,000(3.153) = \$3,153$$

(*b*) $T = 65 - 35 = 30$.

$$p_{t=30} = A\left[\sum_{t=1}^{30}(1.05)^{30-t}\right] = \$1,000(66.439) = \$66,439$$

SOLVED PROBLEM 4.14

A single person who has had a high level of earnings and paid Social Security taxes throughout his life expects to retire at age 65 and receive \$10,000 per year until he dies. Assume this person lives to age 80 and use a 10% discount rate to find the present value of the benefit received by the person when he retires.

SOLUTION

We have $i = 10\% = .10$, $A = \$10,000$, and $T = 80 - 65 = 15$ years.

$$p_0 = A\left[\sum_{t=1}^{T}\frac{1}{(1+i)^t}\right] = \$10,000\left[\sum_{t=1}^{15}\frac{1}{(1.1)^t}\right]$$
$$= \$10,000(7.606) = \$76,060$$

SOLVED PROBLEM 4.15

Ralph and Susan are both 35 years old, married, and are budgeting to provide a comfortable retirement for themselves. If they can save a total of \$7,000 each year until they retire and can earn 10 percent interest on these savings, how much will they have when they reach age 65?

SOLUTION

We have $i = 10\% = .10$, $A = \$7,000$, and $T = 65 - 35 = 30$ years.

$$p_T = A\sum_{t=1}^{T}(1+i)^{T-t} = \$7,000\sum_{t=1}^{30}(1.10)^{T-t}$$
$$= \$7,000(164.494) = \$1,151,458$$

SOLVED PROBLEM 4.16

Andrew is 35 years old and wants to have \$2 million when he retires at age 65. If he can earn 10 percent interest on all the money he saves for retirement, how much must Andrew save each year to reach his \$2 million goal?

SOLUTION

We have $T = 65 - 35 = 30$ years, $i = 10\% = .10$, and $p_T = \$2,000,000$. The answer to Andrew's question can be found by solving Eq. (*4.4a*) for the value of A, as shown below:

$$p_T = A\sum_{t=1}^{T}(1+i)^{T-t} \tag{4.4a}$$

$$\$2,000,000 = A\sum_{t=1}^{30}(1.10)^{30-t} = A(164.494)$$

Looking up the value of $\Sigma_{t=1}^{30}(1.10)^{30-t}$ in Table 4.6 we find 164.494, which we divide into \$2 million to get $A = \$12,158.50$.

If Andrew can save \$12,158.50 every year, he will be a multimillionaire.

SOLVED PROBLEM 4.17

A medical (or auto or home) insurance company advertises that the firm will return every penny you ever pay for the insurance if you *never* file a claim. Thus, if you pay \$500 per year for the next 10 years and never file a claim you can recover \$5,000 (\$500 × 10 years). Is this a good deal if your opportunity cost for the money is 10 percent interest.

SOLUTION

We have $i = 10\% = .10$, $A = \$500$, and $T = 10$. To begin with we must find the future value of the annuity stream.

$$p_T = A\sum_{t=1}^{T}(1+i)^{T-t} = \$500\sum_{t=1}^{10}(1.10)^{T-t}$$
$$= \$500(15.937) = \$7{,}968.50$$

This means the insurance company has accumulated \$7,968.50 by investing your insurance premiums at 10 percent. After the company refunds the \$5,000 to you, you will still have lost the \$2,968.50 (\$7,968.50 − \$5,000) of interest income that stays with the insurance company.

SOLVED PROBLEM 4.18

Sheila is wondering whether she should keep \$10,000 she has in a savings account that earns 10 percent interest or invest the \$10,000 in Treasury bonds. The bond she is considering pays \$90 per year in coupon interest payments until it matures in 10 years, when the \$10,000 principal and the last coupon are paid to her. The T-bonds cost \$4,980 a piece.

SOLUTION

Since Sheila can earn $i = 10\% = .10$ interst on her savings, that is her opportunity cost if she buys the bond. The bond is like an annuity with $A = \$90$ for $T = 10$ years with an additional \$10,000 lump-sum final payment. The present value of the annuitylike bond coupons is found with Table 4.4.

$$p_0 = A\sum_{t=1}^{T}\frac{1}{(1+i)^t} = \$90\sum_{t=1}^{10}\frac{1}{(1.10)^t}$$
$$= \$90(6.145) = \$553.05$$

The present value of the principal is calculated with Eq. (*4.2*) and Table 4.2:

$$p_0 = \frac{p_t}{(1+i)^t} = \frac{\$10{,}000}{(1.10)^{10}}$$
$$= \$10{,}000(.386) = \$3{,}860$$

Adding the present values of the coupons (\$553.05) and the principal (\$3,860) we find that the present value of the bond investment is \$553.05 + \$3,860 which equals \$4,413.05; this is less than the \$4,980 price of the bond. So, the bond is a bad investment. Sheila should leave her money in the savings account.

SOLVED PROBLEM 4.19

John is trying to estimate the value of a share of nonredeemable preferred stock issued by the Acme Corporation, a blue-chip company. The stock pays a cumulative 9 percent cash dividend rate on its face value of \$100 per share. This Acme preferred stock has a selling price of \$106. The stock has yielded a compounded rate of return of 8 percent per annum (including cash dividends) compounded over the last 10 years. Is the stock over- or underpriced at \$106.

SOLUTION

The cash dividends are 9 percent of the \$100 face value, or $A = \$9$ per year for the Acme preferred. The risk of default is nil since Acme is a blue-chip firm. The risk that the dividends might not be paid is practically nonexistent since they are cumulative and the stock is nonredeemable, $T = \infty$. Since Acme preferred has been earning 8 percent over the last decade, that is to be the proper risk-adjusted discount rate to use to find the present value of the stock, $i = 8\% = .08$. Acme preferred is like a \$9 per year annuity to infinity. The present value of a share of an infinite annuity equals the present value of its expected cash flows payable to infinity, calculated with Eq. (*4.3a*):

$$p_0 = A\sum_{t=1}^{T=\infty}\frac{1}{(1+i)^t} = \$9\sum_{t=1}^{\infty}\frac{1}{(1.08)^t}$$
$$= \$9\left(\frac{1}{.08}\right) = \$9(12.5) = \$112.50$$

Since the present value of \$112.50 exceeds the price of \$106, the Acme preferred stock is undervalued. John should invest.

True-False Questions

4.1 The old saying that "A penny saved is a penny earned" is a little oversimplified in view of the time value of money.

4.2 The present value of $5 to be received with certainty 5 years in the future is $3.105 if the discount rate is 10 percent.

4.3 The present value of $1,000 is greater if compounding is quarterly rather than semiannually when the discount rate is greater than zero.

4.4 The present value of $250 to be received at the end of each year for 10 years at 12 percent is $1,500.

4.5 The future value of $10,000 compounded quarterly at 16 percent for 5 years is $21,911.23.

Multiple Choice Questions

4.1 How much is a dollar worth today if you can expect to receive it a year from now from a FDIC-insured bank with no risk of default?
(*a*) Less than $1.00
(*b*) $1.00
(*c*) More than $1.00
(*d*) Not enough information given to tell

4.2 How is the present value of a particular stream of cash flows affected by the timing of the receipt of the cash flows if everything else affecting the cash flows is held constant?
(*a*) The present value of the cash flows increases directly with the length of time in the future until the cash flows are received.
(*b*) The present value of the cash flows varies inversely with the length of time in the future until the cash flows are received.
(*c*) The present value of the cash flows is not affected by the length of time in the future until the cash flows are received.
(*d*) None of the above are true.

4.3 What is the present value of a $1 cash flow to be received annually at the end of each of the next 3 years if the discount rate is 15%?
(*a*) $1.859
(*b*) $1.736
(*c*) $1.626
(*d*) $2.283

4.4 Determine the present value of the following cash flows if the assumed discount rate is 14 percent:

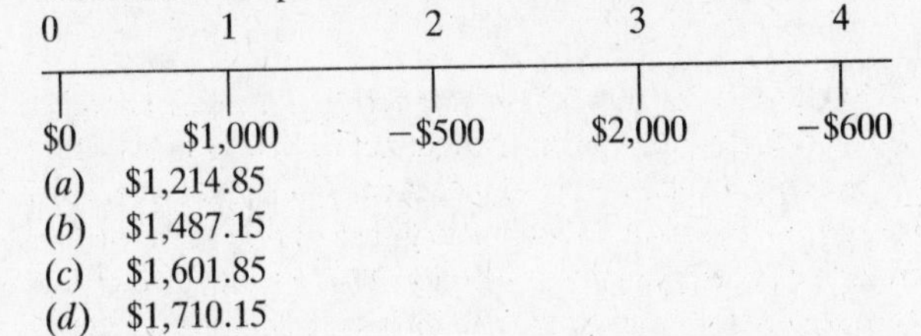

(*a*) $1,214.85
(*b*) $1,487.15
(*c*) $1,601.85
(*d*) $1,710.15
(*e*) $1,487.14

4.5 Refer to Question 4.4. What is the present value of these cash flows if the discount rate is 9 percent?
(*a*) $1,615.90
(*b*) $1,715.60
(*c*) $1,600.25
(*d*) $1,800.15
(*e*) $1,688.12

4.6 Determine the present value of $1,500 to be received at the end of 10 years if the compound rate of interest is 9 percent.
(*a*) $674.00
(*b*) $633.62
(*c*) $710.25
(*d*) $583.12
(*e*) $550.23

4.7 Refer to Question 4.6. Determine the present value if the rate of interest is 12 percent compounded quarterly.
(*a*) $426.13
(*b*) $545.00
(*c*) $565.12
(*d*) $459.84
(*e*) $604.83

4.8 How much would you be willing to pay for an investment with an expected cash flow of $500 per year for the next 10 years if the assumed discount rate was 12 percent?
(*a*) $2,500.11
(*b*) $2,635.14
(*c*) $2,710.45
(*d*) $2,750.12
(*e*) $2,825.11

4.9 Determine the future value of $8,000 compounded annually for 15 years at 14 percent.
(*a*) $57,103.50
(*b*) $59,200.41
(*c*) $61,000.25
(*d*) $56,455.00
(*e*) $58,801.25

4.10 Determine the rate of return on a $10,000 investment that generated cash flows of $2,500 per year for 8 years.
(*a*) 20.53 percent
(*b*) 17.59 percent
(*c*) 21.77 percent
(*d*) 18.62 percent
(*e*) 17.12 percent

Answers

True-False

4.1. T 4.2. T 4.3. F 4.4. F 4.5. T

Multiple Choice

4.1. a 4.2. b 4.3. d 4.4. b 4.5. a 4.6. b 4.7. d 4.8. e 4.9. a 4.10. d

Chapter 5

U.S. Treasury, Agency, and Related Bonds

5.1 CHARACTERISTICS OF GOVERNMENTAL SECURITIES IN THE UNITED STATES

The total debt of the U.S. federal government grew to exceed three trillion dollars (that is, three thousand billions of dollars) in 1990 and continues to grow. Most of this federal debt is in the form of interest-bearing securities issued by the U.S. Treasury; the various securities are called bonds, notes, bills, certificates of indebtedness, and U.S. savings bonds.

SOLVED PROBLEM 5.1

What is the main way that corporate and municipal bonds differ from U.S. government securities?

SOLUTION

In contrast to corporate and municipal bonds, U.S. government securities are of such high quality that their yield is a *default-free* interest rate. They are free from the risk of default because the U.S. government has unlimited power to tax or to print money whenever such action becomes necessary in order to obtain the money to pay its bills. In addition, there are tax differences. Municipal bonds are exempt from federal and state income taxes. U.S. government bonds are exempt from state taxes. Corporate bonds, however, are not exempt from taxes.

5.2 THE MARKETABILITY OF TREASURY SECURITIES

Assets that can be sold quickly without paying substantial selling fees or without significantly lowering the price are called *marketable* (or *liquid*) assets. Assets that are not readily marketable are *illiquid;* it is costly to turn these assets into cash in a short period of time. Houses, antiques, and stamp collections are examples of investments that are not readily marketable. If one of these illiquid assets had to be sold within a 24-hour period of time large commissions and even larger price reductions that could wipe out more than half of the asset's assessed market value would probably be necessary to effect a quick sale. In order to avoid costly liquidation expenses, it is highly desirable for an investment to be readily marketable.

SOLVED PROBLEM 5.2

While most Treasury securities are among the most marketable assets in the world, certain Treasury securities are not marketable at all. Which Treasury securities are not marketable?

SOLUTION

Roughly one-third of the federal debt consists of nonmarketable issues. These cannot be traded in the securities market; they are not transferable or negotiable; they cannot be used as collateral for a loan; they can be purchased only from the Treasury; and they can be redeemed only by the Treasury. Unlike most illiquid federal assets, U.S. savings bonds are well known. U.S. savings bonds are not marketable only because the law says they may be redeemed only at U.S. government offices.

The major portion of nonmarketable securities are U.S. saving bonds—they are Series E and H and the newer Series EE and HH bonds. EE savings bonds were introduced in 1982 to replace the old series E bonds; they are allowed to pay higher interest rates than their predecessors. The E and EE savings bonds pay no coupons; they are sold at discounts from their face values. The face values range from $50 up to $10,000 denominations. The EE government savings bonds are sold at deep discounts (of 50 percent) to yield at least 85 percent of whatever the market yield on 5-year Treasury securities is on the date the EE bond is purchased. Furthermore, the EE savings bonds guarantee a minimum yield of 7.5 percent if held to maturity, no matter how low the other market interest rates may fall. If a savings bond is redeemed before its maturity date, the investor is penalized for the early redemption.

The Series HH savings bonds pay the same interest rates as the EE bonds. However, the HH bonds (1) have 10 years to maturity and (2) pay semiannual–annual coupons; the coupon income must be reported to the IRS annually and $500 is the smallest denomination.

Marketable Treasury Issues

Marketable issues make up about two-thirds of the federal debt. They are usually purchased from outstanding supplies through a dealer or broker. However, the purchaser may subscribe for new issues through any one of the twelve Federal Reserve banks around the United States. Securities issued by the U.S. Treasury are so highly marketable that they possess many of the same qualities of U.S. money, which is the most liquid asset in the world.

The holder of marketable government securities stands to gain not only from the interest paid on these bonds, like the owner of nonmarketable bonds, but also from price appreciation. Bid and ask prices for these marketable issues are published daily in national newspapers such as *The New York Times* and *The Wall Street Journal*. The prices of the T-notes and T-bonds are quoted in thirty-seconds of one percent of their face value; fractions are written as though they were decimals. For example, 70.16 means $70\frac{16}{32}$ percent of par. However, the prices of T-bills are not published; the bid and asked yields-to-maturity are published to the nearest basis point.

5.3 TREASURY BILLS

T-bills are extremely liquid, short-term notes that mature in 13, 26, or 52 weeks from date of issue. The Treasury usually offers new bills every week, auctioning them on a discount from face value basis. Auctions are held at the Federal Reserve Bank of New York. T-bills are issued only on a "book entry" basis—the buyer never actually receives the security, only a receipt. The Treasury agent records the purchasers' transactions and issues receipts to the Treasury bill buyers instead of the actual T-bill.

T-bills are only sold on a discount basis. The discount to investors is the difference between the price they have paid and the face amount they will receive at maturity.

SOLVED PROBLEM 5.3

A $10,000 90-day T-bill can be purchased at its asked yield of 10.6 percent at an annual rate. At the end of the 90 days the buyer would be repaid the $10,000 face value by the U.S. Treasury.

(*a*) What is the present value of this T-bill?

(*b*) What is the purchase price of this T-bill?

(*c*) If the bid-asked spread on this transaction is 30 basis points on the annual rates, what is the bid-asked spread in dollars?

SOLUTION

(*a*) We have $T = 13$ weeks $= \frac{1}{4}$ of 1 year; the annual rate of interest is $i_a = .106 = 10.6$ percent; $p_1 = \$10{,}000$; and p_0 is unknown.

$$P_0 = \frac{\$10{,}000}{(1.0 + i_a)^{1/4}} = \frac{\$10{,}000}{(1.106)^{1/4}}$$
$$= \$10{,}000(.975127) = \$9{,}751.27$$

The present value of the $10,000 T-bill is $9,751.27.

(*b*) Calculate the purchase price for Wall Street by using Eq. (*5.1*) to obtain the quarterly rate qr from the annual rate ar:

$$(\text{ar})\,(\text{fraction of year}) = \text{qr} \tag{5.1}$$

$$(\text{ar})\left(\frac{13 \text{ weeks}}{52 \text{ weeks}}\right) = (10.6\%)\left(\tfrac{1}{4}\right) = 2.65\% = .0265 = \text{qr}$$

The purchase price is then calculated with Eq. (*5.2*):

$$(\text{Face})\,(1.0 - \text{qr}) = \text{purchase price} \tag{5.2}$$

$$\$10{,}000(1.0 - .0265) = \$10{,}000(.9735) = \$9{,}735$$

The asked price associated with the asked yield of 10.6 percent is $9,735. The investor could expect the $265 ($10,000 − $9,735) discount from the face value as price appreciation income.

(*c*) If the bid-asked yield is 30 basis points, the bid yield must be 30 basis points above the asked yield. Therefore, the bid yield is 10.9 percent.

$$(\text{Bid ar})(\text{fraction of year}) = \text{bid qr} \tag{5.2a}$$

$$(10.9\%)\left(\tfrac{1}{4}\right) = 2.2725\% = .02725 = \text{bid qr}$$

$$(\text{Face})(1.0 - \text{bid qr}) = \text{bid price} \tag{5.2b}$$

$$(10{,}000)(1.0 - .02725) = (10{,}000)(.97275) = \$9{,}727.50 \quad \text{(bid price)}$$

The bid-ask spread in dollars is

$$\text{Asked price} - \text{bid price} = \text{bid-asked spread} \tag{5.2c}$$

The asked price comes from Eq. (*5.2*) above. Therefore,

$$9{,}735.00 - 9{,}727.50 = 7.50 = \text{bid-asked spread}$$

Treasury bills are money market securites that were introduced in Chapter 1—additional details about T-bills can be obtained there.

5.4 CERTIFICATES OF INDEBTEDNESS

Certificates of indebtedness are issued at par (or face) value. Later, after they are issued, certificates are traded in the market at prices which vary minute-by-minute. Certificates bear fixed coupon rates. The *coupon rate* tells what percent of the certificate's face value will be paid out in two semiannual–annual coupon interest payments each year. Certificates usually mature 1 year after their date of issue, but the Treasury can set the period of time to be any length of time up to 1 year. Certificates have been issued infrequently by the Treasury in recent years.

5.5 TREASURY NOTES

Treasury notes are similar to certificates of indebtedness except with regard to their time until maturity. T-notes are bonds that typically have a maturity of from 1 to 10 years. Notes are available in bearer, registered, or book-entry form.

5.6 TREASURY BONDS

Treasury bonds comprise about 10 percent of the federal debt. Bonds differ from notes and certificates with respect to maturity; bond issues run from 10 to 30 years from their date of issue to their maturity. Another significant difference is that some T-bond issues are *callable* prior to the maturity date of the issue. Treasury bond issues that are callable may be called anytime during the last 5 years of the life of the issue. If callable T-bonds are selling in the market above par, their yield-to-maturity is calculated to the nearest call date. If they are selling at a discount, the yield-to-maturity is calculated on the basis of their maturity date. The yield-to-maturity is a compound average rate of return calculated over the bond's entire life.

SOLVED PROBLEM 5.4

How do the press report the maturity date of an issue of callable T-bonds?

SOLUTION

The 12 percent coupon rate T-bonds scheduled to mature in 2013, for instance, are callable anytime after 2008. These bonds are called the "12s of 2008–13" in the newspapers.

5.7 NEWSPAPER PRICE QUOTATIONS FOR TREASURY SECURITIES

Figure 5-1 shows one day's closing price quotations for U.S. government and agency bonds from a newspaper. The left-hand column gives the maturity date of the issue. The lowercase letter n is printed after those issues which are Treasury notes. If the securities are coupon-paying bonds, then the second column gives the coupon rate. T-bills have no coupon rates since they are sold at discount so as to pay interest income in the form of price appreciation rather than by coupon payments.

Government Agency Bonds

Prices in 32d of a point, bill yields in basis points.

BONDS & NOTES

Date			Rate	Bid	Ask	Chg.	Yield
Aug	91	p	7 1/2	99-31	100-03		2.56
Aug	91	p	8 3/4	100	100-04		1.16
Aug	91	n	14 7/8	100-04	100-08		1.81
Aug	91	p	8 1/4	100-01	100-05		4.68
Sep	91	p	8 3/8	100-10	100-14		4.80
Sep	91	p	9 1/8	100-13	100-17		4.80
Oct	91	p	7 5/8	100-12	100-16		5.13
Oct	91	p	12 1/4	101-02	101-06	-01	4.98
Nov	91	p	6 1/2	100-05	100-09		5.29
Nov	91	p	8 1/2	100-21	100-25		5.26
Nov	91	n	14 1/4	102-01	102-09	-01	4.94
Nov	91	p	7 3/4	100-17	100-21		5.40
Dec	91	p	7 5/8	100-22	100-26		5.38
Dec	91	p	8 1/4	100-29	101-01		5.41
Jan	92	p	8 1/8	101-02	101-06	-01	5.47
Jan	92	p	11 5/8	102-13	102-17		5.39
Feb	92	p	6 5/8	100-12	100-16		5.60
Feb	92	p	8 1/2	101-13	101-17		5.60
Feb	92	p	9 1/8	101-19	101-23		5.61
Feb	92	n	14 5/8	104-11	104-21	-01	5.12
Mar	92	p	7 7/8	101-09	101-13		5.55
Mar	92	p	8 1/2	101-21	101-25		5.56
Apr	92	p	8 7/8	102-04	102-08		5.59
Apr	92	k	11 3/4	103-25	103-29	-02	5.69

TREASURY BILLS

Date		Bid	Ask	Chg.	Yield
-1991-					
Aug	15	5.39	5.34	+0.27	5.43
Aug	29	5.34	5.31	-0.02	5.41
Aug	22	5.35	5.28	-0.02	5.38
Sep	26	5.29	5.25	-0.01	5.37
Sep	5	5.28	5.25	-0.04	5.35
Sep	12	5.25	5.22	-0.03	5.33
Sep	19	5.25	5.22	-0.01	5.33
Oct	3	5.29	5.25	-0.01	5.38
Oct	10	5.29	5.25		5.38
Oct	17	5.30	5.28		5.42
Oct	24	5.32	5.28	+0.02	5.43
Nov	21	5.31	5.28	-0.02	5.45
Nov	7	5.31	5.28	-0.01	5.44
Nov	14	5.31	5.28		5.44
Oct	31	5.31	5.28		5.43
Nov	29	5.33	5.31	+0.01	5.49
Dec	5	5.33	5.31		5.49
Dec	12	5.34	5.31	+0.01	5.50
Dec	19	5.32	5.28		5.47
Dec	26	5.32	5.28	-0.01	5.48
-1992-					
Jan	2	5.32	5.28	-0.03	5.48
Jan	9	5.37	5.34		5.55

FEDERAL NATIONAL MTGS

Date		Rate	Bid	Ask	Chg.	Yield
Aug	91	17	100-06	100-10	-11	4.15
Sep	91	7	100-02	100-05		4.69
Oct	91	7.80	100-09	100-15		4.64
Oct	91	7 3/8	100-07	100-10		5.22
Nov	91	9.55	100-28	100-31	-01	5.40
Dec	91	11 3/4	101-27	101-31	-02	5.42
Jan	92	8 1/2	101-04	101-08	+01	5.31
Mar	92	7	100-22	100-25		5.58
Apr	92	12	103-29	104		5.67
May	92	8.45	101-28	101-31	+01	5.68
May	92	8 1/2	101-29	102	+01	5.69
Jun	92	7.05	100-28	100-31		5.81
Jun	92	10 1/8	103-09	103-12		5.84
Jul	92	8.45	102-05	102-08	+01	5.85
Aug	92	7 3/4	101-21	101-25	+01	5.87
Sep	92	9.15	103-04	103-07		6.00
Oct	92	10.60	104-26	105		6.06
Nov	92	8.20	102-11	102-15	+02	6.09
Dec	92	9 7/8	104-14	104-17	+01	6.24
Jan	93	10.90	106-01	106-04		6.28
Feb	93	7.95	102-05	102-08		6.34
Mar	93	7.90	102-03	102-09	-01	6.35
Mar	93	10.95	106-20	106-23		6.38

Fig. 5-1 Newspaper excerpt showing U.S. government and agency bond price quotations for 1 day.

The bid and asked prices are in the next two columns of Fig. 5-1. For coupon-paying bonds, the bid and asked prices are stated as percentages of the bond's face value. For T-bills the bid and asked values are the market interest rates which the investor will earn if the T-bills are purchased at their respective bid or asked prices. The *bid price* is the highest price (stated as a percentage of face value) that any potential investor is willing to pay. The *asked price* is the lowest price that any potential seller is willing to take.[1] The column headed "Chg." contains the amount of price change from the previous day's closing price (or yield for T-bills) to the current day's closing price (or yield). The right-hand column headed "Yield" contains the yield-to-maturity the investor would earn if the security were purchased at the current market price and held to the maturity date.

5.8 DIFFERENT BOND RATE OF RETURN MEASURES

Discussions about bonds are complicated by the fact that every bond has different ways to measure its yield. More specifically, every bond has four different ways to measure its rate of return.

The Coupon Rate

The coupon rate or nominal rate is that fixed rate of interest which is printed on the bond certificate. Coupon rates are contractual rates that cannot be changed after the bond is issued.

$$\text{Coupon rate} = \frac{\text{annual coupon interest payment}}{\text{face value of the bond}} \tag{5.3}$$

Coupon rates do not exist for T-bills and other zero coupon bonds.

The Current Yield

Every bond that pays coupon interest has a current yield or coupon yield.

$$\text{Current yield} = \frac{\text{dollars of coupon interest per year}}{\text{current market price}} \tag{5.4}$$

For example, a 6.0 percent coupon bond with $1,000 face value which is selling at the discounted price of $900 has a current yield of 6.66 percent ($60/$900 = .0666). The current yield is an annual cash flow measure based on current market prices.

The Yield-to-Maturity

The internal rate of return or *yield-to-maturity* (YTM) of a bond is the discount rate that equates the present value of a bond's cash flows to the bond's current market price. The YTM is a compounded multiperiod effective rate of return that is earned if the bond (1) is held to its maturity date and (2) does not default. For a

[1] For T-bills and other money market securities the bid and asked prices are stated as interest rates instead of percentages of face value in some newspapers. The bid and asked price stated as interest rates are simply the yield-to-maturity an investor would earn if the T-bill was purchased at the current bid and asked market prices, respectively.

bond to earn its YTM over the life of the bond, the bond's interim interest payments must be invested at the YTM of the bond.

The One-Period Rate of Return

The single-period (for example, the 1-month or 1-year) rate-of-return formula for a bond is shown below:

$$\begin{pmatrix}\text{One-}\\\text{period}\\\text{rate of}\\\text{return}\end{pmatrix} = \frac{(\text{capital gain or loss}) + (\text{coupon int., if any})}{\text{purchase price}} \tag{5.5}$$

The one-period rate of return varies from positive to negative in each period as the bond experiences capital gains and losses, respectively.

Figure 5-2 illustrates how three of these four different interest rate measures interact with the market price of their related bond. Figure 5-2 illustrates three price–interest rate relationships for a default-free bond with \$1,000 face value, 6.0 percent coupon rate, and 25 years until maturity. The one-period rate of return is not shown in this figure because it depends on both the beginning and the end-of-period prices of the bond, which can not be conveyed in the figure. Figure 5-2 depicts graphically the fact that the market price of a bond *varies inversely* with both its yield-to-maturity and its current yield. Some other bond price, coupon rate, and YTM relationships are given below:

(1) For any given difference between the coupon rate and the YTM, the accompanying price change will be greater the longer the term to maturity.

(2) The percentage price changes described in (1) increase at a diminishing rate as the term to maturity increases.

(3) For any given maturity, a decrease in yield causes a capital gain which is larger than the capital loss resulting from an equal increase in yield.

(4) The higher the coupon rate on a bond, the smaller will be the percentage price change for any given change in yield (except for 1-year and perpetual bonds).

Bond relationship (3) is also related to a bond's convexity. The shape of the bond YTM curve in Fig. 5-2 is the bond's convexity. The bond YTM curve is negatively sloped and convex relative to the origin. A bond's convexity toward the YTM axis tends to increase (decrease) as its YTM decreases (increases).

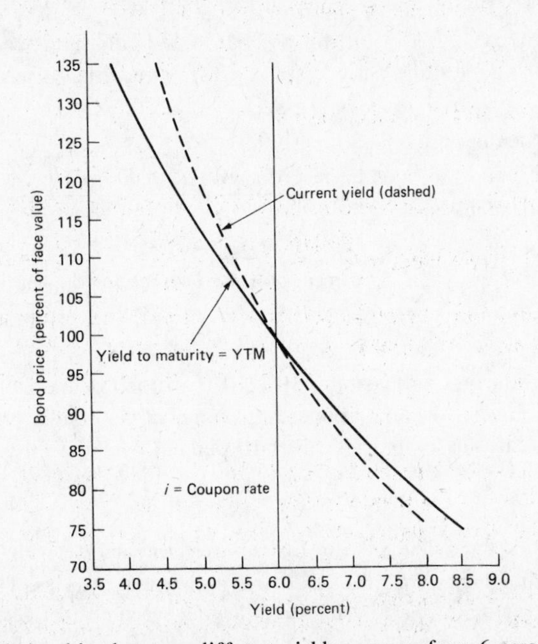

Fig. 5-2 The relationships between different yield measures for a 6 percent coupon bond.

SOLVED PROBLEM 5.5

Jane Poole purchased a bond with $1,000 face value that paid $60 per year of coupon interest and was selling at the discounted price of $900. What was this bond's coupon rate?

SOLUTION

The bond's market price is irrelevant to the coupon rate. If the annual coupon interest equals 6 percent of the bond's face value ($\frac{60}{100} = .06$), then the coupon rate printed on the face of the bond is 6 percent, and it never changes as the price of the bond fluctuates.

SOLVED PROBLEM 5.6

Jane Poole bought a $10,000 T-bond with a 5 percent coupon rate for $9,500 on June 14 and sold it prior to its maturity on June 14 of the next year for $9,950.

(*a*) What was Jane's one-period rate or return from this T-bond investment?

(*b*) If the market price of Jane's T-bond had fallen to $8,525 instead of rising to $9,950, what would her one year's rate of return have been?

SOLUTION

(*a*) If a bond sells at $9,950 on June 14 of some year after being purchased for $9,500 on June 14 of the preceding year the bond experienced a capital gain of $450. In addition, the bond paid $500 of coupon interest during that year.

$$\begin{pmatrix}\text{One-}\\ \text{period}\\ \text{rate of}\\ \text{return}\end{pmatrix} = \frac{(\text{cap. gain or loss}) + (\text{cpn. int., if any})}{\text{purchase price}} \tag{5.5}$$

$$\frac{(\$9{,}950 - \$9{,}500) + \$500}{\$9{,}500} = \frac{\$450 + \$500}{\$9{,}500} = \frac{\$950}{\$9{,}500} = .10 = 10.0\%$$

Jane's one-year rate of return is 10 percent.

(*b*) If the T-bond's market price had fallen to $8,525 instead of rising to $9,950, Jane's return would be as follows:

$$\frac{(\$8{,}525 - \$9{,}500) + (.05 \times \$1{,}000)}{\$9{,}500} = \frac{-\$975 + \$500}{\$9{,}500} = \frac{-\$475}{\$9{,}500} = -.05 = -5.0\%$$

Jane's return would be a negative 5 percent. The one-period rate of return is sometimes called the *holding period return.*

SOLVED PROBLEM 5.7

Jane Poole also bought a $10,000 T-bill for $9,751.34 and held it 13 weeks until it matured and repaid its principal. What was Jane's one-period rate of return over this 13-week-long time period?

SOLUTION

T-bills pay no coupon interest.

$$\frac{(\text{Capital gain or loss}) + (\text{coupon interest, if any})}{\text{Purchase price}} = \frac{(\$10{,}000 - \$9{,}751.34) + (\text{zero})}{\$9{,}751.34} = \frac{\$248.66}{\$9{,}751.34}$$

$$= .0255 = 2.55\%$$

Jane's one-period rate of return was 2.55 percent over the 13-week investment period.

SOLVED PROBLEM 5.8

Elsie Calhoun is considering purchasing a 10% 20-year bond of the Harvey Corporation. If Elsie purchases the bond and reinvests the annual interest payment at the bond's annual coupon rate of 10 percent, prove that Elsie will earn an annual return of 10 percent over the 20-year period. Assume Elsie paid $1,000 for the bond.

SOLUTION

First, we need to find the ending value of Elsie's investment and then calculate the return.

(1) Determine the ending lump-sum value of the interim interest payments. This is the future value of an ordinary annuity and can be calculated using the following equation from Chapter 4:

$$p_T = (\text{FV annuity}) = A \sum_{t=1}^{T} (1 + i)^{T-t} \tag{4.4}$$

where A is payment (or annual interest in this situation), i is the annual rate of return, and T denotes the number of interest payments. In the problem, $A = .10 \times 1{,}000 = \$100$, $i = .10$, and $T = 20$.

$$p_T = \$100 \times \sum_{t=1}^{20} (1 + .10)^{20-t} = \$100 \times 57.275 \quad \text{(from Appendix D)}$$
$$= \$5{,}727.50$$

In 20 years, Elsie will also have $1,000 for the bond itself. Therefore, the investment will have a future value of $5,727.50 + $1,000 = $6,727.50.

(2) If Elsie invests $1,000 ($p_0$) at 10 percent ($i = .10$) for 20 years ($t = 20$), then the ending value of her investment will be as follows:

$$p_{20} = \$1{,}000(1 + .10)^{20} \quad \text{[Eq. (4.1) from Chapter 4]}$$
$$= \$1{,}000(6.7275) \quad \text{(from Appendix A)}$$
$$= \$6{,}727.50$$

5.9 SPECIAL ISSUES

Approximately 20 percent of the government debt consists of *special issues*. These federal obligations cannot be purchased by the public and are sold by the Treasury to those special government funds that have cash to invest. The Government Employees' Retirement Fund, the Federal Old-Age and Survivors Insurance Fund, and the National Service Life Insurance Fund are examples of such funds.

5.10 AGENCY SECURITIES

The Federal Land Banks, the Federal Home Loan Banks, the Central Bank for Cooperatives, the Federal National Mortgage Association (called FNMA or Fannie Mae), Government National Mortgage Association (called GNMA or Ginnie Mae), the Postal Service, and the Federal Intermediate Credit Bank are all U.S. government agencies allowed to issue their own debt obligations. Such bonds are similar in substance to other government bonds. However, the federal government makes no guarantee that the interest and principal of these "independent" bonds are free from default. Therefore, the bonds of federal agencies must pay higher yields than federal bonds in order to induce investors to accept their higher level of default risk. In practice, it would be poor political and economic policy for the government to allow any of its own agencies to default. There have been instances in which the Treasury has provided the funds needed to prevent any such financial embarrassment. Thus, the default risk of agency securities is low. The debt of two agencies is *officially* guaranteed by the Treasury: the oustanding debt of the District of Columbia Armory Board and some of the Federal Housing Administration (FHA) bonds. The income from federal agency bonds is fully taxable, as are the coupons from all other federal government bonds.

5.11 ZERO COUPON BONDS

A zero coupon bond is a bond that does not make interim interest payments and is sold with a large discount. For example, in order to buy a so-called *zero* that matured in 2004 with a face value of $14,000, an investor need only have spent $1,000 in 1982 to buy the certificate. Such a purchase would have yielded an average annual return of 12.7 percent per year over the 22 years, if the bond is held to maturity and does not default. The disadvantage of investing in zero coupon bonds is that taxable investors must pay income taxes on the coupon interest each year (unless the bond is held in a tax-exempt account, like an IRA)—even though the investor does not actually receive the interest. So, zero coupon bonds cannot be used to delay income tax payments—only the income that is being taxed is postponed.

In 1985, the U.S. Department of the Treasury started the Separate Trading of Registered Interest and Principal of Securities (STRIPS) program. Since the introduction of STRIPS, the Treasury has dominated the market for zero coupon bonds. Zero coupon bonds are also issued by some corporations and municipalities.

SOLVED PROBLEM 5.9

For a market price of $860 Jane Poole purchased a zero coupon bond that matured in 4 years with a face value of $1,000. She held it until it matured. What was Jane's income tax on this zero coupon bond in the first year she owned it?

SOLUTION

It is impossible to tell from the information given what the tax on this zero coupon bond would be because we cannot tell what annual coupon payment to *impute* to Jane. The teaching point, however, is that some annual coupon will be attributed to the owner even if it was not actually paid. This is a disadvantage of investing in zeros.

True-False Questions

5.1 *Term bonds* are Treasury bond issues that have a single maturity date.

5.2 *Serial bonds* are issues that have spaced maturities occurring in different years.

5.3 Treasury bonds are issued in either registered or bearer form.

5.4 Public announcements of offerings of Treasury securities are made 10 to 20 days prior to the issue date to give potential bidders the opportunity to prepare their bid.

5.5 All bidders for Treasury securities except commercial banks must post cash deposits of a few percent of the value of the bid when their bid is submitted.

5.6 The old Series E and H savings bonds offered higher rates of interest than the new Series EE and HH savings bonds.

5.7 The Treasury sometimes puts T-notes in denominations as small as $1,000 up for bids when it wants to encourage small savers to invest.

5.8 The Treasury security prices quoted in the financial newspapers are over-the-counter prices that were observed during the afternoon of the previous day and may not represent an opportunity that is available anymore to potential investors.

5.9 Very little trading of Treasury securities occurs in the organized exchanges.

5.10 The bidder that bids the lowest yield-to-maturity at an auction of Treasury securities is assured of getting nothing.

5.11 The coupon interest paid on U.S. government agency bonds is exempt from state and local income taxes.

5.12 Investors who buy zero coupon bonds must pay income taxes on the coupons from their zeros every year even though they receive no interest income.

Multiple Choice Questions

5.1 Sales of Treasury securities in the secondary market requires that payment be made by which of the following methods?
(*a*) *Cash settlement* transactions must be paid for on the date of the transaction.
(*b*) Terms of "2/10 percent, net 30 days" allow the buyer to take a 2 percent discount for paying cash within 10 days after the transaction, otherwise the transaction must be fully paid within 30 days.
(*c*) *Skip-day settlement* means that payment is not due until 2 business days after the date of the trade.
(*d*) Both *a* and *c* are true.
(*e*) None of the above are true.

5.2 How are the prices of Treasury securities quoted in the financial press?
(*a*) T-bill prices are not quoted; the bills' bid and asked yields are what is quoted in the newspapers.
(*b*) The prices of T-bonds are quoted in $\frac{1}{32}$s of 1 percentage point of the face value.
(*c*) The prices of "flower bonds" are quoted to the penny.

(*d*) Both *a* and *b* are true.
(*e*) None of the above are true.

5.3 The *stop-out price* is which of the following?
(*a*) The type of order you might give to your securities broker that is also called a "stop-loss order."
(*b*) The price below which the Treasury decides not to accept any more bids at a Treasury auction.
(*c*) The same thing as a "Dutch auction."
(*d*) An uncompetitively high asking price that a dealer posts when he temporarily decides not to transact any more sales.

5.4 If the *current yield* on a bond declines from one day to the next, how do other measures of the same bond's yield behave over the simultaneous time interval?
(*a*) The coupon rate will also decline.
(*b*) The YTM will also decline.
(*c*) The one-period rate of return over that day will be positive.
(*d*) All of the above are true.
(*e*) None of the above are true.

5.5 Series EE savings bonds are best described by which of the following statements?
(*a*) They are nonmarketable securities that can only be redeemed at an office of the U.S. government.
(*b*) They pay a guaranteed minimum rate of interest of at least 7.5 percent, if they are held to their maturity date.
(*c*) They pay a guaranteed minimum rate of interest equal to at least 85 percent of the market interest rate on 5-year Treasury securities outstanding on the date when the savings bonds were issued, if they are held to their maturity date.
(*d*) All of the above are true.
(*e*) None of the above are true.

5.6 When agencies of the U.S. government have a primary offering, how do they sell the securities?
(*a*) The agency uses an investment banker (just like a Fortune 500 corporation would do if it issued bonds).
(*b*) The Treasury sells the agency issue using the Federal Reserve banks as agents (similar to the way a Treasury issue is handled).
(*c*) Either *a* or *b* may be used.
(*d*) The agency accepts bids for the issue directly from the public.
(*e*) All of the above are used sometimes.

5.7 Which of the following statements describes how the U.S. Congress exercises some controls over the Treasury's security offerings?
(*a*) Congress has set a 4.25 percent interest rate ceiling on T-bond issues. The Treasury cannot violate this ceiling unless it obtains special advance permission for a specific issue of T-bonds that pays a higher rate.
(*b*) The Congress sets a limit on the size of the nation's debt. The Treasury cannot exceed this limit by selling securities that would push the debt over that ceiling.
(*c*) Both *a* and *b* are true.
(*d*) None of the above are true.

5.8 A security will not earn the yield-to-maturity that was promised when the security was purchased if which of the following conditions occurs?
(*a*) The issuer defaults on either the interest or principal payments.
(*b*) The investor sells the security prior to its maturity date.
(*c*) Cash flows from the security paid to the investor prior to its maturity date are held in cash or spent on consumption goods rather than reinvested.
(*d*) All of the above are true.
(*e*) None of the above are true.

5.9 The size of the bid-asked spread determines which of the following factors?
(*a*) Smaller spreads indicate greater market liquidity in that issue at that time.
(*b*) The spreads tend to be larger on small transactions.
(*c*) The broker and the dealer that participated in the transaction obtain their remuneration from the spread.
(*d*) All of the above are true.
(*e*) None of the above are true.

5.10 Treasury bond investors face which of the following types of investment risks?
(*a*) Purchasing power risk
(*b*) Interest rate risk
(*c*) Reinvestment risk
(*d*) All of the above
(*e*) None of the above

Answers

True-False

5.1. T 5.2. T 5.3. T 5.4. T 5.5. T 5.6. F 5.7. T 5.8. T 5.9. T 5.10 F
5.11. T 5.12. T

Multiple Choice

5.1. d 5.2. d 5.3. b 5.4. b 5.5. d 5.6. a 5.7. c 5.8. d 5.9. d 5.10. d

Chapter 6

Municipal Bonds

6.1 MUNICIPAL SECURITIES DEFINED

States, counties, parishes, cities, towns, townships, boroughs, villages, and any special tax districts such as toll bridge authorities, college dormitory authorities, and sewer districts are all *municipalities.* The bonds issued by municipalities to finance their public works projects are called *municipal bonds,* or simply *municipals.* All municipal securities are bonds because municipalities are not authorized to sell equity securities to finance community projects. More generally, "munis" include the debt obligations of state and local commissions, agencies, and authorities as well as state and community colleges.

Municipal Bond Interest Is Exempt from Federal Income Taxes

Federal laws stipulate that the coupon interest income derived from the debt obligation of a political subdivision is exempted from federal income taxes, but any capital gains that might be earned are taxable. *Munis* are frequently purchased by wealthy individuals, partnerships, and corporations whose income is subject to high tax rates.

Equation (*6.1*) shows the mathematical relationship between (1) a municipal bond's interest rate, (2) a taxable bond's interest rate, and (3) the investor's income tax rate that will allow a bond investor to determine if they are equally well off regardless of which bond is purchased.

$$\begin{pmatrix}\text{Tax-exempt municipal} \\ \text{bond rate, } i_M\end{pmatrix} = (\text{taxable bond rate, } i_T)(1.0 - \text{investor's tax rate, } T) \qquad (6.1)$$

or

$$i_M = i_T(1 - T)$$

SOLVED PROBLEM 6.1

Ralph is in the 15 percent income tax bracket. Would Ralph be better off to invest in a corporate bond that pays an interest rate of 10 percent or a municipal bond that pays 7.3 percent interest? The two bonds are equally likely to default and are similar in all other respects except their interest rates and taxability.

SOLUTION

We have $i_M = 7.3\%$, $i_T = 10.0\%$, and $T = 15.0\% = .15$. Substituting these values into Eq. (*6.1*) indicates that Ralph should prefer the corporate bond. The left side of Eq. (*6.1*) = 7.3%. In the right side, $i_T(1 - T) = 10\%(1.0 - .15) = 8.5\%$ after taxes. Since $8.5\% > 7.3\%$, Ralph will earn a higher after-tax rate of interest, 8.5 percent, from the taxable corporate bond.

SOLVED PROBLEM 6.2

Mariko is in the 18 percent tax bracket. She is trying to decide whether to invest in a municipal bond yielding 5.2 percent or a corporate bond with the same amount of default risk that yields 8.5 percent.

SOLUTION

We have $i_M = 5.2\%$, $i_T = 8.5\%$, and $T = 18\% = .18$.

$$i_M = i_T(1.0 - T) = 8.5\%(1.0 - .18) = 6.97\%$$

Mariko will earn an after-tax yield of 6.97 percent from the taxable bond. Mariko is in too low a tax bracket to benefit from a tax-exempt bond that yields only 5.2 percent; she would be better off buying the taxable corporate bond and getting 1.77 percent (6.97% − 5.2%) more after-tax yield.

Bearer Bonds Versus Registered Bonds

The interest on bonds can be paid in two ways: (1) by check to the bond's registered owner, or (2) by coupons attached to a bearer bond. Years ago, income tax evaders preferred their munis in the form of *bearer bonds* because they did not have to report to the federal government that they owned the bonds, since the interest income was tax-exempt. In addition, when the owner of the municipals sold or gave them to another party, it was easy to avoid paying the capital gains or gift tax, respectively, because there was no registered list of owners which could be consulted by the Internal Revenue Service (I.R.S.) to discern ownership changes. The federal government curtailed the issue of new bearer bonds by municipalities after 1981 by removing the tax-exempt status, unless the issue was registered. However, bearer bonds issued before 1981 will be traded until they are all retired.

The disadvantage of owning bearer bonds is that thieves find them easy to steal and resell since the bond owner's name is not recorded on a registration list. In contrast, the owners of *registered bonds* are protected from getting their bonds stolen because all registered owners must notify the trustee of the bond issue of any change in ownership. Furthermore, the new investor in the bond must have his or her name added to the list of registered owners. This registration procedure prevents stolen bonds from being easy to resell, and also makes tax evasion easier for the I.R.S. to detect.

Municipal bonds' tax-exemption advantage works to the benefit of the issuers. The bonds are generally regarded by investors as being particularly desirable because their coupons are exempt from income taxes. Tax exemption allows these bonds to command a price premium that is reflected in the form of lower market interest rates. High-quality munis usually have the lowest rates of interest in the bond market.

Municipal Bonds Involve Some Default Risk

Not all municipal bonds are high-quality investments. Some local governments are already too burdened with debt or have a tax base so limited that expert bond raters, like S&P and Moodys, refuse to consider the bonds as top rate. Other issues are supported only by limited revenue-producing property and are not considered able to guarantee payment.

EXAMPLE 6.1 In 1975 New York City offered a bond issue with a tax-exempt coupon interest rate of over 9 percent. In spite of this high after-tax yield, the city was still unable to sell the issue to investors because the city was teetering on the verge of bankruptcy.

General Obligation Bonds Versus Limited Obligation Bonds

Municipal bonds fall into one of two categories: (1) general obligation bonds or (2) limited obligation bonds.

(1) *General obligation bonds.* Often referred to as *full faith and credit bonds* because of the unlimited nature of their pledge, general obligation securities originate from government units that have unlimited power to tax property to meet their obligations. General obligation bonds are also called G.O. bonds. Cities are one of the most frequent issuers of G.O. bonds because they have the revenue-generating (that is, taxing) power to go to the politically feasible limit to collect the taxes needed to pay their debts.

(2) *Limited obligation bonds.* The term *limited obligation bonds* is applied when the bond issuer is in some way restricted in raising revenues used to pay its debts. *Revenue bonds* are the most popular form of limited obligation bonds. The distinguishing aspect of such bonds is that they are only entitled to the revenue generated from the specific property they financed. These bonds are widely used to finance one specific municipally owned utility such as a water works, electrical facility, gas facility, sewage disposal systems, or a public convenience like a swimming pool or toll bridge.

The One-Period Rate-of-Return Formula

Municipal bonds pay income to their investors in two forms: interest payments and capital gains (or losses). The one-period rate of return from a municipal bond investment is computed with Eq. (*6.2*) if income taxes are ignored:

$$\begin{pmatrix}\text{One-period}\\ \text{rate of}\\ \text{return}\end{pmatrix} = \frac{(\text{cap. gain or loss}) + (\text{coupon int., if any})}{\text{purchase price}} \tag{6.2}$$

Although the interest payments made to municipal bond investors are normally exempt from federal income taxes, the income from price changes is not tax-exempt. Equation (*6.3*) defines the after-tax one-period rate of return for an investor with an income tax rate of *T*:

$$\begin{pmatrix}\text{After-}\\ \text{tax}\\ \text{rate of}\\ \text{return}\end{pmatrix} = \frac{(\text{cap. gain or loss})(1.0 - T) + (\text{coupon int.})}{\text{purchase price}} \tag{6.3}$$

SOLVED PROBLEM 6.3

Jane Poole was in the 28 percent income tax bracket when she bought a $1,000 municipal bond with a 5 percent coupon rate for $950 on June 14 and sold it prior to its maturity on June 14 of the next year for $995.

(*a*) What was Jane's pre-tax 1-year rate of return from this municipal bond?
(*b*) What was Jane's after-tax rate of return from the municipal bond?

SOLUTION

(*a*) If a bond sells at $995 on June 14 of some year after being purchased for $950 on June 14 of the preceding year the bond experienced a capital gain of $45 ($995 − $950). In addition, the bond paid $50 of coupon interest (5% of the $1,000 face value) during that year.

$$\begin{pmatrix}\text{Pre-tax}\\ \text{rate of}\\ \text{return}\end{pmatrix} = \frac{(\text{cap. gain}) + (\text{coupon int.})}{\text{purchase price}} \tag{6.2}$$

$$\frac{(\$995 - \$950) + \$50}{\$950} = \frac{\$45 + \$50}{\$950} = \frac{\$95}{\$950} = .10 = 10.0\%$$

This municipal bond's 1-year rate of return is 10 percent before taxes.

(*b*) Since Jane's tax rate is $T = .28$, the same municipal bond's after-tax rate of return over the same 1-year holding period was less than the 10 percent pre-tax return; the capital gains (but not the coupon interest) income from a municipal bond is taxable.

$$\begin{pmatrix}\text{After-}\\ \text{tax}\\ \text{rate of}\\ \text{return}\end{pmatrix} = \frac{(\text{cap. gain})(1.0 - .28) + (\text{cpn. int.})}{\text{purchase price}} \tag{6.3a}$$

$$= \frac{(\$995 - \$950)(.72) + \$50}{\$950} = \frac{\$82.40}{\$950} = .0867 = 8.67\% \text{ after taxes}$$

The bond's after-tax rate of return is 8.67 percent.

6.2 INSURED MUNICIPAL BOND ISSUES

Even though the tax-exempt income from a municipal bond may be quite attractive to some investors, they may still shy away from these bonds if there is much prospect that the bond issue might default and not be able to repay its obligations. This understandable risk-aversion makes it difficult for municipalities whose bonds do not receive the highest quality ratings to issue bonds.

AMBAC and the MBIA Go into Business

In the 1970s two firms set up business to insure bonds issued by municipalities that were not worthy of the highest-quality credit ratings. The two firms are the American Municipal Bond Assurance Association, often called AMBAC, and the Municipal Bond Insurance Association, or MBIA. Insuring municipal bond issues proved to be such a profitable business that several competing municipal bond insurance firms were started up in the 1980s.

The Agreement with the Municipal Bond Rating Agencies

Standard & Poors and some other bond rating agencies have given any municipal bond issue that high-quality municipal bond insurance companies insures their highest-quality credit rating. Thus, for instance, if

AMBAC or the MBIA or another top flight insurer agrees to back a municipality's bond issue, the issue will get a top credit rating that it might never have been able to obtain based only on its own merits. Essentially, the credit rating agencies are giving the issue the credit rating of the insurance company that insured the bonds. Having a high-quality rating assigned to a bond issue makes it much easier for small and risky municipalities to find investors to buy their bonds, and also, to be able to sell their issues at lower interest rates. In fact, good municipal bond insurance can raise an issue's quality rating and lower its interest rate so much that the issuing municipality's savings in interest expense help pay for the insurance.

SOLVED PROBLEM 6.4

The president of First Federal Savings and Loan Association of Elmherst (FFSLE) was active in local politics. As a result of its president's local interests the FFSLE had a large portion of its assets invested in bonds issued by the small municipalities that were located around the FFSLE's offices. Although these local municipal projects were risky investments, their municipal bonds were rated AAA by Standard & Poors because they were insured by AMBAC.

The executive vice-president at FFSLE objected to his president's investment policy of investing in risky, local municipal bonds that were insured by AMBAC because (1) FFSLE's portfolio was poorly diversified, and (2) FFSLE's portfolio was too risky. Are the executive vice-president's fears and objections valid?

SOLUTION

The executive vice-president's fears are valid because all insured municipal bonds are no stronger than the strength of the underlying insurance company. If some Act of God (such as a flood or earthquake, for instance) destroyed all the municipal projects in which the FFSLE had invested, the associated insurance losses could significantly weaken the company that insured these bond issues. As a result of all of these simultaneous insurance losses the municipal bond insurance company might have its own bond quality rating lowered (and perhaps even default). If the company that insured the municipal bonds had its quality rating lowered, all the risky municipal bond issues that were insured would simultaneously suffer lowered quality ratings and falling market prices.

The executive vice-president should do a financial analysis of AMBAC to determine (1) if the municipal bond insurance company laid off (that is, diversified away) some of its risks by reinsuring portions of the bond issues it insured with other insurance companies, and (2) if the insurance company was in a strong financial position.

6.3 DEFAULT RISK ANALYSIS FOR MUNICIPAL BONDS

Municipalities are only allowed to issue municipal bonds to raise funds. These municipal bonds are different from the corporate bonds issued by businesses in the respects listed below:

1. Municipalities do not earn profits like a business; rather, they endeavor to provide optimum service at minimum cost.
2. Unlike the interest from corporate bonds, the interest income investors earn from municipal bonds is exempt from federal income taxes.
3. Municipal projects are usually narrow rather than broad in scope. For example, the proceeds from sewer-district bonds might go for the construction of only one sewer. The cash from the sale of the bonds cannot be spent for any other purpose. In contrast, the proceeds from an issue of corporate bonds might be spent on a wider range of projects.

Because of their unique characteristics, municipal bonds are analyzed differently from corporate bonds.

Analyzing Limited Obligation Bonds

With respect to the probability of default, municipal bonds can be divided into two main categories that were introduced above: (1) general obligation (or simply G.O.) bonds and (2) limited obligation bonds.

Revenue bonds are the prime example of limited obligation bonds. The interest and principal on revenue bonds must be repaid from the revenues generated by the project financed by the revenue bonds.

EXAMPLE 6.2 Toll bridge collections are the only source of revenue from which a toll bridge authority's revenue bonds can be repaid. The city in which the toll bridge is located cannot tax the local residents to pay off revenue bonds that were issued to finance a toll bridge. If people do not use the toll bridge, the toll bridge authority will default on its bonds because the bridge generated insufficient revenue.

(1) *General obligation (G.O.) bonds* are so called because it is a general legal obligation of the entire municipality to see that the bonds do not go into default. Suppose that a toll bridge were built by a city (rather than by a toll bridge authority). Further suppose that because of a lack of use the toll bridge revenues were insufficient to pay off the G.O. bonds used to finance the toll bridge. Then the city could collect sales taxes, property taxes, dog taxes, or any other kind of taxes from its residents to pay off the toll bridge bonds. The full faith and credit of the bond's issuer, which in this case was assumed to be a city, stands behind G.O. bonds—not merely the revenues from the project financed.

(2) *Revenue bonds.* When an issue of revenue bonds defaults, the courts are reluctant to auction off the bankrupt assets in order to see that the bond's investors are repaid. The municipal assets that were supposed to support the issue of revenue bonds are usually viewed by the courts as being vital public facilities that should be used only for public welfare. So, as a practical matter, municipal bonds' collateral should be viewed as essentially untouchable in the event of bankruptcy (this is true for both G.O. and revenue bonds). Stated differently, whatever income the project that an issue of revenue bonds financed is usually the only source of funds from which to pay revenue bond investors.

    In analyzing the potential income behind an issue of revenue bonds, the analyst focuses on the asset that is supposed to generate the revenue. For example, if the revenue bond's proceeds are to be used to pay for a toll bridge, the important questions are: How much will the toll bridge be used? How much toll will be charged? What chance is there that a competing toll bridge or ferry boat will make the toll bridge suffer losses?

Municipal Bond Ratings

Standard & Poor's, Moodys, Fitch's, and other municipal bond rating services publish quality ratings on thousands of different municipal bond issues. These ratings are important to investors who don't have time to do their own financial analysis. The various municipal bond rating services obtain audited financial statements from the issuing municipality in order to obtain facts on which to base their published ratings.

Most municipal bonds are traded inactively in small over-the-counter bond markets located in the issuing municipality. Local banks, wealthy local individuals, and large local businesses that have some interest in the municipality frequently buy entire issues of municipal bonds. Such directly placed investments are usually held to maturity. Many of these directly placed issues never even receive quality ratings. As a result, the markets for many municipal bonds are localized and, sometimes, even nonexistent. Thus, it is important to see if a given municipal bond is actively traded before undertaking any further investigation. Unrated issues are most likely to be illiquid.

True-False Questions

6.1 Sometimes a municipality will guarantee the principal and interest payments from an issue of revenue bonds and thereby upgrade its status to general obligation bond.

6.2 Revenue bond issues are usually governed by debt limitations imposed by laws in the state that granted the authority for the bond issue.

6.3 Sometimes cities issue short-term municipal bonds called *tax anticipation notes* that mature when the next tax collection arrives to pay off the issue.

6.4 *Industrial development bonds* are municipal bonds that are issued by states and cities to finance the private investments of new businesses that a commmunity is endeavoring to attract.

6.5 The municipal bonds that most brokers and dealers are offering for sale are listed in *The Blue List*.

6.6 General obligation bonds are guaranteed by the U.S. government.

6.7 AMBAC and the MBIA diversify their risks by reinsuring portions of the issues they insure with several other insurance companies.

6.8 One of the more important functions of the *bond attorney* in any municipal bond underwriting is to attest that the issue qualifies for the federal income tax exemption on its interest payments.

6.9 It is easy to obtain complete audited financial statements from the municipalities that issue bonds because federal regulations require complete disclosure of all relevant information.

6.10 One of the best sources of information about municipal bond issues and their issuers is a periodical named *The Daily Bond Buyer.*

6.11 Municipalities sometimes offer issues of zero coupon bonds.

6.12 Issues of municipal bonds never provide for *sinking funds* to which the issuer contributes funds specifically to retire all or part of the issue.

6.13 When the yield-to-maturity on a municipal bond rises, its market price also rises.

Multiple Choice Questions

6.1 *Special tax securities* are best described by which of the following statements?
(*a*) They are a type of limited obligation municipal bond.
(*b*) The principal and interest are paid from special taxes that the municipality may elect to collect each year.
(*c*) The principal and interest can only be paid from taxes on special goods such as cigarette taxes or sales taxes.
(*d*) Both *a* and *c* are true.
(*e*) They are bonds sold to finance special projects, such as a flood or drought emergency.

6.2 *Special assessment bonds* are best described by which of the following?
(*a*) These are bonds issued to finance a particular project such as a sewer system or water works.
(*b*) They are usually a type of limited obligation municipal bond that can only have their principal and interest paid from special taxes assessed on the residents of the community.
(*c*) Occasionally an issue of special assessment bonds is backed by the full faith and credit of the issuing community.
(*d*) All of the above are true.
(*e*) None of the above are true.

6.3 Municipal bonds are not usually investments that are recommended for small investors because of which of the following reasons?
(*a*) Many municipal bond issues are illiquid.
(*b*) The small investor typically is in a low income tax bracket and does not need the tax exemption.
(*c*) The normal denomination unit of $10,000 for municipal bonds is too expensive for small investors.
(*d*) All the above are true.
(*e*) None of the above are true.

6.4 The indenture contracts that govern municipal bond issues typically provide for which of the following?
(*a*) The authority governing the project shall not have the right to raise the rates charged for the service after the bonds are issued.
(*b*) The authority governing the project shall not have the right to sell more bonds at a later date to finance additions to the project.
(*c*) Both *a* and *b* are false.
(*d*) Both *a* and *b* are true.

6.5 Which of the following statements best describes the criteria used by AMBAC and the MBIA in accepting which municipal bond issues to insure?
(*a*) The insured issues must be geographically diversified.
(*b*) The insured issues must cover different and unrelated types of projects.
(*c*) The insured issues must be capable of obtaining a Standard & Poors rating of BBB (or a Moodys rating of Baa) or better on their own merits.
(*d*) All the above are true.
(*e*) None of the above are true.

6.6 Which of the following reasons best explains why municipalities are willing to pay expensive insurance premiums to have their issues insured?
(*a*) To reduce the risk to the investor and thereby increase the issue's marketability.
(*b*) The insurance is required by regulations issued by the Securities and Exchange Commission.
(*c*) To get the issue's quality rating raised to AAA-grade and thus obtain interest rate savings.
(*d*) Both *a* and *c* are true.
(*e*) All the above are true.

6.7 Which of the following statements best describes how municipal bond issues are underwritten?
(*a*) Most municipal bond issues are put up for competitive bidding and competing bids are submitted by the investment bankers that want to distribute the issue to the investing public.
(*b*) Municipalities that issue the largest bond issues, as measured by aggregate dollar values, often place these issues with an investment banker that is selected through direct negotiations rather than through some competitive bidding process.
(*c*) Many municipalities sell their bond issues locally through public newspaper announcements stating the location where the bonds can be purchased, the denominations available, how payment for the bonds must be made, how the securities will be allocated if excess bids are forthcoming at the opening of the sale, and other details.
(*d*) All the above are true.
(*e*) Both *a* and *b* are true.

6.8 An *option tender bond* is best described by which of the following statements?
(*a*) An "option tender bond" is the same thing as a "put bond."
(*b*) The bondholder has the right to sell the bond back to its issuer at a fixed price before the bond's maturity date.
(*c*) A provision in the issue's indenture contract tends to provide a price support (or "floor") beneath the bond's market price and thus reduce the investors' risk from price fluctuations.
(*d*) All of the above are true.
(*e*) None of the above are true.

6.9 *Super sinkers* are best defined by which of the following descriptions?
(*a*) Revenue bonds issued to finance a pool of mortgages on single-family residences
(*b*) Bonds that have long times until they mature but have a high probability of being paid off before they reach their maturity date if the issuer obtains the funds before the retirement date is reached
(*c*) Pass-through mortgage-backed securities that have a provision in the indenture contract for early redemption under special circumstances
(*d*) All the above
(*e*) None of the above

6.10 *Variable-rate municipal bonds* are best described by which of the following descriptions?
(*a*) They are also called "floating rate municipals."
(*b*) Bond issues that are designed to offer investors reduced price fluctuations because they have coupon rates that fluctuate with other current market rates of interest.
(*c*) Bonds used to finance pools of home mortgages that experience widely differing default rates from year to year.
(*d*) Both *a* and *b* are true.
(*e*) All the above are true.

6.11 Mutual funds that invest solely in municipal bonds provide which of the following advantages to investors?
(*a*) Tax-exempt interest income
(*b*) Freedom from interest-rate risk
(*c*) Diversification to reduce default risk
(*d*) None of the above
(*e*) Both *a* and *c*

6.12 Which of the following municipal bonds do not enjoy the federal income tax exemption for the interest they pay their investors?
(*a*) None; the interest payments from all municipal bonds are exempt from federal income taxes.
(*b*) The municipal bonds issued by swimming pool authorities, yacht basin authorities, and other recreational projects are not entitled to the federal income tax exemption.
(*c*) Industrial development bonds issued by municipalities after 1986 to finance business development are not exempt from federal income taxation.
(*d*) If the proceeds from a municipal bond issue goes to finance a project that the Internal Revenue Service deems more appropriate for some other municipality to finance the I.R.S. may disallow that bond issue's tax-exempt status.

6.13 The market price of a municipal bond depends on which of the following factors?
(*a*) The coupon rate.
(*b*) The protective provisions in the indenture.
(*c*) The maturity date of the issue.
(*d*) The collateral that backs the bond issue.
(*e*) *a*, *b*, and *c* are all true.

Answers

True-False

6.1. T 6.2. T 6.3. T 6.4. T 6.5 T 6.6 F 6.7. T 6.8. T 6.9. F 6.10. T
6.11. T 6.12. F 6.13 F

Multiple Choice

6.1. d 6.2. d 6.3. d 6.4. c 6.5. d 6.6. d 6.7. e 6.8. d 6.9. d 6.10. d
6.11. e 6.12. c 6.13. e

Chapter 7

Issuing and Trading Securities

7.1 INVESTMENT BANKERS MAKE PRIMARY MARKETS

When a corporation sells new securities to raise cash, the offering is called a *primary issue.* The agent responsible for finding buyers for these securities is called the *investment banker* or *underwriter.* The name "investment banker" is unfortunate because these people are not investors and they are not bankers. Essentially, investment bankers purchase *primary issues* from security issuers such as companies and governments, and, then, arrange to immediately resell these securities to the investing public. The First Boston Corporation; Merrill Lynch, Pierce, Fenner & Smith; Goldman Sachs; Morgan Stanley; and Salomon Brothers are investment banking companies. These few large firms do most of the underwriting in the United States. The investment banking industry is made up of several thousand different firms in the United States, but most of them are small and not widely known.

In addition to being investment bankers, almost all of the large firms perform brokerage services and other financial functions as well. Merrill Lynch, Pierce, Fenner & Smith has diversified its activities extensively. For example, Merrill Lynch runs one of the largest brokerage operations in each of the following markets: government securities, municipal bonds, commodity futures contracts, options, financial futures, corporate bonds, preferred stocks, common stocks, and corporate bonds. Also, through its subsidiaries, Merrill Lynch provides real estate financing and investment advisory services. Thus, investment banking is only a small part of the huge Merrill Lynch operation. Merrill Lynch has thousands of stockbrokers who arrange trades between investors in the *secondary market* but only a few hundred investment bankers.

SOLVED PROBLEM 7.1

What tasks do investment bankers perform to assist their client companies raise capital?

SOLUTION

Advisory. In a corporation's first meeting with an investment banker, the banker will serve in an advisory capacity. The underwriter will help the firm considering the issue of new securities to analyze its financing needs and make suggestions about various means of financing. The underwriter may also function as an advisor in mergers, acquisitions, and refinancing operations.

Administrative. Federal laws require substantial investigations, filing of information about an initial public offering (IPO) with the Securities and Exchange Commission (SEC), dissemination of information about the issue in a pamphlet called a "prospectus," and other "red tape" to precede a primary securities issue.

Underwriting. This refers to the guarantee by the investment banker that the issuer will receive a certain minimum amount of cash for their new securities. This guarantee involves a significant degree of risk for the investment banker. It is the underwriter's intention to buy the securities from the issuer at a few percentage points less than the expected selling price. This intention is sometimes frustrated, however. If so, underwriting losses occur.

Not all new security issues are underwritten. If the investment banker finds one or more buyers for a new issue and arranges for a single transaction between issuer and investors, this is called a *private placement.* In a private placement the investment banker is compensated for acting as the middle link in bringing buyer and seller together, for skill and speed in determining a fair price, and for execution of the transaction.

Even in a *public offering,* the investment banker may not assume the role of underwriter. Instead the investment banker may agree to use certain facilities and services in distributing new shares on a *best efforts basis* while assuming no financial responsibility if all the securities cannot be sold. In these best efforts offerings the investment banker's charges are typically more than they would have charged for a direct placement but less than they would have charged for a fully underwritten public offering. Best efforts offerings are the exception rather than the rule, however.

Distribution. Distributing securities to investors is an important function of investment bankers. The success of the investment banking firm ultimately depends upon its ability to find investors/buyers for the new securities.

Market stabilization. During the distribution period, the manager of an underwriting firm occasionally must stabilize the price of the issue to prevent its drifting downward. To achieve this objective, the underwriting syndicate's manager *pegs the price* by placing orders to buy the newly issued security at a specified price in the secondary market where the securities are trading.

EXAMPLE 7.1 On October 4, 1979, Salomon Brothers managed a $1 billion underwriting of bonds for the IBM Corporation—the largest debt offering in the United States up to that time. IBM took a check for its $990 million proceeds ($1 billion less the investment bankers' fees of $10 million) from the issue and walked away with the money safely in hand. Then, the investment banker had a hard time selling the IBM bonds.

On October 4, 1979, the same day the IBM bond issue came out, the U.S. Treasury auctioned $2.5 billion of 4-year notes; the T-note issue alone sopped up much of the cash available for investing on Wall Street that day. Coincidently, the Federal Reserve started to rapidly tighten credit conditions. On October 6, 1979, the Fed raised the discount rate from 11 to 12 percent, for instance. Credit conditions tightened further and on October 9 the prime rate went up from 13.5 to 14.5 percent. The market value of the IBM bonds was falling as market interest rates rose. As a result the investment bankers were experiencing millions of dollars of losses on the new IBM bonds they still held.

On October 10, 1979, the underwriting syndicate (composed of 227 different investment banking firms) was disbanded with about $650 million of the IBM bonds still unsold in the underwriters' inventories. The market prices of the new IBM bonds fell another $5 per $1,000 bond when the syndicate disbanded.[1] This caused more millions of losses for the underwriters.

The investment bankers' multimillion dollar losses continued after the underwriting syndicate was dissolved. The IBM bonds were finally sold with the aid of unprofitable swapping arrangements that had been made to get clients to take some of the new issues. In these *swaps* the investment banker exchanges (or swaps) into its account some bonds that the investing client already owned in order to rid itself of the primary issue. Later, when the securities the investment banker took in on the swap are resold they must be sold at a loss that can be attributed to the difficulties in distributing the primary offering.

EXAMPLE 7.2 Mr. Smyth and his associates of the Smyth & Westrik Corporation agreed they needed $100 million to build a new factory. They sought advice about how to raise this much capital from the investment banking house of Ambrose, Trout & Company.

Early conferences. The investment house that first reaches an agreement with the issuer is called the *originator*. The originator ultimately manages the flotation and coordinates the *underwriting syndicate* and *selling group*. At the outset, however, the originator and the issuer must determine how much capital should be raised, whether it should be raised by debt or equity, and whether Smyth & Westrik Corporation is in a sound financial position. Investigations are conducted by accountants, engineers, and attorneys. The accountants assess the firm's financial condition. If the funds are to be used to acquire new assets, Ambrose, Trout & Company's engineering consultants investigate the proposed acquisition. Attorneys will be asked to give interpretations and judgments about various documents involved in the flotation. Also, Ambrose, Trout & Company will make an investigation of the firm's future prospects. Finally, the originator will draw up a tentative underwriting agreement between the issuer and the investment banking house, specifying all terms of the issue except the specific price that will be set on the debenture.

The underwriting syndicate. With most large issues the investment banker forms a purchase syndicate made up of a group of investment banking houses, usually 4 to 100 of its competitors. There are at least three advantages to forming an underwriting syndicate. First, since it spreads around the purchase cost, Ambrose, Trout & Company is not faced with an enormous cash drain while the securities are being underwritten. Second, it lessens the risk of loss, because several firms would bear the size of the potential loss in case of failure since Ambrose, Trout & Company has partners in the effort. Third, the utilization of several underwriters and each of their selling groups encourages a wider ownership of the new securities. Figure 7-1 illustrates these relationships.

[1]The IBM case is simplified for the sake of expeditious reading. Actually, Merrill Lynch assisted Salomon Brothers in managing the underwriting with each firm underwriting $125 million. Morgan-Stanley underwrote $40 million; First Boston took $20 million; Goldman Sachs handled $20 million; and over 200 other investment bankers took the remaining millions. The $1 billion offering was broken down into two equal-sized parts: (1) $500 million of 7-year notes, and (2) $500 of 25-year debentures. For more details see "Prices Drop Further as Record IBM Offer Encounters Surprising Buyer Resistance," *The Wall Street Journal*, October 5, 1979, p. 37. Also see *Business Week*, October 29, 1979, p. 50. This IBM case was composed from these and other articles in the IBM Prospectus, *The Wall Street Journal*, and *The New York Times*.

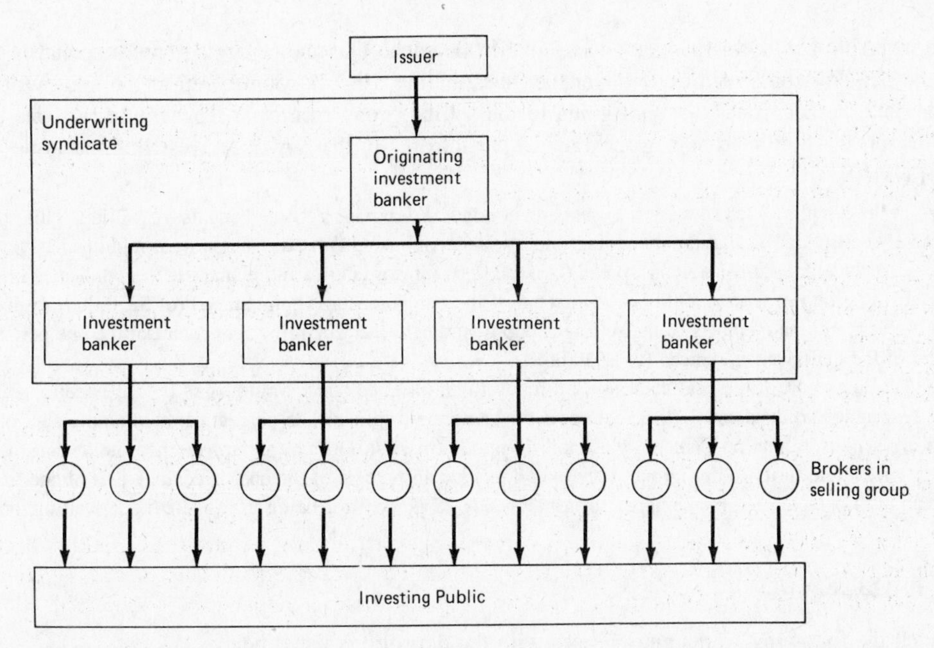

Fig. 7-1 Flowchart for a primary offering made through a syndicate of investment bankers.

The selling group. After the underwriters have purchased the issue from Smyth & Westrik, each uses its own selling group for distribution to the investing public. The selling group consists of other investment bankers, dealers, and brokers. Some firms, such as Merrill Lynch, Pierce, Fenner & Smith, perform all these functions—from managing underwriter in some issues to being brokers in others.

Disclosure requirements. The federal government's Securities and Exchange Commission (SEC) requires that a registration statement be filed with the Commission. This *registration statement* must disclose enough information for an investor to judge the investment quality of the new issue. After the filing of the statement, there is usually only a brief delay until the new issue may be offered for sale. During this period the SEC analyzes the registration statement to determine if the legally required disclosure of information was provided. The SEC may act to delay approval or request an amendment to the statement, in which case the waiting period may last weeks or months. In fact, most delays are caused by the large number of statements filed that must be processed by the SEC staff.

A portion of the registration statement is the *prospectus.* After gaining the SEC's approval and setting the price for the issue, the prospectus is printed in quantity and delivered to potential investors. The law requires that all potential investors must have a prospectus before they can invest. The prospectus contains information about Smyth & Westrik's history, about those individuals who hold large blocks of Smyth & Westrik stock, and other facts pertinent to the evaluation of the new issue. It should be emphasized that SEC approval of the registration statement and the prospectus within is not an endorsement by the SEC of the investment value of the securities offered. Its approval implies only that adequate information has been disclosed to enable investors to make their own judgment about the value of the security offer.

Setting the price. Perhaps the most difficult decision in a flotation is setting the "right" price. The right price is one that is not too low; this would be unnecessarily costly to the issuer. It also cannot be too high; this might cause losses for the underwriters. Therefore, a delicate balance is necessary. The price is generally set at the end of the registration period. The syndicate prefers to wait to set the final price until the issue is ready for the market so that it may have the latest, most up-to-the-minute information from the market. As a rule, when the price is right, market conditions are good, and the issuer and underwriters are reputable, the flotation will be sold in a few days, or even several hours. When one or more of these conditions is lacking, it may become a "sticky issue," taking a week, month, or even more to sell, and it may result in multimillion dollar losses for the underwriting syndicate if the issue is a big deal.

SOLVED PROBLEM 7.2

Consider the investment banking firm of Ambrose, Trout & Company from Example 7.2. Suppose that Ambrose, Trout bought the Smyth & Westrik Corporation's bonds for $990 each and they were sold to the investing public for their face value of $1,000 each. The one percentage point spread is the investment bankers' compensation to cover the investigations, the discount given to the underwriting syndicate, and the additional discount given to the selling group members. How might this one percentage point spread be divided among the various participants in the Smyth & Westrik bond issue?

SOLUTION

In the Smyth & Westrik case the one percent bond *underwriters' spread* equals $1 million. This spread would typically be divided so that the managing underwriter, Ambrose, Trout & Company, would keep 20 percent of the one percentage point underwriters' spread (or $200,000) for originating and managing the syndicate. The entire underwriting group of firms would get 25 percent of the one percentage point spread (or $250,000) to divide among themselves; and the members of the selling group would earn the remaining 55 percent of the one percentage point bond of the underwriters' spread (or $550,000).

Whatever part of the deal that is sold directly to an ultimate buyer would bring the investment banker the full one percentage point spread—20 percent of it for being the originator, 25 percent for being a member of the underwriting syndicate, and 55 percent as a retail sales commission. On that part of the new issue that the managing underwriter sold to its selling group, they would receive 45 percent of the one percentage point bond underwriters' spread—20 percent of it for being the originator plus 25 percent for being part of the underwriting syndicate.

SOLVED PROBLEM 7.3

Match the following words and phrases with the definitions listed below.

1. Dilution
2. Letter stock
3. Regulation A
4. Registrar for the issuer
5. Tombstone
6. Best efforts offering
7. Shelf registration
8. Red herring

Definitions for the words above:

(A) An investment banker accepts the responsibility to sell an issue, but not to underwrite the risk of the distribution.

(B) A bank is appointed to monitor the issuance of shares and ensure that no unauthorized shares are created.

(C) A preliminary version of the issuer's prospectus.

(D) Small issues are exempted from the SEC's registration procedures.

(E) The investor in a private placement cannot trade the securities for some stipulated time (usually a year or two) after buying it.

(F) One or more primary issues are registered in advance of their issue at the SEC.

(G) A public announcement of a consummated deal that is published in a financial newspaper or magazine.

(H) The issuance of common stock shares not backed by tangible earning assets reduces the value and earnings per share.

SOLUTION

1. H 2. E 3. D 4. B 5. G 6. A 7. F 8. C

7.2 PRIMARY AND SECONDARY MARKETS CONTRASTED

Most people who are interested in investing in securities go directly to a nearby brokerage house and request the services of one of its brokers. After the initial paperwork has been completed, the investor's order will be relayed to one of the dealers handling the securities in which the investor is interested and the purchase will be consummated.

Individual investors most frequently utilize (through their brokers) the services of either the organized exchanges or the over-the-counter markets. These markets are called the *secondary markets.* Investors buy brand new securities through investment bankers. In the secondary market investors buy and sell securities between themselves so that the issuer never gets any cash from these trades. This discussion of the secondary markets begins with the organized exchanges, of which the largest and best known is the New York Stock Exchange (NYSE), also known as the Big Board. The next chapter discusses the over-the-counter market, another important segment of the secondary market.

7.3 ORGANIZED SECURITIES EXCHANGES

In recent years the NYSE handles about half of the volume of securities (measured in number of shares) traded on organized exchanges in the United States. The American Stock Exchange (AMEX) follows with less than 5 percent of the total volume from all organized exchanges. The other exchanges listed in Table 7.1 are called regional exchanges; they make up the balance. The vast majority of their trading volume is in stocks which are *dually listed* on the NYSE and the smaller exchanges.

Table 7.1 List of Organized Exchanges in the United States

New York City Exchanges
New York Stock Exchange (NYSE)
American Stock Exchange (AMEX)
Regional Exchanges
Midwest Stock Exchange
Pacific Stock Exchange
Philadelphia Stock Exchange
Boston Stock Exchange
Cincinatti Stock Exchange

Functions of a Securities Exchange

The function performed by any exchange is the creation of a continuous market where investors have the opportunity to buy or sell securities immediately at a price that varies little from the previous trade. Continuous markets allow investments to be liquid and marketable. That is, the investors are not obligated to hold their securities, they can sell their securities anytime they would prefer to have cash. A securities exchange also helps determine fair market prices. Price is determined by supply and demand from different investors. The exchanges bring together buyers and sellers from all over the nation and from foreign countries; anonymity between buyers and sellers is preserved as their agents transact the trades.

The organized exchanges in the United States follow the organizational pattern of the New York Stock Exchange.

EXAMPLE 7.3

NYSE organization. The New York Stock Exchange has been described as a *voluntary association.* More specifically, it is a corporation that endeavors to maintain a smoothly operating marketplace. The NYSE is directed by a Board of Governors elected by its members. The NYSE board is composed of governors representing member firms and the public. The board is the chief policy-making body of the exchange. It approves or rejects applications of new members; it accepts or rejects budget proposals; it disciplines members through fines, suspension, or expulsion; it accepts or rejects proposals for new security listings; it submits requests to the SEC for changes; and, among other duties, it assigns securities to the various posts on the trading floor.

NYSE trading floor. The main trading floor of the NYSE is about the size of a football field. There is an annex in which bonds and less actively traded stocks are bought and sold. Around the edge of both rooms are telephone booths, used primarily to transmit orders from the broker's office to the exchange floor and back again to the broker's office after execution of the order. On the floor are 18 U-shaped counters; each counter has many *trading posts.* One or a few of the 1,600 or so (it changes constantly) domestic corporations listed on the NYSE are assigned to be traded at each of the posts on the trading floor.

NYSE listing requirements. All firms whose stock is traded on an organized exchange must have at one time filed an application to have their securities listed on that exchange. Most firms traded at the NYSE are listed on more than one exchange. The NYSE has the most stringent listing requirements of all the exchanges. These requirements are given in Table 7.2.

Table 7.2 New York Stock Exchange Listing Requirements

1.	Earnings before taxes of at least $2.5 million in the most recent year
2.	Earnings before taxes of at least $2.0 million during the two preceding years
3.	Net tangible assets of at least $16.0 million
4.	Total market value of common stock of at least $16.0 million
5.	Publicly held shares of at least $1.0 million
6.	More than 2,000 holders of 100 shares or more

Once a company has met all the requirements for listing and is allowed to have its securities traded on the NYSE, it must meet certain requirements established by the exchange and the SEC in order to maintain the listing privilege. For example, the listed firm must publish quarterly earnings reports; it must fully disclose financial information annually; it must obtain approval by the SEC of proxy forms before they can be sent to stockholders; and, among other things, insiders of the firm are prohibited from short selling.

With the strict listing requirements and other requirements after membership, one wonders why firms seek listing on organized exchanges rather than settle for trading in the over-the-counter market. Part of the answer lies in the fact that the listed firm benefits from a certain amount of "free" advertising and publicity. This exposure probably has a favorable effect on the sale of its products to the extent that the company's name and its products are associated in the public's mind.

NYSE membership. There are 1,366 members of the NYSE. Memberships are frequently referred to as *seats*, although trading is conducted without the benefit of chairs. In 1969, seats sold at a high of $515,000, but by 1977 they were down to only $35,000. Recently, seat prices have been greater than $1 million. In most years there are over 100 transfers of exchange memberships. The composition of the membership varies as to function.

SOLVED PROBLEM 7.4

Match the following words and phrases with the definitions listed below.

1. Specialist
2. Listing requirements
3. Odd lot
4. Midwest Stock Exchange
5. Volume
6. Brokers
7. Dealers

Definitions for the words above are listed below.

(A) Sales people who earn commission income and never take possession of the securities they sell

(B) Less than 100 shares of stock

(C) A member of an organized securities exchange who acts as a dealer, a broker, and a market-maker in some security

(D) Minimum acceptable standards for an issuer's size and profits

(E) A regional exchange located in Chicago

(F) Sales people who sell securities from an inventory that they own

(G) The number of shares traded

SOLUTION

1. C 2. D 3. B 4. E 5. G 6. A 7. F

True-False Questions

7.1 An investment banking firm is a company that specializes in helping other companies raise capital at the most advantageous terms available.

7.2 When the SEC reviews the registration statement it might delay the offering by sending out a deficiency letter.

7.3 The order in which the names of the investment banking firms are listed on a prospectus is called the "pecking order" and reflects the prestige of the firms.

7.4 Copies of the registration statement must be submitted to both the SEC and the National Association of Security Dealers (NASD).

7.5 The NASD regulations allow its member investment banking firms to join in any underwriting syndicate they desire, even if all of the members are not members of the NASD.

7.6 Securities exchanges do not buy or sell securities.

7.7 The various stock exchanges in the United States operate on an auction basis.

7.8 Primary issues can be marketed on the floor of a securities exchange.

7.9 The NYSE makes markets in bonds with the aid of bond specialists.

7.10 The *intermarket trading system (ITS)* is a computer network that allows the NYSE and other participating exchanges to compare the bid and asked prices for stocks that are available on different exchanges.

7.11 The *Committee on Uniform Securities Identification Procedures (CUSIP)* is operated by Standard & Poors Corporation and assigns uniform identification numbers to all securities traded at the NYSE, AMEX, and NASD to expedite clearing transactions.

7.12 The primary market and the secondary markets for any particular common stock are really the same market.

7.13 The SEC required the organized exchanges to stop charging fixed minimum commission rates on May 1, 1975, and, as a result, many customers have been paying significantly lower commission rates since 1975.

7.14 The specialists at the organized exchanges have access to valuable inside information about the companies in which they make a market.

7.15 The number of seats (or memberships) at the NYSE changes in proportion to the number of securities listed there and the volume of shares traded.

Multiple Choice Questions

7.1 An issuer can elect to make a new issue of securities through any one of three ways listed in which of the following alternatives?
(*a*) Common stock, preferred stock, or bonds
(*b*) Competitive offering, negotiated offering, or direct placement
(*c*) Primary market, secondary market, or direct placement
(*d*) Both *a* and *b*
(*e*) None of the above

7.2 When an issuer selects an underwriter by using competitive bidding, the price at which the new securities are sold is determined by which of the following?
(*a*) Negotiations between the issuer and the investment banker.
(*b*) Bids from competing investment bankers.
(*c*) The Securities and Exchange Commission.
(*d*) All of the above play a role in setting the price.
(*e*) None of the above are true.

7.3 Investment bankers consult with their clients about which of the following problems?
(*a*) Whether it is best to issue bonds, preferred stock, or common stock
(*b*) Whether it is better to have a rights offering combined with a standby offering, or whether to have a fully underwritten offering
(*c*) When is the best time to schedule the new issue
(*d*) All of the above
(*e*) None of the above

7.4 New issues of securities are handled by which of the following departments in an investment banking firm?
(*a*) Mergers and acquisitions department.
(*b*) Corporate finance department.
(*c*) Secondary issues department.
(*d*) None of the above are true, investment banking firms are not departmentalized.

7.5 The syndicate manager considers which of the following factors when assembling the selling group?
(*a*) The amount of capital the selling firm has
(*b*) The size and strength of the selling firm's brokerage organization
(*c*) The reputation of the selling firm
(*d*) All of the above
(*e*) None of the above

7.6 The prospectus derived from a registration statement which has been filed but has not yet become effective and therefore has red ink stamped on its face is best described by which of the following?
(*a*) It is sent to major potential investors to elicit interest before the issue comes to market.
(*b*) It is called a *red herring*.
(*c*) It is a rough copy being passed back and forth between the investment banking firm and the printer.
(*d*) Both *a* and *b* are true.

7.7 The geographic location of the primary market is best described by which one of the following statements?
(*a*) It transacts business in New York City.
(*b*) It transacts its business at the investment bankers' offices around the world.
(*c*) It transacts its business at country clubs, on airplanes, or in restaurants.
(*d*) All of the above are true.

7.8 Which of the following statements best describes people who are allowed to conduct trades at the NYSE but do not own a seat?
(*a*) *Physical access members* can rent from the NYSE the right to go on the floor and trade like a member.
(*b*) *Electronic access members* can rent from the NYSE the right to install a wire to the trading floor of the NYSE, but they cannot go on the floor themselves.
(*c*) Qualified people can rent a member's seat and thereby gain the privilege of going on the NYSE floor and trading like a member.
(*d*) All of the above are true.
(*e*) None of the above are true.

7.9 A *block trade* is defined as which of the following?
(*a*) Any trade worth $10,000 or more
(*b*) Any trade worth $100,000 or more
(*c*) Any trade of 1,000 or more shares
(*d*) Any trade of 10,000 or more shares
(*e*) Any trade of 100 shares

7.10 The *consolidated ticker tape* is best described by which one of the following statements?
(*a*) It is a telecommunications network between different organized exchanges and over-the-counter markets.
(*b*) It prints out every transaction on every NYSE-listed stock.
(*c*) It prints out transactions that occurred on the NYSE and other organized exchanges and in the over-the-counter market as well.
(*d*) All of the above are true.
(*e*) None of the above are true.

7.11 The requirements that the NYSE imposes on the employees working there are best described by which one of the following statements?
(*a*) All employees of all member firms must pass a multiple choice examination that lasts several hours, to ensure a familiarity with the exchange's procedures.
(*b*) Any employee of any member firm may be dismissed for failure to maintain high standards of business conduct.
(*c*) All employees must be college graduates.
(*d*) Both *a* and *b* are true.

7.12 *Allied members* are best described by which one of the following statements?
(*a*) They are senior officers in a firm that owns a seat on the exchange.
(*b*) They cannot go on the trading floor unless the seat is in their name.
(*c*) They are subject to the same rules and regulations as the people who own seats.
(*d*) All of the above are true.
(*e*) None of the above are true, there are no "allied members."

7.13 Regulation of the organized exchanges in the United States is best described by which one of the following statements?
(*a*) All organized exchanges must register with the SEC before they can operate.
(*b*) The SEC can go in and rewrite any rules and regulations of any organized exchange operating in the United States.
(*c*) The SEC can close down any organized exchange in the United States if it deems the exchange's operations to be unfair to the interests of the public.
(*d*) All of the above are true.
(*e*) None of the above are true.

7.14 Investors are insured against losses if their securities brokerage firm goes bankrupt by which of the following organizations?
(*a*) FDIC
(*b*) FSLIC
(*c*) SIPC
(*d*) The Federal Reserve
(*e*) SEC

7.15 A trade of 210 shares of common stock would be called which of the following?
(*a*) An odd lot of 210 shares
(*b*) A round lot of 210 shares
(*c*) Two round lots and an odd lot of 10 shares
(*d*) One round lot of 200 shares and one odd lot of 10 shares
(*e*) Two round lots and ten odd lots

Answers

True-False

7.1. T 7.2. T 7.3. T 7.4. T 7.5. F 7.6. T 7.7. T 7.8. F 7.9. F
7.10. T 7.11. T 7.12. F 7.13. T 7.14. F 7.15. F

Multiple Choice

7.1. d 7.2. b 7.3. d 7.4. b 7.5. d 7.6. d 7.7. d 7.8. d 7.9. d
7.10. d 7.11. d 7.12. d 7.13. d 7.14. c 7.15. c

Chapter 8

Secondary Security Markets

8.1 INTRODUCTION

This chapter extends Chapter 7's discussion of secondary security markets. The over-the-counter market, the third market, and the fourth market are other important secondary security markets that are the topic of Chapter 8.

8.2 OVER-THE-COUNTER MARKETS

An *over-the-counter* (OTC hereafter) market is a way of trading securities that involves no organized exchange. The broker-dealers who engage in OTC common stock trades are linked by a network of telephones and computer terminals through which they deal directly with one another and with customers. Thus, prices are arrived at by a process which takes place over communication lines that span thousands of miles and allows investors to select between competing market-makers.

Securities Traded OTC

The securities traded OTC range from the default-free U.S. government bonds to the most speculative common stocks. Virtually all U.S. government, state, and municipal obligations are traded OTC, although U.S. government bonds are also traded at organized exchanges. More than 90 percent of corporate bonds are traded OTC, although many of them are also listed on the NYSE.

The OTC stock market is not quite as large as the OTC bond market. Many preferred stock issues are traded OTC. About one-third of the common stock trading in the United States is OTC; over 30,000 different common stock issues are traded OTC. But, many of these issues are small and generate virtually no trading activity.

Broker-Dealers

Some broker-dealers are organized as sole proprietorships, some as partnerships, and some as corporations. Many of them have memberships in one or more stock exchanges. Some are wholesalers (that is, they buy from and sell to other dealers), some are retailers (selling mostly to the investing public), and some serve both types of clients. If the dealer buys and sells a particular security regularly, they are said to *make a market* in that security, serving somewhat the same function as the market-makers (namely, the specialists) on an organized exchange. Broker-dealer firms can be categorized according to their specialities. For example, a pure OTC house specializes in OTC issues and rarely belongs to an organized exchange; an investment banking house that specializes in the underwriting of new security issues may (or may not) diversify by acting as dealer in both listed and OTC securities; a commercial bank or a trust company may make a market in U.S. government, state, and local obligations; a stock exchange member house may have a separate department specifically formed to carry on trading in OTC markets. There are houses that deal almost exclusively in municipal issues or federal government bond issues.

National Association of Security Dealers (NASD)

The National Association of Security Dealers (NASD hereafter) is a voluntary organization of security dealers that performs a self-regulating function for the OTC markets. To qualify as a *registered representative* (that is, as a partner, officer, or employee of a broker-dealer firm which does business directly with the public), the candidate files an application with the NASD and must pass a written qualifying examination prepared by the NASD. The applicant must be recommended by a partner, owner, or voting stockholder of a member organization. Once a member, any individual who violates the rules of fair practice outlined by the NASD is subject to censure, fine, suspension, or expulsion, and so are the member firms. The NASD is designed to protect the interests of its members by creating a favorable public image for the OTC market.

OTC Price Quotations

Prices are determined by negotiated bid and asked prices on the OTC markets rather than by a monopolistic market-making specialist, as on the organized exchanges. In 1971 a computerized communications network called NASDAQ became operative in the OTC market. NASDAQ stands for the initials NASD plus AQ from the words "automated quotations." It provides up-to-the-minute bid and asked prices for thousands of securities in response to the simple pressing of appropriate keys on a computer terminal. When an inquiry is made the NASDAQ computer system instantly flashes prices on the screen of any computer terminal that is linked to NASDAQ's central computer. Thus, the OTC security sales representative can quickly obtain bid and ask quotations from all dealers making a market in the stock they wish to trade. After obtaining this information the OTC broker then contacts the dealer offering the best price and negotiates a trade. The advantage NASDAQ offers to investors is the assurance that they are receiving the best price available.

SOLVED PROBLEM 8.1

Match the following words and phrases to the definitions below.

1. OTC market
2. NASD
3. National daily list
4. Pink sheets
5. NASDAQ
6. The 5 percent markup policy.
7. Level 3 of NASDAQ

Definitions to be matched to the words above are listed below.

(A) A NASD guideline for its dealers to follow in establishing the prices they ask for their securities.

(B) A geographically dispersed market that communicates through a central computer.

(C) The OTC stocks that are traded actively enough to be reported in national newspapers.

(D) NASD authorized market-makers are given access to current bid and asked price quotations.

(E) A computer in Connecticut that centrally clears OTC quotations and transactions from around the world.

(F) A list of infrequently traded OTC securities.

(G) A trade association for OTC brokers and dealers that came into existence under the Maloney Act.

SOLUTION

1. B 2. G 3. C 4. F 5. E 6. A 7. D

8.3 TRADING ARRANGEMENTS

Before a buy or sell order can be executed, the securities broker must have explicit orders about the trading arrangements. For example, the broker must be told whether the customer wants to specify a market, limit, or stop order and also whether the customer prefers to buy on margin or pay cash. These trading arrangements are explained below.

Types of Orders

Investors have several options when placing a buy or sell order.

Market orders. This type of order is the most common and most easily executed. With a market order, the customer is simply requesting that the securities be traded at the best possible price as soon as the order reaches the trading floor of the exchange. Market orders are usually traded very rapidly, sometimes in minutes after the order is given the broker.

Stop orders. Sometimes called stop-loss orders, these are usually designed either to protect a customer's existing profit or to reduce the amount of loss.

EXAMPLE 8.1 Ms. Burr buys a stock for $50 and its current market price rises to $75, she has a *paper profit* of $25 per share. If Ms. Burr fears a drop in the current market price, she could request a stop order to sell at, say, $70. This stop order would in effect become a market order after the security fell to $70 (or "sells through $70"), and it would be executed as soon as possible after the stock's market price reached $70. The $70 liquidating price is not guaranteed, however. The stock might be down to $69 or $68 or even lower by the time the order could be executed. However, the investor's profit position is protected to a large extent. The danger of using stop-loss orders is that the investor runs the risk of selling a security with a future of long-run price appreciation in a temporary decline.

The market-makers (called specialists) on the organized exchanges must keep a record of their clients' orders. These orders are executed in order of priority, the first order received at a given price is the first order executed. An accumulation of stop orders at a certain price can cause a sharp break in the market of the issue involved. In such an event, it is quite likely that the exchange would suspend the stop orders, just at the time the traders most needed the protection. The value of a stop order can be considerably diminished by such a contingency.

Stop limit orders. These orders specify both the stop price and the limit price at which the customer is willing to buy or sell. The customer must be willing to run the risk that the security will not reach the limit price, resulting in no trade. If the trade cannot be executed by the broker when the order reaches the trading floor, the broker will turn the order over to the specialist, who will execute the order if the limit price or better is reached.

EXAMPLE 8.2 Mr. Morgan owned 2,000 shares of a stock that was selling at $40, but he feared that the price was poised for a decline. To allay his fears, Mr. Morgan places an order: "Sell 2,000 at $38, stop and limit."

As soon as the price of the stock falls to $38 the broker will attempt to execute the order at a price of $38 or better, but in no case at a price below $38. If the stock cannot be sold for $38 or better, there is no sale.

Mr. Morgan's example of a stop limit order would have been more effective if it had been placed as follows. "Sell 2,000 shares at $39 stop, $38 limit." If the price of the stock falls to $39 the broker will immediately endeavor to execute the stop portion of the stop limit order. If the stop order isn't executed at $39 for some reason, it may be executed at the $38 limit price or better. But, under no condition will the stock be sold at a price below $38. This second stop limit order is superior to Mr. Morgan's stop limit order in Example 8.2 because it has more opportunity to be executed.

A *stop limit order to buy* is executed in the reverse order of the stop limit order to sell. As soon the stock's price reaches the stop level or higher, the stop order to buy is executed at the limit level or better—that is, at a price below the limit price, if possible. Unfortunately, the danger does exist that in a fast-moving market the prices may move so fast that even a well-placed stop limit order gets passed over without being exercised.

Open order or good-till-canceled (GTC) order. These terms refer to the time in which the order is to remain in effect. An *open order* or a *GTC order* remains in effect indefinitely, whereas a *day order* remains in effect only for the day that it is brought to the exchange floor. The vast majority of orders are *day orders,* probably because the customer feels that conditions are right for trading on that specific day. Market conditions may change the next day. However, customers may prefer a GTC order, particularly for limit orders, when they are willing to wait until the price is right for trading. GTC orders must be confirmed at various intervals to remain in effect.

SOLVED PROBLEM 8.2

Match the following words and phrases to the definitions listed below.

1. Day order
2. Market order
3. GTC order
4. "Sell at $60, stop and limit"
5. Limit order

Definitions for the words and phrases above are listed below.

(A) Also called a "stop limit order to buy (or sell, whichever the case may be)."

(B) An order that is canceled if it is not executed on the same day it was issued.

(C) The type of order that is executed most quickly and most surely.

(D) An open order.

(E) It would be safer to "sell at $60 stop, $59 limit."

SOLUTION

1. B 2. C 3. D 4. E 5. A

Margin Buying

Technically, margin trading includes both margin buying and margin short selling.

When investors buy stock on *margin,* they buy some shares with cash and borrow to pay for additional shares, using the paid shares as *collateral.* The shares paid for with the investor's money are analogous to the equity or down payment in an installment purchase agreement. The Federal Reserve Board of Governors controls the amount that may be borrowed. For example, if the Federal Reserve Board stipulates a 55 percent margin requirement, the investor must pay cash equal to at least 55 percent of the value of the securities purchased. The buyer may borrow funds to pay for no more than 45 percent of the cost of the securities. The Federal Reserve's margin requirements have varied from a low of 25 percent in the 1930s to a high of 100 percent in the 1940s.

The investor who wishes to buy on margin is required to open a *margin account* with a stockbroker. Then the investor is required by the NYSE to make a minimum down payment of $2,000. Some brokerage firms require initial margin deposits in excess of the NYSE $2,000 minimum.

EXAMPLE 8.3 The margin requirement is 55 percent and Mr. Reiter wishes to purchase 100 shares of a $100 stock. He wishes to make a total investment of $10,000 ($100 times 100 shares), but he has only $5,500 cash of his own. Because of the Federal Reserve Board's 55 percent margin requirement, Mr. Reiter can still buy 100 shares by paying cash for 55 shares and using them as collateral for a loan to pay for the other 45 shares.

An example of a rising price. If the price of Mr. Reiter's shares rises from $100 to $200, his total profit will be $10,000 ($100 profit per share times 100 shares) before interest, commissions, and taxes. Compare this $10,000 gross gain from the margined position with a gross gain of only $5,500 ($100 profit per share times 55 shares) if he had not bought on margin (that is, if he had invested only his $5,500 cash). Mr. Reiter's gross profit increased because he bought on margin. If Mr. Reiter pays cash, his total gain of $5,500 represents a 100 percent return on the invested cash.

But, if Mr. Reiter uses margin, his total gain of $10,000 represents a 182 percent return on the invested cash ($5,500), an example of favorable financial leverage.

An example of a price drop.. If Mr. Reiter's shares decrease in price from $100 to $50 per share, the current market value of his investment drops from $10,000 (100 shares times $100 per share) to $5,000 (100 shares times $50). Compare again his position as a margin buyer with that of a nonmargin buyer. As a margin buyer, he has a $50 per share loss times 100 shares, or a $5,000 loss. If he had not bought on margin and had purchased only 55 shares, his loss would have been $50 loss per share times 55 shares, or only $2,750. Thus we see that by buying stock on 55 percent margin, Mr. Reiter increases his loss if the price moves adversely. If Mr. Reiter pays cash, his total loss of $2,750 is a 50 percent loss of his invested cash. But, if Mr. Reiter uses margin, his total loss of $5,000 is a 91 percent loss of the invested cash because of adverse financial leverage.

The Federal Reserve Board's Regulation T establishes the *initial margin requirement. Maintenance margin requirements* established by the exchanges define the margin requirements that must be maintained after the initial purchase.

EXAMPLE 8.4 Reconsider Mr. Reiter from Example 8.3. If Mr. Reiter's stock decreases in value sufficiently, he will receive a *margin call* from his broker—brokers also call it a *maintenance call.* That is, the broker calls and informs the client that it is necessary to put up more margin (that is, to produce additional cash "down payment"). If Mr. Reiter cannot come up with the additional cash immediately, the broker must liquidate enough of the stocks Mr. Reiter owns at the depressed price that triggered the margin call in order to bring the equity in the account up to the required level. Selling Mr. Reiter's margined shares is easily accomplished; margin customers are required to keep their stock at the broker's office as collateral for the loan from the broker. If anything is left over after the sale and subsequent loan payment, the investor receives the balance.

According to the NYSE's *maintenance margin* requirement, a margin call must occur when the equity in the account is less than 25 percent of the market value of the account. In Mr. Reiter's case, a margin call would have been required when his $10,000 margined purchase of common stock decreased in market value to below $6,000. Of the original $10,000 margin purchase, $5,500 is equity and $4,500 is a loan. The $4,500 loan is fixed—it does not vary as the stock's price changes. Therefore, if the market value of the stock drops to $6,000, Mr. Reiter's loan is still $4,500; his equity position is now $1,500—25 percent of the account's market value of $6,000. If the account drops below $6,000, Mr. Reiter's equity position would decline even further to below the 25 percent maintenance margin required by the NYSE. A margin call would then occur.

The primary benefit of buying on margin is that it allows investors to magnify their profits by the reciprocal of the margin requirement (that is, 2 times if the margin requirement is $\frac{1}{2}$, 3 times if it is $\frac{1}{3}$, and so forth). The major disadvantage is that it causes magnified losses of the same reciprocal if stock price moves adversely. There is the added disadvantage of fixed interest payments whether stock prices advance or decline. In sum, margin trading increases risk.

SOLVED PROBLEM 8.3

Mr. Reiter purchased a $100 stock on 55 percent margin and then its price doubled to $200. The interest rate Mr. Reiter's brokerage firm charged him for the loan was 10 percent. No cash dividends were received while Mr. Reiter held the stock.

(*a*) What is Mr. Reiter's one-period rate of return if he paid cash for the stock?

(*b*) What is Mr. Reiter's one-period rate of return if he paid only 55 percent margin for the stock?

SOLUTION

(*a*) When an investor buys a share of stock the one-period rate of return is defined in Eq. (*8.1*):

$$\begin{pmatrix}\text{One-period}\\ \text{rate of}\\ \text{return}\end{pmatrix} = \frac{\begin{pmatrix}\text{price}\\ \text{change}\end{pmatrix} + \begin{pmatrix}\text{cash}\\ \text{dividend}\end{pmatrix}}{\text{purchase price}} \tag{8.1}$$

$$= \frac{(\$200 - \$100) + 0}{\$100} = \frac{\$100}{\$100} = 1.0 = 100\%$$

Mr. Reiter made a 100 percent rate of return from his cash position purchase.

(*b*) When Mr. Reiter bought on margin the one-period rate of return is defined in Eq. (*8.2*):

$$\begin{pmatrix}\text{One-period}\\ \text{rate of}\\ \text{return}\end{pmatrix} = \frac{\begin{pmatrix}\text{price}\\ \text{change}\end{pmatrix} + \begin{pmatrix}\text{cash}\\ \text{dividend}\end{pmatrix} - \begin{pmatrix}\text{interest}\\ \text{expense}\end{pmatrix}}{\text{margin money paid}} \tag{8.2}$$

Equation (*8.2*) is reproduced below as Eq. (*8.2a*) to reflect the case from above in which Mr. Reiter purchased a $100 stock on 55 percent margin and then its price doubled to $200. Mr. Reiter's brokerage firm charged him a 10 percent interest rate for the $45 per share ($100 − $55) it loaned to him.

$$\frac{(\$200 - \$100) + 0 - [(10\%)(\$45)]}{\$55} = \frac{\$95.50}{\$55} = 1.736 = 173.6\% \tag{8.2a}$$

Equation (*8.2a*) shows that Mr. Reiter made a 173.6 percent return when the price of the stock he bought doubled. Stated differently, margin transformed a 100 percent price rise into a 173.6 percent gain.

SOLVED PROBLEM 8.4

Thomas Kinney opened a margin account, bought 200 shares of stock in the Abington Corporation at $80 per share by paying 70 percent initial margin for the stock, and shortly thereafter received a margin call from his broker. The broker explained that Tom's new account did not meet the maintenance margin requirements of 30 percent because the price of Abington's stock fell right after Tom bought it. What percentage decline must Abington experience for Tom to violate the 30 percent maintenance margin requirement?

SOLUTION

Tom paid 70 percent initial margin for the stock.

$80	per share purchase price
×.7	equals 70 percent initial margin
$56	equals the initial margin paid for each share

On the purchase date Tom's debt was $24 ($80 purchase price less $56 initial margin) per share. The investor's *debt remains constant* as the price of the margined stock declines; all losses come out of the equity balance (or margin) in the account. Therefore we must find an unknown price p such that after $24 of constant debt is deducted from p we will have a remaining equity balance equal to 30 percent of p. We must solve the problem algebraically: $p - \$24 = .3p$, or equivalently, $.7p = \$24$; $p = \$24/.7 = \$34.28$ per share is the new low price for Abington. When the price falls below $34.28, Tom's equity is below 30 percent.

A new low price of $34.28 is 42.85 ($34.28/$80 = .4285) percent of the price at which Tom purchased Abington. Therefore, Abington's price had to decline by at least 57.15 percent (100% less 42.85%) in order to bring Tom's remaining equity in the account down to the 30 percent maintenance margin requirement level that triggered Tom's margin call.

8.4 FULL-SERVICE AND DISCOUNT BROKERAGE SERVICES

Investors can choose to buy their securities through either expensive full-service brokerages or discount brokers.

Full-Service Brokerage Services

The investor services provided by full-service brokerage houses include the following:

1. *Free safe-deposit vaults for securities.* If investors leave their securities with the broker for safekeeping they are relieved of the responsibility for finding some other means of storage, and they do not have to physically transfer their securities to the broker's office every time they wish to sell. The full-service brokerage firms will also collect any dividends and interest and then credit it to the customer's account free of charge.
2. *Free research literature.* This literature ranges from a booklet of essential information for the beginning investor to computer printouts of the most up-to-date information on securities compiled by the financial analysts of the firm's research staff. Some brokerage houses also provide free newsletters about commodity prices, foreign exchange, and various industry reports.
3. *A market for all types of trading.* Most brokerages can arrange trades for anything from the most speculative commodities to risk-free bonds.
4. *A credit agency.* When a customer is buying on margin, the brokerage firm will gladly loan the funds.
5. *Services competition.* By law a broker is not allowed to give any client more than $25 worth of gifts per year—to make a more costly gift could be viewed as buying or bribing customers. However, some brokers "loan" cars to a favored customer for months at a time, "wine and dine" their best customers, and provide other services in order to get lucrative customers.

Merrill Lynch Pierce Fenner and Smith, Goldman-Sachs, and Shearson Lehman Hutton are examples of full-service brokerages.

Discount Brokers

Discount brokers are brokers in the secondary market that maintain downward pressure on the commission rates. Discount brokerages seek to attract clients by offering lower brokerage commissions than the full-service brokerages. In contrast to the full-service brokers the discount brokers do not provide quite as many amenities for their clients—they just do the clerical paperwork that every brokerage must do and charge minimal commission rates for this minimal service. Charles Schwab & Co., or Quick & Reilly Inc., or Source Securities are examples of discount brokerage firms.

8.5 SPECIALTY BROKERAGE SERVICES

Figure 8-1 illustrates the relationship between the OTC market, the organized exchanges, the third market, and the fourth market.

The Third Market

In the third-market exchange listed securities are traded over the counter. The third market is made up of securities dealers making markets in anywhere from one to a few hundred securities. These third-market dealers stand ready to buy or sell for their own account in sizes ranging from an odd lot to large blocks. In those listed securities in which it chooses to deal, each dealer owns an inventory (including short positions). Thus,

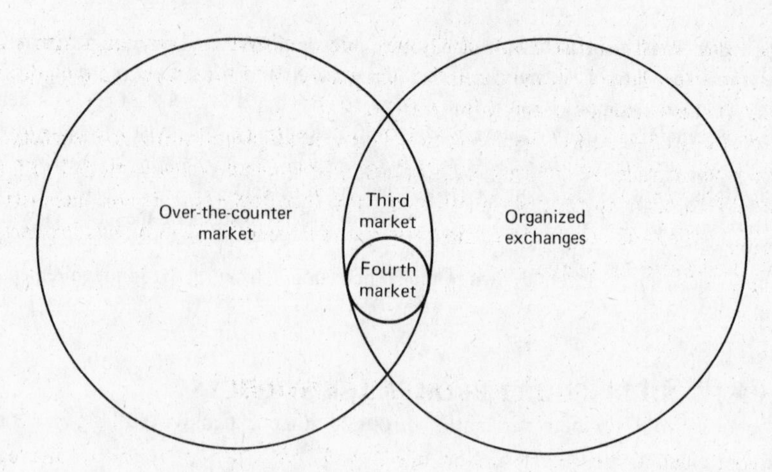

Fig. 8-1 Subsets of the secondary market.

the third-market broker-dealers are market-makers who are in direct competition with the specialists that make markets on the organized exchanges.

The third market developed as a response to the absence of commission-rate discounts on the NYSE. Prior to May 1, 1975, the NYSE's commission charge for, say, 20,000 shares was 200 times its round-lot charge for 100 shares. This system made trading in large blocks very expensive. One way to achieve lower commission charges, then, was to seek an OTC market-maker that made markets in NYSE-listed securities. The OTC dealers were not bound to the minimum commission rates which members of the NYSE set for themselves prior to May 1, 1975. After May 1, 1975 (called "May Day"), the SEC required the NYSE members to negotiate their commission rates downward; the importance of the third market diminished as a result.

The Fourth Market

The fourth market refers to those institutional investors and wealthy individuals who buy and sell securities *directly* from each another. The *fourth market* is essentially a communication network among institutional investors that trade large blocks without the aid of a brokerage house. The functions of inventory carrying, risk-bearing, investment research, credit provision, and dealing in other markets are lacking in the fourth market. The fourth-market maker is usually one individual or a few persons who communicate the buy-and-sell desires of their clientele to block traders and thus facilitate directly negotiated sales. The fourth-market organizer may collect a small commission or a flat annual fee for helping to arrange these large transactions. Generally, the costs of trading large blocks are smaller in the fourth market than in other markets. Other reasons for operating in the fourth market include the expectation of obtaining a better price through direct negotiation, savings on commissions, rapid execution, or a desire to retain anonymity.

EXAMPLE 8.5 Instinet is a fourth-market firm that operates out of New York City via a computer network and geographically dispersed terminals. If an Instinet subscriber wants to buy or sell, they begin by querying their Instinet computer terminal. The subscriber starts the inquiry by entering the name of the stock, its bid or asked price, and the number of shares into Instinet's computer network, plus a secret code number through which they can be contacted. This entry, which is essentially an offer to buy or sell, prints out on the computer terminals of other Instinet subscribers around the world.

If a second Instinet subscriber is interested, they may contact the first subscriber by addressing the identification number that typed out with the inquiry. The inquirer and the responding party can then negotiate over the price via the computer terminals in their offices. If they agree on the price and size of a trade, the market-maker's computer automatically closes the trade and prints out confirmation slips for both subscribers. The deal is completed without a middle party (such as an exchange's specialist) who charges a commission, carries inventories, or provides other services. The buying and selling subscribers never even need learn each others identity. Instinet will contact both parties and expedite the exchange of securities and money. The anonymity is valued by some fourth-market clients.

The Block Positioners

Whenever 10,000 or more shares of one stock are traded in one transaction, it is called a *block trade*. Because multiple buyers must usually be lined up to purchase a block, a special type of broker called "block positioner" has developed. *Block positioners* routinely handle large blocks and rarely cause the market price of the issue to change significantly. Most block positioners are employees of brokerage firms that have seats on the NYSE—these large firms have both the capital to carry a block in inventory and the connections to distribute it. Block positioners also operate in the third market.

The commission rates charged by block positioners are small. One-fourth of 1 percent is not an unusual commission rate for a block trade. In contrast, odd-lot commissions are typically from 1 to 6 percent—because there are no economies of scale in these small transactions. The low commission rates offered by the block positioners are another source of economic competitive pressure that helps maintain low negotiated brokerage commissions on the organized exchanges.

True-False Questions

8.1 The 1964 Amendments to the Security Exchange Act of 1934 changed the disclosure requirements so that OTC securities must disclose essentially the same information as the exchange-listed securities.

8.2 The OTC market is located in New York City.

8.3 The OTC market is where all secondary sales are transacted.

8.4 The same types of broker orders (such as market orders, limit orders, etc.) are used on the organized exchanges and in the OTC market.

8.5 Most of the trades going through NASDAQ are for NYSE-listed stocks.

8.6 The majority of OTC stocks have price quotations through NASDAQ.

8.7 When a limit order is placed, it must be accompanied by a time specification to determine the length of its life.

8.8 Margin trading does not change the riskiness of the underlying security, but it does increase the riskiness of the investor's margined position.

8.9 The margin requirements that constrain investors change after they initially establish a margined position.

8.10 Investors who open margin accounts must sign written statements giving their broker permission to liquidate their account without their permission in the event they cannot meet a margin call.

8.11 NYSE-listed stocks cannot be traded outside of the NYSE.

8.12 Fourth-market makers transact their business as dealers.

8.13 At any given moment General Motors common stock can be purchased in either the NYSE, some regional exchanges, the OTC market, the third market, or the fourth market.

8.14 Discount brokers charge lower commission rates than full-service brokers because they execute trades slower and at security prices that are frequently not as favorable to the client as the full-service brokers.

8.15 Discount brokers are small local organizations that never have offices in many different states and large computerized central offices.

Multiple Choice Questions

8.1 The OTC market is best described by which of the following statements?
(*a*) It is a market where prices may be negotiated rather than determined by an auction.
(*b*) It is a market where unlisted securities are traded.
(*c*) In order to survive in the OTC market it is essential to be a member of a trade association called the NASD.
(*d*) All of the above are true.

8.2 A broker-dealer can handle a client's purchase order in which of the following ways?

(*a*) The order can be filled from inventory if the dealer owns shares of the security.
(*b*) The dealer can act as a broker (or agent) and obtain the security for the client from some other seller or a dealer.
(*c*) A dealer that does not carry the desired security in inventory can buy it for their own inventory and then resell it to the client.
(*d*) All of the above are true.

8.3 The *NASD 5 percent markup policy* is best described by which of the following?

(*a*) The 5 percent markup policy is a guideline, not a rule. Markups in excess of 5 percent may be fair in some circumstances (for instance, when an inactively traded security was carried in inventory for some time).
(*b*) The NASD member's contemporaneous cost for the security is the primary factor on which the 5 percent markup should be based.
(*c*) Markups of less than 3 percent (or even less) will be excessive and unfair in some cases (for instance, in a large transaction involving an actively traded bond in which the NASD member only acted as a broker).
(*d*) All of the above are true.
(*e*) None of the above are true.

8.4 Approximately how many NASDAQ display terminals are located in broker's offices?

(*a*) Hundreds of terminals
(*b*) Thousands of terminals
(*c*) Tens of thousands of terminals
(*d*) Hundreds of thousands of terminals
(*e*) Millions of terminals

8.5 What information does NASDAQ provide to its users?

(*a*) Representative bid and asked prices, and also the highest bid and the lowest offer, for each security.
(*b*) The identification of every market-maker in each security and every market-makers' bid and asked prices.
(*c*) The identification of every market-maker in each security and every market-makers' bid and asked prices, and the ability for market-makers to enter their own bid and asked quotations directly.
(*d*) Every one of the above services is provided for certain classes of NASDAQ subscribers.
(*e*) Only one price that is the average of the bid and asked prices is provided for each security.

8.6 Block positioners are best described by which one of the following statements?

(*a*) They act only as brokers.
(*b*) They act only as dealers.
(*c*) Sometimes they act as brokers, and sometimes they act as dealers.
(*d*) They act through the organized exchanges.

8.7 If a customer of an OTC broker or dealer places a buy order for an OTC stock, which of the following statements best describes the way the customer's order for that security is filled?

(*a*) A dealer can buy the stock the client desires in the market if it is not already in the dealer's inventory.
(*b*) The broker or dealer sells the desired stock to the client at their asked price.
(*c*) An OTC dealer that does not have the desired stock in inventory, keeps the bid-asked spread when their customer buys a stock.
(*d*) All of the above are true.

8.8 Stop orders are treated like market orders when which one of the following conditions occurs?

(*a*) The stock's current price approaches within 50 cents of the specified price.
(*b*) As soon as the stock's current price reaches the specified price.
(*c*) The stock's current price "sells through" and passes 50 cents past the specified price.
(*d*) How the order is handled depends on whether it is handled by a specialist in an organized exchange or a dealer in the OTC market.

8.9 Margin trading is best described by which one of the following statements?

(*a*) Margin buying increases the investor's rate of return if the price of the underlying security moves advantageously.

(*b*) If the price of the underlying security moves adversely margin buying increases the investor's losses over what they would have been without the use of margins.

(*c*) Margin buying increases the investor's expected rate of return if and only if the rate of return from the underlying asset exceeds the rate of interest the margined buyer is paying.

(*d*) All of the above are true.

(*e*) None of the above are true.

8.10 At any given moment, if a specified quantity of some given stock could be purchased at the same price per share on either the NYSE or in the fourth market, which of the following statements best describes the total cost (including commissions) of the transaction?

(*a*) The total cost of the transaction will be more in the NYSE.

(*b*) The total cost of the transaction will be less in the NYSE.

(*c*) The total cost of the transaction will be the same in either market.

(*d*) It is impossible to tell in advance, any of the above may be true.

Answers

True-False

8.1. T 8.2. F 8.3. F 8.4. T 8.5. T 8.6. F 8.7. T 8.8. T 8.9. T
8.10. T 8.11. F 8.12. F 8.13. T 8.14. F 8.15. F

Multiple Choice

8.1. d 8.2. d 8.3. d 8.4. c 8.5. d 8.6. c 8.7. d 8.8. b 8.9 d 8.10. a

Chapter 9

Federal Investments Regulations

9.1 INTRODUCTION

To maintain and augment its capital markets, the U.S. government has taken various legal steps to ensure that the markets are fair and honest places where small savers and big investors alike can participate safely. In particular, laws forbidding fraud and price manipulation have been passed and federal agencies have been established specifically to enforce these securities laws. This chapter explains the various laws that govern the investment industry in the United States. The laws are presented in the chronological order in which they were enacted so you can follow the development of the investment law system to its present form.

9.2 THE GLASS-STEAGALL ACT OF 1933

In 1933 Representative Steagall and Senator Glass pushed a law through Congress which was officially named *The Banking Act of 1933*. The *Glass-Steagall Act,* as it is more popularly called, forbade commercial banks from conducting two important activities: (1) paying interest on demand deposits and (2) performing investment banking activities. The law also established the Federal Deposit Insurance Corporation (FDIC) to insure the deposits of those banks that elect to pay the FDIC insurance premiums and established ceilings on the interest rates that banks can pay on checking account deposits.

EXAMPLE 9.1 The mighty House of Morgan, owned by the famous financier J. P. Morgan, was split as a result of the Glass-Steagall Act. J. P. Morgan & Company was one of the largest, most profitable, and most powerful financial houses on Wall Street in the 1920s. In order to split the J. P. Morgan commercial banking activities away from the investment banking operations, the House of Morgan was split into two firms, both of which are still famous and powerful in financial circles around the world today. Morgan-Guaranty Bank is America's fourth largest bank—a feat this aristocratic bank accomplishes without having any branches. And, Morgan-Stanley is a large and highly prestigious investment banking firm.

9.3 THE SECURITIES ACT OF 1933

The Securities Act of 1933 (the Securities Act, hereafter) deals largely with primary issues of securities. This act, also known as the "truth in securities law," was supplemented by the Securities Exchange Act of 1934 (SEA). The SEA extends some of the disclosure requirements for primary issues to many secondary issues. The primary purpose of these two laws is to require security issuers to *fully disclose all information* about themselves that affects the value of their securities. The Securities Act of 1933 also prohibits certain types of fraud; let us consider the Securities Act in some detail before discussing the SEA.

Registration of new issues. The main objective of the Securities Act of 1933 is to provide the potential investor in *primary issues* with a full disclosure of the information needed to make an informed decision about new securities. To achieve this objective, the Securities Act of 1933 specifies that the issuing firm and the investment banker must "register" the issue. Registering an issue involves filing with the Securities and Exchange Commission (SEC) audited financial statements, other information about the firm, and information about the underwriting agreement. Information required in the registration is listed below:

1. A statement as to the nature of the issuer's business, its organization, and its financial structure
2. A list of directors and officers of the issuer, their addresses, and their salaries
3. Details about the issuer's arrangements for bonuses, stock options, and profit-sharing
4. Contracts the issuer may have with subcontractors, consultants, and others
5. Audited balance sheets and income statements of the issuing firm for preceding years

6. Copies of the issuer's articles of incorporation, bylaws, trust indentures, and agreement with the investment banker
7. A statement about other securities the issuer has outstanding and their rights
8. A statement about the terms on which the issuer offers the new shares to the public
9. Any other statements the SEC may require and any other information which may materially affect the value of the securities

Prospectus. The first part of the registration statement is prepared in the form of a booklet for public dissemination and is called a *prospectus.* The prospectus contains most of the information in the registration statement. The Securities Act of 1933 requires that a prospectus must be given to every investor to whom the investment banker's syndicate sells the new securities.

After a potential issuer registers the required information with the SEC, it must wait at least 20 days before issuing the securities. During this waiting period the SEC investigates the proposed prospectus to ensure that all the required information has been disclosed. The proposed prospectus may be circulated by the potential issuer during this waiting period, but it must have a note in red ink on its front cover stating that it has not yet received SEC approval for issuance as a final prospectus. These tentative prospectuses are called *red herrings.*

By permitting securities to be issued, the SEC in no way implies its approval of them as a good investment. SEC disapproval of a proposed prospectus merely indicates that in the opinion of the SEC insufficient information has been disclosed for investors to analyze.

Shelf registrations. The SEC adopted its Rule 415 in 1982 to allow large corporations to file registration statements with details about the firm's long-run financing plans. Then, at a later date, a corporation that previously filed one of these so-called *shelf registration* statements can issue the stocks and/or bonds detailed in its long-run plan without filing another separate registration statement for each issue.

Small issues exemption According to Regulation A of the SEC, a firm issuing less than $1,500,000 per year of new securities need not comply with the full registration requirement. Such issuers are required only to furnish potential investors with an offering circular containing a limited amount of unaudited financial information.

Secondary sales are also exempt from registration under the Securities Act of 1933. However, the SEA of 1934 extended the Securities Act of 1933 law's provisions for primary issues by requiring issuers of securities traded in secondary markets to register and file information with the SEC too.

Private offering exemption. The Securities Act of 1933 also exempts from the registration requirements stock issues that are offered to a small group of private subscribers who are sufficiently experienced or informed that the disclosure requirements are not necessary for their protection and who are purchasing the shares as an investment and not for resale. Purchasers in a private offering are required to sign a letter stating that they are purchasing the shares for investment purposes—shares issued under this exemption are called *letter stock.* The SEC has required that letter stock investors not sell their shares for at least 2 years after purchase, as proof of their investment motives.

"No sale" exemption. The Securities Act of 1933 did not require the registration of securities issued in exchange for outstanding stock of the issuer as, for example, in a merger or consolidation. However, in 1972 Rule 145 was passed requiring SEC registrations for business combinations such as mergers and acquisitions. Thus, mergers and acquisitions are now viewed as security sales that are subject to the full disclosure of information requirements of the Securities Act of 1933.

Antifraud provisions. In addition to the requirements pertaining to full disclosure of information, the Securities Act contains antifraud provisions. It provides court remedies against those who disseminate untrue or misleading information about securities. The Securities Act of 1933 also limits the techniques that can be used to sell securities. It provides the basis for a later SEC ruling that all public securities dealers imply, by offering their services to the public, that they will deal fairly. This "fair deal" ruling provides a basis for prosecuting security salespersons who issue misleading advice.

9.4 THE SECURITIES EXCHANGE ACT OF 1934

After the Securities Act of 1933 was passed some deficiencies in the Act were apparent immediately. So the Congress reconvened the next year to enact the Securities Exchange Act of 1934 (SEA) to rectify the deficiencies in the 1933 Act. The primary objectives of the SEA are to (1) *establish the Securities and Exchange*

Commission (SEC), (2) provide adequate information about securities being traded in *secondary markets* in order to facilitate their evaluation and discourage price manipulation, (3) require organized exchanges to register with the SEC, (4) regulate the use of credit for security purchases, (5) protect against misuse of shareholders' proxy voting power, (6) outlaw the use of insider information, and (7) provide additional antifraud provisions.
SEC established. The SEA charged the SEC with the responsibility for regulating securities markets. The SEC is located in Washington, D.C., and is headed by five commissioners who are appointed by the President with the consent of Congress. In recent years the SEC has had a staff well in excess of a thousand people and a multimillion dollar annual budget.
Disclosure requirements for secondary securities. In order to ensure full disclosure of information for securities being traded in secondary markets, the SEA requires that an annual registration statement and other periodic reports be filed for public inspection with the SEC as a prerequisite for the listing of a security for trading. The Securities Acts Amendments of 1964 extended these registration requirements to securities traded in over-the-counter markets if the issuing firm has total consolidated assets in excess of $3 million and meets other requirements.

Since the SEA was passed the SEC has developed the 8-K, 10-K, and 10-Q forms on which corporations are required to report their activities. Corporations must file their periodic financial statements on the 10-K forms. Significant current developments must be reported on the 8-K forms as they occur. Unaudited financial reports must be filed quarterly on the 10-Q forms. These forms are available to the public.
Registration of organized exchanges. The SEA grants the SEC considerable authority over organized security exchanges. The SEA requires all exchanges to (1) register with the SEC, (2) comply with the letter and spirit of the law, (3) adopt bylaws or rules for expelling and disciplining members of the exchange who do not conduct their activities in a legal and ethical manner, and (4) furnish the SEC with copies of its rules and bylaws and any amendments which are adopted. Within these guidelines the exchanges are free to regulate themselves. However, the SEC can intervene in the affairs of the exchange and alter penalties, expel members of the exchange, or even close the exchange. As a matter of practice, the SEC rarely has intervened.[1]
Credit regulation. As securities rise in price most securities brokerage firms count the capital gains as additional equity in the client's account. This added equity entitles the borrower to borrow even more money. This pyramiding of debt on top of unrealized paper profits can be disastrous when the market prices decline.

EXAMPLE 9.2 Before the Great Crash in 1929 some speculators purchased securities by making tiny down payments. When securities prices began to fall in 1929 security price declines equal to speculators' tiny down payments occurred quickly and were common. Thus, the first market decline bankrupted imprudent speculators who had overextended themselves by pyramiding debt. When lenders, many of them banks, tried to sell the securities they held as collateral, they often found that the price of the securities were not sufficient to cover the debt. In order to avoid further capital losses, lenders who held securities as collateral hurriedly liquidated the shares. This dumping accelerated the market's decline and further aggravated the financial crisis. The instability in the banking system and the money supply caused by pyramids of debt which came crashing down deepened the recession of the early 1930s.

The congressmen who wrote the SEA wanted to prohibit dangerous debt pyramids. Since the Federal Reserve Board is charged with controlling the money supply and credit conditions, the SEA also gave it the authority to set *margin requirements* for credit purchases of securities. The Federal Reserve then wrote Federal Reserve Regulations T and U to cover initial margin requirements. The initial margin is the percentage of the purchase price which investors must be able to pay with their own funds. Regulations T and U allow the Board of Governors of the Federal Reserve to set the *initial margin requirements* for loans for the purpose of purchasing securities. In recent years the margin requirement has varied between 50 and 80 percent.

SOLVED PROBLEM 9.1

Assume that (1) the Federal Reserve has set *initial margin* requirements at 55 percent for common stock purchases, (2) the organized stock exchanges require a *maintenance (or variation) margin* re-

[1]The SEC intervened by forcing the organized security exchanges to abandon their fixed minimum commission schedules no later than May 1, 1975—this date is well-known on Wall Street *as May Day.* Another example of the SEC imposing its rules on the organized exchanges occurred in 1979 when the SEC's Rule 19c-3 took effect. Rule 19c-3 required the organized exchanges to allow their member firms to trade any new stock listed after April 26, 1979, either on-the-floor or off-of-the-floor of the exchange. The purpose of these two rules was to force the organized exchanges to comply with Securities Acts Amendments of 1975 and establish a competitive national market system.

quirement of 30 percent, (3) Thomas Bookbinder buys 100 shares of a common stock named Futuristic Conductors Inc., for $40 per share on margin, and (4) Futuristic stock's price falls to $10 per share 1 month after Mr. Bookbinder bought it.

(*a*) What is the maximum amount that Mr. Bookbinder can borrow from his broker to finance his initial purchase of 100 shares of Futuristic?

(*b*) If Bookbinder puts down the minimum initial margin requirement will he receive a margin call because Futuristic's price declines?

(*c*) What is the purpose for "having margin calls"?

SOLUTION

(*a*) The minimum initial margin requirement is $22 (55 percent times $40 per share) per share. This means that the maximum amount that can be borrowed is $18 ($40 per share less $22 minimum initial margin) per share, or $1,800 ($18 per share times 100 shares) to finance the round lot.

(*b*) Since the minimum maintenance margin is 30 percent the investor's debt cannot exceed 70 percent (100 percent less 30 percent) of whatever price the security may reach after it is initially purchased. If Mr. Bookbinder puts down the minimum initial margin of $22 per share he must have $18 ($40 less $22) of debt per share outstanding against his Futuristic stock. This $18 of debt per share equals 70 percent of a market price of $25.71 per share, because if $.70p = \$18$, then $p = \$25.714$. Therefore, Thomas will receive a margin call to put up more margin money when the price of Futuristic stock falls to a price of $25.71 per share. If Thomas does not give his broker more margin money within about 48 hours after the margin call the brokerage firm will liquidate his position.

(*c*) The position of any investor receiving a margin call would be liquidated to protect the lending brokerage firm from potential losses if the investor defaults on a debt agreement.

Dealer's indebtedness restrictions. The SEA also limited security dealers' total indebtedness to 20 times their net capital. This provision is intended to keep securities firms from using excessive debt to carry inventories of securities which could bankrupt the firm if the market value of their inventory declined significantly.

Proxy solicitation. The SEA requires that the SEC establish rules to govern proxy solicitations by those security issuers that are required to register with the SEC. The top corporate executives normally seek proxies in order that they may exercise the votes of those investors who are absent from the annual stockholders' meeting. These permissions from absentee voters are called *proxy votes,* or simply "proxies." Any party holding a proxy controls the voting power of the absent investor's shares on matters to come before the shareholders meeting (such as election of directors). The SEC requires that all proxy solicitations contain (1) a reasonable amount of information about the issues to be voted upon, (2) an explanation of whether management or the stockholders proposed the issue, (3) a place for the shareholder to express approval or disapproval of each issue with the exception of election of directors, and (4) a complete list of candidates if the proxy solicitation is for election of directors. All proxy solicitations and consent forms must be submitted to the SEC for approval before they are sent to shareholders.

Exemptions from the regulations. Securities of the federal, state, and local governments; securities that are not traded across state lines; and any other securities the SEC wishes to specify are exempt from registering with the SEC. Certain organized exchanges may also be exempted from registering if the SEC chooses. As a matter of practice a few small, local exchanges have been exempted from SEC registration. As a result of this exemption some of the provisions of the SEA do not apply to the securities traded at the exempted securities exchanges.

Insider activities. Corporation directors, officers, executives, other employees, and external technicians (such as auditors, investment bankers, and consultants) who have access to inside information about the firm that employs them are forbidden by the SEA from earning speculative profits from trading in the firm's securities. To enforce this prohibition, the SEA requires that every insider and every owner of more than 10 percent of a listed firm must file a statement, called an *insider report,* of his or her holdings of that firm's securities in each month in which a change in those holdings occurs. These insider reports are made public. For example, *The Wall Street Journal* prints insider reports.

Section 16 of the SEA of 1934 forbids insiders from making short sales in their firm's shares. The Act also entitles stockholders to recover any speculative profits (that is, gains on holdings of less than 6 month's duration), or losses avoided, that were obtained with the aid of insider information. And a 1984 Amendment to the SEA provides for treble damages—that is, the corporation that employs the inside trader can recover $3 for every $1 the insider gained. These provisions have greatly diminished the occurrence of price manipulation schemes involving insiders. However, insider information violations of a different variety do still occur.

EXAMPLE 9.3 In 1986 Mr. David Lash was a 31-year-old vice-president in the Merger and Acquisition Department of Drexer Burner. David was paid a salary and bonus in excess of $1 million for his services to the firm in 1986. David was a courteous gentleman, a good husband and father, and he was a "nice guy" who had many friends. In addition, David had a secret account at the Caribbean branch of a Swiss bank where it was disclosed he had over $12 million sequestered away; he had accumulated the money between 1981 and 1985 by secretly trading illegally on inside information he had gained about merging companies while he was doing his job at Drexer Burner.

David Lash had what seemed like a fool-proof scheme going. He would call his Swiss bank collect from a pay phone so that no phone records would be created in the United States that might connect him to his dealings with the Swiss bank where he had his secret account. From the pay phone he would instruct his Swiss banker to buy securities in corporations he had learned inside information about in his role as a merger specialist at Drexer Burner. Mr. Lash bought shares in public corporations that he had learned were destined to be the object of takeover offers that would, in all probability, bid up the price of the firms' stock. After the stock's price rose, David would tell his Swiss banker to sell the securities. He accumulated a multimillion dollar fortune with his clandestine one-man scheme.

Unfortunately for Mr. Lash a zealous young attorney at the SEC tracked David's series of profitable transactions to his Swiss bank. Then the U.S. government made the president of that Swiss bank reveal the identity of Mr. Lash. The U.S. government threatened to freeze millions of dollars that Mr. Lash's Swiss bank held in various deposits within the United States until the bank revealed David Lash's identity and handed over to the SEC records of Mr. Lash's illegal transactions. The SEC brought public charges against David in May 1986, for illegal use of inside information. Mr. Lash was caught red-handed; he pleaded guilty. In November 1986, a U.S. court took away Mr. Lash's assets and sentenced him to several years in prison. David Lash's position changed from being a "rising star" on Wall Street who was worth over $10 million to being humiliated and in jail—all in about 6 months.

Such actions indicate that the SEC tends to give a strict interpretation to the law forbidding the use of insider information.[2]

Price manipulation. The SEA specifically forbids certain price manipulation schemes such as wash sales, pools, circulation of manipulative information, and making false and misleading statements about securities. However, it does allow investment bankers to manipulate prices, but only to temporarily stabilize a security's price for a few weeks immediately following a primary offering.

The SEA also authorizes the SEC to supervise trading in the put and call option markets.[3]

SOLVED PROBLEM 9.2

Match the definitions listed below to the appropriate terms.

Terms	Description of Terms
1. Churning	A. A phony transaction carried out to create the illusion that a significant transaction occurred; a buy and an offsetting sale.
2. Cornering the market	B. The Dow-Jones Industrial Average fell 90 percent from a high reached in 1929.
3. The depression	C. The common practice of brokers to get their clients to generate commissions by fruitless security trading.
4. Insider	D. An executive, owner of shares, or either an internal or an external employee having access to information that may affect the firm's security prices.

[2]Section 10b of the SEA involves more subtle legal issues than the application of Sec. 16. Section 16 permits the stockholders to recover short-term profits earned by an insider regardless of whether or not the inside information was misused. On the other hand, Sec. 10b deals with fraudulent activities perpetrated by insiders or outsiders. The misuse of inside information is only one area covered by Sec. 10b.

In general, the SEC deals harshly with the users of inside information. In one case, the printer that printed a prospectus was prosecuted for using information gained from that prospectus while working on it before its release to the public.

[3]In 1981 the SEC and the Commodity Futures Trading Commission (CFTC) announced an administrative pact between the two governmental agencies that clarified their jurisdiction over recently developed financial futures and option products. Essentially, the SEC oversees almost all options trading, while the CFTC regulates almost all futures contracts and options on futures.

5. Pool	E. A tentative prospectus that has not received final approval by the SEC.
6. Wash sale	F. These are set by the Federal Reserve Board.
7. The Great Crash	G. Buy almost all the supply of a good that is available.
8. Red herring	H. Several years in the early 1930s when unemployment reached 24 percent and bankruptcies were rampant.
9. Margin requirement	I. An association of people formed to profit from manipulating security prices.

SOLUTION

1. C 2. G 3. H 4. D 5. I 6. A 7. B 8. E 9. F

9.5 THE PUBLIC UTILITY HOLDING COMPANY ACT OF 1935

Congress enacted the Public Utility Holding Company Act of 1935 (called simply the 1935 Act hereafter) to prevent public utilities from abusing whatever power they may possess as the sole supplier of an essential service. Section 11(a) of the Public Utility Holding Company Act gave the SEC the responsibility and the authority "to determine the extent to which the corporate structure . . . may be simplified, unnecessary complexities thereby eliminated, voting power fairly and equitably distributed ... and the properties and business thereof confined to those necessary and appropriate to the operations of an integrated public utility system."

The 1935 Act also gave the SEC the power to regulate the terms and form of securities issued by utility companies, regulate the accounting systems they use, approve all acquisitions and dispositions of assets and securities, and to regulate intercompany transactions such as the payment of cash dividends and the making of loans. Thus, the 1935 Act puts the SEC in a position of potential importance with respect to the regulation of America's public utilities.

9.6 THE MALONEY ACT OF 1938

The *Maloney Act,* an amendment to the SEA of 1934, was adopted at the request of the over-the-counter (OTC) security dealers and provides for the OTC industry's self-regulation. This Act stipulates that one or more associations of qualified OTC brokers and dealers may apply for registration with the SEC. These groups may regulate themselves within the guidelines laid down by the SEC, and may grant discounts on securities traded among group members. OTC dealers who are not members of an association deal with members of an association by paying full retail prices for any securities they purchase. The price concessions for members provide a strong incentive for all OTC brokers and dealers to belong to an association. The NASD is the only group operating under the Maloney act.

9.7 THE TRUST INDENTURE ACT OF 1939

An *indenture* is a contract, written by a firm which issues bonds, stipulating certain promises the firm makes to its bondholders. A common provision of an indenture is that the issuing corporation can pay no dividends on common stock if the bond's interest payments are in arrears. An independent third party called a *trustee* (for example, a bank) is appointed to monitor the issuing corporation on behalf of the bondholders and to make certain that the provisions of the indenture are not violated. If a provision is violated, the trustee should bring a suit against the issuing corporation on behalf of the owners of the indentured securities.

Prior to the 1939 Act unethical corporations might appoint their own banks as their trustee. Such a bank was dependent upon the indentured corporation for income and was therefore reluctant to sue it if it violated its indenture. To overcome such weakness, the Trust Indenture Act of 1939 requires that the indenture clearly specify the rights of the owners of the indentured securities, that the issuing corporation provide the trustee periodic financial reports, and that the trustee not impair its willingness or legal right to sue the issuing corporation.

9.8 THE INVESTMENT COMPANY ACT OF 1940

The *Investment Company Act of 1940* (ICA) is the main piece of legislation governing mutual funds and closed-end investment companies. The ICA extends the provisions of the Securities Act and the SEA. These earlier acts require that investment companies (like other issuers of securities) register with the SEC, limit sales commissions to no more than 9 percent, avoid fraudulent practices, fully disclose their financial statements, refrain from making short sales, and give their prospectuses to potential investors. The ICA also requires that investment companies publish statements outlining their investment goals (for example, growth, income, or safety of principal), not change their published goals without the consent of the shareholders, obtain the stockholders' approval of contracts for management advice for the fund, include outsiders on their boards of directors, follow uniform accounting procedures, submit to audits at least annually, and operate the fund for the benefit of its shareholders rather than for the benefit of its managers.

The ICA of 1940 was modified slightly by the Investment Company Amendments Acts of 1970 and 1975. The 1970 Amendments (1) asked for a standard of "reasonableness" with respect to the management fees charged to manage the assets of a mutual fund, and (2) restricted the adoption of new management contracts. The 1975 Amendment said that the sales charges that could be deducted from a fund investor's money must be related to the service the fund provides for the shareholder.

9.9 THE INVESTMENT ADVISORS ACT OF 1940

The *Investment Advisors Act of 1940* (IAA) requires individuals or firms that *sell advice* about securities or investments to register with the SEC. These investment advisors are required to observe the legal guidelines pertaining to fraud, price manipulation, and other factors. Either a set fee or a percentage of the assets managed is a permissible compensation plan for advisors under this law.

9.10 THE REAL ESTATE INVESTMENT TRUST ACT OF 1960

Real estate investment trusts, called *REITs,* are investment companies that specialize in holding and managing various types of real estate. According to the 1960 REIT Act every new REIT must have at least 100 different investors—also called *certificate holders* or shareholders. No group of five or fewer of these investors may control more than 50 percent of the shares in any REIT. The Act also says that any REIT is exempt from federal income taxes if it obtains at least 75 percent of its income from rent and mortgage interest, has 75 percent or more of its assets invested in real estate, and pays out 90 percent or more of each year's income to its shareholders.

9.11 THE SECURITIES INVESTOR PROTECTION CORPORATION ACT OF 1970

The *Securities Investor Protection Corporation* (SIPC) was established in 1970 by an act of Congress to assist the clients of bankrupt brokerage firms. The act requires that all registered securities brokers and dealers and all members of national securities exchanges join SIPC and pay dues (which are like insurance premiums) equal to approximately 1 percent of the firm's gross revenues. Mutual fund salespeople, insurance agents, and investment advisors need not join SIPC. SIPC dues are accumulated in a fund that is used to repay clients of a bankrupt brokerage firm if the firm loses the client's money or securities and does not have the capital to repay the loss. SIPC was formed to free investors from worry about selecting a brokerage firm by providing insurance to protect investors in case their brokerage firm fails.

9.12 THE COMMODITY FUTURES TRADING COMMISSION ACT OF 1974

The Commodity Exchange Authority (CEA) Act of 1936 established the CEA as a regulatory branch of the U.S. Department of Agriculture (USDA) that regulated trading in domestic agriculture commodities from 1936 until 1974. The CEA had the authority to grant approval for new futures contracts to be publicly traded, police the registration of the commodity futures commission merchants, investigate charges of cheating and fraud in commodity trading, and prevent price manipulation in domestic U.S. commodity trading. Commodity futures trading grew rapidly and the Commodity Futures Trading Commission Act of 1974 was enacted in order to pass all of the CEA's regulatory authority onto a new, larger regulatory agency called the Commodity Futures Trading Commission (CFTC). The CFTC is an independent federal regulatory agency overseen by five commissioners who are appointed by the President of the United States. The CFTC has a staff of economists and other regulatory officials who research the commodity markets in an effort to discern what rules and regulations about commodity futures trading will best promote the public welfare.

In addition to establishing the CFTC and giving it the powers that had previously been assigned to the CEA, the 1974 Act also gave the CFTC authority to sue any person or organization that violated the CFTC Act; take charge of a commodity market in an "emergency" situation and direct whatever actions it deems necessary to restore an orderly market; and issue "cease and desist" orders. Moreover, one of the most sweeping changes brought about by the CFTC Act was to grant the CFTC authority over the *entire* futures trading industry—that is, all commodities in the world that are traded in the United States, rather than merely domestically produced commodities.

9.13 EMPLOYMENT RETIREMENT INCOME SECURITY ACT OF 1974

Pension fund abuses by the managers of the funds result in the loss of pension benefits to hapless and unsuspecting employees. Not infrequently, these abuses stem from the imprudent risks taken by fund managers in deploying the funds entrusted to them. In an attempt to eliminate such disasters, Congress passed the *Employee Retirement Income Security Act of 1974* (called simply ERISA) to protect workers' pensions. Among ERISA's provisions is the so-called "prudent man rule."

While the word "prudent" has been left somewhat vaguely defined by Congress and the state legislatures that refer to the "prudent man rule," it apparently refers to some "average" rate of return with an "average" assumption of risk. The returns from Standard & Poor's 500 market index, for example, might be such an average yardstick.

9.14 THE SECURITIES REFORM ACT OF 1975

The *Municipal Securities Rule Making Board* (MSRB) was established under the *Securities Reform Act of 1975*. The MSRB is an independent self-regulating organization that is run by a SEC-appointed board of 15 members. The MSRB has passed rules requiring municipal securities dealers and brokers to register with the SEC, disclose their connections with new issues of municipals they might be selling, pass the NASD's periodic examinations, keep adequate records of their dealings, take disciplinary action against fraud and deception, and adopt uniform clearing procedures.

9.15 THE SECURITIES ACTS AMENDMENTS OF 1975

The *Security Acts Amendments* (SAA) of 1975 mandated the development of the *national market system* (NMS). The SAA did not specify the details of the NMS, leaving that to be determined by the competitive economic forces in the security markets themselves—subject, of course, to the approval of the SEC. The SAA merely indicated that the NMS should comprise a competitive environment which would result in maximum efficiency and liquidity. As a result of the SAA, organized exchanges discontinued their fixed minimum commission-rate schedules, began to allow exchange-listed stocks to be traded off-the-floor of the exchanges by their member firms, supported development of the Consolidated Tape, developed the Intermarket Trading System, and implemented other changes to spur competition.

9.16 THE NATIONAL BANKRUPTCY LAWS

In addition to the securities laws outlined above, there is some commerical law which is sometimes relevant for investors. The Bankruptcy Act of 1938, which was revised and updated by the Bankruptcy Act of 1978, is one example of a business law which sometimes affects investors. Essentially, the Bankruptcy Act requires that courts or court-appointed trustees oversee the affairs of firms against which bankruptcy charges have been filed. Furthermore, the law requires that in bankruptcies involving listed securities the bankruptcy courts ask the SEC for an advisory opinion concerning whatever financial reorganization may result from the bankruptcy proceeding. Significantly different types of bankruptcy proceedings are provided for by the different chapters of the bankruptcy law.

SOLVED PROBLEM 9.3

Match each of the brief definitions listed below to the appropriate word or phrase:

Words		Definitions
1. Default	A.	An agreement in which the majority of the unsecured creditors accept partial and/or late payment of their debts.
2. Arrangement	B.	The liquidation of a firm that was ordered by a bankruptcy court's decision.
3. Reorganization	C.	A plan for financial rehabilitation in which bonds might be downgraded to become preferred stock.
4. Bankruptcy auction	D.	A debtor makes a scheduled payment that is late and/or inadequate.

SOLUTION

1. D 2. A 3. C 4. B

SOLVED PROBLEM 9.4

Match the following fourteen brief descriptions of securities laws to the title of the appropriate law:

Acts		Brief Descriptions of Securities Laws
1. Glass-Steagall Act	A.	Requires that courts or a court-appointed trustee oversee the affairs of firms against which bankruptcy charges have been filed.
2. Securities Act of 1933	B.	Under this act, the MSRB was established.
3. Securities Exchange Act	C.	Sellers of investment advice are required to register with the SEC.
4. Public Utility Holding Company Act	D.	The federal insurance program to reimburse clients for losses resulting from bankrupted brokerage firms was established.
5. Maloney Act	E.	Pension fund management was brought under federal control.
6. Trust Indenture Act	F.	The law establishing a federal agency to oversee futures markets.
7. Investment Company Act	G.	The SEC was directed to establish a new national market system (NMS) with negotiated commission rates.
8. Investment Advisors Act	H.	Forbids commercial banks from engaging in investment banking.
9. Securities Investor Protection Corporation (SIPC)	I.	Firms issuing securities must register new issues with federal authorities. Registration information is made available to the public in the form of a prospectus.
10. Employee Retirement Income Security Act (ERISA)	J.	The SEC was set up to regulate the securities industry. All security exchanges must register with the SEC. The SEC must regulate proxy voting. Regulations of earlier laws were extended to cover secondary sales.
11. Commodity Futures Trading Trading Act	K.	Empowered the SEC to oversee the finances, accounting, organization, and activities of public utilities to ensure the public welfare is served.
12. National Bankruptcy Law	L.	Associations of qualified over-the-counter brokers and dealers can register with the SEC and regulate themselves within SEC guidelines.

13. Securities Reform Act — M. The contracts governing the bond issues clearly specify the rights of bond owners. Trustees must not allow anything to impair their willingness or legal right to sue the issuer.

14. Securities Acts Amendments — N. Mutual funds and closed-end investment companies were brought under federal control.

SOLUTION

1. H 2. I 3. J 4. K 5. L 6. M 7. N 8. C 9. D 10. E
11. F 12. A 13. B 14. G

True-False Questions

9.1 Margin requirements are regulated by the U.S. Treasury Department.

9.2 FDIC is to commerical banks what the SIPC is to stock brokerage firms.

9.3 The Securities Act of 1933 and Securities Exchange Act of 1934 are the most important pieces of legislation governing the securities market in America.

9.4 The Glass-Steagall Act is a synonym for The Banking Act of 1933.

9.5 According to the Securities Act of 1933 security exchanges are required to register with the SEC.

9.6 The SEC has very little legal authority over the New York Stock Exchange because it was in operation before the SEC was established.

9.7 Insiders, who the law forbids from earning short-term trading profits from their privileged information, include outsiders like external consultants and employees of an external accounting firm who do the auditing.

9.8 The Investment Advisors Act of 1940 allows practically anyone (even obvious incompetents) to register with the SEC as investment advisors.

9.9 ERISA is a 1975 Act of Congress which forbids pension funds from allowing mutual funds and certain other outsiders to manage their investments.

9.10 Churning is a common-place activity even though it is illegal.

Multiple Choice Questions

9.1 The Securities Act of 1933 is a law that
(*a*) Was passed to protect security investors in case their stockbrokers went bankrupt.
(*b*) Requires primary issuers to advertise in a national newspaper such as *The Wall Street Journal.*
(*c*) Ensures full disclosure of information with respect to new secondary issues.
(*d*) Allows the SEC to analyze issues and let only the good investments go to market.
(*e*) None of the above are true.

9.2 The NASD is best described by which one of the following?
(*a*) A trade association of security dealers.
(*b*) The organization that oversees and regulates the over-the-counter market.
(*c*) The provider of a computerized clearinghouse for a geographically fragmented market.
(*d*) All of the above are true.
(*e*) Nonactive security dealers are limited partners who have no voice in the management of the firm.

9.3 The law that establishes rules and regulations for mutual funds is the
(*a*) Securities Act of 1933
(*b*) Investment Advisors Act of 1940
(*c*) The Investment Company Act Amendments of 1970 and 1975
(*d*) Investment Company Act of 1940
(*e*) Both *c* and *d*

9.4 Investors are insured against loss if their brokerage firm goes bankrupt by which one of the following bodies?
(*a*) SIPC
(*b*) FDIC
(*c*) SEC
(*d*) U.S. Treasury
(*e*) Federal Reserve

9.5 When margin requirements are 50 percent and a stock sells for $40, an investor with $1,000 can
(*a*) Purchase 25 shares without borrowing any funds.
(*b*) Purchase 50 shares using an additional $1,000 borrowed from their brokerage firm.
(*c*) Will have higher returns if the stock price increases using a margin purchase.
(*d*) All of the above.
(*e*) Both *a* and *b* are true.

9.6 If the margin requirement is 60 percent, what is the maximum amount that could be borrowed in order to purchase 200 shares of a stock that is currently selling for $19.79 if brokerage commissions are assumed to be zero?
(*a*) $3,958
(*b*) $1,583
(*c*) $3,951
(*d*) $1,988
(*e*) $2,375

9.7 Which one of the following statements is false?
(*a*) An investor that illegally corners the market in some security or commodity buys all that item that is for sale.
(*b*) Short sellers are speculators who sell an asset they do not actually own.
(*c*) Short selling is illegal.
(*d*) Churning was made illegal by the Securities Exchange Act of 1934.
(*e*) Investment bankers are allowed to take actions to keep the market price of a security they recently issued from changing.

9.8 The Securities Exchange Commission was established by which one of the following laws?
(*a*) The Securities Act of 1933
(*b*) The Securities Exchange Act of 1934
(*c*) The Maloney Act of 1936
(*d*) The Trust Indenture Act of 1939
(*e*) The Securities Investor Protection Corporation Act

9.9 Insider activities are required to be reported under which of the following laws?
(*a*) The Securities Act of 1933
(*b*) Securities Exchange Act of 1934
(*c*) Maloney Act of 1938
(*d*) Trust Indenture Act of 1939
(*e*) The Securities Investor Protection Corporation Act

9.10 The National Association of Securities Dealers registered with the SEC under the provision of which one of the following laws?
(*a*) Securities Act of 1933
(*b*) Securities Exchange Act of 1934
(*c*) Maloney Act of 1938
(*d*) Trust Indenture Act of 1939
(*e*) Investment Advisors Act of 1940.

Answers

True-False

9.1. F 9.2. T 9.3. T 9.4. T 9.5. F 9.6. F 9.7. T 9.8. T 9.9. F
9.10. T

Multiple Choice

9.1. e 9.2. d 9.3. e 9.4. a 9.5. d 9.6. b 9.7. c 9.8. b 9.9. b 9.10. c

Chapter 10

Security Market Indexes

10.1 INTRODUCTION

Security market indicators are of two basic types—averages and indexes. A stock market *average* is merely a weighted or unweighted average price for a group of stocks. Stock market indexes typically employ more refined methods to measure the level in stock prices than do stock market averages.

Index numbers are void of dollar values or other units of measure. Stock market indexes are usually calculated as ratios of dollar values. They are "pure numbers" that are used for making comparisons between indexes, averages, or other numbers. An index is usually a weighted average ratio that is calculated from an average of a large number of different stocks. The index numbers are typically a time series constructed from the same base value (which is usually set to be 100, 10, or 1). Some year in the past is selected as the base year from which the index's base value is calculated in order to impart a time perspective to the index.

10.2 DIFFERENT AVERAGES AND INDEXES EXIST

Many different security market indexes and averages are published. Some are listed below:

The Dow Jones industrial average (DJIA)
The Dow Jones transportation average
The Dow Jones utility average
Moody's industrial average
Moody's railroad stock average
Moody's utility stock average
Standard & Poor's stock price average from 90 different industries
Standard & Poor's 400 industrial stocks average
Standard & Poor's 20 transportation stocks average
Standard & Poor's 40 utility stocks average
Standard & Poor's financial stocks average
Standard & Poor's 500 composite stocks average
The New York Times index
Value Line index
Wilshire 5000 equity index
New York Stock Exchange index
Center for Research on Security Prices (CRSP) index
National Quotation Board index of over-the-counter stocks
NASDAQ Price indexes
American Stock Exchange (ASE) index
Barron's 50-stock average

Some bond indexes follow:

Dow Jones 40 bonds index

Salomon Brothers corporate bond index

Standard & Poor's municipal bond index

Standard & Poor's U.S. government bond index

Hundreds of other bond indexes exist[1]

The following commodity indexes are available:

Dow Jones indices of spot commodity prices

Dow Jones futures commodity index

Commodity Research Bureau futures index

The security market indicators listed above are published in financial newspapers (like *Barrons*) and business periodicals (such as the various Standard & Poors, and Moodys Corporation publications). International investors can also find similar indicators that are prepared for every market that is significant in the world economy.

10.3 THE CONSTRUCTION OF INDEXES

Every market index is constructed differently. A well-constructed market index will give an indication of the prices of all the items in the *population* under consideration. A poorly constructed index will only furnish erratic indications of what an unrepresentative sample of the population does. In the design or selection of a market index the following five factors should be considered:

1. *Sample size.* The sample should be a statistically significant fraction of the population studied because larger samples tend to produce more accurate indications about the underlying population. The well-known Dow-Jones Industrial Average, for example, is constructed from a tiny sample of only 30 of the approximately 1,700 stocks listed on the NYSE. At the other extreme, if a sample is too large it can be costly to compile. (However, computers have reduced this cost considerably.)
2. *Representativeness.* The sample should contain heterogeneous elements representing all segments of the population. The Dow Jones Industrial Average, for example, is constructed from an unrepresentative sample of NYSE stocks because it contains only large, old, blue-chip firms. Thus, this average provides a poor indication of what the stocks issued by the smaller NYSE listed firms are doing.
3. *Weighting.* The various elements in the sample should be assigned weights that correspond to investment opportunities in the population under study.
   - *a.* A security's weight in some index might be proportional to the total market value of all the firms' shares that are outstanding stated as a fraction of the total market value of all the securities being traded in its market. Such *value-weighting* of an index is done to reflect investment opportunities in existence at any moment. The S&P500 Composite stocks average is an example of a value-weighted index.
   - *b.* *Equal weights* could be used to represent the probability of selecting any given security with random sampling (or equivalently, selecting stocks by throwing an unaimed dart). An equally weighted index represents a "no skill" or naive buy and hold investment strategy. The Center for Research on Security Prices (CRSP) index is calculated in both an equally weighted and a value-weighted form.

[1]See Frank Fabozzi and Irving Pollack, *The Handbook of Fixed Income Securities,* 2d ed. (Homewood, Ill.: Dow Jones–Irwin, 1987), appendix entitled "Fixed Income Indexes" by Arthur Williams and Noreen M. Conwell, pp. 1288–1342. The appendix lists details of approximately 400 different indexes for corporate bonds and government bonds; U.S. government, U.S. government agencies, and corporate bonds; municipal bonds; Yankee bonds; Eurodollar bonds; foreign bonds; zero coupon bonds; and high-yield bonds. Salomon Brothers has 45, Standard & Poor's has 15, Shearson Lehman has 36, Moody's has 19, and Merrill Lynch has 95 bond indexes which they maintain and publish.

4. *Convenient units.* An index should be stated in units that are easy to understand and which facilitate answering questions. The Dow Jones Industrial Average furnishes an example of an index that is quoted in terms of inconvenient and implausible economic units.
5. *Computation of the mean.* Most security market indicators are calculated as some sort of arithmetic average. The *geometric average* is an alternative computational procedure; it results in a smaller but similar value that is less volatile than an arithmetic average calculated from the same sample of securities. (See Chapter 25 for more details about geometric means.)

SOLVED PROBLEM 10.1

Calculate the values of three different stock price indexes for the three common stocks listed below for the time period from July 1, 1965, to July 1, 1992. The three stocks below were selected to expedite the computations because the three corporations (1) issued no additional shares and (2) had no stock dividends or splits. Cash dividend payments should be ignored in the computations.

STOCK	TOTAL SHARES OUTSTANDING ON BOTH DATES	BASE PERIOD MARKET PRICE JULY 1, 1965	MORE RECENT PERIOD MARKET PRICE JULY 1, 1992	PERCENTAGE PRICE CHANGE
Holland	60,000	$30	$45	+50%
Manard	20,000	$25	$80	+220%
Redbud	90,000	$65	$85	+31%

(*a*) If the three-stock index is value-weighted, what will its value be on July 1, 1992?
(*b*) If the three-stock index is price-weighted, what will its value be on July 1, 1992?
(*c*) If the three-stock index is equally weighted, what will its value be on July 1, 1992?
(*d*) Compare and contrast the price-weighted, the value-weighted, and the equally weighted index numbers you obtained from the same three stocks and explain why they differ.

SOLUTION

(*a*) The value-weighted three-stock index is calculated below:

STOCK	TOTAL SHARES OUTSTANDING ON BOTH DATES	MORE RECENT MARKET PRICE JULY 1, 1992	TOTAL VALUE EQUALS (NO. OF SHARES) × (PRICE PER SHARE)	WEIGHTS EQUAL TOTAL VALUE / $11,950,000
Holland	60,000	$ 45	$ 2,700,000	2.7/11.95 = .226
Manard	20,000	$ 80	$ 1,600,000	1.6/11.95 = .134
Redbud	90,000	$ 85	$ 7,650,000	7.65/11.95 = .64
Totals	170,000	$210	$11,950,000	1.0

STOCK	TOTAL SHARES OUTSTANDING ON BOTH DATES	BASE PERIOD MARKET PRICE JULY 1, 1965	TOTAL VALUE EQUALS (NO. OF SHARES) × (PRICE PER SHARE)	WEIGHTS EQUAL TOTAL VALUE / $8,150,000
Holland	60,000	$ 30	$1,800,000	1.8/8.15 = .221
Manard	20,000	$ 25	$ 500,000	.5/8.15 = .061
Redbud	90,000	$ 65	$5,850,000	5.85/8.15 = .718
Totals	170,000	$120	$8,150,000	1.0

The value-weighted index would be calculated to be 1.4663, as shown below:

$$\frac{\text{July 1, 1992 market value}}{\text{July 1, 1965 market value}} = \frac{\$11,950,000}{\$8,150,000} = 1.4663$$

The value-weighted index's value of 1.4663 implies the three stocks increased 46.63 percent from their base date of July 1, 1965, on average. Note that stock splits and stock dividends in any of the stocks would not affect the way the value-weighted index is calculated or its value. (This is the way the S&P500 index is calculated.)

(*b*) The price-weighted three-stock index is calculated below:

STOCK	MORE RECENT MARKET PRICE JULY 1, 1992	WEIGHTS EQUAL TOTAL VALUE $11,950,000
Holland	$ 45	45/210 = .2143
Manard	$ 80	80/210 = .3809
Redbud	$ 85	85/210 = .4048
Totals	$210	1.0

STOCK	BASE PERIOD MARKET PRICE JULY 1, 1965	WEIGHTS EQUAL TOTAL VALUE $8,150,000
Holland	$ 30	30/120 = .2500
Manard	$ 25	25/120 = .2083
Redbud	$ 65	65/120 = .5417
Totals	$120	1.0

The price-weighted index is calculated as shown below:

$$\frac{\text{Total value of the three shares in 1992}}{\text{Total value of the three shares in 1965}} = \frac{\$210}{\$120} = 1.75$$

The price-weighted index's value of 1.75 implies that the three stocks increased an average of 75 percent from its base date of July 1, 1965. The computations would have been much more complicated if any stock dividends or stock splits had occurred. (This is the way the DJIA is calculated.)

(*c*) The equally weighted three-stock index is calculated below:

STOCK	PERCENTAGE PRICE CHANGE PER SHARE FROM 1965 TO 1992	EQUAL WEIGHTS	PRODUCTS OF (PERCENT CHANGE) × (EQUAL WEIGHT)
Holland	+50%	$\frac{1}{3}$	16.667
Manard	+220%	$\frac{1}{3}$	73.333
Redbud	+31%	$\frac{1}{3}$	10.333
Totals	+301%	1.0	100.333%

The equally weighted index's value of 100.333 percent implies that the three-stock index increased 100.333 percent from its base date of July 1, 1965. The computations would have been more complicated if any stock dividends or stock splits had occurred.

(*d*) The values of the three different indexes are summarized below:

STOCK	PERCENTAGE PRICE CHANGE	INDEX	VALUE OF THE INDEX
Holland	+50%	Value-weighted	46.63%
Manard	+220%	Equally weighted	100.333%
Redbud	+31%	Price-weighted	75.0%

The value-weighted index suggested the smallest rate of price appreciation, 46.63 percent, because the value-weighting procedure assigned the largest weight to the stock that happened to have the smallest percentage gain, Redbud. The equally weighted index registered the largest percentage price gain, 100.333 percent, because it gave equal weights to the large 220 percent gain of the Manard stock and the more modest gains from the two larger issuers. The price-weighted index yielded an intermediate value of 75 percent. The value-weighted index is the only one of the three methods that is not complicated by changes in the units of account used by the individual corporations.

10.4 MAINTENANCE PROBLEMS WITH SECURITY MARKET INDEXES

After a security market index is constructed, situations normally arise requiring that it be revised. The three most common problems that cause an existing index to need revision are (1) changing the number of stocks in the sampled list, (2) adjusting for stock splits and stock dividends within the index, and (3) making of substitutions to replace securities that have become unsatisfactory. The way these three problems have affected the Dow Jones Industrial Average (DJIA) and the Standard & Poors 500 Composite stocks (S&P500) index are compared below.

Changing the Size of the Sample

When the DJIA was first constructed in 1884 it contained 12 stocks. The sample size was increased to 20 stocks in 1916. The present sample size of 30 stocks was adopted in 1928. These changes all provided samples that many people considered inadequate.

The S&P500 was computed in 1923 with a sample of 233 stocks. This sample was gradually increased to 500 stocks in 1957. The 500-stock sample is 16.6 times larger than the DJIA sample of 30. The total market value of all the NYSE and over-the-counter stocks that comprise the S&P500 equals approximately 75 percent of the total market value of all NYSE stocks. The S&P500 has been historically formulated and revised to provide a more adequate sample size than the DJIA.

Adjustments for Stock Splits

The strange way that stock splits are reflected in the divisor of the DJIA results from the original formulation of that index. In 1928, when the 30-stock DJIA was constructed, the 30 market prices were simply summed up and divided by 30 to obtain the DJIA, as shown below.

$$\text{DJIA}_t = \sum_{i=1}^{30} \frac{p_{i,t}}{\text{divisor}_t}$$

where divisor = 30 in 1928

divisor = .505 in 1991

Equal weights were assigned to the 30 securities that were used to form the DJIA in 1928. However, over the years as some of the 30 securities underwent stock splits and stock dividends, the weights had to be changed. A simplified numerical example in Table 10.1 demonstrates the arbitrary manner in which the weights in the DJIA are changed by stock dividends and splits.

Table 10.1 Example of How the Divisor for a Three-Stock Average That Is Calculated Like the DJIA Changes When One Stock Is Split

Three Stocks	Prices Before Stock Zeta Is Split 3-for-1 at 11:00 AM on Split Day	Prices After Stock Zeta Is Split 3-for-1 at 11:00 AM on Split Day
Zeta	$ 60	$20
Tau	$ 40	$40
Epsilon	$ 25	$25
Totals	$125/3 = 41.67	$85/divisor = 41.67
Divisors	3	2.04

As a result of the Dow Jones procedure the relative importance of stocks that split is decreased in the computation of the DJIA, and the importance of nonsplit stocks increases. There is no economic or statistical logic behind these shifts in the relative weights.

In contrast to the Dow Jones procedure, the S&P500 index is computed in a manner that handles stock splits logically. The S&P500 is an index that is calculated from a base 1941–1943 base value of 10, as shown below:

$$\text{S\&P500} = \frac{\sum_{i=1}^{500} p_{i,t} q_{i,t}}{\sum_{i=1}^{500} p_{i,0} q_{i,0}} \times 10 = \frac{p_{1,t}\, q_{1,t} + p_{2,t}\, q_{2,t} + \cdots + p_{500,t}\, q_{500,t}}{p_{1,0}\, q_{1,0} + p_{2,0}\, q_{2,0} + \cdots + p_{500,0}\, q_{500,0}}$$

where $p_{i,t}$ and $q_{i,t}$ represent the market price per share and quantity of shares outstanding at time period t for the ith stock issue; the index is calculated over $i = 1, 2, \ldots, 500$ issues; and $p_{i,0}$ and $q_{i,0}$ denote the market prices per share and quantity of shares of the 500 stocks that were used in the computations during the 1941–1943 base period.

The S&P500 index is calculated using both the presplit and the postsplit market prices to nullify any changes in the unit of account (namely, the stock dividends or splits). As shown in the S&P500 formula on page 92, the market prices (denoted p) are multiplied times the associated number of shares outstanding (denoted q). Thus, every market-value-weighted security in the S&P500 index is unaffected by stock splits since the total value of a corporation is unaffected by changes in its unit of account.

Substitutions

Substitutions can be a recurrent and troublesome problem, especially for an index computed from a small sample—like the DJIA. There have been many substitutions in the DJIA over the decades.

One of the more interesting substitutions involved IBM's stock. IBM was *added* to the DJIA in 1932 and then *deleted* in 1939 in order to make room for American Telephone and Telegraph (ATT). The logic behind this substitution was too tortured to understand.[2] But then, IBM was *added back* into the DJIA again in 1979.

Substitutions in the S&P500 are more logical, and, also, of only minor importance because of the small weight given to each individual stock. Essentially, stocks are added to or deleted from the S&P500 index only when they are listed or delisted from the NYSE or disappear because of mergers or acquisitions.

SOLVED PROBLEM 10.2

Consider the effect of a 20 percent rise in the price of one stock on the computation of the following three-stock security price indicators:

Stocks	Begin. Value or Average at Time $t = 0$	Average at Time $t = 1$ after 20% Rise in	
		Colby's Price	Barton's Price:
Barton	\$110	\$110	\$110(1.2) = \$132
Brown	\$ 40	\$ 40	\$ 40
Colby	\$ 30	\$30(1.2) = \$ 36	\$ 30
Totals	\$180	\$186	\$202
Divisor	3	3	3
Average	60	62.00	67.33
Percent increase in the average		3.33%	12.22%

To what do you attribute the fact that the average rose only 3.33 percent when the price of Colby's stock rose 20 percent, but the same average rose 12.22 percent when the price of Barton went up by 20 percent?

SOLUTION

When the Colby Corporation's \$30 stock rose 20 percent it had a small impact on the average because the average is a price-weighted average and Colby is a low-priced stock. In contrast, when the price of the \$110 Barton stock rose 20 percent this change had a larger effect on the average because Barton is a high-priced stock.

The DJIA is a price-weighted average and therefore it reacts to changes in the prices of its component stocks like the three-stock average in this example. Most price-weighted averages are not based on any rational economic model or logical reflection of investment opportunities. Price-weighting is arbitrary and inappropriate in most applications and can result in misleading values.

SOLVED PROBLEM 10.3

The following data currently exist for the common stock of three companies. Assume that no dividends were paid by the three companies.

[2] The sample used in the so-called Dow Jones *Industrial* Average does not even contain all industrial stocks, as its name implies it should. More specifically, the public utility stock of ATT which is used in the DJIA is not an industrial stock. It appears that another substitution is in order—or else a more truthful name change for the DJIA.

Time (End of Year)	Price			Shares Outstanding		
	Alpha	Beta	Delta	Alpha	Beta	Delta
19X0	$50	$40	$35	1,000	3,000	2,000
19X1	20*	40	30	3,000	3,000	2,000
19X2	24	45	33	3,000	3,000	2,000

*A 3-for-1 split took place on the first day of the year.

(*a*) Determine a price index for the three stocks using the price-weighted approach used by the Dow Jones Industrial Average (DJIA).

(*b*) Calculate an index for the three stocks using the value-weighted method employed to determine the S&P500 index.

SOLUTION

(*a*) The DJIA at 19X0 = ($50 + $40 + $35)/3 = $125/3 = $41.67.

The DJIA at 19X1: First, a new denominator must be determined by solving for D as shown below:

$$\$41.67 = \frac{\$16.67 + \$40 + \$35}{D}$$

$$D = \frac{\$91.67}{\$41.67} = 2.20$$

The DJIA for 19X1 is

$$\frac{\$20 + \$40 + \$30}{2.20} = \frac{\$90}{2.20} = \$40.91$$

The DJIA for 19X2 is

$$\frac{\$24 + \$45 + \$33}{2.20} = \frac{\$102}{2.20} = \$46.36$$

(*b*) The base value for 19X0 is

$50(1,000) + $40(3,000) + $35(2,000) = $50,000 + $120,000 + $70,000 = $240,000 = aggregate value

The index is 10 = 10($240,000)/($240,000).

The S&P500 for 19X1 is

$$10\left[\frac{\$20(3{,}000) + \$40(3{,}000) + \$30(2{,}000)}{\$240{,}000}\right] = 10\left(\frac{\$60{,}000 + \$120{,}000 + \$60{,}000}{\$240{,}000}\right)$$

$$= 10\left(\frac{\$240{,}000}{\$240{,}000}\right) = 10$$

The S&P500 for 19X2 is

$$10\left[\frac{\$24(3{,}000) + \$45(3{,}000) + \$33(2{,}000)}{\$240{,}000}\right] = 10\left(\frac{\$72{,}000 + \$135{,}000 + \$66{,}000}{\$240{,}000}\right)$$

$$= 10\left(\frac{\$273{,}000}{\$240{,}000}\right) = 10(1.138) = 11.38$$

SOLVED PROBLEM 10.4

Refer to Solved Problem 10.3. Determine the rate of return for the two averages for the years 19X1 and 19X2.

SOLUTION

Using the price-weighted approach:

$$\text{Return for 19X1} = \frac{\text{price for 19X1}}{\text{price for 19X0}} - 1 = \frac{\$40.91}{\$41.67} - 1$$

$$= .9818 - 1 = -.0182 \quad \text{or} \quad -1.82\%$$

$$\text{Return for 19X2} = \frac{\text{price for 19X2}}{\text{price for 19X1}} - 1 = \frac{\$46.36}{\$40.91} - 1$$

$$= 1.1332 - 1 = .1332 \quad \text{or} \quad 13.32\%$$

Using the value-weighted approach:

$$\text{Return for 19X1} = \frac{\text{index for 19X1}}{\text{index for 19X0}} - 1 = \frac{10}{10} - 1 = 0\%$$

$$\text{Return for 19X2} = \frac{\text{index for 19X2}}{\text{index for 19X1}} - 1 = \frac{11.38}{10} - 1$$

$$= 1.138 - 1 = .138 \quad \text{or} \quad 13.8\%$$

10.5 CONTRASTING DIFFERENT MARKET INDICATORS

The preceding comparison of the DJIA and the S&P500 stock market indicators makes the DJIA seem weak and inadequate. Surprisingly, however, the two indicators are highly positively correlated with each other.[3] In fact, almost all of the stock market indicators for stock markets in the United States are highly positively correlated with each other. Consider the nine stock market indicators listed below; their correlation coefficients with each other are shown in Table 10.2.

1) Dow Jones Industrial Average (DJIA)
2) Standard & Poors 400 Industrial Stocks Average
3) Standard & Poors 500 Composite Stocks Average
4) New York Stock Exchange (NYSE) Average
5) American Stock Exchange (ASE) Average
6) Over-the-Counter (OTC) Industrial Stocks Average
7) OTC Composite Stocks Average
8) CRSP Equally Weighted Stocks Index
9) CRSP Value Weighted Stocks Index

Table 10.2 shows that the American Stock Exchange (ASE), which has the lowest correlations with the other U.S. stock markets, nevertheless has a robust .675 as its lowest correlation coefficient with another stock market indicator. The other U.S. stock market indicators are even more highly correlated with each other.

Table 10.2 Correlation Coefficients Between Different Stock Market Indicators

	DJIA	SP400	SP500	NYSE	ASE	OTCIND	OTCCOMP	CRSPEQ	CRSPVW
DJIA	1.0								
SP400	.958	1.0							
SP500	.963	.987	1.0						
NYSE	.949	.989	.981	1.0					
ASE	.675	.798	.796	.836	1.0				
OTCIND	.773	.801	.819	.837	.702	1.0			
TCCOMP	.798	.827	.856	.846	.762	.821	1.0		
CRSPEQ	.934	.946	.955	.949	.854	.743	.806	1.0	
CRSPVW	.945	.948	.957	.953	.858	.760	.815	.920	1.0

10.6 THE NAIVE BUY-AND-HOLD STRATEGY

Naive buy-and-hold strategy is a phrase that describes a purposefully unaggressive and uninformed approach to investing. The first requirement for a naive buy-and-hold portfolio is that all the investments be se-

[3] The correlation coefficient is an index number that varies from positive one, $+1.0 = \rho$, for perfectly positively correlated variables and negative one, $-1.0 = \rho$, for perfectly inversely correlated variables.

lected by an uninformed investor who randomly picked from a diversified list of assets (by throwing an unaimed dart at the stock exchange listing page in a newspaper, for instance). The second requirement for naive buy-and-hold portfolio is that all the randomly selected investments be retained in the portfolio regardless of whatever new information about future prospects for bankruptcies or better investments became available. Such naive buy-and-hold portfolios are constructed and used as standards of comparison against which other investment strategies may be compared. The Standard & Poors 500 Composite Stocks Average (S&P500) is one well-known example of a naive buy-and-hold portfolio that is constructed so that is could be used as a fair standard against which to gauge the performance of other common stock and mutual fund investments, for example.

SOLVED PROBLEM 10.5

One way an investor can pursue a naive buy-and-hold strategy is to purchase the S&P500. Realistically, how might an investor accomplish this?

SOLUTION

This can be accomplished by purchasing all the common stocks in the S&P500 with the relative weight for each stock being the same as that for the S&P500 index. With this approach, periodic rebalancing would be necessary and this could be very troublesome. Only a few wealthy investors could accomplish this. However, this approach is not necessary since *index mutual funds* exist. For example, with a minimum investment of $3,000, an investor can purchase Vanguard's *no-load* index trust, a fund that mimics the S&P500 index. A number of different index mutual funds exist. They have been very popular in recent years because they have outperformed almost every other mutual fund.

10.7 COMPARING INVESTMENT ALTERNATIVES

A question that is often asked by investors is: "What rate of return can I expect to earn if I invest in a portfolio of investment assets of some particular type?" Various market indexes have been prepared to answer such questions.

Table 10.3 contains summary statistics that were calculated for different investment indexes. The geometric mean rate of return, the arithmetic average rate of return, and the standard deviations of the year-to-year rates of return for each different index are in the table.[4] The geometric mean and the arithmetic mean are two similar, but slightly different, ways of calculating the average rate of return. The standard deviation is a statistic which measures the variability of returns (or the range of returns) for each investment. Riskier investments have larger standard deviations of returns than the less risky investments. The standard deviation of returns is a popular statistical measure of investments' total risk.

Table 10.4 shows the correlation coefficients between investment returns from several different markets in the United States. The table shows that the stock markets are all highly positively correlated—just as did the different study which was summarized above in Table 10.2. Table 10.4 also shows that the stock market returns are not so highly correlated with the returns from other markets. In fact, the stock market returns are slightly negatively correlated, on average, with the returns from several types of bonds and real estate investments in Table 10.4.

By comparing the summary statistics in Tables 10.3 and 10.4 an investor can gain insights into different investment possibilities that could take a lifetime of experience to accumulate.

SOLVED PROBLEM 10.6

What does Table 10.4 suggest to an investor regarding diversification?

SOLUTION

For one thing, with lower correlation between domestic equities and foreign equities and foreign bonds, an investor's portfolio should probably include all three in order to reduce risk. In general, because correlation coefficients are lower, diversification across asset classes is indicated as a way to reduce risk. With *no-load* mutual funds, this can be accomplished at a reasonable cost.

[4]The geometric mean rate of return is discussed in more detail in Chapter 25.

Table 10.3 Risk and Average Return Statistics for Different Categories of Investments, 1960–1984*

Asset Category	Geometric Mean Return, %	Arithmetic Mean Return, %	Standard Deviation of Returns, %
Common Stocks			
United States			
NYSE	8.71	9.99	16.30
AMEX	7.28	9.95	23.49
OTC	11.47	13.88	22.42
U.S. total	8.81	10.20	16.89
Foreign			
Europe	7.83	8.94	15.58
Asia	15.14	18.42	30.74
Other	8.14	10.21	20.88
Foreign total	9.84	11.02	16.07
Common stock total	9.08	10.21	15.28
Bonds			
Corporate			
Intermediate-term	6.37	6.80	7.15
Long-term	5.03	5.58	11.26
Corporate total†	5.35	5.75	9.63
Government			
Treasury notes	6.32	6.44	5.27
Treasury bonds	4.70	5.11	9.70
U.S. agencies	6.88	7.04	6.15
Government total	5.91	6.10	6.43
U.S. total	5.70	5.93	7.16
Foreign			
Corporate domestic	8.35	8.58	7.26
Government domestic	5.79	6.04	7.41
Crossborder	7.51	7.66	5.76
Foreign total	6.80	7.01	6.88
Bonds total	6.36	6.50	5.56
Cash Equivalents			
United States			
Treasury bills	6.25	6.29	3.10
Commercial paper	7.03	7.08	3.20
U.S. cash equiv. total	6.49	6.54	3.22
Foreign	6.00	6.23	7.10
Cash total	6.38	6.42	2.92
Real Estate‡			
Business	8.49	8.57	4.16
Residential	8.86	8.93	3.77
Farm	11.86	12.13	7.88
Real estate total	9.44	9.49	3.45
Metals			
Gold	9.08	12.62	29.87
Silver	9.14	20.51	75.34
Metals total	9.11	12.63	29.69
U.S. total wealth portfolio	8.63	8.74	5.06
Foreign total wealth	7.76	8.09	8.48
World Wealth Portfolio			
Excluding metals	8.34	8.47	5.24
Including metals	8.39	8.54	5.80
U.S. inflation rate	5.24	5.30	3.60

*See Table 10.4 for the correlation coefficients among these assets' rates of return.

†Including preferred stock. ‡United States only.

Source: Roger G. Ibbotson, Laurence Siegel, and Kathryn S. Love, "World Wealth: Market Values and Returns," *Journal of Portfolio Management,* Fall 1985, table 4, p. 17. This copyrighted material is reprinted with permission from Institutional Investor, Inc.

Table 10.4 Correlation Coefficients Between the Returns from Different Investments, 1960–1984

	NYSE	AMEX	OTC	U.S. Total Equities	Europe Equities	Asia Equities	Other Equities	Foreign Total Equities	World Equities	U.S. Treasury Notes	U.S. Treasury Bonds	U.S. Agencies	U.S Total Govt. Bonds
NYSE	1.000												
AMEX	.851	1.000											
OTC	.900	.897	1.000										
U.S. Equities	.997	.883	.929	1.000									
Europe Equities	.618	.689	.651	.640	1.000								
Asia Equities	.237	.123	.244	.237	.391	1.000							
Other Equities	.792	.848	.766	.807	.731	.320	1.000						
Foreign Equities	.656	.657	.666	.672	.908	.695	.765	1.000					
World Total Equities	.955	.879	.914	.964	.787	.409	.853	.841	1.000				
U.S. Treasury Notes	1.05	−.102	−.117	.068	−.159	−.108	−.252	−.192	−.037	1.000			
U.S. Treasury Bonds	.091	−.153	−.094	.056	−.130	−.005	−.266	−.165	−.041	.904	1.000		
U.S. Agencies	.007	−.201	−.187	−.030	−.280	−.178	−.342	−.327	−.156	.962	.904	1.000	
U.S. Total Govt. Bonds	.033	−.183	−.189	−.006	−.201	−.067	−.296	−.226	−.105	.972	.950	.964	1.000
U.S. Intermediate-Term Corp. Bonds	.361	.078	.132	.322	.099	.045	−.028	.072	.242	.900	.865	.848	.887
U.S. Long-Term Corp. Bonds	.341	.058	.110	.302	.095	.022	−.033	.052	.219	.858	.912	.808	.859
U.S. Total Corp. Bonds	.361	.083	.132	.323	.117	.033	−.019	.075	.243	.865	.902	.809	.863
U.S. Total Bonds	.206	−.047	−.031	.166	−.045	−.007	−.160	−.074	.075	.954	.956	.915	.967
Foreign Domestic Corp. Bonds	.044	.025	.107	.050	.315	.269	−.028	.314	.156	.035	.172	−.008	.085
Foreign Domestic Govt. Bonds	.010	.078	.097	.024	.345	.084	.058	.255	.115	.061	.190	.044	.117
Foreign Crossborder Bonds	.270	.116	.172	.255	.253	.154	.017	.215	.249	.560	.716	.552	.607
Foreign Total Bonds	.042	.067	.112	.052	.343	.153	.028	.281	.144	.097	.239	.072	.153
World Total Bonds	.136	.035	.069	.124	.248	.122	−.041	.194	.155	.511	.619	.473	.561
U.S. Busines Real Estate	.159	.227	.138	.164	.268	.218	.243	.332	.233	.262	.036	.179	.206
U.S. Residential Real Estate	.123	.213	.090	.125	.207	−.080	.356	.141	.133	.068	−.039	.095	.066
U.S. Farm Real Estate	−.164	−.093	−.223	−.171	−.097	−.003	−.063	−.065	−.139	−.315	−.256	−.273	−.267
U.S. Real Estate Total	.054	.166	.006	.054	.156	−.033	.288	.129	.083	−.051	−.138	−.024	−.040
U.S. Treasury Bills	−.055	−.063	−.160	−.070	−.169	−.157	−.101	−.153	−.114	.395	.111	.328	.325
U.S. Commercial Paper	−.112	−.130	−.210	−.127	−.211	−.176	−.150	−.199	−.174	.394	.115	.348	.330
U.S. Total Cash	−.064	−.080	−.170	−.079	−.178	−.159	−.112	−.162	−.125	.400	.119	.340	.332
Foreign Total Cash	−.393	−.355	−.289	−.386	−.127	.009	−.270	−.107	−.311	−.203	−.183	−.154	−.143

Table 10.4 (continued)

	NYSE	AMEX	OTC	U.S. Total Equities	Europe Equities	Asia Equities	Other Equities	Foreign Total Equities	World Equities	U.S. Treasury Notes	U.S. Treasury Bonds	U.S. Agencies	U.S Total Govt. Bonds
World Total Cash	−.225	−.240	−.284	−.238	−.212	−.115	−.225	−.180	−.242	.270	.032	.237	.236
Gold	−.094	−.024	−.067	−.088	.032	.046	.140	.044	−.058	−.277	−.252	−.178	−.206
Silver	.093	.374	.142	.116	.052	−.181	.410	−.020	.070	−.131	−.140	−.064	−.109
World Total Metals	−.093	−.011	−.064	−.086	.032	.036	.152	.039	−.058	−.279	−.253	−.177	−.207
U.S. Market Wealth Portfolio	.915	.837	.831	.917	.605	.209	.754	.626	.886	.214	.162	.139	.152
Foreign Market Wealth Portfolio	.493	.498	.544	.510	.823	.602	.556	.865	.678	−.086	.021	−.201	−.083
World Market Wealth Port. (W/O Metals)	.853	.799	.814	.861	.782	.406	.765	.815	.914	.109	.119	.007	.066
World Market Wealth Port. (W/ Metals)	.747	.723	.727	.757	.706	.351	.753	.732	.805	−.010	.016	−.059	−.023

	U.S. Intermed.-Term Corp. Bonds	U.S. Long-Term Corp. Bonds	U.S. Total Corp. Bonds	U.S. Total Bonds	Foreign Corp. Bonds	Foreign Govt. Bonds	Cross-border Bonds	Foreign Total Bonds	World Total Bonds	Bus. Real Estate	Resi-dential Structures	Farm Real Estate	Total U.S. Real Estate
U.S. Intermediate-Term Corp. Bonds	1.000												
U.S. Long-Term Corp. Bonds	.941	1.000											
U.S. Total Corp. Bonds	.960	.996	1.000										
U.S. Total Bonds	.956	.956	.962	1.000									
Foreign Domestic Corp. Bonds	.211	.263	.264	.180	1.000								
Foreign Domestic Govt. Bonds	.203	.269	.266	.192	.890	1.000							
Foreign Crossborder Bonds	.741	.814	.807	.721	.626	.628	1.000						
Foreign Total Bonds	.260	.326	.323	.242	.950	.985	.689	1.000					
World Total Bonds	.635	.693	.692	.646	.829	.860	.866	.895	1.000				
U.S. Business Real Estate	.335	.107	.152	.192	.165	.249	.203	.228	.256	1.000			
U.S. Residential Real Estate	.085	−.039	−.030	.017	.091	.293	.108	.225	.191	.493	1.000		
U.S. Farm Real Estate	−.252	−.255	−.273	−.274	.176	.103	.049	.125	−.013	.016	.214	1.000	
U.S. Real Estate Total	−.004	−.129	−.123	−.082	.164	.303	.123	.256	.172	.518	.916	.570	1.000
U.S. Treasury Bills	.336	.094	.135	.244	−.269	−.224	−.060	−.240	−.091	.685	.428	−.053	.389

Table 10.4 (continued)

	U.S. Intermed.-Term Corp. Bonds	U.S. Long-Term Corp. Bonds	U.S. Total Corp. Bonds	U.S. Total Bonds	Foreign Corp. Bonds	Foreign Govt. Bonds	Cross-border Bonds	Foreign Total Bonds	World Total Bonds	Bus. Real Estate	Resi-dential Structures	Farm Real Estate	Total U.S. Real Estate
U.S. Commercial Paper	.313	.070	.108	.230	−.289	−.232	−.078	−.254	−.108	.655	.462	−.040	.415
U.S. Total Cash	.339	.096	.136	.247	−.265	−.217	−.054	−.234	−.085	.681	.447	−.046	.405
Foreign Total Cash	−.191	−.225	−.225	−.192	.616	.617	.101	.608	.393	.231	.317	.306	.399
World Total Cash	.222	−.005	.029	.141	.048	.080	.007	.065	.106	.705	.528	.096	.529
Gold	−.235	−.316	−.323	−.280	.001	.107	−.046	.062	−.079	.219	.586	.517	.684
Silver	−.150	−.177	−.187	−.153	−.286	−.054	−.076	−.136	−.177	.188	.532	.351	.580
World Total Metals	−.239	−.318	−.326	−.282	−.011	.104	−.047	.056	−.085	.220	.596	.526	.696
U.S. Market Wealth Portfolio	.446	.367	.393	.284	.153	.171	.395	.191	.288	.394	.422	−.019	.371
Foreign Market Wealth Portfolio	.192	.221	.236	.080	.723	.687	.517	.718	.603	.329	.174	−.008	.177
World Market Wealth Port. (W/O Metals)	.390	.354	.377	.231	.431	.428	.504	.455	.471	.407	.365	−.014	.332
World Market Wealth Port. (W/ Metal)	.238	.193	.207	.093	.380	.426	.404	.429	.389	.390	.552	.133	.531

	U.S. Treasury Bills	U.S. Commercial Paper	U.S. Total Cash	Foreign Total Cash	World Total Cash	Gold	Silver	World Total Metals	U.S. Market Wealth Portfolio	Foreign Market Wealth Portfolio	World Market Excl. Metals	World Market Incl. Metals
U.S. Treasury Bills	1.000											
U.S. Commercial Paper	.990	1.000										
U.S. Total Cash	.999	.995	1.000									
Foreign Total Cash	−.008	.033	.010	1.000								
World Total Cash	.881	.895	.891	.460	1.000							
Gold	.179	.256	.210	.419	.366	1.000						
Silver	.125	.127	.123	−.203	−.014	.438	1.000					
World Total Metals	.177	.253	.207	.401	.355	.999	.477	1.000				
U.S. Market Wealth Portfolio	.133	.088	.130	−.233	.013	.104	.291	.111	1.000			
Foreign Market Wealth Portfolio	−.254	−.298	−.258	.218	−.122	.025	−.110	.018	.533	1.000		
World Market Wealth Port. (W/O Metals)	−.033	−.083	−.037	−.059	−.053	.075	.142	.077	.925	.812	1.000	
World Market Wealth Port. (W/ Metals)	−.014	−.027	−.004	.105	.046	.427	.283	.427	.873	.727	.924	1.000

Source: R. G. Ibbotson, L. Siegel, and K. S. Love, "World Wealth: Market Values and Returns," *Journal of Portfolio Management,* Fall 1985, table 5, pp. 19–20.

True-False Questions

10.1 The phrase "stock market average" is synonymous with the phrase "stock market index."

10.2 An investor that employed a naive buy-and-hold strategy would be employing a *passive investment management* strategy.

10.3 The Dow Jones Industrial Average has a misleading name because it has contained nonindustrial utility stocks like ATT at various times.

10.4 Since it assigns equal weights to a large sample of heterogeneous securities, the Value Line index represents a naive buy-and-hold strategy.

10.5 Treasury bill returns can sometimes be negatively correlated with stock market returns in the United States.

10.6 The Dow Jones Industrial Average (DJIA) and the Standard & Poors 500 Composite stocks (S&P500) indexes are so different from each other that they are empirically uncorrelated with each other.

10.7 It is undesirable to state a security price indicator in dollar terms because it will become distorted and lose perspective with the passage of time as the level of prices changes significantly.

10.8 A good security market indicator can be prepared from a small but statistically significant fraction of the population being surveyed.

10.9 The correlation coefficient is an index number that varies between zero and positive one.

Multiple Choice Questions

10.1 An *index fund* is best described by which of the following?
(*a*) A mutual fund constructed to achieve a particular investment goal
(*b*) A portfolio that attempts to match the performance of some stock market index by investing in the same stocks and in the same proportions as those that comprise the selected market index
(*c*) Both of the above
(*d*) An investment portfolio that appreciates in value at least as rapidly as some inflation index (such as the Consumer Price Index, for instance)
(*e*) Both *a* and *d*

10.2 The weights used in constructing a *value-weighted* stock market index are best described by which of the following statements?
(*a*) The same (or equal) weights are assigned to every security in the index.
(*b*) The weight assigned to each stock is proportionate to its price per share.
(*c*) The share price of every stock in the index is multiplied times the number of shares outstanding to determine the weight of that issue based on its total value stated as a proportion of the aggregate market value of all the stocks in the index.
(*d*) The weight assigned to each stock in the index is proportional to the number of shares that issue has outstanding stated as a proportion of the aggregate number of shares outstanding for all issues that comprise the index.
(*e*) Both *a* and *d* are true.

10.3 The Value Line Composite index differs from the Standard & Poors and the Dow Jones indexes in which of the following respects?
(*a*) The size of the sample is larger.
(*b*) A geometric mean and also an arithmetic mean index are published.
(*c*) The Value Line Composite index is rebalanced daily.
(*d*) The Value Line geometric mean index experiences less variability than its arithmetic mean counterpart.
(*e*) All the above are true.

10.4 Table 10.4 shows that the correlation coefficients between the common stock market indicators, commodity market indicators, bond market indicators, and the other major categories of investment indicators tend to differ substantially and not be highly positively correlated. The market indicators between these different markets are uncorrelated while the different stock market indicators shown in Table 10.2 are all highly positively correlated because of which of the following reasons?

(*a*) Statistical sampling error accounts for most of the differences between the correlations.
(*b*) The same systematic economic forces tend to affect the prices of all equity shares.
(*c*) The prices of real physical goods (like real estate and the physical commodities) respond differently to the influences of the inflation rate and other important factors than do the prices of monetary assets (like bonds).
(*d*) Both *b* and *c* are true.
(*e*) All the above are true.

10.5 Why do you think the Asian common stocks pay the highest (arithmetic and geometric) rate of return of any category of assets shown in Table 10.3?

(*a*) Because foreign exchange rate changes magnified the returns of investors who invested U.S dollars during the period sampled
(*b*) Because increasing investor interest bid up the prices of the Asian stocks
(*c*) Both *a* and *b*
(*d*) Because high rates of inflation in Asia inflated the prices of common stocks there
(*e*) All the above

10.6 Summary statistics like the ones shown in Tables 10.3 and 10.4 are best described by which of the following statements?

(*a*) If the statistics are calculated over a long sample period that includes several complete business cycles they may be representative of the market's long-run equilibrium tendencies.
(*b*) If the statistics are calculated over sample periods so short that they do not include at least one complete business cycle then they are unique summary statistics that will probably be unrepresentative of any long-run equilibrium relationships.
(*c*) Geometric mean rates of return will be larger than arithmetic mean returns calculated on the identical sample.
(*d*) Both *a* and *b* are true.
(*e*) All the above are true.

10.7 A well-constructed stock market index has all the following characteristics except which one?

(*a*) It is denominated in U.S. dollars rather than some foreign currency.
(*b*) If has a weighting system that corresponds to meaningful investment opportunities.
(*c*) It contains a representative sample of securities.
(*d*) The sample size is sufficiently large to reduce sampling errors to a modest level.

10.8 Maintaining and continually updating a stock price index is made difficult by which one of the following problems?

(*a*) Stock splits and stock dividends
(*b*) Substitutions for troublesome stocks
(*c*) Providing a significant sample size
(*d*) All of the above

10.9 All stock market indexes for the different stock markets in the United States are most accurately characterized by which of the following statements about the degree to which they covary together?

(*a*) They are perfectly positively correlated.
(*b*) They are highly positively correlated.
(*c*) They are uncorrelated.
(*d*) They are negatively correlated.
(*e*) It is impossible to generalize, some are highly positively correlated and some are negatively correlated.

10.10 Which of the following phrases most accurately describes the correlation coefficients between the various domestic and foreign stock, domestic and foreign bond, commodity, and real estate value indexes for the United States?

(*a*) They are perfectly positively correlated.
(*b*) Mostly, but not always, they are significantly positively correlated.
(*c*) They are uncorrelated.
(*d*) Mostly, but not always, they are negatively correlated.

Answers

True-False

10.1. F 10.2. T 10.3. T 10.4. T 10.5. T 10.6. F 10.7. T 10.8. T 10.9. F

Multiple Choice

10.1. c 10.2. c 10.3. e 10.4. d 10.5. c 10.6. d 10.7. a 10.8. d 10.9. b
10.10. b

Chapter 11

Analysis of Financial Statements

11.1 INTRODUCTION

One of the most insightful sources of information about most firms are their own financial statements. This chapter reviews the balance sheet and the income and expense statement and the ratios that are useful in assessing the financial condition of a firm.

The Balance Sheet

A company's *balance sheet* represents an accounting picture of all the firm's sources of external funds (called liabilities and stockholders' equity) and uses of funds (that is, the assets it has purchased) on one particular day. The basic equation that identifies the balance sheet is shown below as Eq. (*11.1*):

$$\text{Total assets} = \text{total liabilities} + \text{stockholders' equity} \qquad (11.1)$$

Stockholders' equity or net worth is the equity section of the balance sheet. Table 11.1 shows the balance sheets for the Interstate Business (IB) Corporation for two consecutive years.

Table 11.1 Balance Sheet of Interstate Business Corporation (IBC) on December 31, 19X1 and 19X2

	Assets (Uses of Funds)		19X1		19X2
1	Cash		$ 10,900		$ 12,500
2	Marketable securities		5,877		7,425
3	Accounts receivable		32,975		30,950
4	Inventories		58,950		56,320
5	Other current assets		7,150		9,345
	Total current assets		$115,852		$116,540
6	Investments		27,900		29,500
7	Property, plant, and equipment		509,200		522,200
8	Total assets (TA)		$652,952		$668,240
	Liabilities (Sources of Funds)		**19X1**		**19X2**
9	Accounts payable		$ 40,500		$ 44,700
10	Other current liabilities		38,650		39,400
	Accrued expenses	$17,700		$18,900	
	Notes payable	19,900		19,400	
	Income taxes payable	1,050		1,100	
	Total current liabilities		$ 79,150		$ 84,100
11	Long-term debt		$232,000		$212,000
12	Deferred tax		39,050		45,900
	Total long-term liabilities		$271,050		$257,900
13	Shareholder equity (EQ) or total net worth		302,752		326,240
	Total liabilities and equity		$652,952		$668,240

The Income Statement

In the past, the *income statement* was called the *profit and loss statement* because the so-called *bottom line* of the statement revealed either the profits or losses from the firm's operations over the accounting period. The profit and loss statement's proper name is the *income and expense statement.* The accounting definition that underlies the income and expense statement is shown below:

$$\text{Sales} - \text{expenses} = \text{income or loss} \qquad (11.2)$$

Table 11.2 shows the IBC's income statements for all the operations of the firm in the years 19X1 and 19X2.

Table 11.2 Income and Expense Statements for Interstate Business Corporation (IBC) for the Years Ending December 31, 19X1 and 19X2

		19X1	19X2
14	Sales	$1,025,125	$1,075,400
15	Plus: Other income	350	1,200
	Equals: Total revenue	$1,025,475	$1,076,600
16	Cost of goods sold*	$ 690,300	$ 725,700
17	Excise taxes	195,200	198,600
18	Marketing and administrative expenses	99,875	105,550
	Total operating expenses	$ 985,375	$1,029,850
	Earnings before interest and taxes	$ 40,100	$ 46,750
19	Interest expense	$ 17,375	$ 14,620
20	Other expenses	400	9,225
	Total expenses	$1,003,150	$1,053,695
21	Equals: Earnings before tax (EBT)	$ 22,325	$ 22,905
22	Less: Corporate income taxes	9,800	10,200
23	Equals: Net income (NI) after taxes	$ 12,525	$ 12,705
24	Less: Cash dividend payments	6,250	6,750
25	Equals: Addition to retained earnings	$ 6,275	$ 5,955
	Per Share Data for Common Stock	19X1	19X2
26	Number of shares (NS) outstanding	17,100	17,100
27	Market price (*P*) per share of stock	$9.10	$9.50
28	Earnings per share (EPS) after tax	$.732	$.743
29	Cash dividends per share (CDPS)	$.365	$.3947
30	Price-earnings (P/E) ratio	12.43	12.786

*Includes depreciation of $62,000 in 19X1 and $68,000 in 19X2.

EXAMPLE 11.1 Another way to view the balance sheet and income and expense statements is through a re-formation designed to make the values a *common-sized statement.* With a *common-sized statement* each item on the statement is expressed as a percentage of one number. For the balance sheet, each item is typically expressed as a percent of total assets; the income statement is usually expressed as a percent of sales. In Table 11.3, IBC's income and expense statement for 19X2 is expressed as a percent of sales or total revenue.

SOLVED PROBLEM 11.1

Briefly contrast the balance sheet and the income statement.

SOLUTION

The income statement reports *flows* of funds that have occurred over the accounting period. In contrast, the balance sheet reports no flows. Balance sheets report *stocks* of assets and liabilities that exist at one particular date.

Table 11.3 Common-Sized Income Statement for Interstate Business Corporation's (IBC) 19X2 Operations, Percent of Sales

	Income and Expense Items	Percentage of Total Revenues, 19X2
C14	Sales	99.9%
C15	Plus: Other income	0.1%
	Total revenue	100.0%
C16	Cost of goods sold	67.4%
C17	Excise taxes	18.4%
C18	Marketing, administrative, and general expenses	9.8%
C19	Interest expense	1.4%
C20	Other expense	.9%
	Total expense	97.9%
C21	Earnings before taxes	2.1%
C22	Less: Income taxes	.9%
C23	Equals: Net income	1.2%
C24	Less: Cash dividend payments	.6%
C25	Equals: Retained earnings	.6%

11.2 FINANCIAL RATIOS

Most financial ratios have descriptive names that give the user clues about how to calculate the ratio and/or how to interpret its numerical value. The individual item numbers from the financial statements in Tables 11.1 and 11.2 are used in calculating the ratios below for 19X2 to demonstrate clearly the source of the values used in the ratios.

Solvency Ratios

One of the best-known and widely used measures of a firm's solvency is the *current ratio:*

$$\text{Current ratio} = \frac{\text{current assets}}{\text{current liabilities}} = \frac{(1) + (2) + (3) + (4) + (5)}{(9) + (10)}$$

$$= \frac{\$116{,}540}{\$84{,}100} = 1.386 = 138.6\% \tag{11.3}$$

The integer numbers in the parentheses above indicate that current assets, for instance, are a combination of line items (1), (2), (3), (4), and (5) from IBC's balance sheet, Table 11.1. The current ratio for IBC indicates that the firm had $1.386 of current assets for every $1.00 of bills that are coming due in 19X2. This seems to indicate that the firm had plenty of current assets to pay its bills and, thus, was solvent.

The *quick ratio* is somewhat similar to the current ratio because both have the same denominator. However, the numerator in the quick ratio includes only those liquid assets that can be *quickly* turned into cash—they are sometimes called "quick assets." Quick assets include all current assets except inventory.

$$\text{Quick ratio} = \frac{\text{current assets} - \text{inventory}}{\text{current liabilities}} = \frac{\text{quick assets}}{\text{current liabilities}}$$

$$= \frac{(1) + (2) + (3) + (5)}{(9) + (10)} \tag{11.4}$$

$$= \frac{\$60{,}220}{\$84{,}100} = .716 = 71.6\%$$

The quick ratio calculations above indicate that in 19X2 IBC had 72 cents of quick assets for every dollar of liabilities coming due that year. The quick ratio of .72 suggests that if the firm's inventory became worthless, IBC could possibly suffer a financial embarrassment called "insolvency." *Insolvency* occurs when the firm has insufficient cash to pay all of its bills when they come due.

Coverage Ratios

A *coverage ratio* measures how many times the firm's annual earnings cover its debt-servicing charges (namely, any interest, sinking fund, and lease charges). The popular *times-interest-earned ratio* is defined below:

$$\text{Times-interest-earned ratio} = \frac{\text{annual operating income}}{\text{annual interest payments}} \tag{11.5}$$

A firm's *operating income* is earnings from its ordinary operations. Extraordinary income is not included and nonoperating costs such as interest expenses and taxes are not deducted in the determination of operating income. Therefore, a firm's operating income is sometimes called its *earnings before interest and taxes (EBIT)*. In terms of the line item numbers from Table 11.2, IBC's operating income equals item (14) less the quantity [(16) + (17) + (18)], as shown in the numerator below:

$$\text{Times-interest-earned ratio} = \frac{(14) - [(16) + (17) + (18)]}{(19)}$$

$$= \frac{\$1{,}075{,}400 - \$1{,}029{,}850}{\$14{,}620} = 3.12 \text{ times}$$

The 19X2 value of 3.12 for IBC's times-interest-earned ratio suggests that the corporation's operating earnings could drop off by about 68 percent {that is, 100% less 32%, which equals, 1.0 less [1.0/(3.12 times)]} and the firm would still be able to pay the interest on its debts.

Most financial analysts have their own favorite variations of the ratios discussed here that they prefer to use. The times-interest-earned ratio is a case in point. Some bond analysts use the firm's operating income while others prefer to use the firm's pretax fixed charge coverage in the numerator of the times-interest-earned ratio. *Pretax fixed charge coverage* is an income measure defined as the firm's net income plus income taxes plus gross interest charges. And, some analysts define the debt-service charges they use in the denominator to include only interest specified contractually in bond indentures while others use gross interest expenses to measure the debt-service charges. The *pretax fixed charge coverage ratio* is defined in Eq. (*11.6*):

$$\text{Pretax fixed charge coverage} = \frac{\text{pretax income} + \text{gross interest expense}}{\text{gross interest expense}} \tag{11.6}$$

SOLVED PROBLEM 11.2

Determine (*a*) the current ratio, (*b*) the quick ratio, and (*c*) the times-interest-earned ratio for the IB Corporation for the year 19X1.

SOLUTION

(*a*)

$$\text{Current ratio} = \frac{\text{current assets}}{\text{current liabilities}} = \frac{(1) + (2) + (3) + (4) + (5)}{(9) + (10)}$$

$$= \frac{\$115{,}852}{\$79{,}150} = 1.464$$

(*b*)

$$\text{Quick ratio} = \frac{\text{current assets} - \text{inventory}}{\text{current liabilities}} = \frac{[(1) + (2) + (3) + (5)]}{[(9) + (10)]}$$

$$= \frac{\$56{,}902}{\$79{,}150} = .719$$

(*c*)

$$\text{Times-interest-earned ratio} = \frac{\text{annual operating income}}{\text{annual interest payments}} = \frac{(14) - [(16) + (17) + (18)]}{(19)}$$

$$= \frac{\$1{,}025{,}125 - \$985{,}375}{\$17{,}375} = 2.29$$

Turnover Ratios

Turnover ratios measure business activity within the firm. The general idea underlying the several different turnover ratios is that unused or inactive assets are non-earning assets and actions should be taken to either utilize these assets more effectively or eliminate them. Turnover ratios are sometimes called *efficiency ratios* and *activity ratios*.

The *receivable turnover* ratio is used to scrutinize the liquidity of accounts receivable. If the credit customers are all paying their bills, then the accounts receivable should be turning over. The receivables turnover ratio is defined below:

$$\text{Receivables turnover} = \frac{\text{annual sales}}{\text{accounts receivable}} = \frac{(14)}{(3)} \tag{11.7}$$

$$= \frac{\$1{,}075{,}400}{\$30{,}950} = 34.7 \text{ times}$$

The calculations above show that IBC's accounts receivable turned over 34.7 times in 19X2. The fact that there are 52 weeks in a year implies that if a firm's accounts receivables turned over every week they would turn over 52 times a year. This reasoning indicates that IBC's receivables turned over less than once per week, since 34.7 times is less than 52 times. Whether or not a receivables turnover of 34.7 times per year is too fast or too slow cannot be determined without knowing the company's credit conditions and the customs within the industry in which it competes.

The financial ratio to compute the number of days in a firm's *collection period* is below:

$$\text{Collection period} = \frac{\text{accounts receivable}}{\text{average day's sales}} \tag{11.8}$$

$$= \frac{\text{accounts receivable}}{(\text{annual sales})/(360 \text{ days})} = \frac{(3)}{(14)/(360 \text{ days})}$$

$$= \frac{\$30{,}950}{\$1{,}075{,}400/(360 \text{ days})} = \frac{\$30{,}950}{\$2{,}987.22}$$

$$= 10.36 \text{ days}$$

IBC's average collection period was a little over 10 days during 19X2. This means that the corporation collects its bills within an average of one and one-half weeks.

The *inventory turnover ratio* ia a gauge of how efficiently the firm is employing its inventory. It is usually preferable to measure the firm's sales at the cost-of-goods-sold (instead of at the inventory's retail) value in computing this ratio; this is because inventories are usually carried on the firm's books at their cost values. If retail sales were divided by the inventory valued at cost the resulting ratio would be erroneously inflated.

$$\text{Inventory turnover} = \frac{\text{annual sales(preferably at cost, not retail)}}{\text{average inventory(usually valued at cost)}}$$

$$= \frac{\text{cost of goods sold}}{\text{average inventory}} = \frac{(16)}{(4)} \tag{11.9}$$

$$= \frac{\$725{,}700}{\$56{,}320} = 12.89 \text{ times}$$

The calculation above indicates that in 19X2 IBC turned its inventory over 12.89 times per year, or a little more than once per month.

EXAMPLE 11.2 If IBC manufactures whiskeys with an inventory turnover of 12.89 times per year, the company must be producing their product so hastily that it isn't fit to drink. In contrast, if the firm is in the fresh vegetable business a month old inventory is probably garbage. A similarly calculated industry average inventory turnover figure would make an appropriate yardstick with which to compare IBC's inventory turnover.

The *asset turnover ratio* is used to measure the productivity of the firm's total assets:

$$\text{Asset turnover} = \frac{\text{annual sales}}{\text{total assets}} = \frac{(14)}{(8)} \tag{11.10}$$

$$= \frac{\$1{,}075{,}400}{\$668{,}240} = 1.61 \text{ times per year}$$

The turnover of total assets per year varies from a low value like once per year for heavy manufacturing industries (like steel mills) to over a dozen times a year for advertising agencies which typically own virtually no tangible assets.

The "equity turnover ratio" is a turnover ratio which is useful in analyzing aspects of a firm's financial position that are explained more fully later in this chapter. The *equity turnover* ratio shown below measures the relationship between the dollar values of a firm's sales and its owners' equity investment (EQ):

$$\text{Equity turnover} = \frac{\text{sales}}{\text{equity}} = \frac{\text{sales}}{\text{EQ}} \tag{11.11}$$

$$= \frac{(14)}{(13)} = \frac{\$1{,}075{,}400}{\$326{,}240} = 3.30 \text{ times}$$

The computations above show that IBC has sales that were 3.30 times larger than its equity (or net worth) in 19X2. The reason that the firm's equity turns over faster than do its assets is because the firm uses financial leverage obtained from debt financing. The components of IBC's 19X2 equity turnover ratio are decomposed below:

$$\text{Equity turnover} = \frac{\text{sales}}{\text{EQ}} = \left(\frac{\text{sales}}{\text{total assets}}\right) \times \left(\frac{\text{total assets}}{\text{EQ}}\right) \tag{11.12}$$

$$= (\text{total asset turnover}) \times \begin{pmatrix}\text{financial}\\ \text{leverage}\\ \text{ratio}\\ \text{or equity}\\ \text{multiplier}\end{pmatrix}$$

In 19X2:

$$3.30 \text{ times} = (1.61 \text{ times}) \times (2.05 \text{ times})$$

After the financial leverage ratio (equity multiplier) is explained in more detail below, we will reconsider the information it conveys.

SOLVED PROBLEM 11.3

If the Jones Corporation has credit sales of \$3,000,000 per year and a collection period (CP) of 40 days, what is its level of accounts receivable (AR)? Assume a 360-day year.

SOLUTION

$$\text{CP} = \frac{\text{AR}}{\text{sales per day (SPD)}}$$

$$\text{AR} = \text{CP} \times \text{SPD} = 40 \times \left(\frac{\$3{,}000{,}000}{360}\right) = 40 \times \$8{,}333.33$$

$$= \$333{,}333$$

SOLVED PROBLEM 11.4

The current assets and liabilities of the Organic Beauty Products (OBP) Corporation are listed below:

Current assets:		Current liabilities:	
Cash	\$ 9,000	Accounts payable	\$39,000
Accounts receivable	71,000	Accrued expenses	29,000
Inventories*	79,000	Total	\$68,000
Total	\$159,000		

*Inventory is all raw materials, valued at cost. The firm's products are produced to fill telephone orders from beauty salons.

The Organic Beauty Products Corporation has annual sales of \$650,000 and the cost of these goods sold is \$325,000. It is the custom in the beauty salon products industry for the beauty salons to pay cash on delivery (COD) for the goods when the manufacturer's truck delivers the products. OBP's chief executive officer and primary stockholder, Mr. Robert Davis, pays all of his bills quickly enough to enable him to take any cash discounts that are available. Organic Beauty's accounts payable and accrued expenses include rent, employees wages, utility bills, and taxes that are currently due. Calculate OBP's (*a*) current ratio, (*b*) quick ratio, (*c*) inventory turnover ratio, and (*d*) age of inventory. (*e*) Assume that 10 percent of Organic's sales are made on credit and calculate its accounts receivable turnover, and (*f*) calculate OBP's age of accounts receivable. Do you think Organic's current assets and liabilities are well-managed? Explain.

SOLUTION

It would be easier to analyze Organic Beauty Products if some industry average ratios or OBP's own historical ratios were made available. However, even without employing any industry standards it is possible to reach some conclusions.

(*a*)
$$\frac{\text{Current assets}}{\text{Current liabilities}} = \frac{\$159{,}000}{\$68{,}000} = 2.34 \text{ times}$$

The current ratio of 2.34 times seems too high; a value of 2 is considered "normal" in many industries.

(*b*)
$$\frac{\text{Curr. assets} - \text{inventory}}{\text{Curr. liabilities}} = \frac{\$159{,}000 - \$79{,}000}{\$68{,}000} = 1.18 \text{ times}$$

Organic's quick ratio of 1.18 times current liabilities also seems too high; a value of 1 is considered "normal" in many industries.

(*c*)
$$\frac{\text{Cost of goods sold}}{\text{Inventory (at cost)}} = \text{inventory turnover} = \frac{\$325{,}000}{\$79{,}000} = 4.11 \text{ times}$$

Organic's inventory turnover of 4.11 times per year seems too slow.

(*d*) An inventory turnover of 4.11 times per year implies that the average age of the inventory is about 88 days old.

$$\frac{\text{360 days per year}}{\text{Inventory turnover}} = \frac{360}{4.11 \text{ times}} = 87.59 \text{ days old}$$

Very few firms need an inventory of 3 months of raw materials to operate profitably. Excess inventory can be stolen, can rot, is subject to property taxes and insurance, and must be stored in a warehouse that is costly to operate. Therefore, it appears that Organic Beauty Products has too much inventory. Without any standards of comparison it is clear that Organic's $71,000 investment in accounts receivable is too large. If all of OBP's sales are made COD, as explained in the problem, the firm should have accounts receivable of 0.

(*e*)
$$\frac{\text{Annual credit sales}}{\text{Average accounts receivable}} = \frac{\$65{,}000}{\$71{,}000} = .92 \text{ times per year}$$

Even if $65,000 (that is, 10 percent) of OBP's annual sales are made on credit, the firm's accounts receivable turnover would be only .92 times per year—too slow.

(*f*)
$$\frac{\text{360 days}}{\text{Accounts receivable turnover}} = \frac{\text{360 days}}{.92 \text{ times}} = 391.3 \text{ days}$$

An accounts receivable turnover of .92 times per year implies that the average age of OBP's accounts receivable would be 391.3 days old. Customers should not be given credit in excess of 1 year in a COD business. Mr. Davis appears to be *too nice* to the credit customers and appears to have accumulated some bad debts as a result.

Profitability Ratios

Profitability ratios compare a firm's earnings with various factors that generate earnings. The resulting ratios can reveal which aspects of the business are particularly profitable or unprofitable. The *net profit margin* is a popular profitability ratio. It is calculated for IBC below:

$$\text{Net profit margin} = \frac{\text{net income}}{\text{sales}} = \frac{\text{NI}}{\text{sales}} = \frac{(23)}{(14)} \tag{11.13}$$

$$= \frac{\$12{,}705}{\$1{,}075{,}400} = .011814 = 1.18\%$$

The above computations measure the contribution to after-tax income that each sales dollar generates. IBC's net after-tax profit margin was about 1.2 percent of each sales dollar in 19X2.

As the name *rate of return on assets* suggests, the ratio measures net income after taxes (NI) as a percentage of the company's total asset (TA) investment:

$$\text{Return on assets} = \frac{\text{net income}}{\text{total assets}} = \frac{\text{NI}}{\text{TA}} = \frac{(23)}{(8)} \qquad (11.14)$$

$$= \frac{\$12{,}705}{\$668{,}240} = .019013 = 1.90\%$$

IBC's rate of return on total assets in 19X2 means that the firm's average dollars worth of assets yielded about 1.9 cents of after-tax earnings in 19X2.

The *rate of return on equity (ROE)* measures the rate of return on earnings after taxes the firm earns on the owners' equity investment:

$$\text{Return on equity (ROE)} = \frac{\text{net income}}{\text{equity}} = \frac{\text{NI}}{\text{EQ}} = \frac{(23)}{(13)} \qquad (11.15)$$

$$= \frac{\$12{,}705}{\$326{,}240} = .038944 = 3.89\%$$

The difference between a firm's rate of return on assets and its rate of return on equity, the two preceding ratios, is attributable to the firm's use of borrowed money (or synonymously, financial leverage). If a firm had no debts these two ratios would yield identical values. Comparing IBC's 19X2 return on assets of 1.9 percent with its 19X2 return on equity of 3.89 percent indicates that the company employed borrowed money advantageously to leverage its rate of return to its stockholders up to a level above the positive rate of return it earned on its assets.[1]

SOLVED PROBLEM 11.5

Determine IBC's (*a*) net profit margin, (*b*) return on assets, and (*c*) return on equity for the year 19X1.

SOLUTION

(*a*)

$$\text{Net profit margin} = \frac{\text{net income}}{\text{sales}} = \frac{(23)}{(14)} = \frac{\$12{,}525}{\$1{,}025{,}125}$$

$$= .012218 = 1.22\%$$

(*b*)

$$\text{Return on assets} = \frac{\text{net income}}{\text{total assets}} = \frac{(23)}{(8)} = \frac{\$12{,}525}{\$652{,}952}$$

$$= .019182 = 1.92\%$$

(*c*)

$$\text{ROE} = \frac{\text{net income}}{\text{equity}} = \frac{(23)}{(13)} = \frac{\$12{,}525}{\$302{,}752} = .04137 = 4.14\%$$

SOLVED PROBLEM 11.6

If the Jenkins Corporation has a net profit margin (M) of 6 percent and a return on assets (ROA) of 14 percent, what is its total asset turnover (T)?

SOLUTION

$$M = \frac{\text{net income}}{\text{sales}} \qquad T = \frac{\text{sales}}{\text{total assets}} \qquad \text{ROA} = M \times T$$

$$T = \frac{\text{ROA}}{M} = \frac{14\%}{6\%} = 2.333$$

[1]Financial leverage is counterproductive when a firm is suffering losses. Financial leverage magnifies both positive and negative rates of return on assets.

Leverage Ratios

Leverage ratios gauge the extent to which a firm finances its operations with borrowed money rather than with owners' equity. The *total debt to total asset* ratio defined below indicates what percent of a firm's assets are financed by creditors:

$$\text{Debt to assets} = \frac{\text{total debt}}{\text{total assets}} = \frac{(9) + (10) + (11) + (12)}{(8)} \qquad (11.16)$$

$$= \frac{\$342{,}000}{\$668{,}240} = .511792 = 51.18\%$$

Slightly over 51 cents out of every dollars worth of assets that IBC owned in 19X2 was financed with borrowed money.

The *total debt to equity* ratio is defined in Eq. (*11.17*). The numerator is the same as the numerator in Eq. (*11.16*).

$$\text{Debt to equity} = \frac{\text{total debt}}{\text{equity}} = \frac{(9) + (10) + (11) + (12)}{(13)} \qquad (11.17)$$

$$= \frac{\$342{,}000}{\$326{,}240} = 1.0483 = 104.83\%$$

The above computations indicate that in 19X2 creditors put up 104.83 percent as much money as the owners of IBC had invested in the firm. That seems like a substantial use of borrowed money. However, much of the borrowed money may be interest-free trade credit and short-term accounts payable. The next ratio will throw some light on the question of long-term versus short-term debt.

The *long-term debt to equity* ratio is calculated to ascertain the extent to which the firm has employed long-term (LT) borrowings (which are usually more fixed than short-term borrowings).

$$\text{LT debt to equity} = \frac{\text{long-term debt}}{\text{equity}} = \frac{(11) + (12)}{(13)} \qquad (11.18)$$

$$= \frac{\$257{,}900}{\$326{,}240} = .7905 = 79.05\%$$

Since the LT debt to equity ratio has a significantly smaller value than total debt to equity ratio for 19X2, this means that much of IBC's debts are short-term debts. (In order to maximize IBC's income we hope that these short-term debts are not interest-bearing debts.) Nevertheless, long-term lenders provided IBC with 79.05 percent as much funds as its owners in 19X2.

The *long-term debt to capitalization* ratio is similar to the long-term debt to equity ratio above. The long-term debt to capitalization ratio is calculated below to determine what fraction of the firm's permanent capital is from debt:

$$\text{LT debt to capitalization} = \frac{\text{long-term debt}}{\text{capitalization}} = \frac{(11) + (12)}{(11) + (12) + (13)} \qquad (11.19)$$

$$= \frac{\$257{,}900}{\$584{,}140} = .4415 = 44.15\%$$

Capitalization refers to a firm's permanently committed capital funds. A firm's capitalization is the sum of its long-term debt, preferred stock, and stockholders' equity.

Another ratio that is used to evaluate the degree of indebtedness that a firm has incurred is the *total asset to equity (or net worth)* ratio. This ratio is sometimes called the *equity multiplier* and is given below:

$$\begin{array}{c}\text{Total assets to equity} \\ \text{(Equity multiplier)}\end{array} = \frac{\text{total assets}}{\text{equity}} = \frac{\text{TA}}{\text{EQ}} = \frac{(8)}{(13)} \qquad (11.20)$$

$$= \frac{\$668{,}240}{\$326{,}240} = 2.0483 = 204.83\%$$

The value of IBC's total assets to stockholders' equity ratio shows that in 19X2 the firm had acquired 2.048 times as much assets as it had in net worth (or equity). Total assets 2.048 times larger than the stockholders' equity is a significant amount of indebtedness. The fixed interest expenses that arise from such substantial long-term debts increases the risky possibility that IBC could default if its profitability slipped enough that it could not pay its fixed interest expenses.

Common Stock per Share Data

Common stock investors are particularly concerned about a few values that have a strong effect on the market price of their common stock. The *earnings per share (EPS)* after income taxes is one of the most important determinants of a common stock's value because it measures the earning power underlying each share of stock.

$$\text{Earnings per share} = \frac{\text{net income to common stockholders}}{\text{number of common shares outstanding}} = \frac{(23)}{(26)} \tag{11.21}$$

$$= \frac{\text{NI}}{\text{NS}} = \frac{\$12{,}705}{17{,}100 \text{ shares}} = \$.743 \text{ per share}$$

The earnings per share computations above indicate that IBC earned $.743 per share after taxes in 19X2.

Dividing the company's cash dividend payments by the number of shares of common stock outstanding reveals that IBC's *cash dividend per share* was 39.47 cents in 19X2:

$$\text{Cash dividend per share (CDPS)} = \frac{\text{total corporate cash dividend}}{\text{number of shares outstanding}} \tag{11.22}$$

$$= \frac{(24)}{(26)} = \frac{\$6{,}750}{17{,}100 \text{ shares}} = \$.3947 \text{ per share}$$

The calculations below show the IBC's cash dividend of 39.47 cents per share in 19X2 resulted in a *payout ratio* of 53 percent.

$$\text{Payout ratio} = \frac{\text{cash dividends per share (CDPS)}}{\text{earnings per share (EPS)}} \tag{11.23}$$

$$= \frac{\text{CDPS}}{\text{EPS}} = \frac{(29)}{(28)} = \frac{39.47 \text{ cents per share}}{\$.743 \text{ per share}}$$

$$= .53 \quad \text{or} \quad 53 \text{ percent in 19X2}$$

The retention rate measures the fraction of a corporation's total after-tax earnings (or net income, denoted NI) that are retained within the firm (presumably to finance expansion). The *retention rate (RR)* is defined in terms of the corporation's total dollar values of *retained earnings (RE)* [item (25) in Table 11.2] stated as a fraction of the corporation's net income, as shown below:

$$\text{RR} = \frac{\text{NI} - \text{total cash dividends}}{\text{net income (NI)}} = \frac{\text{retained earnings}}{\text{NI}} \tag{11.24}$$

$$= \frac{\text{RE}}{\text{NI}} = \frac{(25)}{(23)} = \frac{\$5{,}955}{\$12{,}705} = .47 = 47 \text{ percent}$$

The equation below defines the retention ratio (RR) on a per share basis:

$$\text{RR} = \frac{\text{EPS} - \text{CDPS}}{\text{earnings per share}} = \frac{\text{retained earnings per share (REPS)}}{\text{EPS}} \tag{11.25}$$

$$= \frac{\text{REPS}}{\text{EPS}} = \frac{34.83 \text{ cents}}{\$.743} = .47 = 47 \text{ percent}$$

The two equations above that appear to define the retention ratio differently are actually equivalent, they seem to differ only because one uses corporate aggregates while the other uses per share data. Regardless of whether it is measured on an aggregate basis or on a per share basis, the retention ratio equals 1.0 less the payout ratio, as shown below:

$$\text{Retention ratio} = 1.0 - \text{payout ratio}$$

Common stock investors are also interested in their stock's *price-earnings ratio (P/E).*

$$\text{Price-earnings ratio} = \text{P/E} = \frac{\text{market price per share } (P)}{\text{earnings per share (EPS)}} \tag{11.26}$$

$$\frac{(27)}{(28)} = \frac{P}{\text{EPS}} = \frac{\$9.50}{\$.743} = 12.786 \text{ times}$$

The price-earnings ratio is sometimes called the *earnings multiplier.* The calculations above show that in 19X2 IBC's stock was selling at 12.786 times its earnings per share. This is an average value for a price-earnings ratio. Most corporations' stock sells for prices that range between four and sixteen times its earnings.

The Dupont Framework for Analyzing Equity Returns and Growth

Years ago the Dupont Corporation developed a system of decomposing the rate of return on equity for a firm into its financial components in order to reveal some of the sources of a firm's growth. The rate of return on equity definition is reproduced below so it can be analyzed.

$$\text{Return on equity (ROE)} = \frac{\text{net income}}{\text{equity}} = \frac{\text{NI}}{\text{EQ}} = \frac{(23)}{(13)} \tag{11.15}$$

$$= \frac{\$12{,}705}{\$326{,}240} = .03894 = 3.89\%$$

Dividing both the numerator and the denominator of the ROE ratio above by the firm's sales results in the mathematically identical way of stating the ROE ratio, as shown below:

$$\text{ROE} = \frac{\text{NI}}{\text{EQ}} = \left(\frac{\text{sales}}{\text{EQ}}\right) \times \left(\frac{\text{NI}}{\text{sales}}\right) \tag{11.27}$$

$$= \begin{pmatrix}\text{equity}\\ \text{turn-}\\ \text{over}\end{pmatrix} \times \begin{pmatrix}\text{net}\\ \text{profit}\\ \text{margin}\end{pmatrix}$$

$$3.89\% = \begin{pmatrix}3.30\\ \text{times}\end{pmatrix} \times 1.18\%$$

There are different ways to restate the formula to calculate the rate of return on equity (ROE) that yield identical numerical results. The ROE formula above allows a more in-depth financial analysis because it decomposes a company's ROE into two other insightful financial ratios. The ROE formula above can be further decomposed into three financially meaningful segments. The equity turnover ratio, which was briefly introduced earlier in this chapter, is the key to the further decomposition of the ROE ratio.

$$\text{Equity turnover} = \frac{\text{sales}}{\text{EQ}} = \left(\frac{\text{sales}}{\text{total assets}}\right) \times \left(\frac{\text{total assets}}{\text{EQ}}\right) \tag{11.11}$$

$$= \begin{pmatrix}\text{total asset}\\ \text{turnover}\end{pmatrix} \times \begin{pmatrix}\text{financial}\\ \text{leverage}\\ \text{ratio}\end{pmatrix}$$

Algebraically substituting the above formula for the equity turnover ratio into the ROE formula allows the ROE formula to be broken down into the three components shown below:

$$\text{ROE} = \frac{\text{NI}}{\text{EQ}} = \left(\frac{\text{sales}}{\text{EQ}}\right) \times \left(\frac{\text{NI}}{\text{sales}}\right) \qquad (11.28)$$

$$= \begin{pmatrix}\text{equity}\\ \text{turn-}\\ \text{over}\end{pmatrix} \times \begin{pmatrix}\text{net}\\ \text{profit}\\ \text{margin}\end{pmatrix}$$

$$= \left(\frac{\text{sales}}{\text{TA}}\right) \times \left(\frac{\text{TA}}{\text{EQ}}\right) \times \left(\frac{\text{NI}}{\text{sales}}\right) \qquad (11.29)$$

$$= \begin{pmatrix}\text{total}\\ \text{asset}\\ \text{turnover}\end{pmatrix} \times \begin{pmatrix}\text{financial}\\ \text{leverage}\\ \text{ratio}\end{pmatrix} \times \begin{pmatrix}\text{net}\\ \text{profit}\\ \text{margin}\end{pmatrix}$$

$$3.89\% = 1.61 \text{ times} \times 2.048 \text{ times} \times 1.18\%$$

Breaking the formula for the ROE down into three categories shows that a company's ROE can be increased in three different ways: (1) by more efficient asset usage (as measured by faster total asset turnover), (2) by increased use of debt (as measured by the financial leverage ratio), or (3) by increasing the profit margins (as measured by the net profit margin ratio). These ROE components can contribute to the firm's growth if the earnings are reinvested in the firm.

SOLVED PROBLEM 11.7

Suppose that the Acme Supermarket Company (ASC) was located in the same block as Baker's Jewelry Store (BJS) and that both of these retail stores earned the same rate of return on equity (ROE) in the same year.

(*a*) How might you expect the profit margins and turnover ratios of these two establishments to differ?

(*b*) Explain how they could earn the same ROE in spite of the differences in profit margins and turnover you envision.

SOLUTION

(*a*) The jewelry business is traditionally a high markup–low-turnover business. It is normal to mark up the wholesale cost of the jewelry 100 percent to set the retail price and, then, hold the jewelry on display for weeks or months before it sells. In contrast, retail supermarkets are set up to operate as high-volume–low-profit-margin operations. The profit margins on any food items are small but the goods sell within a few days after being placed on display.

(*b*) Equation (*11.29*) shows that any given rate of return on equity can be achieved with either high-turnover-and-low-markup sales (which typifies supermarkets) or low-turnover-and-high-markup operations (like most jewelry stores).

$$\text{ROE} = \frac{\text{NI}}{\text{EQ}} = \left(\frac{\text{sales}}{\text{EQ}}\right) \times \left(\frac{\text{NI}}{\text{sales}}\right) \qquad (11.29)$$

$$= \begin{pmatrix}\text{equity}\\ \text{turn-}\\ \text{over}\end{pmatrix} \times \begin{pmatrix}\text{net}\\ \text{profit}\\ \text{margin}\end{pmatrix}$$

Hypothetically,

$$10\% = .5 \times 20\% \qquad \text{for BJS}$$

$$10\% = 10 \times 1\% \qquad \text{for ASC}$$

SOLVED PROBLEM 11.8

What is the intrinsic value per share for a corporation with EPS of $2 and a P/E ratio of 15?

SOLUTION

$$\text{P/E} = 15 \qquad P = 15 \times E = 15 \times \$2 = \$30$$

SOLVED PROBLEM 11.9

What is the total debt to total asset ratio for a corporation with an equity multiplier of 2.5?

SOLUTION

$$\text{Total debt (TD)} + \text{total equity (TE)} = \text{total assets (TA)}$$

$$\frac{TD}{TA} + \frac{TE}{TA} = 1 \qquad \text{Equity multiplier} = \frac{TA}{TE} = 2.5 \qquad \frac{TE}{TA} = \frac{1}{2.5} = .4$$

$$\frac{TD}{TA} + .4 = 1 \qquad \frac{TD}{TA} = 1 - .4 = .6 \quad \text{or} \quad 60 \text{ percent}$$

SOLVED PROBLEM 11.10

The Paxton Corporation is considering adding a new product division. If a new division is added, it will cause a 20 percent increase in the existing profit margin and a 40 percent increase in total assets. The increase in assets will be financed with debt. Determine the new ROE if sales remain constant. Assume the following ratios existed before the change in assets:

$$\text{Profit margin } (M) = \frac{\text{NI}}{\text{sales}} = .12$$

$$\text{Total assets turnover } (T) = \frac{\text{sales}}{\text{total assets}} = 2.5$$

$$\text{Equity multiplier (EM)} = \frac{\text{total assets}}{\text{equity}} = 1.5$$

SOLUTION

$$\text{ROE} = M \times T \times \text{EM}$$

The new $M = 1.20 \times (\text{old } M) = 1.20 \times .12 = .144$.

Since assets are increasing by 40 percent and equity remains constant, the new EM = old EM $\times$ 1.4 = 1.5 $\times$ 1.4 = 2.1. In addition, since assets are increasing by 40 percent and sales remain constant, the denominator of the total asset turnover will increase by 40 percent to 1.4. Therefore, the new $T = (\text{old } T)/1.4 = 2.5/1.4 = 1.786$. As a result, the new ROE is

$$\text{ROE} = .144 \times 1.786 \times 2.1 = .54 \quad \text{or} \quad 54\%$$

Analysis of Growth

The *growth* of a corporation's common stock value depends on two factors. First, growth depends on the amount of capital retained and reinvested in the firm. This rate of retained earnings is measured by the retention rate (RR) that was defined several paragraphs above.

Second, a corporation's growth rate depends on the rate of return on equity (ROE) earned on funds that are retained and reinvested in the firm. Defining the growth rate in earnings as shown below shows how the ROE and the retention rate (RR) determine the retention-induced growth rate.[2]

$$\text{Growth rate} = \text{RR} \times \text{ROE} \tag{11.30}$$

Substituting a decomposed version of the ROE ratio into the above growth rate formula results in the more enlightening growth rate analysis shown below:

$$\text{Growth rate} = \text{RR} \times \frac{\text{sales}}{\text{TA}} \times \frac{\text{TA}}{\text{EQ}} \times \frac{\text{NI}}{\text{sales}} \tag{11.31}$$

Furthermore, substituting the definition of RR = RE/NI into the above partially decomposed growth rate formula and algebraically rearranging the terms yields the mathematically equivalent formula for the growth rate that is shown below:

$$\text{Growth rate} = \frac{\text{RE}}{\text{NI}} \times \frac{\text{NI}}{\text{sales}} \times \frac{\text{sales}}{\text{TA}} \times \frac{\text{TA}}{\text{EQ}} = \frac{\text{RE}}{\text{EQ}}$$

[2]This earnings growth rate analysis ignores expansion that is financed with funds from external financing sources.

The various equivalent ways that the ROE and growth rate ratios can be restated highlights the manner in which different financial variables can either add or detract from the growth of a common stock's value.

Growing corporations are usually more risky than companies that are not experiencing the changes associated with growth. Regardless of whether a company is risky because of growth, management errors, tough competition, or because of other factors, risk is another aspect of an investment that the financial analyst should consider.

SOLVED PROBLEM 11.11

In recent years the Acme Corporation has earned about a 10 percent rate of return on equity (ROE). Does this mean that the corporation is growing in value at about 10 percent per year? Explain why or why not.

SOLUTION

No. Acme's 10 percent rate of return on equity need not be used to finance the firm's growth. All or part of a corporation's earnings could be paid out as cash dividends, for example. If Acme uses no external sources of financing Eq. (*11.32*) explains the relationship between a firm's rate of return on equity (ROE), its retention rate (RR), and its growth rate:

$$\text{Growth rate} = \text{RR} \times \text{ROE} \qquad (11.32)$$

If Acme uses external financing its ROE is only related to its growth rate indirectly. Lenders' willingness to lend funds to companies is positively related to the profitability of the potential project and the borrower.

11.3 INTERPRETATION OF RATIOS

Financial ratios and common-sized financial statements may be even more informative when they are compared with other relevant financial ratios. Financial analysts often undertake (1) cross-sectional comparisons and (2) time-series comparisons in order to discern unusual levels in a ratio and to detect trends, respectively.

Cross-Sectional Standards of Comparison

A firm's financial ratios can be compared to other firm's ratios. Such *cross-sectional comparisons* may reveal strengths and/or weaknesses relative to the other firms. Two categories of cross-sectional comparison can be insightful.

(1) *Industry average ratios.* Industry ratios averaged over competitors of the firm being analyzed provide good measures of the average *level* of the financial ratios of similar firms. Financial periodicals published by (*a*) Dun & Bradstreet, (*b*) Moodys, (*c*) Robert Morris Associates, (*d*) Standard & Poors, and (*e*) the *Quarterly Financial Report* published by the Federal Trade Commission report representative financial ratios for different industries (and in some cases, individual firms).

(2) *The Ratios of the Firm's Competitors.* By comparing the financial ratios of the firm being analyzed with the ratios from competing firms, a financial analyst may be able to detect differences that explain the success or failure of the firms.

Time-Series Standards of Comparison

A firm's own ratios from other years can be surveyed. Such *time-series comparisons* are useful to highlight (1) trends or (2) once-and-for-all changes within the firm.

(1) *Trends.* Trends may occur slowly from month to month and may go unnoticed by even close observers. However, when a time series of values for a particular ratio is observed annually over several years, significant trends, if any exist, will become apparent.

(2) *Once-and-for-all changes.* When a firm's financial ratios are calculated and compared for adjoining years it will be much easier to spot significant changes in the way the firm operates.

11.4 PROBLEMS WITH FINANCIAL STATEMENT ANALYSIS

While financial analysis is a worthwhile way to gain information, it is not without its potential pitfalls.

Diversification Can Take a Firm into Multiple Industries

Large firms sometimes diversify into different and unrelated products and industries so that it is impossible to find competing firms that are analogous. Stated differently, diversified firms do not fit neatly into any single industry. Furthermore, the consolidated financial statements of a diversified firm can obscure the details of its product-by-product sales and profits. No good standards of comparison exist for such conglomerates.

Inflationary Distortions

Inflation can distort financial statements and the ratios calculated from accounting statements. This is a particular problem with the balance sheet items because some fixed assets are carried on the balance sheet at depreciated historical costs that become increasingly irrelevant as inflation proceeds.

The Definition of Accounting Income Is Vague

The *generally accepted accounting principles* used to define a firm's income are not as exact as they may seem. Whether the firm's accountants use straight-line or accelerated depreciation, and/or LIFO or FIFO inventory valuation, for example, are accounting decisions that modify a company's financial statements and its reported income.

Mergers and Consolidated Financial Statements

Mergers and the acquisition of one company by another create problems with the consolidated financial statements. Intangible items like "goodwill" often appear on the consolidated balance sheet. Financial analysts should be prepared to make adjustments in the firm's published consolidated financial statements to align them more closely with the economic realities of the situation.

SOLVED PROBLEM 11.12

The *statement of cash flows* is another important financial statement contained in a firm's annual report.

(*a*) What is the statement of cash flows?

(*b*) How is it constructed?

(*c*) How can the statement of cash flows be used by an investor?

SOLUTION

(*a*) A firm's statement of cash flows shows the impact that a firm's *investing, operating,* and *financing* activities have on its cash flows over a period of time, such as 1 year.

(*b*) The *indirect* method of generating a cash flows statement proceeds as follows: (1) The net cash flows from operations are determined by first adding net income to depreciation. Then increases in current assets or decreases in current liabilities are subtracted while decreases in current assets and increases in current liabilities are added. The changes in cash and marketable securities and notes payable are not considered in this area. (2) Cash flows from investing are determined by adding decreases in investements and plant and equipment while increases in investments and plant and equipment are subtracted. (3) Cash flows from financing activities are taken into account by adding increases in long-term debt, common stock, and preferred stock while decreases in long-term debt, common stock, and preferred stock are subtracted. In addition, increases in notes payable are added while decreases are subtracted. (4) Finally, all three areas are summed to determine the impact on cash and marketable securities. That is whether cash and marketable securities increases or decreases.

(*c*) An investor can gain a great deal of insight into how the firm has allocated its funds historically by studying several years' cash flows statements. For example, has the firm been financing its long-term assets with long-term funds such as common stock and/or bonds issues or has it been relying too much on short-term financing, which is not permanent capital? In addition, cash flows statements can be projected for the future and potential strengths and weaknesses can be noted.

True-False Questions

11.1 Total assets is assigned the value of 100 percent in a common-sized income statement.

11.2 *Net working capital* equals the excess of a firm's current assets over its current liabilities.

11.3 Depreciation must be entirely omitted from a firm's net income in order to determine how much cash flow the firm generated.

11.4 Although a stock split and a stock dividend are economically equivalent transactions, accountants nevertheless represent them by making different types of entries in the net worth section of the corporation's balance sheet.

11.5 When a firm pays an account payable the transaction does not affect the equity section of its balance sheet in any way.

11.6 A primary issue of bonds or stock would increase both sides of the issuing corporation's balance sheet by the same amount.

11.7 The *retention rate* equals 100 percent less the percent of the corporation's earnings paid out for cash dividends.

11.8 If a corporation has no preferred stock outstanding its *book value per share* equals its total net worth divided by the number of shares of common stock it has outstanding.

11.9 The *asset section* of the balance sheet may be viewed as a list of sources of funds while the *liabilities and net worth section* lists uses the firm has made of its funds.

11.10 The *acid-test ratio* is a synonym for the quick ratio.

Multiple Choice Questions

11.1 Financial analysts alter the financial statements of many firms because of which of the following problems with financial statements?

(*a*) Inflation undermines the validity of the depreciated purchase prices used by accountants.

(*b*) As accountants switch from LIFO to FIFO inventory valuation techniques the reported results might be unrealistic.

(*c*) Mergers result in consolidated financial statements that can contain "goodwill" and other confusing items that are sometimes significant dollar values.

(*d*) An accounting switch from the straight-line depreciation to an accelerated method of depreciation might result in unrealistic reported income for the firm.

(*e*) All the above are true.

11.2 What differences would you expect between the financial ratios of an advertising agency and a manufacturing company.

(*a*) Unlike an advertising agency that rents practically all of its assets, most manufacturing companies would probably have higher leverage ratios since they must borrow to finance the purchase of plant and equipment.

(*b*) An advertising agency can be expected to have slower turnover ratios than a manufacturing company that owns considerable tangible assets.

(*c*) A manufacturing corporation that generated the same dollar amount of annual sales as an advertising agency would probably have a lower break-even point, stated in annual sales dollars.

(*d*) Both *b* and *c* are true.

(*e*) All the above are true.

11.3 Which of the following ratios will increase as a firm uses more financial leverage?

(*a*) The times-interest-earned ratio

(*b*) The debt-to-equity ratio

(*c*) The inventory turnover

(*d*) Both *a* and *b*

(*e*) Both *a* and *c*

11.4 Which of the following factors tends to increase the growth rate of a corporation?

(*a*) External borrowing

(*b*) Increasing the corporation's retention rate

(*c*) Increasing the corporation's rate of return on equity

(*d*) Both *a* and *b*

(*e*) All of the above

11.5 Cash, accounts receivable, inventory, and marketable securities are best described by which of the following statements?
(*a*) The productivity of these earning assets can be measured with various turnover ratios.
(*b*) The liquidity of the firm can be assessed with ratios that employ these current assets.
(*c*) Both *a* and *b* are true.
(*d*) The profitability of the firm is substantially determined by these earning assets.
(*e*) All the above are true.

11.6 A corporation has total assets of $2,000,000. It has $700,000 in long-term debt. If stockholders' equity is $900,000, what is its total debt to total asset ratio?
(*a*) 45 percent
(*b*) 47 percent
(*c*) 59 percent
(*d*) 52 percent
(*e*) 55 percent

11.7 A corporation had a total debt to total asset ratio of .4, total debt of $200,000, and net income of $30,000. Determine the corporation's return on equity.
(*a*) 8 percent
(*b*) 9 percent
(*c*) 10 percent
(*d*) 12 percent
(*e*) 14 percent

11.8 If the equity multiplier is 5, determine the total debt to total asset ratio for a corporation.
(*a*) 50 percent
(*b*) 60 percent
(*c*) 75 percent
(*d*) 80 percent
(*e*) 82 percent

11.9 Assume the following information: stockholders' equity = $2,000; shares outstanding = 40; market price to book value = 2. Determine the market price for the firm's common stock.
(*a*) $75
(*b*) $100
(*c*) $110
(*d*) $115
(*e*) $117

11.10 Which of the following is a *source* of funds?
(*a*) An increase in inventory
(*b*) An increase in accounts receivable
(*c*) An increase in investments
(*d*) An increase in accounts payable
(*e*) None of the above

Answers

True-False

11.1. F 11.2. T 11.3. F 11.4. T 11.5. T 11.6. T 11.7. T 11.8. T 11.9. F
11.10. T

Multiple Choice

11.1. e 11.2. a 11.3. b 11.4. e 11.5. b 11.6. e 11.7. c 11.8. d 11.9. b
11.10. d

Chapter 12

Short Positions, Hedging, and Arbitrage

12.1 INTRODUCTION

Short positions, hedging, and arbitrage are financial positions that investors may assume that differ from the typical position of buying a market asset, holding it, and hoping for price appreciation and/or other income. Each of these positions can be used for different purposes. Some of the positions are profitable if prices rise; some are profitable if prices fall; some are not profitable if prices either rise or fall; and some are profitable if prices do not change appreciably. Whether the position turns out to be a speculation or an investment depends in each case on how long and why the position was kept open.

12.2 LONG AND SHORT POSITIONS

The two basic positions an investor may assume are (1) the long position and (2) the short position. A *long position* involves simply buying and holding the asset in order to profit from any price appreciation, cash dividends, interest, or other income. This is the most popular investment strategy. The short position is more complex.

The Short Position

A *short sale* occurs when one person borrows securities and sells them to a second party. Essentially, short sellers sell something that they do not yet own, with the intention of purchasing the securities later at a lower price in order to profit from an *expected* price decline. If the price of the borrowed securities falls, the short seller can profit by purchasing securities like the ones that were borrowed at a lower price to repay the party who lent the securities.

SOLVED PROBLEM 12.1

What are some of the complicated aspects of short positions?

SOLUTION

First, short sales of NYSE common stock can be made only on an "up-tick"—that is, after a trade in which the stock's price was bid up. This is an NYSE rule designed to keep short sellers from accentuating a downturn in the price of a stock. A second possible complication arises from cash dividends. If a common stock which is sold short pays a cash dividend while it is still on loan to the short seller, the short seller must pay that dividend from their own pocket to the shareowner who lent the shares.

A third possible complication with short selling is that the short seller may be required to put up guarantee money equaling as much as 100 percent of the value of the borrowed shares as collateral to protect the interests of a third party who lent the shares. A fourth problem which can arise with short sales is that the short seller can be involuntarily "forced out" of the short position at any time if the third party who lent the shares demands them back. This is unlikely, however, because similar shares can usually be borrowed elsewhere.

Gain-Loss Illustrations for Long and Short Positions

Figure 12-1 contrasts long and short positions. The vertical axes in these two gain-loss graphs show the dollars of profit above the origin and the dollars of loss below the origin. The horizontal axes show the market prices of the assets held in either the long or the short position.

The gain-loss graph for the long position in Fig. 12-1*a* has a slope of positive unity, indicating that the person holding the long position makes a dollar of profit (loss) for each dollar the market price rises (falls). In contrast, the gain-loss graph for the short position in Fig. 12-1*b* has a slope of negative unity, indicating a dollar of loss (profit) for the short seller for each dollar the market price rises (falls).

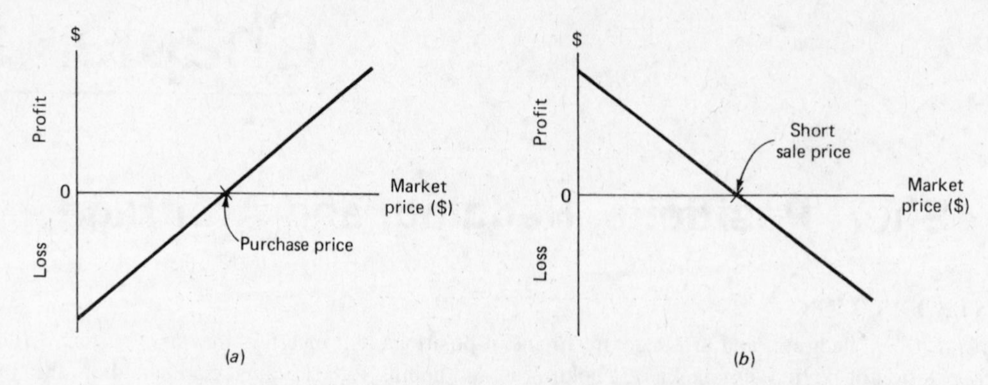

Fig. 12-1 Gain-loss illustrations. (*a*) Long position; (*b*) short position.

EXAMPLE 12.1 On April 21 Mr. Frank Evans sold short 100 shares of the Elton Manufacturing Company's stock for $50 per share. On May 4 the price of Elton's stock fell to $40 per share and Mr. Evans reversed his position by purchasing 100 shares of Elton stock for $40 per share. Frank made a *short-term profit* of $10 ($50 − $40) × 100 shares = $1,000 before taxes and transaction costs. However, if the price of Elton's stock had increased by $10 to $60 and if Frank had reversed his position, he would have lost $10 ($50 − $60) × 100 shares = $1,000 before taxes and transaction costs.

Short sales have been conducted on the floor of the New York Stock Exchange (amidst what is predominantly long buying) for decades. The volume of short sales is reported daily in the financial newspapers under the heading "Short Interest." The *short interest* is the total number of shares brokers have listed in their accounts as being sold short. The short interest is usually below 5 percent of the total volume of shares traded. NYSE specialists do most of the short selling.

There are different reasons why an individual may take a short position. First, and most obvious, is the desire to make a speculative gain from a price fall. Second, a *risk-averse* investor may sell short to "hedge" against possible losses. *Hedging* is a tactic that can be used to limit the investor's risk exposure. This risk-reducing strategy is discussed later in this chapter.

SOLVED PROBLEM 12.2

Mr. Pogue was bearish about the stock issued by the American Technology Corporation (ATC); he expected it to fall significantly within the next 3 months. So, Mr. Pogue sold 100 shares short. Mr. Pogue's stockbroker arranged to loan Mr. Pogue the 100 shares to deliver with the understanding that these shares would be replaced with other ATC shares later. A few days after Mr. Pogue opened his short position ATC announced a cash dividend of $3.50 per share. Does this cash dividend affect people like Mr. Pogue who have sold ATC stock short?

SOLUTION

Mr. Pogue and the all other short sellers must pay $3.50 out of their own pockets for every share they borrowed to sell short. Since Mr. Pogue sold 100 shares short he must pay $350 (100 shares times $3.50). This money must be paid to the account from which the short sellers borrowed shares in order to provide the cash dividends to which the share lender's account is legally entitled.

12.3 HEDGED POSITIONS

Hedging occurs when someone both buys and sells the same or similar assets at the same time. Hedging may be defined as arranging for two different positions such that the potential losses from one of the positions tends to be, more or less, offset by profits from the other position. Alternatively, hedging can be defined as the establishment of offsetting long and short positions in order to diminish the loss that could result from an adverse price movement.

There are many different types of hedges. Some hedges are undertaken to reduce potential losses from adverse price movements. Other hedges are set up with the expectation of reaping profits. The easiest hedge of all to explain is discussed first, it is the perfect hedge from which no profits or losses can be earned. Figure 12-2 is a gain-loss graph for a perfect hedge.

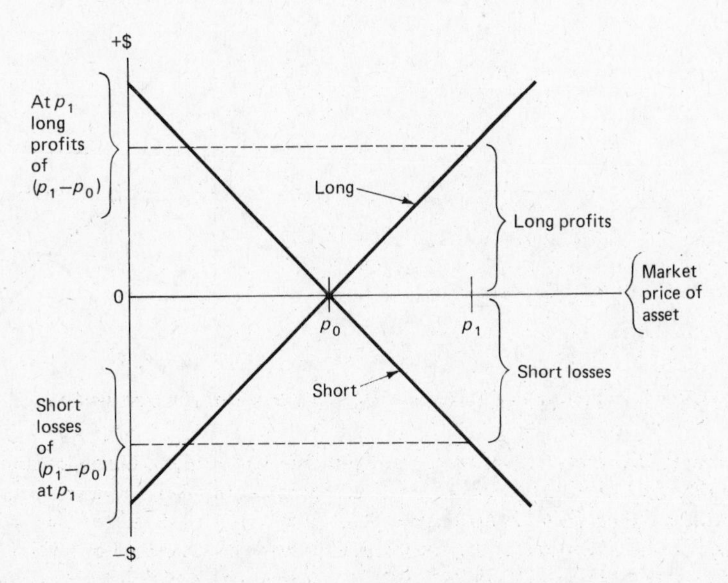

Fig. 12-2 Gain-loss illustration of a perfect hedge.

The Perfect Hedge

Figure 12-2 is a gain-loss graph which combines the long position from Fig. 12-1*a* and the short position from Fig. 12-1*b* at the same purchase and sale prices. The hedger is thus *perfectly hedged* so that the profits and losses from these two positions sum up to zero at any value that the market price may attain. Figure 12-2 might result, for instance, if an investor purchased a long position of 100 shares of the Acme Corporation's common stock at p_0 = $64 per share. Simultaneously, the investor sold 100 shares of Acme's stock short at $64 per share. Figure 12-2 shows that if the market price of the hedged asset rises above the identical prices, p_0 = $64 for both the long position and the short position, to the higher price of, say, p_1 dollars, then the profit on the long position will be exactly offset by the loss on the short position. The hedger can earn neither profits or losses because the hedge is perfect. Even if the issuer of the shorted stock goes bankrupt so that $p_1 = 0$, the perfect hedge position earns no profits nor suffers any losses. Perfect hedges are created by risk-averters. *Risk-averters* are people who are so afraid of risk that they are willing to give up some gains in order to reduce their possible losses.

The conditions essential for a hedge to be perfect are (1) equal dollar amounts must be held in both the long and the short positions and (2) the purchase price for the long position must be identical to the sales price for the short sale.[1] Not all hedges are perfect. In fact, most hedges are imperfect—but that can be more desirable than a perfect hedge.

Imperfect Hedges

A hedge may be imperfect for either of two reasons. First, if the *dollar commitments* to the long and the short positions are not equal, the hedge will be imperfect. Or second, a hedge will be imperfect if the short sales *price* is not equal to the purchase price for the long position. This second imperfection often results from getting into the long and the short positions at different points in time.

Figure 12-3 illustrates two *imperfect hedges.* Since the size of the dollar commitments to the long and the short positions cannot be illustrated in such figures, let us assume that these dollar commitments are equal. The two hedges are imperfect because their short sales price, denoted p_s, differs from the purchase price for the long position, designated p_p in Fig. 12-3.

The hedge in Fig. 12-3*a* involves a purchase price for the long position which is *above* the sales price for the short position, $p_p > p_s$. The resulting hedge will yield an *invariant loss* at whatever value the market price may assume. This loss will equal the excess of the purchase price over the short sale price ($p_p - p_s$).

[1]Technically, the long and short positions do not have to be of equal dollar magnitude to create a perfect hedge. For instance, an investment that involved only half as many dollars in an offsetting short position that had twice the price elasticity could result in a perfect hedge if the two positions were perfectly inversely correlated.

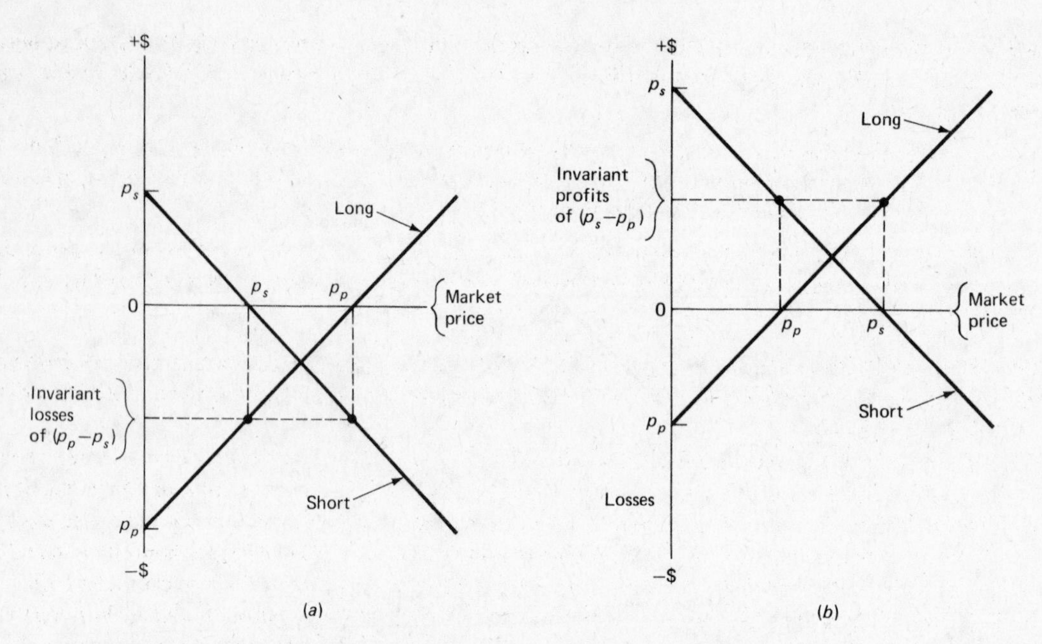

Fig. 12-3 Gain-loss illustrations of imperfect hedges. (*a*) Invariant losses; (*b*) invariant profits.

The hedge in Fig. 12-3*b* is imperfect because its short sales price is *above* the purchase price for its long position. As a result the hedge will yield an *invariant profit* equal to the excess of the short sale price over the purchase price. The imperfect hedge in Fig. 12-3*b* will yield a profit of $p_s - p_p$ regardless of what value the market price of the imperfectly hedged asset assumes.

12.4 ARBITRAGE

Another reason someone may want a short position or a hedge is to carry on arbitrage. *Arbitraging* is like hedging because both the hedger and the arbitrager buy and sell essentially the same items. Arbitrage can be defined as simultaneously buying long and selling short the same (or different, but related) assets in an effort to profit from unrealistic price differentials.

Arbitrage may take place in the same or different markets. For an example of arbitrage between different markets consider a hypothetical disparity in the price of GM's common stock.

International Stock Price Arbitrage

If GM stock is sold in the United States and also in the London Stock Exchange (LSE) at different prices, arbitrage can be profitable. Profit-seeking arbitragers facilitate enforcement of the economic "law of one price" by buying the stock in the market where its price is lowest and simultaneously selling in the market where the stock's price is highest. The *economic law of one price* says that at any given moment in time identical goods should sell at equal prices everywhere in the world.

Arbitragers will go on buying-at-the-low-price and selling-at-the-high-price until the price of GM stock is the same in all free markets around the world. Technically, the price of GM stock may never be exactly identical in all markets because of transactions costs such as brokers commissions, foreign exchange restrictions, long-distance telephone costs, mailing costs, and other "frictions" that slow up arbitrage and erode arbitrage profits. However, with the exception of these transactions costs (of a few cents per share), GM stock should cost the same no matter where in the world it is traded. The law of one price should never be broken or else profit seekers will exploit the following profitable procedure until a single prevailing price is restored.

EXAMPLE 12.2

(1) Sell short in the market where the good is offered at the higher price. For example, sell GM stock short for $100 per share in London if the price of GM is higher in the LSE than it is elsewhere.

(2) Buy a long position in the same quantity of the same good in the market where it is offered at the lowest price. To continue the example, simultaneously buy GM stock for $99 at the NYSE (or anywhere else it sells for less than the short sale price).

(3) Deliver the good that was purchased at the low price for the long position at a higher selling price to fulfill the delivery requirements of the short position. Buy GM for $99 at the NYSE, sell it short for $100 in London, and make $1 per share profit for each share delivered under these terms.

(4) Continue to profit from "buying low and selling high" to make delivery on the short position. Repeat this profitable procedure until the cheap price is bid up by demand, the high price is driven down by the supply, and the same price prevails in all markets.

The arbitrage procedure above can yield *riskless* profits for the arbitrager. The profits need not involve any risk-taking because the arbitrager can, if desired, remain fully hedged while repeating the profitable arbitrage procedure again-and-again.

Some arbitrage is risky and some is riskless. In order to earn riskless trading profits an arbitrager simultaneously sells *equal amounts* of the security short in the market where its price is high and buys the security long in the market where the price is low. Figure 12-3*b* illustrates a profitable hedge of the type that arbitragers strive to establish. Arbitragers keep buying the security in the market where it is cheapest until they bid its price up to a higher level. Simultaneously, the arbitragers keep selling in the market where the price is higher until they drive down the high price. As the short sale price and the long purchase price are thus driven together by the market activities of profit-seeking arbitragers, the arbitrage pays off regardless of what other price fluctuations occur. The general level of the prices could double or fall in half, for instance, and the arbitrage will still be profitable as long as the differing prices come together at any level.

SOLVED PROBLEM 12.3

Read the case below and then fill in the ten blanks.

Mr. Joe Ufora has bought a long position in International Motors (IM) common stock at a purchase price of $50 per share. If the price of IM stock goes up to $70 per share, Fig. 12-4*a* shows that Joe has a profit of __1__ per share before commissions and taxes. But if Joe was bullish when he should have been bearish and the stock's price falls to $40 per share, he has a loss of __2__ per share.

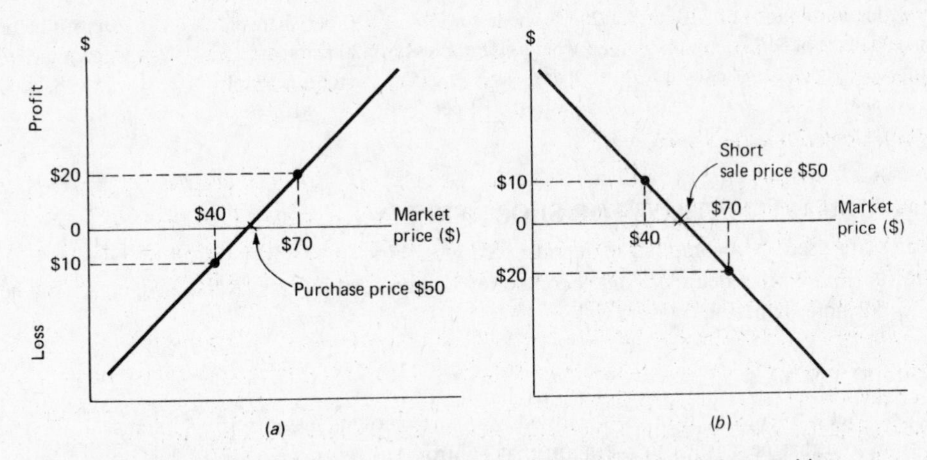

Fig. 12-4 Position graphs for Joe Ufora. (*a*) Long position; (*b*) short position.

If Mr. Ufora were bearish about IM stock he could sell the stock short at $50 per share, as shown in Fig. 12-4*b*. If the price then fell to $40 per share, Joe would have a profit before commissions and taxes of __3__ per share from his short position. But if Joe judged the stock wrong and its price appreciated to $70 per share, he would suffer a loss of ___4___ per share from the short sale. Note the symmetry of Joe's long and short positions; Fig. 12-4 shows that one is the inverse of the other.

Finally, consider Joe's position if he had taken both a long and a short position. Figure 12-5 is a gain-loss graph which combines Joe Ufora's long position from Fig. 12-4*a* with his short position from Fig. 12-4*b*, with both positions being taken simultaneously at the same $50 per share price. Figure 12-5 illustrates what happens if Mr. Joe Ufora hedged himself perfectly. The figure shows that if the market price of the hedged asset rises above the $50 purchase price to the higher price of $70 dollars, then the ___5___ per share profit on the long position will be offset by a ___6___ per share loss on the short position for a net profit of ___7___. In contrast, if the market price of IM fell from $50 to $40, then the loss of ___8___ per share on Joe's long position would have been offset by a gain of ___9___ per share on his short position for a net profit of ___10___.

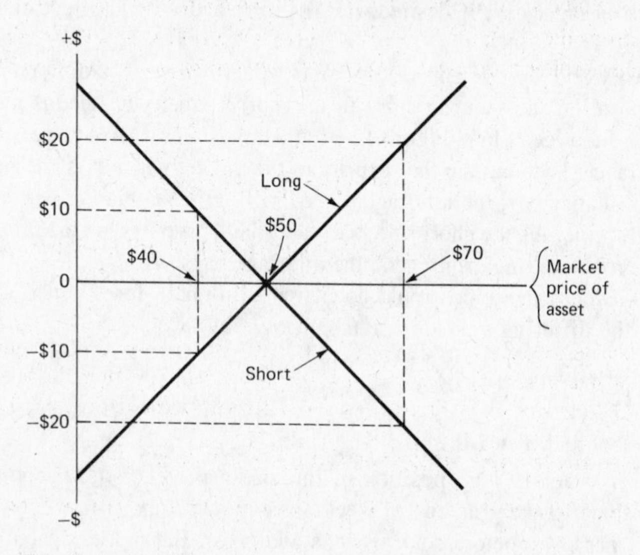

Fig. 12-5 Position graph for Joe Ufora's perfect hedge at $50.

SOLUTION

1. ... Joe has a profit of $20... 2. ... he has a loss of $10 per share... 3. ... profit before commissions and taxes of $10... 4. ... he would suffer a loss of $20 per share... 5. ... then the $20 per share profit... 6. ... offset by a $20 per share loss... 7. ... for a net profit of zero... 8. ... the loss of $10 per share... 9. ... offset by a gain of $10 per share... 10. ... for a net profit of zero...

12.5 DIFFERING MOTIVATIONS FOR SHORT SELLING

Short sales are used to accomplish different objectives. First, they can be used by bearish speculators in search of profits from a price decline. And second, they can be used by risk-averse hedgers. Some hedgers can be seeking to do more than simply avert risks.

SOLVED PROBLEM 12.4

Suppose that a hypothetical investor named Mr. Parrish owns a controlling interest in the Parrish Corporation, and that he wishes to maintain that control. However, because he has access to inside information, Mr. Parrish expects the price of Parrish's stock to suffer a drastic fall. How can Mr. Parrish avoid being hurt by the imminent collapse in Parrish's stock price and still maintain his voting control of his corporation?

SOLUTION

Mr. Parrish can continue to hold onto his shares of Parrish stock and thus maintain the control he desires over his corporation. While maintaining the long position in Parrish stock that he needs to control the corporation, he can simultaneously sell an equal number of shares of Parrish stock short to establish a perfect hedge. This perfect hedge will totally eliminate any possibility that Mr. Parrish loses anything if the price of Parrish stock declines.[2] After he sets up a hedge, if the price falls the losses on Mr. Parrish's long position are matched by gains on his short position. Thus, the investor has maintained voting control through his long position and, at the same time, hedged his loss. Since Mr. Parrish always actually owned shares (presumably they were in his safe-deposit box) exactly like the ones he sold short, he did what is called *selling short against the box*. Selling short against the box is not risky because the short seller is hedged against adverse price moves.

When selling short against the box, short sellers can borrow shares to use for delivery and then later purchase shares to repay the loan, or they may simply deliver the shares they hold in their boxes. It is a common procedure to borrow shares. The borrower may be required to give the lender cash to hold equal to the value of the shares borrowed; this protects the lender. The lender of the shares can use this cash at will while still benefiting from any income from the shares. The lender of the shares may even be able to charge the borrower a fee for using the shares. Many brokers can arrange for such loans of shares in order to complete a short sale—the practice is common.

True-False Questions

12.1 Risk-averters can create riskless hedges simply by assuming a long and a short position in similar securities.

12.2 Imperfect hedges are needed to profit from arbitrage.

12.3 Consider two highly positively correlated common stocks, say Ford and GM. Assume the correlation coefficient between the rates of return from these two automotive stocks was +.8. If you took a long position in GM and a short position in Ford (or vice versa) of exactly equal value you would be perfectly hedged.

12.4 Person who sell short are, in effect, selling something that they do not own.

12.5 Taking a short position involves buying and holding the security for only a short period of time.

12.6 Brokers normally loan securities they are holding for their other clients to short sellers in order to make delivery on the securities that were sold short.

12.7 Imperfect hedges occur when either the quantities sold short and bought long are out of balance, or the purchase and short sale prices differ.

12.8 Arbitrage is an imperfect hedge with a guaranteed profit built into it.

12.9 A perfect hedge requires that the long and the short positions be established in identical rather than merely similar securities.

12.10 Arbitrage is undertaken to profit from price discrepancies.

Multiple Choice Questions

12.1 What characteristics do the long and short positions have in common?

(*a*) The potential profits from a long position and the potential losses from a short position are both infinite if the price of the underlying security rises to infinity.
(*b*) There is a one-to-one correspondence between movements in the price of the underlying security and the investor's profits.
(*c*) Both *b* and *a* are true.
(*d*) The investor loses money if the price of an asset held in either position declines.
(*e*) All the above are true.

[2] If the security involved in the short selling to maintain control is required to be listed with the SEC (see Chap. 9 about the law), then the transaction described is illegal because "insiders" are not allowed to sell short.

12.2 Under which of the following conditions would someone who thought that the price of a stock was going to rise want to become involved in a short position in that stock?
- (*a*) If the short sale were part of a larger plan to sell short against the box in order to maintain voting control through the shares in a long position
- (*b*) If the short sale were part of an imperfect hedge that was expected to yield arbitrage profits
- (*c*) Both *a* and *b*
- (*d*) If the short sale were part of a perfect hedge the investor was setting up in order to reap large profits
- (*e*) All of the above

12.3 Which of the following statements correctly describes short sales?
- (*a*) The volume of short sales is reported daily in the financial newspapers.
- (*b*) NYSE rules stipulate that a short sale can only be made on an up-tick in the security's price.
- (*c*) Short selling is an essential part of hedging and arbitrage.
- (*d*) Both *b* and *c* are true.
- (*e*) All the above are true.

12.4 Which of the following statements correctly describes a short seller's profits?
- (*a*) The per share profit from short selling is limited to an amount equal to the price at which the shares were sold short.
- (*b*) The short seller earns $1 profit for every $1 fall in price of the security.
- (*c*) Short sellers must pay for any cash dividends the stock might declare while they are borrowing it and this decreases the profits from selling short.
- (*d*) Short selling can help arbitragers earn profits.
- (*e*) All the above are true.

12.5 Which of the following conditions are not essential for a hedge to be perfect?
- (*a*) The short sale must be initiated at the same price that was paid for the long position.
- (*b*) The dollar values of the long and the short positions should be of identical dollar value.
- (*c*) If the dollar values of the long and the offsetting short positions differ, then some arrangements must be made so that the price elasticities of the offsetting positions are appropriate.
- (*d*) The long and the short positions must be initiated simultaneously.

12.6 Selling short against the box involves which of the following conditions?
- (*a*) The owner of the securities can continue to own them, and, thus, exercise whatever voting power they might convey.
- (*b*) A short position of equal dollar value and in the identical security that is held in the long position must be established if a perfect hedge is desired.
- (*c*) If the dollar values of the long and the short positions differ an imperfect hedge can be established that leaves the party who is selling short against the box partially exposed to risk.
- (*d*) Both *a* and *b* are ture.
- (*e*) All of the above are true.

12.7 Selling securities short is useful in which of the following activities?
- (*a*) Speculating
- (*b*) Hedging
- (*c*) Selling short against the box
- (*d*) Arbitrage
- (*e*) All the above

12.8 Profitable arbitrage is correctly described by which of the following statements?
- (*a*) If the long and short positions exactly offset each other then profitable arbitrage is impossible.
- (*b*) An imperfect hedge is a necessary ingredient if an arbitrage position is to be profitable.
- (*c*) It involves only small risks.
- (*d*) Both *a* and *b* are true.
- (*e*) All the above are true.

12.9 Which of the following statements about hedging are false?
(*a*) Imperfect hedges can be profitable.
(*b*) Imperfect hedges can yield losses for the hedger.
(*c*) Hedges, of even an imperfect variety, reduce risk below what it would be with an unhedged position.
(*d*) Perfect hedges usually yield a profit.
(*e*) Both *c* and *d*.

12.10 Investors' motives are correctly described by which of the following statements?
(*a*) Uncovered short sellers are bearish.
(*b*) Uncovered buyers of long positions are bullish.
(*c*) Hedgers are bullish.
(*d*) Both *a* and *b* are true.
(*e*) All of the above are true.

Answers

True-False

12.1. F 12.2. T 12.3. F 12.4. T 12.5. F 12.6. T 12.7. T 12.8. T 12.9. T
12.10. T

Multiple Choice

12.1. c 12.2. c 12.3. e 12.4. e 12.5. d 12.6. e 12.7. e 12.8. d 12.9. d
12.10. d

Chapter 13

Total Risk and Risk Factors

13.1 INTRODUCTION

Risk is defined as variability of return. The one-period rate of return is the basic random variable used in measuring an investment's risk. Equation (*13.1*) defines the single-period rate of return for a share of common stock:

$$r_t = \frac{\text{(price change)} + \text{(cash dividend, if any)}}{\text{purchase price at start of the period}} \tag{13.1}$$

The expected rate of return is the sum of the product of the various one-period rates of return times their probabilities. Equation (*13.2*) defines the expected rate of return.

$$E(r) = \sum_{t=1}^{T} P_t r_t \tag{13.2}$$

where r_t is the tth rate of return from a probability distribution, P_t denotes the probability that the tth rate of return will take place, and there are T possible rates of return. Equation (*13.3*) shows how the investor's total variability of return is measured.

$$\sigma^2 = \text{variance} = \sum_{t=1}^{T} P_t[r_t - E(r)]^2 \tag{13.3}$$

where σ^2 represents the variance. The square root of the variance, σ, is the standard deviation of returns.

When historical returns are used, the following formula is used to calculate an average return:

$$\bar{r} = \frac{\sum_{t=1}^{T} r_t}{T} \tag{13.4}$$

where $\bar{r}$ is the average or mean return and T is the number of observed returns. The standard deviation of returns (σ) for assets using historical returns is calculated with Eq. (*13.5*):

$$\sigma = \sqrt{\frac{\sum_{t=1}^{T} (r_t - \bar{r})^2}{T}} \tag{13.5}$$

EXAMPLE 13.1 Calculating a Common Stock's Rates of Return The financial data in Table 13.1 shows how to calculate the annual common stock rates of return for the Interstate Business (IB) Corporation with Eq. (*13.1*).

SOLVED PROBLEM 13.1

Refer to Table 13.1. Determine the three annual rates of return that were left blank.

SOLUTION

Annual returns can be determined with Eq. (*13.1*).

$$r_t = \frac{\text{(price change)} + \text{(cash div., if any)}}{\text{purchase price at the start of the period}}$$

$$r_{19X8} = \frac{(\$80.31836 - \$70.2653) + \$4}{\$70.2653} = \frac{\$14.05306}{\$70.2653} = 20\%$$

$$r_{19X9} = \frac{(\$92.382032 - \$80.31836) + \$4}{\$80.31836} = \frac{\$16.063672}{\$80.31836} = 20\%$$

$$r_{19Y0} = \frac{(\$134.573048 - \$92.382032) + \$4}{\$92.382032} = \frac{\$46.191016}{92.382032} = 50\%$$

Table 13.1 Stock Price and Cash Dividend Data for Calculating the Interstate Business (IB) Corporation's Annual Rates of Return

Year	Year's Closing Prices*	Annual Cash Dividends	Annual Rates of Return, Eq. (*13.1*)
19X0	$ 60.00	$3.00	Insufficient data to calculate.
19X1	69.00	3.00	($9.00 + $3.00)/$60 = 20%
19X2	100.50	3.00	($31.50 + $3.00)/$69 = 50%
19X3	47.25	3.00	(−$53.25 + $3.00)/$100.50 = −50%
19X4	39.525	3.00	(−$7.725 + $3.00)/$47.25 = −10%
19X5	72.0975	3.00	($32.5725 + $3.00)/$39.525 = 90%
19X6	82.517	4.00	($10.4195 + $4.00)/$72.0975 = 20%
19X7	70.2653	4.00	(−$12.2517 + $4.00)/$82.517 = −10%
19X8	80.31836	4.00	
19X9	92.382032	4.00	
19Y0	134.573048	4.00	

*Stock prices are usually quoted in increments of one-eighth of one dollar (that is, the three-decimal-point quantity $.125 is the minimum price change). Unrealistic stock prices that run to six-decimal-point accuracy were used in the table so that the annual rates of return would all work out exactly to be tens of percentage points. This was done to simplify the more complex rate-of-return calculations in Table 13.2.

SOLVED PROBLEM 13.2

Calculate the average (or expected) rate of return, the variance, and the standard deviation of returns for the Interstate Business (IB) Corporation; use the data in Table 13.1.

SOLUTION

In Table 13.2 the expected rate of return and the variance of returns are calculated from the 10 annual rates of return for the IB Corporation that were computed above in Table 13.1 and Solved Problem 13.1. Formulas (*13.2*) and (*13.3*) are being used.

The standard deviation is

$$\sqrt{\text{Var}(r_{\text{IB}})} = \sqrt{.134} = \sigma_{\text{IB}} = .36606$$

Table 13.2 The Interstate Business (IB) Corporation's Common Stock Expected Rate of Return and Risk Statistics Computations

Year	IB's Returns, r	Probability, $1/T$	Prob. × r	Deviations of r from $E(r)$, $r - E(r)$	Probability times Squared Deviation, Prob. × $[r - E(r)]^2$
19X1	.2 = 20%	.1	(.1)(.2) = .02	(.2 − .2) = 0	$(.1)(0)^2 = 0$
19X2	.5 = 50%	.1	(.1)(.5) = .05	(.5 − .2) = .3	$(.1)(.3)^2 = .009$
19X3	−.5 = −50%	.1	(.1)(−.5) = −.05	(−.5 − .2) = −.7	$(.1)(-.7)^2 = .049$
19X4	−.1 = −10%	.1	(.1)(−.1) = −.01	(−.1 − .2) = −.3	$(.1)(-.3)^2 = .009$
19X5	.9 = 90%	.1	(.1)(.9) = .09	(.9 − .2) = .7	$(.1)(.7)^2 = .049$
19X6	.2 = 20%	.1	(.1)(.2) = .02	(.2 − .2) = 0	$(.1)(0)^2 = 0$
19X7	−.1 = −10%	.1	(.1)(−.1) = −.01	(−.1 − .2) = −.3	$(.1)(-.3)^2 = .009$
19X8	.2 = 20%	.1	(.1)(.2) = .02	(.2 − .2) = 0	$(.1)(0)^2 = 0$
19X9	.2 = 20%	.1	(.1)(.2) = .02	(.2 − .2) = 0	$(.1)(0)^2 = 0$
19Y0 = T	.5 = 50%	.1	(.1)(.5) = .05	(.5 − .2) = .3	$(.1)(.3)^2 = .009$
Total		1.0	$E(r_{\text{IB}})$ = .2		$\text{Var}(r_{\text{IB}}) = .134$

Columns 2 and 3 of Table 13.2 contain objective historical return data that are given equal weights (of one-tenth) in calculating the security's ex post average return and risk statistics. An asset's expected (or ex ante) return and risk estimates can also be calculated by using subjectively assigned probabilities that the analyst expects to occur in the future.

SOLVED PROBLEM 13.3

The Holmes Corporation has the following probability distribution of expected future returns:

PROBABILITY	FORECASTED RETURN
.15	−15%
.10	−10
.20	5
.20	12
.15	20
.10	25
.10	30

Determine the expected return and standard deviation of returns for Holmes.

SOLUTION

$$E(r) = \sum_{t=1}^{T=7} P_t r_t \tag{13.2}$$

$$E(r) = (.15)(-15) + (.10)(-10) + (.20)(5) + (.20)(12) + (.15)(20) + (.10)(25) + (.10)(30)$$
$$= -2.25 + -1 + 1 + 2.4 + 3 + 2.5 + 3 = 8.65\%$$

$$\sigma^2 = \sum_{t=1}^{T} P_t[r_t - E(r)]^2 \tag{13.3}$$

$$\sigma^2 = .15(-15 - 8.65)^2 + .10(-10 - 8.65)^2 + .20(5 - 8.65)^2 + .20(12 - 8.65)^2 + .15(20 - 8.65)^2 + .10(25 - 8.65)^2 + .10(30 - 8.65)^2$$
$$= 83.8984 + 34.7823 + 2.6645 + 2.2445 + 19.3234 + 26.7323 + 45.5823 = 215.2277$$
$$\sigma = \sqrt{215.2277} = 14.6706\%$$

SOLVED PROBLEM 13.4

The Quinn Company had the following annual returns over the past 5 years:

YEAR	RETURN
19X1	10%
19X2	−5
19X3	14
19X4	−6
19X5	20

Determine Quinn's average return and standard deviation of returns over the past 5 years.

SOLUTION

$$\bar{r} = \frac{\sum_{t=1}^{T} r_t}{T} \tag{13.4}$$

$$\bar{r} = \frac{10 + (-5) + 14 + (-6) + 20}{5} = 6.6\%$$

$$\sigma = \sqrt{\frac{\sum_{t=1}^{T} (r_t - \bar{r})^2}{T}} \tag{13.5}$$

$$\sigma^2 = \frac{(10 - 6.6)^2 + (-5 - 6.6)^2 + (14 - 6.6)^2 + (-6 - 6.6)^2 + (20 - 6.6)^2}{5}$$

$$= \frac{539.2}{5} = 107.84 \quad \text{(variance)}$$

The square root of the variance, σ, is the standard deviation:

$$\sigma = \sqrt{107.84} = 10.385\%$$

13.2 DEFAULT RISK

Default risk is that portion of an investment's total risk that results from changes in the financial strength of the investment. For example, when a company that issues securities moves either further away from or closer to bankruptcy, these changes in the firm's financial strength are reflected in the market prices of its securities. The *variability of return* that investors experience as a result of changes in the financial strength of a firm that issues securities is a measure of the securities default risk. Default risk might also be called *financial risk* or *bankruptcy risk*.

Defaults and bankruptcies do not usually occur without giving some warning signs. A bankruptcy can normally be foreseen by financial analysts because deteriorating financial ratios and insolvency typically precede it. Practically all the losses suffered by investors as a result of default risk occur months *before* a possible bankruptcy. Default risk losses are primarily caused by security prices falling as the healthy firm that issued the securities weakens financially and, as a result, the market price of its securities declines. By the time an actual bankruptcy occurs, the market price of the troubled firm's securities will have already declined to near zero, so the losses at the time of the bankruptcy would be only a small part of the total losses resulting from the decline.

SOLVED PROBLEM 13.5

When discussing the possible outcomes of a risky investment the "upside" and the "downside" outcomes are sometimes discussed separately. The *upside* outcome refers to the best possible outcome. The *downside risk* is the worst possible outcome. The worst possible outcome is the same for most investments; it is -100 percent.

Consider the stock price of the Chrysler Corporation; the consensus in late 1981 was that the company was near bankruptcy. If a speculator bought Chrysler common stock in December 1981, for $3\frac{3}{8}$ (that is, \$3.375) per share, what was the upside risk and the downside risk?

SOLUTION

The *downside risk* is that Chrysler goes bankrupt and the investor has a negative 100 percent rate of return. The "upside" is that the investor might sell the Chrysler stock purchased in 1981 at \$3.375 per share for \$32 per share in June 1983.

$$\frac{(\text{Selling price}) - (\text{purchase price}) + (\text{cash dividend})}{\text{Purchase price}} = \frac{(\$32) - (\$3.375) + (\text{zero})}{\$3.375}$$

$$= \frac{\$28.625}{\$3.375} = 8.481 = 848.1 \quad \text{percent gain}$$

The resulting \$28.625 price increase equals an 848.1 percent upside rate of return over the 17-month holding period. The investor could have earned even more if the position were held open until 1985. But let's be satisfied with an 848.1 percent gain over 17 months. The *most likely outcome* lies somewhere between the upside and the downside extremes.

SOLVED PROBLEM 13.6

Reconsider the Chrysler common stock investor's upside and downside risks from Solved Problem 13.5. Prepare a subjective estimate of the probability distribution of one-period rates of return that the Chrysler investor faced over the 17-month holding period; use the same December 1981, buying and June 1983, selling dates. In addition, let the expected rate of return be $E(r) = 374$ percent with a probability of $\frac{8}{20}$. From Solved Problem 13.5, we know that the worst possible rate of return is -100 percent; let it have a probability of $\frac{1}{20}$. The best possible return is 848 percent; let it also have a $\frac{1}{20}$ probability.

Now select two other rates of return that each have a probability of $\frac{5}{20}$. They should be equally far above and below the expected rate of return (so the probability distribution is symmetric). Calculate the expected rate of return and the standard deviation of returns from these five rates of return. Sketch what the probability distribution looks like, based on your risk and return statistics.

SOLUTION

There is no single correct subjective estimated probability distribution. However, one plausible answer is suggested below. Note that 298 percent and 450 percent are both symmetric to $E(r) = 374\%$.

RATE OF RETURN	PROBABILITY	
$-100\% = -1.0$	$\frac{1}{20} = .05$	Worst possible outcome
$+298\% = 2.98$	$\frac{5}{20} = .25$	An arbitrarily selected symmetric return
$+374\% = 3.74$	$\frac{8}{20} = .40$	Expected rate of return
$+450\% = 4.50$	$\frac{5}{20} = .25$	An arbitrarily selected symmetric return
$+848\% = 8.48$	$\frac{1}{20} = .05$	Best possible outcome
	$1.0 = 1.0$	

The calculations for the $E(r)$ and the standard deviation follow:

RETURN	PROB.	PRODUCT	DEVIATION	SQUARED DEVIATION	PROBABILITY TIMES SQUARED DEVIATIONS
$-100\% = -1.0$	.05	$-.05$	-4.74	22.4676	1.12338
$298\% = 2.98$	.25	.745	$-.76$	.5776	.1444
$374\% = 3.74$	.40	1.496	0	0	0
$450\% = 4.50$	.25	1.125	.76	.5776	.1444
$848\% = 8.48$	.05	.424	4.74	22.4676	1.12338
Totals	1.0	$E(r) = 3.74 = 374\%$			$\text{Var}(r) = 2.53556$

$$\sqrt{2.53556} = 1.59234 = \text{standard deviation of returns}$$

See Fig. 13-1.

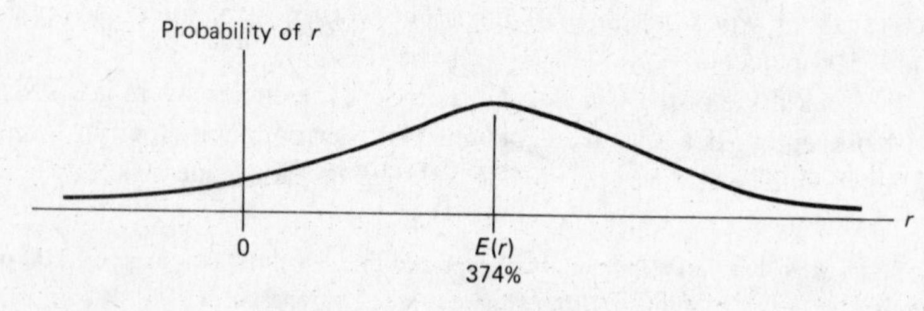

Fig. 13-1

Default Risk Determines the Level of Returns Investors Expect

It would seem that investors should require issuers of high-risk securities to pay higher rates of return than issuers of low-risk securities; otherwise, why should investors assume the greater risk of loss?

Figure 13-2 shows the relationship between risk and corporate bond yields at different times. Corporate bonds yield progressively higher interest rates as their ratings deteriorate. Since bond prices vary inversely with interest rates, the quality ratings directly affect bond prices. The quality ratings determine which risk-adjusted interest rate is appropriate to calculate a bond's value. The Federal Reserve Board's monetary policy, fiscal policy, the supply of and demand for loanable funds, and other factors that constantly change cause the relationship between the discount rate and bond ratings to shift minute by minute every day. But high-risk bonds are always forced to pay the highest returns in order to attract investors.

The tradeoff between the default risk that investors undertake and the rate of return they are paid is not limited to bonds. Stock investors also try to avoid risk. As a result, common stocks must, on average, pay higher rates of return than bonds because if the firm goes bankrupt common stockholders have only a residual claim against whatever assets (if any) the business has left over after all higher-priority (or senior) debt investors are paid.

Diversifiable and Undiversifiable Default Risk

Although default risk is always present for business firms, the probabilities of default are increased under certain conditions. For instance, when a recession slows the flow of purchase orders, firms that are already on the brink of insolvency fall into default as a result of declines in their sales and income. The business recession is an example of a *systematic force* that affects all firms simultaneously and systematically pushes many of them toward default. Systematic influences add an *undiversifiable component* to the amount of *diversifiable default risk* that exists under normal conditions.

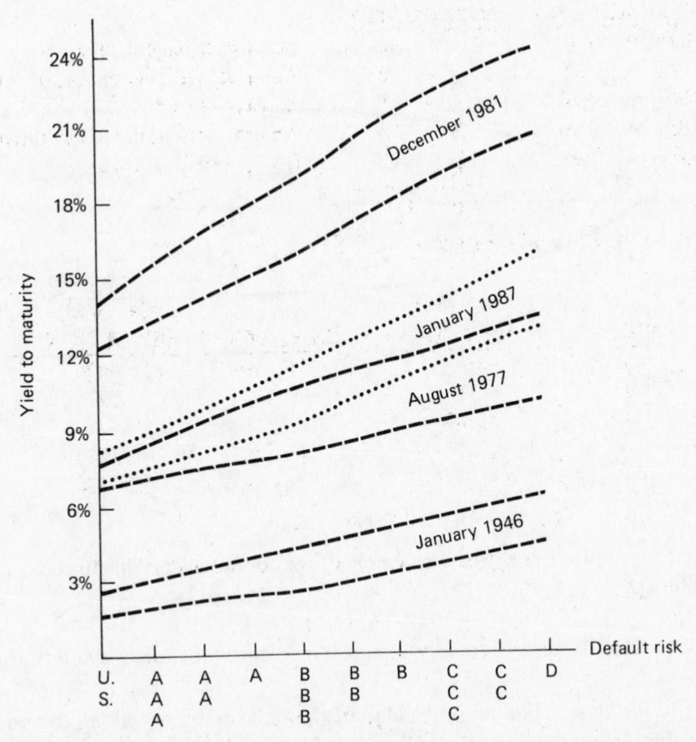

Fig. 13-2 The risk structure of bond yields on (*a*) January 1946, (*b*) August 1977, (*c*) December 1981, and (*d*) January 1987.

13.3 THE INTEREST-RATE RISK FACTOR

Interest-rate risk is the variability in the return of an investment that grows out of fluctuations in the market rate of interest. Chapter 4 showed how present values varied inversely with the interest (or discount) rate. It is through this present-value mechanism that interest rates affect the prices of all assets.

Even Default-Free Bonds Have Interest-Rate Risk

A *bond* is a legal contract that requires the borrower to pay the lender (that is, the bond investor) a fixed annual coupon interest payment every year until the bond matures. At maturity, the bond issuer must repay the principal amount (or face value) of the bond. This is true for both corporate bonds and U.S. Treasury bonds. But corporate bonds and Treasury bonds differ in an important respect: Corporations can default or even go bankrupt. In contrast, U.S. Treasury bonds are free from bankruptcy risk. (See Chaps. 3 and 5 for a more detailed discussion of the different bonds.)

Treasury bonds are sometimes called default-free bonds because the U.S. Treasury should not go bankrupt as long as the U.S. government can print money. Regardless of the fact that they cannot go bankrupt, U.S. bonds still experience interest-rate risk. In fact, interest-rate risk is the main risk to which the default-free Treasury bonds are subject.

Price Change Risk

The factor that makes a $1,000 Treasury bond with decades to maturity vary in price from $800 to $1,200 are the changing market interest rates in the bond market. The market price of a bond can be calculated to the penny by observing the current market interest rate (or yield-to-maturity, as it is more properly called) and using it as the discount rate to find the present value of the bond's cash flows. The *cash flows* are all known in advance—they are the annual coupon interest payments plus the face value at maturity. For instance, a $1,000 Treasury bond with a 10 percent coupon rate will pay $100 per year until it matures and then repay the $1,000 principal. The various present values this default-free bond may assume as its time to maturity varies from 50 to 0 years are illustrated in Fig. 13-3 for market interest rates of 9 percent, 10 percent, and 11 percent.

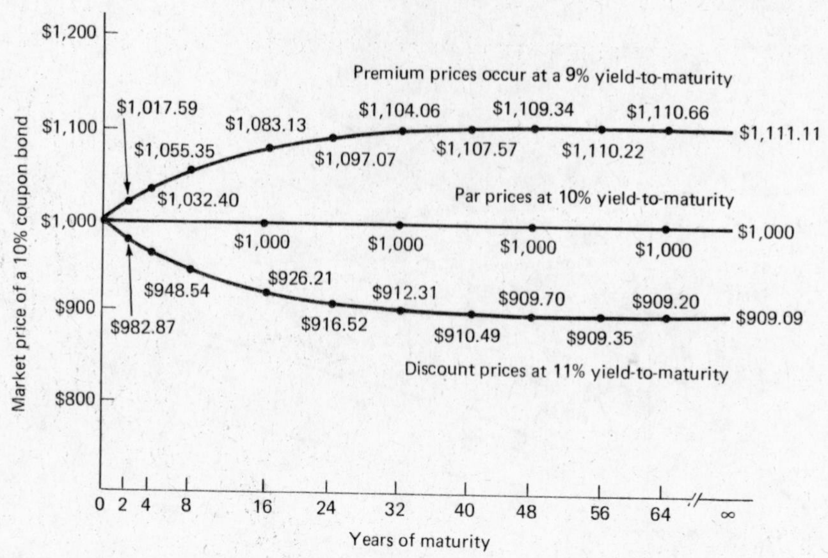

Fig. 13-3 How differing market interest rates affect the market prices for bonds with 10 percent coupon rates and various times to maturity.

The market price of a bond will always exactly equal its present value, so considering these present values is informative.

Present-value principle one. The present value of the bond is higher along the curve calculated with the 9 percent interest rate than it is along the lower curve, which represents the same bond's present values calculated with an 11 percent rate. That is, the bond's present value at any given time to maturity moves inversely with the interest rate that is used to discount the cash flows. The observance of this inverse relationship is so important that we will memorize it by hereafter calling it *present-value principle one.*

Present-value principle two. A second present-value principle is also visible in Fig. 13-3. The 10 percent Treasury bond's present values fluctuate over a much wider range at the longer maturities than at the shorter maturities. That is, the bond has more interest-rate risk as the futurity of its cash flows increases. Stated differently, the *second present-value principle* is that bonds with more futurity or duration have more interest-rate risk. Figure 13-4 shows how the various market interest rates that induce these bond value changes have varied during recent years.

The *price fluctuation risk* caused by varying market interest rates are much less when the bond has only a few years to maturity. This is because the short-term bonds have shorter durations and, thus, less interest-rate risk. Note, for example, how the 9 percent and the 11 percent curves in Fig. 13-3 come together at the bond's maturity date, when the present values and face values become the same.

The Coupon Reinvestment Risk

In addition to price change risk, those who invest in bonds that pay coupon interest face another kind of risk called *coupon rate risk.* The coupon rate risk is simply a reinvestment risk. Investors receiving coupons are forced to reinvest their coupon income at a different and varying series of interest rates that prevail in the market at the times when they receive the coupon interest. The uncertainty attached to these reinvestment opportunities is the coupon rate risk.

Corporate Bonds

Corporate bonds are also subject to the two kinds of interest-rate risk: (1) price change risk and (2) coupon rate risk. The only difference between the default-free Treasury bonds and the more risky corporate bonds is that the corporate bonds must pay higher rates of interest in order to induce investors to assume their additional risk of default. However, since all interest rates tend to rise and fall together (as shown in Fig. 13-4) the corporate bonds' interest rates fluctuate about the same amount; but they fluctuate at a higher level than do the default-free Treasury bonds.

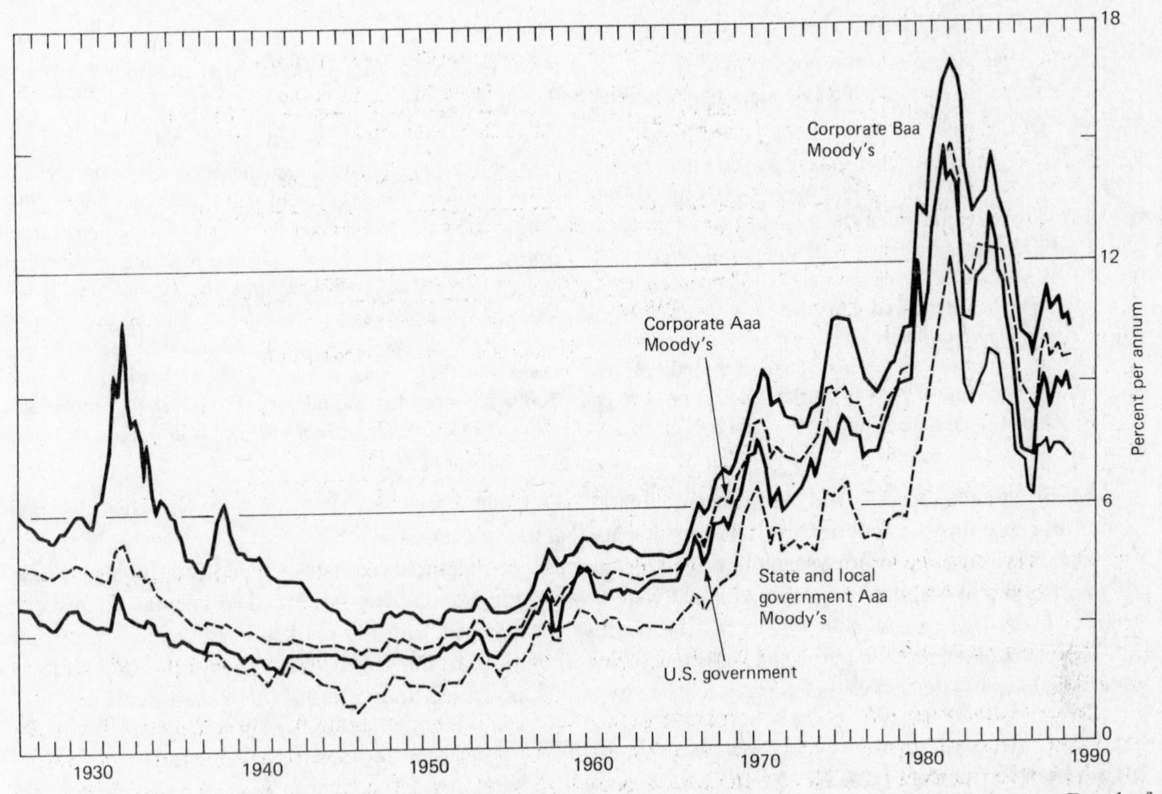

Fig. 13-4 Market yields-to-maturities vary continuously. (*Source: Historical Chart Book,* Federal Reserve Board of Governors, Washington, D.C.)

Stocks

Even preferred and common stocks experience some interest-rate risk. Preferred and common stocks usually pay cash dividends. The *dividend yield* from a share of preferred or common stock is defined below; it is analogous to an interest rate in some respects.

$$\text{Dividend yield} = \frac{\text{cash dividend per share}}{\text{market price per share}}$$

The *coupon yield* (or "current yield") from a bond is

$$\text{Coupon yield} = \frac{\text{coupon interest per year}}{\text{market price per bond}}$$

The dividend yield from a share of stock and the coupon yield from a bond both resemble rates of interest. Yet these two cash yield measures are different because of bankruptcy considerations. This bankruptcy risk makes the cash dividend yield paid to common stockholders considerably more risky than bondholders' coupon yield. Nevertheless, the present-value model is still relevant in determining the prices of stocks. It is through the present-value mechanism that interest-rate risk affects the prices of preferred and common stocks.

Diversifiable and Undiversifiable Interest-Rate Risk

Figure 13-4 shows that when the averages of different interest rates are plotted together through time they all tend to rise and fall together. These systematic interest-rate movements represent *undiversifiable interest-rate risk*. Each of the interest-rate averages plotted in Fig. 13-4 is like the interest rate from a slightly different portfolio of bonds. These interest rates are all positively correlated because the same driving forces propel them together systematically.

SOLVED PROBLEM 13.7

Is it possible for some bonds' market rates of interest to fluctuate independently of the undiversifiable systematic marketwide fluctuations in interest rates? If so, why?

SOLUTION

At any given moment the market interest rate of a few individual bond issues are uncorrelated with the prevailing movements in market interest rates for reasons that are peculiar to the issuers of those particular bonds. The Chrysler Corporation, for example, experienced a rise in the market interest rates on its outstanding bonds from 17.68 percent in January 1980, up to 25.02 percent in April 1980, because the company was teetering on the verge of financial disaster. Investors demanded higher and higher interest rates to induce them to buy these bonds because they perceived Chrysler to be increasingly likely to default and fall into bankruptcy. During the same 4-month period almost all other market interest rates were falling sharply as the United States entered a recession that curtailed most borrower's demand for credit. Thus, Chrysler's market interest rates were uncorrelated with prevailing downward trends in market interest rates in early 1980. The unsystematic behavior of Chrysler Corporation's market interest rates during the first quarter of 1980 is an example of *diversifiable interest-rate risk.*

Major lawsuits, acts of God, and other traumatic events that affect only one or a few individual corporations can cause unsystematic interest-rate movements that are diversifiable.

Bonds with unique or unsystematic price fluctuations can be purchased and included in a highly diversified portfolio of other more normal bonds that were behaving in a systematic fashion. The *average* interest rate from a *diversified portfolio* of bonds will be positively correlated with the market's systematic interest-rate movements. Unsystematic interest-rate movements that are unique to individual issues of bonds will tend to be diversified away—that is why such unsystematic gyrations are called *diversifiable interest-rate risk.*

13.4 PURCHASING POWER RISK

Inflation (or a rise in general prices over time) seems to be the normal way of life in most countries today. However, when inflation takes place, financial assets (such as cash, stocks, and bonds) may lose their ability to command the same amount of real goods and services they did in the past. To put this another way, the *real rate of return* (observed returns less inflation) on financial assets may not adequately compensate the holder of financial assets for inflation.

An investor's real rate of return can be calculated with Eq. (*13.6*):

$$\text{rr} = \frac{1.0 + r}{1.0 + q} - 1 \tag{13.6}$$

where rr denotes the real rate of return, r is the nominal rate of return, and q equals the rate of inflation. Some people like to use a shortcut version of Eq. (*13.6*), Eq. (*13.7*), to quickly approximate nominal returns:

$$r = \text{rr} + q \tag{13.7}$$

EXAMPLE 13.2 Jo Ann James expects to earn a nominal rate of 10 percent on her investments next year. If the rate of inflation is expected to be 6 percent next year, what expected real rate of return will she earn?

For a quick approximation, Eq. (*13.7*) can be used.

$$\begin{aligned} \text{rr} &= r - q \qquad \text{(solving for rr)} \\ &= 10\% - 6\% = 4\% \end{aligned}$$

An exact answer can be determined with Eq. (*13.6*):

$$\text{rr} = \frac{1.10}{1.06} - 1 = 1.0377358 - 1 = .0377358 \quad \text{or} \quad 3.77\%$$

SOLVED PROBLEM 13.8

The CPI index went from 301 to 304 from the end of February to the end of March. Using this information, determine the rate of inflation for March. What annual rate of inflation is implied?

SOLUTION

$$\frac{\text{CPI}_t - \text{CPI}_{t-1}}{\text{CPI}_{t-1}} = \frac{304 - 301}{301} = .00997 \qquad \text{or } .997\% \text{ for the month of March}$$

$$(1 + .00997)^{12} - 1 = .12638 \quad \text{or} \quad 12.638\%$$

The annual rate of inflation implied by the monthly rate is 12.638 percent per annum.

SOLVED PROBLEM 13.9

Mary Hurt recently invested $100,000 in a 1-year CD at a rate of 8 percent. If Mary expects inflation to be 5 percent during the year, what real rate of return does she expect to earn? What is Mary's real after-tax return if she is in a 33 percent tax bracket?

SOLUTION

$$\text{rr} = \frac{1.0 + r}{1.0 + q} - 1 = \frac{1.08}{1.05} - 1 = 1.0285714 - 1$$

$$= .0285714 \qquad \text{or } 2.85714\% \text{ real return}$$

$$\text{After-tax nominal return} = 8\%(1 - \text{tax rate})$$

$$= .08(1 - .33) = 5.333\%$$

Substituting the after-tax nominal return (.0533) for r yields

$$\text{rr} = \frac{1.0 + .0533}{1.0 + .05} - 1 = 1.003171 - 1.0 = .003171$$

or a real after-tax return of .3171 of 1.0 percent.

SOLVED PROBLEM 13.10

Jean Brite has $50,000 to invest for the next 10 years. She is considering two investments: (*a*) a 7 percent municipal bond and (*b*) a 10 percent corporate bond. Both bonds pay annual interest. If the annual rate of inflation over the next 10 years is expected to be 4 percent, which investment should she make? Assume Jean is in a 25 percent tax bracket and that the bonds will be purchased at par and held for 10 years.

SOLUTION

The relevant return is the real after-tax return. Therefore Eq. (*13.6*) should be used and the after-tax return substituted for nominal return (r).

(*a*) With the municipal bond, the after-tax return is 7 percent because "munis" are not taxed. Using Eq. (*13.6*), its after-tax real return is

$$\text{rr} = \frac{1.0 + .07}{1.0 + .04} - 1 = 1.02885 - 1 = .02885 = 2.885\%$$

(*b*) With the corporate bond, the after-tax return is 10%(1 − tax rate) or 10%(1 − .25) equals 7.5%. Substituting 7.5% in Eq. (*13.6*) yields

$$\text{rr} = \frac{1.0 + .075}{1.0 + .04} - 1 = 1.03365 - 1 = .03365 = 3.365\%$$

On the basis of after-tax real return, the corporate bond should be purchased. However, this assumes that the two bonds are identical in every way but return. This, of course, may not be the case. The implied assumption in both cases is that the interim interest payments can be reinvested at the calculated return. The problem would be more complicated if the bonds were not selling at par value. The after-tax yield-to-maturity would be more difficult to calculate.

SOLVED PROBLEM 13.11

Match the following words and phrases to the definitions below:

1. Market risk
2. Management risk

3. Liquidity risk
4. Political risk
5. Callability risk
6. Convertibility Risk

Definitions to be matched to the terms above are listed below.

(A) That portion of an asset's total risk caused by discounts and selling commissions that must be given up to sell an asset quickly

(B) That portion of an asset's total variability of return caused by changes in the political environment (for instance, a new tax law) that affect the asset's market value

(C) Variability of return caused by the fact that a security may legally be redeemed before its maturity date

(D) Variability of return caused by the fact that one security (such as a convertible bond) may be converted to another security (such as common stock)

(E) Arises because alternating bull and bear market conditions tend to affect all securities systematically

(F) Arises when the people who manage an investment asset make errors that affect the asset's value.

SOLUTION

1. E 2. F 3. A 4. B 5. C 6. D

True-False Questions

13.1 An investor in coupon bonds who is trying to reduce his or her reinvestment rate risk can do so by switching to zero coupon bonds.

13.2 A bond selling at a market price that is deeply discounted from its face value is more inclined to have a long time until it reaches maturity rather than a short time until it matures because short-term bonds issued by healthy firms cannot sell for deeply discounted prices.

13.3 The market prices of U.S. Treasury bonds decline as market interest rates rise because present values always move inversely with their discount rate.

13.4 The expected rate of return for an investment should only be calculated with equally weighted historical rates of return.

13.5 The probability of an event occurring in the future can be accurately estimated by calculating the relative frequency that the event occurred in the past if the probability distribution of the event's outcome is stable through time.

13.6 AAA-grade bonds offer investors higher rates of interest than C-grade bonds.

13.7 A savings account earning a guaranteed 5 percent per annum in an FDIC-insured bank is a good example of an asset that is default-free.

13.8 A default-free long-term U.S. Treasury bond is an example of a totally riskless asset.

13.9 The expected value of the number of black dots that turns up when you toss an ordinary six-sided die (that is fair) is 3.0.

Multiple Choice Questions

13.1 How do the market prices of corporations that are involved in bankruptcy proceedings behave?

(*a*) The price of the firm's stock typically collapses and loses most of its market value if and only if the bankruptcy court declares the firm bankrupt and orders a liquidation auction.

(*b*) The price of the firm's stock typically collapses and loses most of its value before the default that led to the action in the bankruptcy court because stock prices tend to anticipate future events.

(*c*) The price of the firm's stock typically will not collapse until after an unsuccessful liquidation sale is completed and it become obvious that the proceeds from the liquidation auction are insufficient to re-pay the common stockholders for their investments.

(*d*) There is no typical pattern to the way that the price of the stock of a firm involved in a bankruptcy proceeding will behave.

13.2 Why do stock prices usually drop when news is released that the issuing corporation's earnings per share dropped a little?

(*a*) Because a reduction in a corporation's earnings means that the firm has less money with which to pay cash dividends and therefore the market fears a reduction in the corporation's future cash dividends.

(*b*) Because the stock market anticipates that a decreased level of earning power might be the first step on the pathway to default and perhaps even bankruptcy.

(*c*) The statement is false. Stock prices do not usually react to announcements about a corporation's current earnings.

(*d*) Both *a* and *b* are true.

13.3 Suppose you read a brand new research report published by a medical school at a major university concluding that cigarette smoking is definitely a cause of lung cancer and heart disease. As a bond quality analyst who specializes in the tobacco corporations at Standard & Poors, how should you react to this medical study?

(*a*) You should do nothing until you see evidence that the earnings of a tobacco firm have actually diminished.

(*b*) You should use the report as a basis for reconsidering whether to downgrade any of the tobacco firms that you think are already near the bottom of their quality rating categories.

(*c*) You should promptly set about to downgrade the quality rating of every tobacco firm by one grade based on the medical report's anticipated effects on the firm's in the industry.

(*d*) You should make a trip to the medical school that published the report and interview the medical researchers to find out their opinion about any additional medical effects of smoking that they might be investigating.

(*e*) Both *b* and *d* are true.

13.4 Interest-rate risk is defined by which of the following statements?

(*a*) Fluctuations in the coupon interest rates that occur from one bond issue to the next

(*b*) Systematic fluctuations in the market prices of bonds as their prices move inversely to the prevailing market interest rates

(*c*) The variability of return that investors experience as a result of fluctuations in market interest rates

(*d*) Both *a* and *b*

(*e*) All of the above

13.5 Assume that you are an investment adviser who has instructed one of your clients to invest their $100,000 in U.S. Treasury notes due to mature in 2 years. If your client becomes worried that a general increase in the level of interest rates will reduce the market value of his bond portfolio, what should you say to allay your client's fears?

(*a*) You could assuage your client's fears by claiming you foresee only stable interest rates ahead.

(*b*) You could instruct your client to liquidate their portfolio of Treasury notes and reinvest the proceeds in an FDIC-insured bank.

(*c*) Both *a* and *b* are true.

(*d*) You could tell your client not to worry because the market prices of short-term bonds do not fluctuate very much.

13.6 Assume you are an investment counselor and one of your clients reads something about interest-rate risk and is worried that if market interest rates declined her coupon interest income will likewise decline. Her bond investments have maturities ranging from 15 to 30 years. What advice is appropriate for this client?

(*a*) Tell the investor to liguidate her coupon-paying bonds and reinvest the money in zero coupon bonds.
(*b*) Tell your client not to worry, her coupon income will not vary until her coupon bonds mature in 15 to 30 years.
(*c*) Both *a* and *b* are true.
(*d*) The client need not worry if market interest rates are expected to rise because coupon rates vary inversely with market interest rates and therefore her coupon interest could increase.
(*e*) All the above are true.

13.7 Calculate the (1) expected rate of return, $E(r)$, and (2) the mode rate of return from the probability distribution of returns below for the Belfast Bearing Corporation's (BBC) common stock. (Note that the mode means the most frequently appearing return.)

FIVE POSSIBILITIES	RATES OF RETURN, *r*	PROBABILITY
$i = 5$	$-.5 = -50\%$	.1
$i = 4$	$-.1 = -10\%$	.25
$i = 3$	$.2 = 20\%$	.3
$i = 2$	$.5 = 50\%$	.25
$i = 1$	$.9 = 90\%$	.1
	Total	1.0

The expected rate of return and mode return for BBC is which one of the following?

(*a*) The $E(r)$ is 5 percent and mode is 9 percent.
(*b*) The $E(r)$ is 20 percent and mode is 20 percent.
(*c*) The $E(r)$ is 5 percent and mode is 5 percent.
(*d*) The $E(r)$ is 10 percent and mode is 9 percent.
(*e*) The $E(r)$ is 12 percent and mode is 9 percent.

13.8 Reconsider the probability distribution of returns for the Belfast Bearing Corporation's (BBC) from the preceding question. Calculate the variance and the standard deviation of BBC's rates of return.

i	RATES OF RETURN, *r*	PROBABILITY	PRODUCTS, $r \times$ PROB.	DEVIATIONS, $r - E(r)$	DEVIATIONS SQUARED $[r - E(r)]^2$	PRODUCTS, Pr. $\times [r - E(r)]^2$
$i = 5$	$-.5 = -50\%$	.1	$-.05$	$-.7$	.49	.049
$i = 4$	$-.1 = -10\%$	.25	$-.025$	$-.3$	.09	.0225
$i = 3$	$.2 = 20\%$	.3	.06	0	0	0
$i = 2$	$.5 = 50\%$	.25	.125	.3	.09	.0225
$i = 1$	$.9 = 90\%$	.1	.09			
	Totals	1.0	$E(r) = .20 = 20\%$			

(*a*) BBC's variance of returns is .143 and its standard deviation is .378.
(*b*) BBC's standard deviation of returns is .378 and its variance is .143.
(*c*) BBC's standard deviation of returns is .307 and its variance is .094.
(*d*) BBC's standard deviation of returns is 1.56 and its variance is 2.433.

13.9 Risk is best described by which one of the following statements?

(*a*) The phrase *total risk* is synonymous with the *variability of return* from an asset.
(*b*) Bond quality ratings essentially measure the probability that an issue of bonds falls into default.
(*c*) Although U.S. Treasury bonds are free from default risk they nevertheless contain substantial amounts of interest-rate risk.
(*d*) Both *a* and *b* are true.
(*e*) All the above are true.

Answers

True-False

13.1. T 13.2. T 13.3. T 13.4. F 13.5. T 13.6. F 13.7. T 13.8. F 13.9. F

Multiple Choice

13.1. b 13.2. d 13.3. e 13.4. e 13.5. d 13.6. b 13.7. b 13.8. a 13.9. e

Chapter 14

Bond Valuation

14.1 BOND VALUES

The value of a bond is simply the present value of all the security's future cash flows, as shown below.[1]

$$\text{Present value} = \frac{\text{coupon}_1}{(1 + \text{YTM})^1} + \frac{\text{coupon}_2}{(1 + \text{YTM})^2} + \cdots + \frac{\text{coupon}_T + \text{face value}}{(1 + \text{YTM})^T} \tag{14.1}$$

The four terms that appear on the right-hand side of the present-value equation (*15.1*) are discussed below.

(1) *Market interest rate:* The discount rate, or interest rate or yield-to-maturity, is a market interest rate that constantly changes. The bond's *yield-to-maturity* is represented by the symbol YTM. The YTM is the discount rate that equates all the bond's future cash flows with the current market price of the bond.[2]

(2) *Face value, F:* The bond's face value (or principal value) is printed on the bond and is invariant throughout the bond's life.

(3) *Coupon:* The dollar amount of a bond's coupon interest payments equals the product of the coupon interest rate, denoted i, and the face value, F. Symbolically, coupon $= iF$.

(4) The number of time periods left until the bond matures and the *terminal* payment occurs is denoted T.

SOLVED PROBLEM 14.1

What is the value of a $1,000 bond with an 8 percent coupon rate, 3 years before maturity? The YTM is 10 percent.

SOLUTION

$$iF = (.08)(\$1{,}000) = \$80 \qquad T = 3 \qquad \text{and} \qquad \text{YTM} = .10$$

Substituting the above values into Eq. (*14.1*) yields

$$\begin{aligned}\text{Present value} &= \frac{\$80}{(1 + .10)^1} + \frac{\$80}{(1 + .10)^2} + \frac{\$80 + \$1000}{(1 + .10)^3} \\ &= \$72.727 + \$66.116 + \$811.420 = \$950.26\end{aligned}$$

SOLVED PROBLEM 14.2

The Palatin Paper Package (PPP) Corporation's $1,000 bonds that pay a coupon rate of 8 percent in a single annual payment and mature in 20 years are selling for a current market price of $1,050. What does an investor in these bonds earn in terms of (*a*) yield-to-maturity (YTM), (*b*) current yield (y), and (*c*) nominal yield or nominal interest rate (i).

[1]This chapter presumes a knowledge of the present-value concept that was introduced in Chap. 4.
[2]See Chap. 5 for more information about YTM.

SOLUTION

We have $i = 8.0\% = .08$, $T = 20$ years, $F = \$1{,}000$, $iF = \$80$ annual coupon and YTM is unknown.

(*a*) The formula for the approximate yield-to-maturity (AYTM) from a bond is shown as Eq. (*14.2*) below.

$$\frac{[(\text{Face value}) - (\text{purchase price})]/(\text{years to maturity}) + (\text{coupon})}{[(\text{Purchase price}) + (\text{face value})]/2} = \text{AYTM}$$

$$\frac{(\text{Average annual price change}) + (\text{annual coupon})}{\text{Average amount of funds invested}} = \text{AYTM} \tag{14.2}$$

$$\frac{[(\$1{,}000 - \$1{,}050)/(20\text{ years})] + \$80}{(\$1{,}050 + \$1{,}000)/2} = \text{AYTM}$$

$$\frac{(\$2.50\text{ per year price deprec.}) + (\$80\text{ coupon})}{\$1{,}025} = \frac{\$77.50}{\$1{,}025} = .0756$$

The approximate yield-to-maturity (AYTM) from the PPP bonds is AYTM = 7.56 percent. More exact methods that utilize bond tables or a computer will indicate that the exact yield-to-maturity is YTM = 7.51 percent. The error of 5 (AYTM − YTM = 7.56% − 7.51% = .05) basis points results from the approximation formula employed above [Eq. (*14.2*)].

(*b*) The current yield (y) from the PPP bond is

$$y = \frac{\text{coupon interest per year}}{\text{purchase price for the bond}} = \frac{\$80}{\$1{,}050} = .07619 = 7.62\%$$

(*c*) The nominal interest rate is synonymous with the coupon interest rate, $i = 8.0$ percent in this case.

SOLVED PROBLEM 14.3

(*a*) Determine the price of a $1,000 zero coupon bond with a YTM of 16 percent and 10 years until maturity.

(*b*) What is the YTM of this bond if its price is $200?

SOLUTION

(*a*)

$$\text{Price} = \frac{\text{face falue}}{(1 + \text{YTM})^{10}} = \frac{\$1{,}000}{(1 + .16)^{10}} = \$226.68$$

(*b*)

$$\left(\frac{\text{Face value}}{\text{Bond value}}\right)^{1/T} - 1 = \text{YTM}$$

$$\left(\frac{\$1{,}000}{\$200}\right)^{1/10} - 1 = \text{YTM}$$

$$(5)^{.1} - 1 = \text{YTM} = 17.46\%$$

Note that YTM can easily be determined on a financial calculator. For example, with Texas Instruments' BA 35, store $1,000 in FV, 10 in N, and $200 in PV. Then, to compute push CPT %i for the YTM (17.46%).

Semiannual Coupon Payments

Semiannual coupon payments are more common than annual coupons. Therefore the present value of a bond model must be modified slightly to accommodate the semiannual coupon payments.

SOLVED PROBLEM 14.4

(*a*) What is the value of a $1,000 bond that is paying $3\frac{1}{2}$ percent annual coupon rate in annual payments over 10 years until it matures if its yield-to-maturity is YTM = 6.0% = .06?

(*b*) What is the bond's present value if the coupons are paid semiannually?

SOLUTION

(*a*) We have YTM = 6.0% = .06, i = 3.5% = .035, and F = $1,000. The dollars of interest per year paid on the bond is i times F, that is, 3.5% × $1,000 or $35 per year. The present value of these annual cash flows is calculated in Eq. (*14.1a*).

$$p_0 = \sum_{t=1}^{T} \frac{iF}{(1 + \text{YTM})^t} + \frac{F}{(1 + \text{YTM})^T} \tag{14.1a}$$

$$= \sum_{t=1}^{T=10 \text{ years}} \frac{\$35}{(1 + .06)^t} + \frac{\$1{,}000}{(1 + .06)^{10}} = \$816.00$$

(*b*) Converting annual compounding [Eq. (*14.1a*)] to the semiannual compounding model for the same bond results in Eq. (*14.3*) below. The bond's $35 annual coupon payments must be halved to get the semiannual coupon payments of $17.50. The bond's compounding period is 6 months. The appropriate market rate of return or discount rate for semiannual coupons is half of the bond's YTM = 6 percent per annum, or YTM/2 = 6.0%/2 = 3.0% = .03 percent per 6-month period. The cash flows in the tth time period, denoted c_t, are c_t = $17.50 for the first $t = 1, 2, \ldots, 19$ half years plus c_{20} = $1,017.50 when the bond matures at the end of 10 years.

$$p_0 = \sum_{t=1}^{2T} \frac{.5iF}{(1 + \text{YTM}/2)^t} + \frac{F}{(1 + \text{YTM}/2)^{2T}} \tag{14.3}$$

$$= \sum_{t=1}^{20 \text{ half years}} \frac{\$17.50}{(1 + .03)^t} + \frac{\$1{,}000}{(1 + .03)^{20}} = \$814.032$$

The present value of $814.032 will be the *asked price* for the $3\frac{1}{2}$ percent coupon bond maturing in twenty 6-month periods. Note that using the more frequent compounding interval reduced the present value of the bond by $1.968 ($816.00 − $814.032) approximately.

Accrued Coupon Interest

Accrued interest is interest that has been earned by an investor but that has not yet been paid to that investor. Bond buyers pay bond sellers accrued interest whenever a bond is purchased on a date that is not a scheduled coupon interest payment date. Thus, if a bond were sold between its semiannual interest payment dates, the purchaser should pay the market price of the bond plus the appropriate fraction of the accrued coupon interest earned but not yet received by the party selling the bond.

SOLVED PROBLEM 14.5

What is the purchase price for a bond that is paying a 6 percent annual coupon rate in semiannual payments if its YTM = 10.0% = .10 and it has 2 years and 10 months from its purchase date until its maturity? What is the accrued interest? Assume the bond is traded in a year of 366 days when calculating the accrued interest.

SOLUTION

Since this bond has 2 months short of 3 full years until it matures, we must first (Step one) calculate its present value on the next interest payment date, which is 2.5 years until maturity. After the present value of a 2.5-year bond has been calculated, (Step two) we will add the interest payment received on that date to the price of the bond. (Step three) Next, the value determined in Step two should be discounted back four months to the purchase date. Figure 14-1 should help clarify the time dimension of this problem.

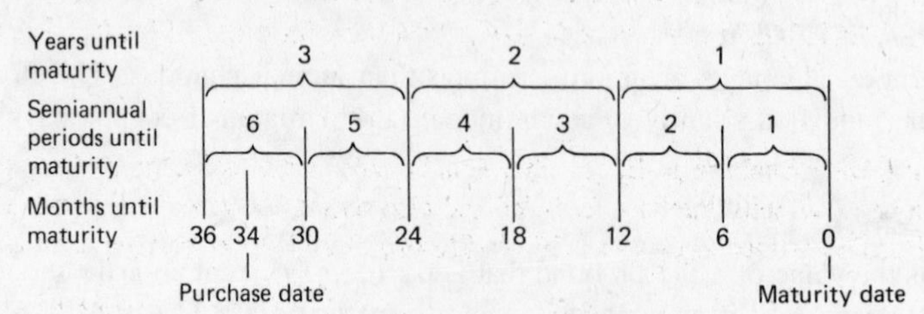

Fig. 14-1

Step one: Use Eq. (*14.3*) to calculate the present value of a bond that has 2.5 years until it matures and pays semiannual interest coupons.

$$p_0 = \sum_{t=1}^{2T} \frac{.5iF}{(1 + \text{YTM}/2)^t} + \frac{F}{(1 + \text{YTM}/2)^{2T}} \tag{14.3}$$

For this case we have $T = 2.5$ years, so $2T = 5$ semiannual periods; the yield-to-maturity is 10 percent so the semiannual discount rate is $\text{YTM}/2 = 10\%/2 = 5\% = .05$; and the coupon payment is $.5iF = (.5)(.06)(\$1{,}000) = \$30$ semiannually.

$$p_0 = \sum_{t=1}^{5 \text{ periods}} \frac{\$30}{(1 + .05)^t} + \frac{\$1{,}000}{(1 + .05)^5}$$

$$= (\$30)(.9524) + (\$30)(.9070) + (\$30)(.8638) + (\$30)(.8227) + (\$30)(.7835) + (\$1{,}000)(.7835)$$

$$= (\$30)(4.3295) + (\$1{,}000)(.7835) = \$129.89 + \$783.50 = \$913.39$$

Step two: The \$30 coupon is added to \$913.39. The sum is \$943.39.

Step three: The value \$943.39 is discounted back four months to the purchase date.

$$\frac{\$943.39}{(1.05)^{2/3}} = \frac{\$943.39}{1.0331} = \$913.16$$

The bond's price, including accrued interest, is \$913.16. Calculate the accrued interest for 2 months. There are 183 days (half of 366 days) between the semiannual coupon payments; thus, the denominator of the first term in Eq. (14.4*a*) below is 183 days. The 2 months that have passed are assumed to be the first 61 days of the partially elapsed semiannual (183 day) coupon payment period; thus, the numerator is 61 days.

$$\frac{\left(\begin{array}{c}\text{Days since last}\\ \text{interest payment}\end{array}\right)}{\left(\begin{array}{c}\text{Days between last}\\ \text{and next coupon}\\ \text{payments}\end{array}\right)} \times \left(\begin{array}{c}\text{coupon}\\ \text{interest}\\ \text{payment}\end{array}\right) = \left(\begin{array}{c}\text{accrued}\\ \text{interest}\end{array}\right) \tag{14.4}$$

$$\frac{61 \text{ days}}{183 \text{ days}} \times \left(\begin{array}{c}\text{Semiannual}\\ \text{coupon of}\\ \$30.00\end{array}\right) = .333 \times \$30.00 = \$10.00 \tag{14.4a}$$

Note that the days in Eq. (*14.4*) are counted from the coupons' delivery dates instead of the trade date or some other date.

Yield-to-Call

Sometimes the issuer of a bond has the option to call (or redeem) the bond before it reaches maturity. This is likely to occur when the coupon interest rate on similar new bonds is substantially below the coupon interest on existing bonds because the corporation can save money on future interest payments. When a bond has an excellent chance of being called, an investor may want to calculate the yield-to-call for the bond. This can be accomplished by modifying the basic bond equation, Eq. (*14.1*), in the following manner: T would now equal the number of time periods until the bond is called and face value would now be the call value.

SOLVED PROBLEM 14.6

The Oak Grove Corporation has a 12 percent semiannual bond issue with $F = \$1{,}000$ that matures in 15 years but is callable in 6 years at \$1,200. If the current price of the bond is \$900, determine its *yield-to-call* (YTC).

SOLUTION

Since this is a semiannual issue, Eq. (*14.3*) should be modified to solve for YTC by setting T equal to the number of semiannual periods until the bond is called and also setting the value of F equal to the call price. YTM is now equal to YTC. The coupon is equal to $.5(.12)(\$1{,}000) = \$60$. After making these changes, Eq. (*14.3*) becomes

$$\$900 = \frac{\$60}{(1 + \text{YTC}/2)^1} + \frac{\$60}{(1 + \text{YTC}/2)^2} + \cdots + \frac{\$60 + \$1{,}200}{(1 + \text{YTC}/2)^{12}}$$

Solving by trial and error, the exact answer is 16.77 percent. This is the rate of return that will make the present value of the bond's expected cash flows equal the bond's price of $900.[3]

The bond's principal amount, its coupon interest payments, and the dates of the cash flows are all printed on the bond and in the bond issue's indenture contract—they are all public knowledge and cannot be changed. The only difference of opinion likely to arise in valuing a bond is in selecting the appropriate interest rate to use for discounting the bond's cash flows.

At any given time, different discount interest rates are appropriate for finding the present value of different bond issues. Different discount rates exist because the yield-to-maturity (YTM) used to find the present value of a bond is a *risk-adjusted discount rate*. The riskiness of bond issues differs for several reasons. First, bond issues from disparate issuers usually involve unequal levels of *default risk* because the issuing firms have different degrees of financial health. Standard & Poors and Moody's bond quality ratings provide default-risk measures. Second, the same bond issuer can have several outstanding bond issues that differ in riskiness because of different *protective provisions* in the indenture contract that governs each issue. And third, the riskiness of various bond issues differs because of different levels of *interest-rate risk*. The next section shows how to measure a bond's interest-rate risk.

14.2 BOND DURATION

Macaulay's duration (MD hereafter) is the average time it takes to receive the cash flows expected from a bond or another asset. Equation (*14.5*) can be used to calculate Macaulay's duration for a bond.

$$\text{MD} = \frac{\sum_{t=1}^{T} [c_t t/(1 + \text{YTM})^t] + FT/(1 + \text{YTM})^T}{v_0} \tag{14.5}$$

In Eq. (*14.5*), c_t is the coupon to be received at time t, F is the face value of the bond, and v_0 is the present value (or equivalently market price) of the bond.

Table 14.1 shows the relationship between Macaulay's duration (MD) and years-to-maturity for semiannual bonds of various coupon rates that have YTM of 9 percent. A bond's duration is less than its years-to-maturity for coupon bonds. MD equals T for zero coupon bonds. MD also increases at a decreasing rate as maturity increases for bonds selling at par or above. For discount bonds, note that duration will eventually decline. The relationship between MD and years-to-maturity is shown graphically in Fig. 14-2 for various bonds.

Table 14.1 Macaulay's Duration (in Years) for Bond Yielding 9 Percent (Semiannual Compounding)

Years to Maturity	Coupon Rates			
	3%	6%	9%	12%
5	4.622	4.345	4.134	3.968
10	8.249	7.347	6.797	6.426
20	12.272	10.437	9.615	9.148
50	12.[illegible]91	11.703	11.469	11.350
70	11.832	11.648	11.587	11.586
100	11.366	11.616	11.609	11.606
∞	12.111	12.111	12.111	12.111

The relationship between a change in the price of a bond relative to a change in its YTM is

$$\frac{dP}{d(\text{YTM})} = -\left(\frac{1}{1 + \text{YTM}}\right) \times \text{MD} \times P \tag{14.6}$$

[3]This can be solved on a financial calculator. With the BA 35, store $60 in PMT, $1,200 in FV, $900 in PV, and 12 in N. Then, compute by pushing CPT %i for an answer of 8.3836 percent. Since this is the semiannual rate, it should be multiplied by 2 in order to determine the annual rate of 16.77 percent. The YTM for a bond could be determined in a similar manner. However, the major difference is that for a YTM calculation, *F*, which is typically $1,000, should be stored in FV.

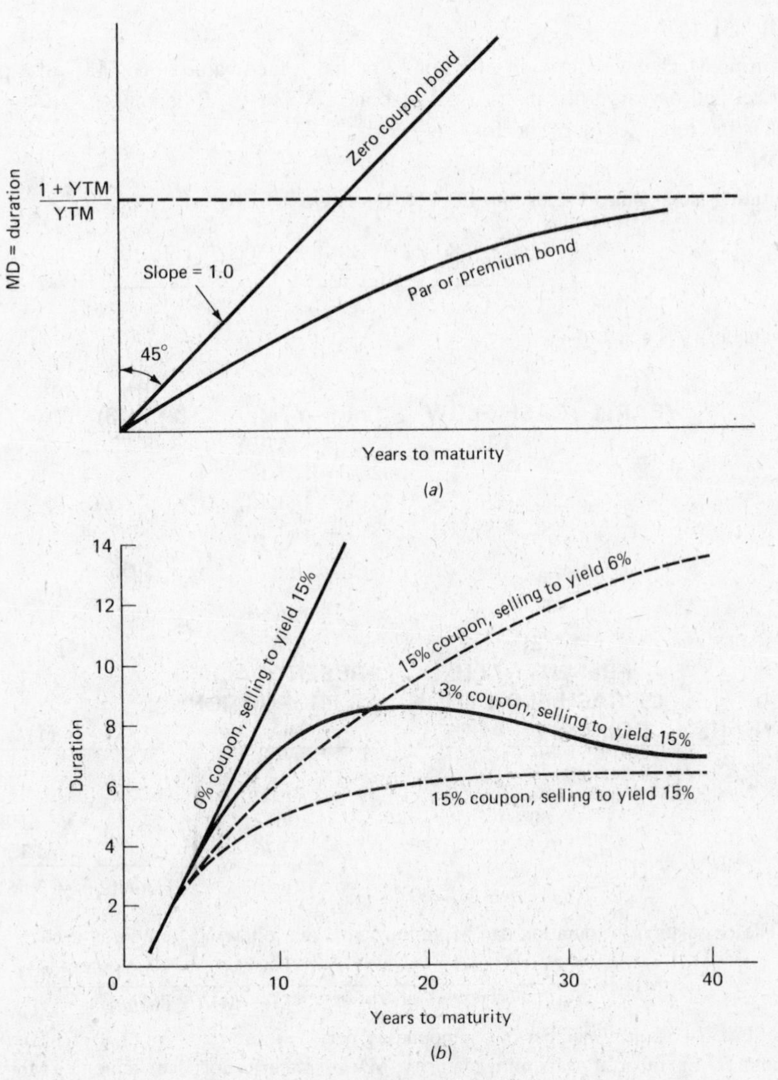

Fig. 14-2 (*a*) Duration and term to maturity for premium, par, and zero coupon bonds. (*b*) Duration versus term to maturity for various bonds. (From *The Revolution in Techniques for Managing Bond Portfolios,* by permission of the Association for Investment Management and Research, Charlottesville, Virginia, 1990, pp. 42.)

where P is the bond's current price and $dP/d(\text{YTM})$ indicates the change in price with respect to the change in YTM. The term

$$\text{MMD} = \frac{\text{MD}}{1 + \text{YTM}}$$

is usually referred to as *modified duration* (MMD) for a bond. By rearranging Eq. (*14.6*) and using the definition of modified duration, the inverse relationship between a bond's price and YTM can be expressed as follows:

$$\frac{dP}{P} = -(\text{modified duration}) \times d(\text{YTM}) \tag{14.7}$$

When using Eq. (*14.7*), it should be noted that $d(\text{YTM})$ is a change in yield as a percent (e.g., a YTM that goes from 9.5 percent to 10 percent is a .5 percent change or .005 decimally). Equation (*14.7*) is an approximation, and the smaller the change in a bond's YTM, the better the approximation.

SOLVED PROBLEM 14.7

(*a*) Determine Macaulay's duration of a bond that has a face value of $1,000, an 8 percent annual coupon rate, and 4 years until maturity. The bond's YTM is 10 percent.

(*b*) What is the modified duration for this bond?

SOLUTION

(*a*) Substituting the assumed values into Eq. (*14.5*) yields

$$\mathrm{MD} = \frac{\sum_{t=1}^{4} [\$80t/(1 + .10)^t] + \$1{,}000T/(1 + .10)^4}{v_0}$$

The value of v_0 is equal to

(1) YEAR, t	(2) CASH FLOW	(3) $1/(1 + \mathrm{YTM})^t$	(4) (2) × (3)
1	$80	$.9091 = 1/(1.10)^1$	$ 72.73
2	80	$.8264 = 1/(1.10)^2$	66.11
3	80	$.7513 = 1/(1.10)^3$	60.10
4	$80 + $1,000	$.6830 = 1/(1.10)^4$	737.64
			v_0 = $936.58

(1) YEAR, t	(2) PRESENT VALUE OF CASH FLOW FROM COLUMN (4) ABOVE	(3) PRESENT VALUE AS PROPORTION OF v_0	(4) (3) × (1)
1	$ 72.73	.0777	.0777
2	66.11	.0706	.1412
3	60.10	.0642	.1926
4	737.64	.7876	3.1504
		1.0	Duration = 3.5619

The calculation for duration can be simplified if the following formula is used:

$$\mathrm{MD} = \frac{c[(Z)^{(T)(m)+1} - Z - (\mathrm{YTM})(T)] + (\mathrm{MV})(T)(m)(\mathrm{YTM}/m)^2}{c(\mathrm{YTM}/m)[(Z)^{(T)(m)} - 1] + \mathrm{MV}(\mathrm{YTM}/m)^2} \qquad (14.8)$$

In Eq. (*14.8*), m = number of compounding periods in a year, $Z = (1 + \mathrm{YTM}/m)$, MD = Macaulay's duration, T = number of years until maturity, MV = maturity (or face) value, YTM = yield-to-maturity at an annual rate, and c = coupon per period.

If Eq. (*14.8*) is used, the above calculation is as follows:

$$\mathrm{MD} = \frac{80[(1.10)^{(4)(1)+1} - 1.10 - (.10)(4)] + (1{,}000)(4)(1)(.10)^2}{80(.10)[(1.1)^4 - 1] + 1{,}000(.10)^2}$$

$$= \frac{48.8408}{13.7128} = 3.5617$$

The tiny difference between this answer and the previous answer is a rounding error.

(*b*)
$$\mathrm{MMD} = \frac{\mathrm{MD}}{1 + \mathrm{YTM}} = \frac{3.5617}{1.10} = 3.238$$

SOLVED PROBLEM 14.8

If the YTM for the bond in Solved Problem 14.7 goes from 10 percent to 11 percent, determine the new price for the bond with the modified duration equation.

SOLUTION

$$\frac{dP}{P} = -\mathrm{MMD} \times d(\mathrm{YTM}) \qquad (14.7)$$

$$dP = -\mathrm{MMD} \times d(\mathrm{YTM}) \times P$$

From Solved Problem 14.7, modified duration was determined to be 3.238, and v_0 (bond's current price) was calculated as $936.58.

$$dP = -3.238 \times .01 \times \$936.58 = -\$30.33$$

The new price is $936.58 − $30.33 = $906.25.

This is a linear approximation to a curvilinear function. The actual price turns out to be $906.93 if the present-value formula is used.

SOLVED PROBLEM 14.9

The Jones Company recently issued a $1,000 12 percent semiannual bond with 20 years to maturity. (*a*) What will be the price of the bond if the market rate of interest is 14 percent? (*b*) Determine the bond's Macaulay's duration when it was issued and (*c*) 2 years later.

SOLUTION

(*a*) The bond's price can be calculated with Eq. (*14.3*):

$$\begin{aligned} p_0 &= \frac{\$60}{(1+.07)^1} + \frac{\$60}{(1+.07)^2} + \cdots + \frac{\$60 + \$1{,}000}{(1+.07)^{40}} \\ &= \sum_{t=1}^{40} \frac{\$60}{(1+.07)^t} + \frac{\$1{,}000}{(1+.07)^{40}} \\ &= \$60 \times \text{PVA}(i, T) + \$1{,}000 \times \text{PV}(i, t) \end{aligned}$$

where $i = 7$ and $t = T = 40$. (For more information on present value, see Chap. 4.)

$$\begin{aligned} p_0 &= \$60 \times \text{PVA}(7, 40) + \$1{,}000 \times \text{PV}(7, 40) \\ &= \$60 \times 13.3317 \quad + \$1{,}000 \times .0668 \\ &= \$799.90 + \$66.80 = \$866.70 \end{aligned}$$

(*b*) Equation (*14.8*) could be used to reduce the needed computations:

$$\begin{aligned} \text{MD} &= \frac{\$60[(1+.07)^{41} - 1.07 - 2.8] + (\$1{,}000)(20)(2)(.0049)}{(\$60)(.07)[(1.07)^{40} - 1] + (\$1{,}000)(.0049)} \\ &= 14.548 \text{ semiannual periods} \quad \text{or} \quad \frac{14.548}{2} = 7.274 \text{ years} \end{aligned}$$

(*c*) Two years after issue the duration is

$$\begin{aligned} \text{MD} &= \frac{\$60[(1.07)^{37} - 1.07 - 2.52] + (\$1{,}000)(18)(2)(.0049)}{(\$60)(.07)[1.07)^{36} - 1] + (\$1{,}000)(.0049)} \\ &= 14.264 \text{ semiannual periods} \quad \text{or} \quad \frac{14.264}{2} = 7.132 \text{ years} \end{aligned}$$

SOLVED PROBLEM 14.10

Mr. Ed Smith will be making a car payment of $316 per month for the next 4 years. If the rate of interest on Ed's loan is 1 percent per month, what is the duration of the loan?

SOLUTION

Equation (*14.8*) should be used. In this situation, YTM = .12 (.01 × 12), $c = \$316$, $T = 4$, MV = 0, and $m = 12$.

$$\begin{aligned} \text{MD} &= \frac{\$316[(1.01)^{49} - 1.01 - (.12)(4)] + (0)(4)(12)(.01)^2}{(\$316)(.01)[(1.01)^{48} - 1] + (0)(.01)^2} \\ &= 22.596 \text{ months} \quad \text{or} \quad \frac{22.596}{12} = 1.883 \text{ years} \end{aligned}$$

SOLVED PROBLEM 14.11

Calculate Macaulay's duration for the following semiannual bonds:

BOND	COUPON, %	TIME TO MATURITY, YEARS	YTM, %
QQ	12	18	12
RR	16	20	14
SS	0	15	12
TT	14	17	15

SOLUTION

Using Eq. (*14.8*), we obtained the following results:

BOND	C	MV	YTM	T	m	MD, YEARS
QQ	$60	$1,000	.12	18	2	7.75
RR	80	1,000	.14	20	2	7.02
SS	0	1,000	.12	15	2	15
TT	70	1,000	.15	17	2	6.62

True-False Questions

14.1 Duration for a zero coupon bond is less than its term to maturity.

14.2 Longer-term bonds are almost always more volatile in terms of price than short-term bonds for a given change in interest rates.

14.3 Bond price volatility is directly related to the bond's coupon.

14.4 Duration for a coupon-paying bond is always less than its term to maturity.

14.5 For any given maturity, bond price movements that result from an equal absolute decrease or increase in the yield-to-maturity are symmetrical.

14.6 There is a direct relationship between a bond's coupon and duration.

14.7 As a bond's YTM increases, if other things are held constant, its duration decreases.

14.8 The duration for a perpetual bond is infinite.

14.9 When a bond is selling at a discount, its YTM exceeds the coupon rate.

14.10 When a bond's YTM equals its coupon rate, the bond's price is less than par value.

Multiple Choice Questions

14.1 A 10 percent semiannual bond with a YTM of 12 percent and 10 years to maturity has a price equal to
(*a*) $1,051.65
(*b*) $1,159.88
(*c*) $885.30
(*d*) $888.89
(*e*) $955.41

14.2 The duration for the bond in Problem 14.1 is
(*a*) 5 years
(*b*) 4.54 years

(*c*) 6.31 years
(*d*) 6 years
(*e*) 3.89 years

14.3 The price of the bond in Problem 14.1 after 2 years, assuming everything else stays the same, is (*Hint:* There will be 8 years until maturity.)
(*a*) $1,130.55
(*b*) $935
(*c*) $757
(*d*) $868
(*e*) $898.94

14.4 The YTM for a zero coupon bond selling at $235 with 10 years to maturity, if it is compounded annually, is
(*a*) 14.25
(*b*) 16.05
(*c*) 17.15
(*d*) 15.58
(*e*) 13.58

14.5 The YTM for a 14 percent noncallable semiannual bond with 10 years to maturity and a market price of $900 is
(*a*) 16.04 percent
(*b*) 14.69 percent
(*c*) 13.45 percent
(*d*) 12.56 percent
(*e*) 17.34 percent

14.6 Determine the duration for the bond in Problem 14.5.
(*a*) 6.89 years
(*b*) 5.44 years
(*c*) 7.45 years
(*d*) 5.96 years
(*e*) 6.52 years

14.7 Determine the yield-to-call (YTC) for a 15 percent coupon bond with a current price of $950 that is callable in 7 years at $1,100 and pays coupons every 6 months.
(*a*) 15.05 percent
(*b*) 17.05 percent
(*c*) 14.25 percent
(*d*) 16.75 percent
(*e*) 16.25 percent

14.8 Determine the duration for the bond in Problem 14.7 if it is called after 7 years.
(*a*) 5.25 years
(*b*) 4.54 years
(*c*) 6.05 years
(*d*) 4.75 years
(*e*) 5.52 years

14.9 Determine the price of a $1,000 face value zero coupon bond with a YTM of 14 percent and 20 years until maturity if it is compounded annually.
(*a*) $72.76
(*b*) $89.08
(*c*) $67.78
(*d*) $112.67
(*e*) $90.87

14.10 Determine the duration for a 12 percent coupon bond that pays coupons semiannually for 30 years and has a YTM of 15 percent.
(*a*) 8.09 years
(*b*) 9.78 years
(*c*) 7.78 years
(*d*) 7.15 years
(*e*) 8.56 years

14.11 A bond's duration measures which one of the following?
(*a*) The time structure of a bond's cash flows
(*b*) The bond's interest-rate risk
(*c*) Both *a* and *b* above
(*d*) The default risk of the bond issue
(*e*) None of the above

14.12 If the market rate of interest falls, a coupon-paying bond will
(*a*) Decrease in value
(*b*) Experience a decrease in duration
(*c*) Experience an increase in duration
(*d*) None of the above
(*e*) Both *a* and *b* above

14.13 A bond's *reinvestment rate risk:*
(*a*) Refers to the problem of being able to purchase another bond with the same or higher YTM when the existing bond matures or is called
(*b*) Is the risk of not being able to reinvest the coupons of a bond at the bond's YTM
(*c*) Is the same as marketability risk
(*d*) Both *a* and *b*
(*e*) None of the above

14.14 If you expect a large decline in interest rates, which of the following investments should you choose?
(*a*) Money market fund
(*b*) Low-coupon short-term bond
(*c*) High-coupon short-term bond
(*d*) Long-term zero coupon bond
(*e*) Short-term zero coupon bond

14.15 Bonds with higher coupons, other things being the same,
(*a*) Have more interest-rate risk than bonds with smaller coupons
(*b*) Have less interest-rate risk than bonds with smaller coupons
(*c*) Have higher duration than smaller-coupon bonds
(*d*) Have lower duration than smaller-coupon bonds
(*e*) Both *b* and *d*

Answers

True-False

14.1. F 14.2. T 14.3. F 14.4. T 14.5. F 14.6. F 14.7. T 14.8. F 14.9. T
14.10. F

Multiple Choice

14.1. c 14.2. c 14.3. e 14.4. d 14.5. a 14.6. b 14.7. b 14.8. b 14.9. a
14.10. d 14.11. c 14.12. c 14.13. d 14.14. d 14.15. e

Chapter 15

Bond Portfolio Management

15.1 THE LEVEL OF MARKET INTEREST RATES

Numerous interest rates exist and they vary continuously. The market rate of interest (or nominal rate) for a security can be expressed symbolically as follows:

$$\text{Nominal interest rate } (r) = \text{real interest rate (rr)} + \text{expected rate of inflation } (q) + \text{various risk premiums (rp)} \qquad (15.1)$$

The real rate of interest is the rate at which physical capital is expected to reproduce in an economy. Since suppliers of funds expect to be compensated for inflation, the expected rate of inflation over the life of the asset should be added to the real rate. Adjustments to a bond's yield-to-maturity (YTM) are also made for the following risk factors:

(1) *Default risk.* This is the risk of bankruptcy and, therefore, the inability of a corporation to pay the contractual interest on debt.

(2) *Liquidity risk.* The risk of not being able to sell an asset quickly at full value.

(3) *Interest-rate risk.* The fluctuation in price, especially for long-term bonds, from changes in the interest rate. Also included is reinvestment rate risk.

(4) *Foreign-exchange risk.* The risk of holding bonds in a foreign currency.

Some other factors affecting YTM are taxes and issue characteristics. Municipal bond coupons are exempt from federal taxes and, therefore, have lower interest rates than taxable corporate bonds. Special features in a bond's indenture such as an embedded call or put can influence its yield. (For more information on risk factors, see Chap. 13.)

SOLVED PROBLEM 15.1

Currently, T-bills with a maturity of 13 weeks have a YTM of 7.5 percent. On the other hand, long-term T-bonds have yields of about 8.5 percent. Using Eq. (*15.1*), explain why these returns differ.

SOLUTION

Two factors given in Eq. (*15.1*) could account for the differences. They are (1) inflationary expectations and (2) interest-rate risk. Since long-term bonds have several more years to maturity than T-bills, expectations for higher rates of inflation in the future could account for some of the differential. In addition, long-term bonds have more interest-rate risk than short-term bonds and, therefore, a greater risk premium is required.

SOLVED PROBLEM 15.2

Long-term BBB-rated corporate bonds yield more that AAA-rated corporate bonds with the same maturity. Explain in terms of Eq. (*15.1*).

SOLUTION

If we assume both issues have identical characteristics, then the main reason the BBB-rated bonds have a higher return is greater default risk than the AAA-rated bonds.

SOLVED PROBLEM 15.3

Several times in U.S. financial history short-term securities such as commercial paper have had a higher return than long-term bonds (both T-bonds and corporates). Explain how this could happen with Eq. (*15.1*).

SOLUTION

The main factor must be decreasing inflationary expectations. If the rate of inflation is expected to fall in the future this makes the expected average rate of inflation smaller for longer-term bonds than short-term securities. For example, the lower rate of inflationary expectations more than offsets the higher default risk and interest-rate risk associated with long-term corporate bonds.

15.2 YIELD SPREADS

Yield spreads are the differences in yields between risky bonds and default-free U.S. Treasury bonds of similar maturity. Equation (*15.2*) defines the yield spread for the *t*th time period:

$$(\text{Yield spread})_t = (\text{yield on a risky bond})_t - (\text{yield on a U.S. Treasury bond})_t \qquad (15.2)$$

For example, suppose an AAA-grade corporate bond's current YTM is 11 percent while the YTM on a similar T-bond is 9 percent. Equation (*15.2*) suggests the yield spread for the pair of bonds is 2 percent or 200 basis points.

Yield spreads tend to vary over the business cycle. They are larger at business troughs than at peaks, and yield spreads take place in a predictable fashion. As a result, bond traders and investors who can act quickly when yield spreads appear to be different from normal can make profits.

EXAMPLE 15.1 Jeff Hand, an astute bond trader, noted that the yield spread between a BBB-rated corporate bond issue and a similar T-bond issue was 250 basis points. However, according to Jeff's careful analysis, the normal yield spread for the two bonds for this stage of the business cycle should be 200 basis points. Jeff feels that he can profit from the abnormal yield spread.

In order for the yield spread to become normal it must decrease. For this to happen, either the BBB corporate bonds must increase in price (yields fall) or the T-bonds must fall in price (yields increase). Therefore, Jeff should purchase the BBB bonds. If, as is likely, the BBB bonds increase in price, he would profit.

SOLVED PROBLEM 15.4

Assume, the following yields currently exist for the bonds below:

BONDS	YTM
Long-term T-bonds	9.00%
Long-term AAA Corp.	10.00%
Long-term BBB Corp.	11.00%

Assume the following are normal yield spreads:

(*a*) Long-term AAA Corp. − long-term T-bonds = 150 basis points

(*b*) Long-term BBB Corp. − long-term AAA Corp. = 50 basis points

In order for an investor to profit from the abnormal yield spreads, what should be done?

SOLUTION

In (*a*), the current yield spread between AAA corporates and long T-bonds is 100 basis points. For the normal yield spread to exist, the current yield spread must increase. This can happen if the AAA-rated bonds fall in price or if the long-term T-bonds increase in price. Therefore, the investor should purchase long-term T-bonds.

With (*b*), the current yield spread is 100 basis points. In order for the current yield spread to narrow to the normal yield spread of 50 basis points, the long-term BBB bonds must increase in price and/or the AAA bonds must fall in price. Therefore, the investor should purchase the BBB bonds and sell short the AAA bonds.

15.3 TERM STRUCTURE OF INTEREST-RATE THEORIES

The relationship at a point in time between the YTMs of homogenous bonds and the years to maturity for the bonds, holding other things constant, is called the *term structure of interest rates* or *yield curve.* Three main explanations or theories of the *term structure* have been given. An explanation of each one of these hypotheses is presented below.

The Expectations Hypothesis

The expectations approach to the term structure of interest rates states that long-term interest rates are the geometric mean of expected forward (or future) short-term interest rates. This can be expressed as follows:

$$\text{YTM}_n = [(1 + \text{YTM}_1)(1 + F_{1,2})(1 + F_{2,3})\cdots(1 + F_{t-1,t})]^{1/n} - 1 \qquad (15.3)$$

where YTM_n = the YTM on a bond maturing in n periods

$F_{t-1,t}$ = the expected forward interest rate on a bond originating in period $t - 1$ and ending in period t

Equation (*15.3*) implies that

$$F_{t-1,t} = \frac{(1 + \text{YTM}_t)^t}{(1 + \text{YTM}_{t-1})^{t-1}} - 1 \qquad (15.4)$$

A general form for Eq. (*15.4*) is

$$F_{t,t+n} = \sqrt[n]{\frac{(1 + \text{YTM}_{t+n})^{(t+n)}}{(1 + \text{YTM}_t)^t}} - 1 \qquad (15.5)$$

where $F_{t,t+n}$ = the expected forward rate on a bond maturing n periods after the start of period t.

SOLVED PROBLEM 15.5

The following yield structure was in existence on August 31, 19X9. Determine the missing forward yields.

YEAR	FORWARD RATE	YTM
1	7.00%	7.00%
2		7.50
3	9.77	8.25
4		8.50
5		9.00

SOLUTION

(1) By using Eq. (*15.4*), the expected one-year forward (or implicit future) rate for year 2 is

$$F_{1,2} = \frac{(1 + \text{YTM}_2)^2}{1 + \text{YTM}_1} - 1 = \frac{(1.075)^2}{1.07} - 1$$

$$= \frac{1.15563}{1.07} - 1 = 1.08 - 1 = .08 \quad \text{or} \quad 8.0\%$$

(2) For year 4, the implied one-year forward rate is

$$F_{3,4} = \frac{(1 + \text{YTM}_4)^4}{(1 + \text{YTM}_3)^3} - 1 = \frac{(1 + .085)^4}{(1.0825)^3} - 1$$

$$= \frac{1.38586}{1.26848} - 1 = 1.0925 - 1 = .0925 \quad \text{or} \quad 9.25\%$$

(3) For year 5, the one-year forward rate is

$$F_{4,5} = \frac{(1 + \text{YTM}_5)^5}{(1 + \text{YTM}_4)^4} - 1 = \frac{(1 + .09)^5}{(1 + .085)^4} - 1$$

$$= \frac{1.53862}{1.38586} - 1 = 1.1102 - 1 = .1102 \quad \text{or} \quad 11.02\%$$

SOLVED PROBLEM 15.6

The YTM on a 7-year T-bond is 9.0 percent and the YTM on a 10-year T-bond is 10.5 percent. Determine the implied average forward rate for a 3-year T-bond starting in year 8.

SOLUTION

Equation (*15.5*) should be used:

$$F_{7,10} = \sqrt[3]{\frac{(1.105)^{10}}{(1.09)^7}} - 1 = \sqrt[3]{\frac{2.714}{1.828}}$$
$$= \sqrt[3]{1.48468} - 1 = 1.1408 - 1 = .1408 \quad \text{or} \quad 14.08\%$$

Note that this is the average for years 8, 9, and 10 at an annual rate.

SOLVED PROBLEM 15.7

If the YTM on a 20-year T-bond is 10 percent and similar 10-year T-bonds are yielding 10.5 percent, what is the rate on a 10-year T-bond starting in year 11?

SOLUTION

Equation (*15.5*) should be used.

$$F_{10,20} = \sqrt[10]{\frac{(1.10)^{20}}{(1.105)^{10}}} - 1 = \sqrt[10]{\frac{6.7275}{2.71408}} - 1$$
$$= \sqrt[10]{2.47874} - 1 = 1.095023 - 1 = .095023 \quad \text{or} \quad 9.50\%$$

SOLVED PROBLEM 15.8

The following two $1,000 face value zero coupon bonds are available:

BOND	PRICE	MATURITY
ABC	$900	1 year
XYZ	785	2 years

Show how the forward rate starting in year 2 could be locked in by a bond trader.

SOLUTION

First, the forward rates must be determined. Bond ABC's YTM is ($1,000/$900) − 1 = 1.1111 − 1 = .1111 or 11.11 percent. Bond XYZ's YTM is $\sqrt{\$1{,}000/\$785} - 1 = \sqrt{1.27389} - 1 = 1.1287 - 1 = .1287$ or 12.87 percent. The forward rate for year 1 is 11.11 percent. Equation (*15.4*) suggests the forward rate for year 2 is as follows:

$$\frac{(1.1287)^2}{1.1111} - 1 = \frac{1.273964}{1.1111} - 1 = 1.146579 - 1 = .146579 \quad \text{or} \quad 14.66\%$$

To lock in the 14.66 percent in year 2, sell the 1-year bond short for $900 and purchase 1.1465 ($900/$785) 2-year bonds with the proceeds. At the end of year 1, when the 1-year bond matures, $1,000 must be spent to cover the short sale. At the end of year 2, $1,146.50 (1.1465 × $1,000) will be received when the 2-year bond matures. The $1,000 outflow in year 1 and a $1,146.50 inflow in year 2 produces a $146.50 gain. This is a return of 14.65 percent in year 2. The slight difference is due to rounding.

SOLVED PROBLEM 15.9

Suppose the real rate is fixed at 3 percent. If the following inflation rates are expected for each of the next 5 years, determine the yield curve for risk-free bonds:

YEAR	EXPECTED INFLATION
1	4.0%
2	4.5
3	5.0
4	6.0
5	5.5

SOLUTION

Using Eq. (*15.1*) and setting rp = 0, you have $r = \text{rr} + q$. The expected inflation rate for each year will be the geometric average of the expected 1-year rates as follows:

$$\text{Exp. inf. for 2 years} = \sqrt{(1.04)(1.045)} - 1 = \sqrt{1.0868} - 1$$
$$= 1.0425 - 1 = .0425 \quad \text{or} \quad 4.25\% = q_2$$
$$\text{Exp. inf. for 3 years} = \sqrt[3]{(1.04)(1.045)(1.05)} - 1$$
$$= \sqrt[3]{1.14114} - 1 = 1.045 - 1 = .045 \quad \text{or} \quad 4.5\% = q_3$$
$$\text{Exp. inf. for 4 years} = \sqrt[4]{(1.04)(1.045)(1.05)(1.06)} - 1$$
$$= \sqrt[4]{1.2096084} - 1 = 1.0487 - 1$$
$$= .0487 \quad \text{or} \quad 4.87\% = q_4$$
$$\text{Exp. inf. for 5 years} = \sqrt[5]{(1.04)(1.045)(1.05)(1.06)(1.055)} - 1$$
$$= \sqrt[5]{1.27613686} - 1 = 1.05 - 1 = .05 \quad \text{or} \quad 5\% = q_5$$

	(1)	(2)	(3) = (1) + (2)
YEAR	rr	*q*	*r*
1	3%	4.00%	7.00%
2	3	4.25	7.25
3	3	4.50	7.50
4	3	4.87	7.87
5	3	5.00	8.00

The Liquidity Premium Hypothesis

While the expectations approach to the term structure of interest rates implies a flat yield curve if interest rates are not expected to change in the future, the *liquidity preference theory,* under similar circumstances, implies a rising yield curve. According to the liquidity preference theory, investors demand a risk premium from long-term securities. As long-term bonds have more interest-rate risk, investors require higher returns.

The Segmentation Hypothesis

According to the *segmented market theory,* certain investors and financial institutions prefer to invest in certain segments of the yield curve. For example, due to the stable long-term nature of their liabilities, pension funds prefer to invest in long-term securities. On the other hand, commercial bank's short-term liabilities (namely, demand deposits) create a need for short-term assets. As a result, supply and demand for funds within each segment of the market determines the level and structure of interest rates for that segment.

15.4 BOND PORTFOLIO IMMUNIZATION

The interest-rate risk from coupon-paying bonds is composed of two components: (1) price risk and (2) coupon reinvestment rate risk. These two components of interest-rate risk vary inversely. If a bond investor wants the promised YTM and the realized YTM to remain equal over the life of a coupon bond, interim interest payments must be invested at the promised YTM. If interim rates change, the realized YTM can be either greater or less than the promised YTM.

One way to assure the bond investor that the portfolio held will achieve the desired realized yield is to *immunize* the portfolio. Immunization takes place when the desired holding period of the portfolio equals the bond portfolio's Macaulay's duration.[1] For example, immunizing a portfolio for 5 years requires the purchase of a series of bonds with an average Macaulay's duration of 5 years, not an average maturity of 5 years. Immunization achieves this result because reinvestment risk and price risk exactly offset one another whenever a bond portfolio's desired holding period is equal to its duration.

[1]This section assumes a knowledge of duration. For more on duration, see Chap. 14.

There are limitations to immunization. Every time market interest rates change the duration of every bond changes. Duration tends to diminish more slowly than calendar time for coupon-paying bonds when interest rates do not change. Therefore, periodic *rebalancing* will be necessary to continuously immunize a portfolio of bonds. In addition, yield curves are not necessarily flat and do not shift in a parallel fashion, so the use of duration will not be exact.

EXAMPLE 15.2 Suppose the Howell Corporation must make a $20 million pension fund payment each year for the next 4 years. Determine the average Macaulay duration (MD) for this four-payment liability. Suppose Howell decided to immunize the payments by currently investing in zero coupon bonds with 2-year and 5-year maturities. What percent should Howell allocate to each zero coupon bond? What will be the accumulated face value of the bonds? Assume the yield curve is flat at 11 percent.

The duration of the payments can be determined by treating each payment like a zero coupon bond with a maturity date equal to the maturity date of the payment.

(1) YEAR	(2) PAYMENT	(3) PRESENT VALUE OF (2) AT 11%	(4) PERCENT OF TOTAL	(5) PAYMENTS MD (1) × (4)
1	$20M	$18.02M*	.29	.29
2	$20M	$16.23M	.26	.52
3	$20M	$14.62M	.24	.72
4	$20M	$13.17M	.21	.84
		Total = $62.04	1.00	2.37 = MD

*$20M × 1/(1.11)^1 = $20 × .9009 = $18.02M

To determine an immunizing asset allocation, we let X equal the percent of the 2-year bonds that are needed: This implies that $(1 - X)$ will be the percent of 5-year bonds because the two weights must sum to 1.

$$(\text{MD of 2-yr. bonds})(X) + (\text{MD of 5-yr. bonds})(1 - X) = 2.37 \text{ years}$$
$$(2 \text{ years})(X) + (5 \text{ years})(1 - X) = 2.37$$
$$2X + 5 - 5X = 2.37$$
$$X = \frac{2.63}{3} = .88 = 88\% \qquad 1 - X = .12 = 12\%$$

88 percent of the portfolio will be 2-year bonds and 12 percent will be 5-year bonds. Note that the duration for a zero coupon bond is equal to its time to maturity.

The 2-year bonds will have a present value of .88 × $62.04M = $54.6M. The present value of the 5-year bonds is .12 × $62.04M = $7.44M. The face value of the 2-year bonds is $54.6M × (1.11)^2 = $54.6M × 1.2321 = $67.27M. The 5-year bonds' face value is $7.44 × (1.11)^5 = $7.44 × 1.6851 = $12.54M.

SOLVED PROBLEM 15.10

The James Insurance Company is required to pay $36,560.78 in 7 years. Show that this liability will be immunized with $20,000 of 10-year maturity 9 percent coupon par value bonds, even if interest rates were to change immediately to (*a*) 8 percent, (*b*) 10 percent, or (*c*) remain at 9 percent, and stay at these assumed levels for 7 years.

SOLUTION

In all three of these interest-rate scenarios, we need to determine the future value of the $20,000 investment. This requires a determination of (1) the future value (FV) of the interim interest payments and (2) the ending prices of the bonds. The future value of an ordinary annuity (FVA) is used to determine (1). The FVA for a particular interest rate and time period is designated FVA (i, T). (See Chap. 4, for more details on the FVA.)

(*a*) If interest rates fall to 8 percent:

$$\begin{aligned} \text{FV of int. payments} &= \text{total int. pay.} \times \text{FVA}(8, 7) \\ &= (.09)(\$20{,}000) \times 8.9228 \\ &= \$1{,}800 \times 8.9228 = \$16{,}061.04 \end{aligned} \qquad (1)$$

$$\text{Bond prices (end of yr. 7)} = \frac{\$1,800}{(1.08)^1} + \frac{\$1,800}{(1.08)^2} + \frac{\$1,800 + \$20,000}{(1.08)^3}$$
$$= \$1,666.67 + \$1,543.21 + \$17,305.54$$
$$= \$20,515.42 \qquad (2)$$
$$(1) + (2) = \$36,576.46$$

(*b*) If rates rise to 10 percent:

$$\text{FV of int. payments} = \text{total int. pay} \times \text{FVA}(10, 7)$$
$$= (.09)(\$20,000) \times 9.4872$$
$$= \$1,800 \times 9.4872 = \$17,076.96 \qquad (3)$$
$$\text{Bond prices (end of yr. 7)} = \frac{\$1,800}{(1.10)^1} + \frac{\$1,800}{(1.10)^2} + \frac{\$1,800 + \$20,000}{(1.10)^3}$$
$$= \$1,636.36 + \$1,487.60 + \$16,378.66$$
$$= \$19,502.62 \qquad (4)$$
$$(3) + (4) = \$36,579.58$$

(*c*) If rates remain at 9 percent:

$$\text{FV of int. payments} = \text{total int. pay} \times \text{FVA}(9, 7)$$
$$= (.09)(\$20,000) \times 9.2004$$
$$= \$1,800 \times 9.2004 = \$16,560.72 \qquad (5)$$
$$\text{Bond prices (end of yr. 7)} = \frac{\$1,800}{(1.09)^1} + \frac{\$1,800}{(1.09)^2} + \frac{\$1,800 + \$20,000}{(1.09)^3}$$
$$= \$1,651.38 + \$1,515.02 + \$16,833.60$$
$$= \$20,000 \qquad (6)$$
$$(5) + (6) = \$36,560.72$$

Note that with the interest rates of 8 percent and 10 percent, there is a small surplus. As noted in Chap. 14, duration is only exact for very small changes in interest rates. When interest rates changed, so did the bond's MD, making the duration-matching strategy an approximate immunization.

SOLVED PROBLEM 15.11

You are managing a portfolio of \$20M. If a target duration of 10 years has been established and you can choose from two zero coupon bonds, one with 5 years to maturity and the other with 20 years to maturity, what percent of your portfolio should be allocated to each bond? Both bonds yield 10 percent.

SOLUTION

If X equals the weight of the 5-year bond, then $1 - X$ must be the weight for the 20-year bond because both must sum to 1. Since we know that zero coupon bonds have durations equal to time to maturity, $5(X) + 20(1 - X) = 10 = 5X + 20 - 20X; X + \frac{10}{15} = .67$ and $1 - X$ is equal to .33.

SOLVED PROBLEM 15.12

Refer to Problem 15.11 and its solution. What will be the face value of each bond?

SOLUTION

The 5-year bond has a present value of .67 × \$20M = \$13.4M. The 20-year bond has a present value of .33 × \$20M = \$6.6M. The face values of the two bonds are as follows:

$$(5\text{ yr.})(\$13.4) \times (1.10)^5 = \$13.4\text{M} \times 1.6105 = \$21.58\text{M}$$
$$(20\text{ yr.})(\$6.6\text{M}) \times (1.10)^{20} = \$6.6\text{M} \times 6.7275 = \$44.4\text{M}$$

SOLVED PROBLEM 15.13

Suppose the Dale Corporation must pay \$25M at the end of each of the next 2 years. Bonds are currently yielding 12 percent.

(*a*) What is the present value and MD of this liability?
(*b*) What maturity zero coupon bond would immunize this portfolio? Determine its face value.

SOLUTION

(*a*)

(1) YEAR	(2) LIABILITY (MILLIONS)	(3) PRESENT VALUE OF (2) AT 12%		(4) (3)'S PERCENT OF TOTAL	(5) LIAB. MD (1) × (4)
1	\$25	\$25 × 1/(1 + .12) =		.53	.53
		\$25 × .8929	= \$22.32		
2	\$25	\$25 × $1/(1 + .12)^2$ =			
		\$25 × .7972	= \$19.93	.47	.94
	Total = (present value)		\$42.25	1.00	1.47 years = (weighted avg. MD)

(*b*) In order to immunize the portfolio, a 12 percent zero coupon bond with a maturity of 1.47 years should be used. The face value of the zero coupon bond is \$42.25M × $(1.12)^{1.47}$ = \$42.25 × 1.1813 = \$49.91M.

SOLVED PROBLEM 15.14

Assume that the Roberts Corporation must make the payments given below at the end of each of the next 5 years:

YEAR	PAYMENT
1	\$10 Million
2	9
3	8
4	8
5	7

(*a*) If market interest rates are 9 percent over all maturities, determine the duration for this series of liability payments.

(*b*) How could this liability be immunized?

SOLUTION

(*a*) To calculate the weighted average duration for this series of payments, we will assume that the payments could be funded by investing in a series of zero coupon bonds with face values equal to the desired payments. The duration for a zero coupon bond is equal to its time to maturity.

(1) PAY. YR.	(2) PAYMENTS	(3)* PRESENT VALUE OF (2) AT 9%	(4)† PERCENT OF TOTAL	(5) (1) × (4)
1	\$10M	\$ 9.17M	.28	.28
2	9M	7.58M	.23	.46
3	8M	6.18M	.19	.57
4	8M	5.67M	.17	.68
5	7M	4.55M	.14	.70
		Total = \$33.15	1.01‡	2.69 years = (wt. av. MD)

*For example, the present value for year 2 is $\$9M/(1.09)^2$ = \$7.58M.

†The percent (in decimal form) in (4) is determined by dividing the individual value in (3) by the total of (3).

‡Note that each year's percentage is rounded. The exact total is 1.00.

(*b*) Immunization will take place by investing in a bond or series of bonds with a weighted average MD of 2.69 years. However, this immunization could be complicated by rebalancing as interest rates change. In addition, interest rates will probably not shift in a parallel fashion, which will make the task more difficult. If corporate bonds were used, several different corporations would be needed to diversify away part of the default risk. Only non-callable bonds should be selected.

SOLVED PROBLEM 15.15

Refer to Solved Problem 15.14 and its solution. If you decided to immunize the payments with two zero coupon bonds, one with a maturity of 2 years and the other with a maturity of 3 years, what percent should you invest in each bond?

SOLUTION

For zero coupon bonds, time to maturity is equal to duration. If X equals the percent invested in the 2-year bond, then $1 - X$ is the percent invested in the 3-year bond, because both must sum to 1. The solution is as follows:

$$(X) \times (\text{dur. 2-year bond}) + (1 - X) \times (\text{dur. of 3-year bond}) = \text{desired dur.}$$

$$(2 \text{ years}) \times (X) + (3 \text{ years}) \times (1 - X) = 2.68 = 2X + 3 - 3X$$

$$X = .32 = 32\% \qquad \text{and} \qquad 1 - X = .68 = 68\%$$

SOLVED PROBLEM 15.16

The modified duration (MMD) of a bond portfolio is 6.5 years and the average YTM of the bond portfolio is 11 percent. Estimate the percent decrease in the bond portfolio's value if the portfolio's average YTM increases to 12 percent.

SOLUTION

An equation that was given in Chap. 14 can be used to answer this question.

$$\frac{dP}{P} = -\text{MMD} \times d(\text{YTM}) \qquad (14.7)$$

where dP is the change in the portfolio's value, MMD is modified duration, P equals the value of the portfolio, YTM is the average YTM for the bond portfolio, and $d(\text{YTM})$ is the change in the portfolio's YTM.

$$\frac{dP}{P} = -6.5 \times 1\% = -6.5\%$$

This is an approximation because we are dealing with a curvilinear relationship.

True-False Questions

15.1 The segmented market hypothesis about the term structure of interest rates asserts that the yield curve will always be upward sloping.

15.2 It is impossible for the yield curve to have a negative slope.

15.3 One of the problems with immunization is the cost associated with rebalancing.

15.4 According to the expectations approach to the term structure of interest rates, a falling yield curve forecasts falling interest rates in the years ahead.

15.5 Yield spreads tend to widen during a boom period in the economy.

15.6 Yield spread differentials are mainly caused by differences in the marketability of long-term debt.

15.7 The average duration for a portfolio of zero coupon bonds will remain constant as interest rates change.

15.8 If the interest rate is 10 percent, the weighted average duration for a portfolio of two $40 million face value zero coupon bonds with maturities of 4 and 8 years, respectively, is 5.64 years.

15.9 The liquidity preference theory about the term structure of interest rates asserts that if short-term interest rates are expected to remain the same in the future, the yield curve should be flat.

15.10 Long-term bonds have more price change risk than short-term bonds.

Multiple Choice Questions

The following yield curve T-bond information should be used with the next four problems.

YEARS-TO-MATURITY	YIELD-TO-MATURITY
1	7%
2	8%
3	8.5%
4	9%
6	10%
10	11.5%

15.1 Determine the implied forward rate for year 2.
(*a*) 8.5 percent
(*b*) 9.0 percent
(*c*) 9.2 percent
(*d*) 8.6 percent
(*e*) 8.7 percent

15.2 Determine the implied forward rate for year 4.
(*a*) 10.5 percent
(*b*) 10.7 percent
(*c*) 9.7 percent
(*d*) 9.2 percent
(*e*) 10.8 percent

15.3 Determine the implied yield on a 2-year bond at the start of year 5.
(*a*) 10.7 percent
(*b*) 11.4 percent
(*c*) 12.0 percent
(*d*) 13.2 percent
(*e*) 11.8 percent

15.4 Determine the implied yield on a 4-year bond at the start of year 7.
(*a*) 12.0 percent
(*b*) 12.5 percent
(*c*) 11.7 percent
(*d*) 13.8 percent
(*e*) 13.2 percent

The following information should be used with the next two questions:
On June 6, 19X3, the following yields-to-maturity existed for long-term bonds:

U.S. T-bonds	9.50%
AAA corporate	10.10%
AA corporate	10.70%
A corporate	11.40%
BBB corporate	12.46%

15.5 Determine the yield spread for AAA- and AA-rated bonds on this date relative to U.S. T-bonds.
(*a*) .50 percent; 1.20 percent
(*b*) .65 percent; 1.25 percent
(*c*) .60 percent; 1.20 percent
(*d*) .90 percent; 1.35 percent
(*e*) None of the above

15.6 Determine the yield spread for A- and BBB-rated bonds on this date relative to U.S. T-bonds.
(*a*) 1.90 percent; 2.96 percent
(*b*) 1.85 percent; 2.92 percent
(*c*) 1.90 percent; 2.80 percent
(*d*) 1.85 percent; 2.96 percent
(*e*) None of the above

The information below should be used with the next three questions:
The Warren Corporation has the following zero coupon bond portfolio. The current yield for each of these bonds is 10 percent and the yield curve is expected to remain flat.

BOND'S FACE VALUE	YEARS UNTIL MATURITY
$10 Million	3
$20 Million	4
$25 Million	5
$30 Million	7
$50 Million	9

15.7 Determine the current (present) value of the bond portfolio.
(*a*) $70.1M
(*b*) $69.5M
(*c*) $68.1M
(*d*) $73.3M
(*e*) $65.2M

15.8 What is the weighted average duration for the bond portfolio?
(*a*) 6.2 years
(*b*) 8.2 years
(*c*) 6.8 years
(*d*) 7.2 years
(*e*) 5.7 years

15.9 If the yield curve remains flat, what will be the weighted average duration for the bond portfolio in 2 years? (*Hint:* The $10M bond will have 1 year to maturity.)
(*a*) 4.8 years
(*b*) 4.9 years
(*c*) 4.5 years
(*d*) 4.2 years
(*e*) 5.1 years

The following information should be used with the next three questions:
The modified duration of a bond portfolio is 7.25 years and the average YTM of the bonds held is 10.5 percent.

15.10 Estimate the percentage change in the bond portfolio's value if the portfolio's average YTM increases to 12 percent.
(*a*) 11.6 percent
(*b*) 10.7 percent
(*c*) −10.9 percent
(*d*) −11.5 percent
(*e*) −12.2 percent

15.11 Estimate the percentage change in the portfolio's value if the portfolio's average YTM decreases to 8.5 percent.
(*a*) 20.0 percent
(*b*) 14.9 percent
(*c*) 14.5 percent
(*d*) 12.5 percent
(*e*) −13.2 percent

15.12 Estimate the percentage change in the portfolio's value if the portfolio's average YTM increases to 12.75 percent.
(*a*) 16.2 percent
(*b*) −17.2 percent
(*c*) −15.2 percent
(*d*) −15.7 percent
(*e*) −16.3 percent

The following information will be used with the next three questions:
You are managing a portfolio of bonds with a current value of $45 million. The current YTM is 12 percent and the yield curve is expected to remain flat.

15.13 If a target duration of 7 years is assumed, and you can choose from two zero coupon bonds of 4 and 8 years to maturity, what percent of your investment should be in each bond to achieve your target duration?
(*a*) 20 percent (4 years); 80 percent (8 years)
(*b*) 30 percent (4 years); 70 percent (8 years)
(*c*) 40 percent (4 years); 60 percent (8 years)
(*d*) 25 percent (4 years); 75 percent (8 years)
(*e*) 50 percent (4 years); 50 percent (8 years)

15.14 Determine the face value of the two zero coupon bonds in Problem 15.13.
(*a*) $15.1M (4 years); $70.4M (8 years)
(*b*) $17.7M (4 years); $83.6M (8 years)
(*c*) $20.2M (4 years); $60.5M (8 years)
(*d*) $30.2M (4 years); $50.6M (8 years)
(*e*) $40.1M (4 years); $40.7M (8 years)

15.15 If a target duration of 5 years is assumed and you can choose from two zero coupon bonds with maturities of 3 and 6 years, what percent of your investment should be in each bond to achieve the target duration?
(*a*) 33 percent (3 years); 67 percent (6 years)
(*b*) 25 percent (3 years); 75 percent (6 years)
(*c*) 30 percent (3 years); 70 percent (6 years)
(*d*) 50 percent (3 years); 50 percent (6 years)
(*e*) 60 percent (3 years); 40 percent (6 years)

Answers

True-False

15.1. F 15.2. F 15.3. T 15.4. T 15.5. F 15.6. F 15.7. F 15.8. T
15.9. F 15.10. T

Multiple Choice

15.1. b 15.2. a 15.3. c 15.4. d 15.5. c 15.6. a 15.7. d 15.8. a
15.9. d 15.10. c 15.11. c 15.12. e 15.13. d 15.14. b 15.15. a

Chapter 16

Common Stock Valuation

16.1 PRESENT VALUE OF CASH DIVIDENDS

The *discounted cash flow approach* to stock valuation suggests that the value of an asset is the present value of all the cash flows an investor can expect from that asset. With common stock the expected cash flows are the cash dividends and the selling price. However, since common stock can have an infinite life expectancy, the stock's price can be expressed in terms of dividends as follows:

$$P_0 = \frac{D_1}{(1+k)^1} + \frac{D_2}{(1+k)^2} + \cdots + \frac{D_\infty}{(1+k)^\infty} \tag{16.1}$$

Equation (*16.1*) can be expressed in the following more convenient form:

$$P_0 = \sum_{t=1}^{\infty} \frac{D_t}{(1+k)^t} \tag{16.2}$$

In Eq. (*16.2*) P_0 denotes the expected stock's price or value, D_t represents expected dividends per share for time period t, and k is the stock's required rate of return (or risk-adjusted cost of capital).

One-Stage Model

If we assume that dividends will grow at a constant rate forever and that the stock's required return will be greater than the dividend growth rate, then, Eqs. (*16.1*) and (*16.2*) can be reduced to the following equivalent expression:

$$P_0 = \frac{D_0(1+g)}{k-g} = \frac{D_1}{k-g} \tag{16.3}$$

In Eq. (*16.3*) D_0 = current dividend per share at time $t = 0$ and g = expected annual growth rate in dividends.

SOLVED PROBLEM 16.1

Derive Eq. (*16.3*). You may assume a constant growth rate for cash dividends to simplify the algebra. (*Hint:* Consider geometric expansions.)

SOLUTION

If dividends grow at some constant rate, denoted g, then future dividends are shown below.

$$P_0 = \sum_{t=1}^{\infty} \frac{D_0(1+g)^t}{(1+k)^t} \tag{1}$$

$\Sigma D_0 x = D_0 \Sigma x$ because D_0 is a constant. This relation means that Eq. (*1*) may be written as shown below.

$$P_0 = D_0 \sum_{t=1}^{\infty} \frac{(1+g)^t}{(1+k)^t} \tag{2}$$

$$P_0 = D_0 \left[\frac{1+g}{1+k} + \frac{(1+g)^2}{(1+k)^2} + \frac{(1+g)^3}{(1+k)^3} + \cdots \right] \tag{3}$$

Multiplying Eq. (*3*) by $(1+k)/(1+g)$ yields Eq. (*4*):

$$P_0 \left(\frac{1+k}{1+g} \right) = D_0 \left[1.0 + \frac{1+g}{1+k} + \frac{(1+g)^2}{(1+k)^2} + \cdots \right] \tag{4}$$

Subtracting Eq. (*3*) from Eq. (*4*) yields Eq. (*5*):

$$\left(\frac{1+k}{1+g} - 1 \right) P_0 = D_0 \tag{5}$$

By assuming that $k > g$, the preceding equation can be rearranged as

$$\left[\frac{(1+k)-(1+g)}{1+g}\right]P_0 = \left[\frac{k-g}{1+g}\right]P_0 = D_0 \tag{6}$$

Multiplying Eq. (6) by the quantity $(1 + g)$ and rearranging yields Eq. (7):

$$P_0(k-g) = D_0(1+g) = D_1 \tag{7}$$

where $D_0(1 + g)^1 = D_1$ denotes the "next period's" dividends per share. Equation (16.3) can be obtained by rearranging Eq. (7) as follows:

$$P_0 = \frac{D_1}{k-g}$$

SOLVED PROBLEM 16.2

The Edward Corporation recently paid a dividend of $4 per share. Dividends have been growing at an annual rate of 8 percent and this growth rate is expected to continue in the foreseeable future. If the required rate of return for Edward's stock is 14 percent, what is the value of its stock?

SOLUTION

We have $D_0 = \$4$, $g = 8$ percent, and $k = 14$ percent. This stock can be valued with Eq. (16.3):

$$P_0 = \frac{D_0(1+g)}{k-g} = \frac{\$4(1+.08)}{.14-.08} = \frac{\$4.32}{.06} = \$72$$

SOLVED PROBLEM 16.3

The Krehbiel Corporation's risk-adjusted cost of capital (or required rate of return) is 10 percent. Krehbiel's current cash dividends per share are $2.50 and have been growing at 3 percent per year. However, a technological breakthrough is expected to increase Krehbiel's growth rate to 6 percent for the foreseeable future. Krehbiel's common stock has been selling at a $35 to $38 range.

(a) What do you expect the stock price will be after Krehbiel's new technological development is announced publicly?

(b) Does the stock price change you suggested in part (a) seem rational in view of the fact that the Krehbiel Corporation will still have the same management, the same physical assets, and the same products as it did before the announcement of the new technology?

SOLUTION

$$P_0 = \frac{D_1}{k-g} = \frac{\$2.50(1.03)}{.10-.03} = \frac{\$2.575}{.07} = \$36.7857$$

Krehbiel's stock was worth $36.79 before the new technology.

(a)

$$P_0 = \frac{D_1}{k-g} = \frac{\$2.50(1.06)}{.10-.06} = \frac{\$2.65}{.04} = \$66.25$$

After the new technology elevates Krehbiel's growth rate to 6 percent, the stock will be worth $66.25.

(b) The sudden 80 percent increase in the value of Krehbiel's common stock reflects an increase in the growth rate from 3 percent to 6 percent that should enable the corporation to be more profitable for many years. Therefore, the $30 price increase is rational and sustainable, unless the new technology fails to produce as expected.

SOLVED PROBLEM 16.4

The Jackson Corporation has a required rate of return of 16 percent and its current dividend is $3 per share. If the current price of Jackson's stock is $55 per share, what is the growth rate of its dividends?

SOLUTION

Solving Eq. (*16.3*) for g yields the following:

$$P_0 = \frac{D_0(1+g)}{k-g}$$

$$\$55 = \frac{\$3(1+g)}{(.16-g)}$$

$$\$55(.16-g) = \$3(1+g)$$

$$\$8.8 - \$55g = \$3 + \$3g$$

$$\$58g = \$5.8$$

$$g = .10 \quad \text{or} \quad 10\%$$

If 10 percent isn't a realistic rate of growth then it may be concluded that the stock price does not equal its value.

SOLVED PROBLEM 16.5

The common stock of the Bensen Corporation is currently selling for $60 per share. Dividends per share have grown from $1.50 to the current level of $4.00 over the past 10 years, and this dividend growth is expected to continue in the future. What is the required return for the Bensen Corporation?

SOLUTION

First, find the growth rate:

$$g = \left(\frac{\text{future value}}{\text{present value}}\right)^{1/N} - 1$$

$$= \left(\frac{\$4}{\$1.50}\right)^{1/10} - 1$$

$$= 1.1031 - 1 = .1031 = 10.31\%$$

Second, solve Eq. (*16.3*) for k and then evaluate it:

$$k = \frac{D_0(1+g)}{P_0 + g}$$

$$= \frac{\$4.00(1.1031)}{\$60 + .1031} = .1766 \quad \text{or} \quad 17.66\%$$

SOLVED PROBLEM 16.6

The Tucker Mining Company has been experiencing a 6 percent per year decline in its cash dividend growth rate for the past few years; this decline is expected to continue. Tucker has a current dividend per share of $3. If Tucker's required rate of return is 14.5 percent, what is a share of the stock worth?

SOLUTION

Using Eq. (*16.3*) with $g = -6$ percent, $D = \$3$, and $k = .145$, we find

$$P_0 = \frac{D_0(1+g)}{k-g} = \frac{\$3[1+(-.06)]}{.145-(-.06)} = \frac{\$3(.94)}{.205} = \$13.76$$

SOLVED PROBLEM 16.7

Refer to Solved Problem 16.6. If conditions remain the same, what will Tucker's price be 3 years from now?

SOLUTION

Using Eq. (*16.3*),

$$P_3 = \frac{D_4}{k-g} = \frac{D_0(1+g)^4}{k-g}$$

$$= \frac{\$3(.94)^4}{.145-(-.06)} = \frac{\$3(.781)}{.205} = \$11.43$$

Two-Stage Cash Dividend Model

Equation (*16.3*) cannot be used to value a growth stock because sometimes g is greater than k. A two-stage dividend valuation model, where dividends can grow at an above normal rate for several years before dropping to a more normal rate, is more realistic in cases of this nature. A two-stage model is given by Eq. (*16.4*):

$$P_0 = \sum_{t=1}^{N} \frac{D_t(1 + g_1)^t}{(1 + k)^t} + \frac{D_N(1 + g_2)}{(k - g_2)(1 + k)^N} \tag{16.4}$$

In Eq. (*16.4*) D_N stands for dividends per share in time period N, g_1 denotes the initial dividend growth rate, g_2 represents the longer-run dividend growth rate, and N is the number of years that the g_1 growth lasts.

SOLVED PROBLEM 16.8

The Babet Computer Corporation has been experiencing an above normal dividend growth rate of 20 percent per year for the last 5 years. This above normal growth rate is expected to continue for another 5 years before it levels off at a more normal rate of 6 percent. Babet's last dividend was \$.50 per share. Determine the current value of Babet's stock if its required rate of return is 15 percent.

SOLUTION

Using Eq. (*16.4*), we have $g_1 = 20$ percent, $g_2 = 6$ percent, $D_0 = \$.05$, $k = 15$ percent, and $N = 5$.

$$P_0 = \sum_{t=1}^{N} \frac{D_t(1 + g_1)^t}{(1 + k)^t} + \frac{D_N(1 + g)_2}{(k - g_2)(1 + k)^N}$$

$$= \sum_{t=1}^{5} \frac{\$.50(1 + .20)^t}{(1.15)^t} + \frac{D_5(1.06)}{(.15 - .06)(1.15)^5}$$

$$= \frac{\$.50(1.20)}{1.15} + \frac{\$.50(1.20)^2}{(1.15)^2} + \frac{\$.50(1.20)^3}{(1.15)^3} + \frac{\$.50(1.20)^4}{(1.15)^4} + \frac{\$.50(1.20)^5}{(1.15)^5} + \frac{\$.50(1.20)^5(1.06)}{(.15 - .06)(2.011)}$$

$$= \$.522 + \$.544 + \$.568 + \$.593 + \$.619 + \$7.29 = \$10.14$$

SOLVED PROBLEM 16.9

Dividends per share for the Crawford Corporation are expected to grow at an annual rate of 25 percent for 4 more years. After this period of time, dividends should grow at a more normal rate of 5 percent. Crawford's last dividend (D_0) was \$.75 per share.

(*a*) If Crawford's current price is \$25 per share, what is its current required rate of return?

(*b*) If your required rate of return is 10 percent, should you invest in Crawford's stock? Why?

SOLUTION

Using Eq. (*16.4*), we have $D_0 = \$.75$, $g_1 = 25$ percent, $g_2 = 5$ percent, $N = 4$, and $P_0 = \$25$.

$$P_0 = \sum_{t=1}^{N} \frac{D_t(1 + g_1)^t}{(1 + k)^t} + \frac{D_N(1 + g_2)}{(k - g_2)(1 + k)^N}$$

$$\$25 = \sum_{t=1}^{4} \frac{\$.75(1.25)^t}{(1 + k)^t} + \frac{\$.75(1.25)^4(1.05)}{(k - .05)(1 + k)^4}$$

(*a*) The required rate of return must be solved by trial and error. Find a value of k that will make the right-hand side of the equation equal to \$25. The answer is 11.0416 percent.

(*b*) Yes, because 11.0416% > 10%.

16.2 EARNINGS APPROACH

Some investors like to use an earnings approach to common stock valuation. The one-stage model can be stated in terms of earnings, by definition, $D = E(1 - b)$, where D is dividend per share, E is earnings per share, and b is the earnings retention rate [$(1 - b)$ is the dividend-payout ratio]. Therefore, an equivalent earnings-based valuation model is

$$P_0 = \frac{E_1(1 - b)}{k - g} \tag{16.5}$$

In Eq. (*16.5*) P_0 stands for the stock's present value, E_1 represents earnings expected at the end of year 1, $b = (1.0 -$ payout ratio) is the retention rate, g denotes the expected earnings growth rate, and k is the stock's required rate of return. It is also true that $E_1 = E_0(1 + g)$, where E_0 is current earnings per share.

Equation (*16.5*) can also be stated in terms of a price-earnings ratio or earnings multiplier. By noting that $(1 - b) = D_0/E_0$ and $E_1 = E_0(1 + g)$, if we divide Eq. (*16.5*) by E_0, we have the following *P/E* version of the one-stage model:

$$\frac{P_0}{E_0} = \frac{(1 + g)(D_0/E_0)}{k - g} \tag{16.6}$$

SOLVED PROBLEM 16.10

The Krehbiel Corporation's cash dividend payout ratio is 60 percent, its risk-adjusted cost of capital is 10 percent, the current earnings per share are $4.04 and have been growing at 3 percent per year. A technological breakthrough is expected to increase Krehbiel's growth rate to 6 percent for the foreseeable future. Krehbiel's common stock has been selling at 8 to 9 times its earnings. What do you expect the price-earnings ratio will be after Krehbiel's new technological development is announced publicly?

SOLUTION

Using the fact that $D_1 = D_0(1 + g)$, $D_1 = (.60 \times \$4.04)(1.03) = \$2.50$.

$$\frac{P_0}{E_0} = \frac{D_1/E_0}{k - g} = \frac{\$2.50/\$4.04}{.10 - .03} = \frac{.62}{.07} = 8.86 \text{ times}$$

Krehbiel's stock was selling at about 8.9 times its earnings per share before the new technology.

$$D_1 = (.60 \times \$4.04)(1.06) = \$2.569$$

$$\frac{P_0}{E_0} = \frac{D_1/E_0}{k - g} = \frac{\$2.569/\$4.04}{.10 - .06} = \frac{.636}{.04} = 15.9 \text{ times}$$

After the new technology elevates Krehbiel's growth rate to 6 percent the common stock will be worth 15.9 times its earnings per share.

SOLVED PROBLEM 16.11

The Logan Corporation currently has earnings that are $4 per share. In recent years earnings have been growing at a rate of 7.5 percent, and this rate is expected to continue in the future. If the Logan Corporation has a retention rate of 40 percent and a required rate of return of 14 percent, what is its current value?

SOLUTION

We have $E_0 = \$4.00$, $g = .075$, $b = .40$, and $k = .14$.

$$P_0 = \frac{E_1(1 - b)}{k - g} = \frac{\$4(1.075)(1 - .4)}{.14 - .075} = \frac{\$2.58}{.065} = \$39.69$$

SOLVED PROBLEM 16.12

The Logan Corporation has current earnings of $4, a current earnings growth rate of 7.5 percent that is expected to continue in the future, a retention rate of 40 percent, and a required rate of return of 14 percent. If the Logan Corporation continues to do as expected in the future, what will its price be in 4 years?

SOLUTION

$$P_4 = \frac{E_5(1 - b)}{k - g} = \frac{E_0(1 + g)^5(1 - b)}{k - g}$$

$$= \frac{\$4(1.075)^5(.6)}{.14 - .075} = \frac{\$3.4455}{.065} = \$53.01$$

SOLVED PROBLEM 16.13

The Evans Company is expecting earnings per share next year to be $5. If earnings have been growing at a rate of 8 percent per year in the past and this growth is expected to continue in the future, determine the current required rate of return for this company's stock. Assume a dividend payout of 60 percent and a current price of $65.

SOLUTION

We have $E_1 = \$5.00$, $g = .08$, $1 - b = .60$, and $P_0 = \$65$. Solving Eq. (*16.5*) for k and substituting gives us

$$k = \frac{E_1(1 - b)}{P_0} + g = \frac{\$5(.6)}{\$65} + .08 = \frac{\$3}{\$65} + .08 = .1262 \quad \text{or} \quad 12.62\%$$

Finite Earnings Model

Rather than using a perpetual constant earnings growth model like the ones given by Eqs. (*16.5*) and (*16.6*), an investor may prefer to use a finite earnings growth model given by Eq. (*16.7*):

$$P_0 = \sum_{t=1}^{N} \frac{E_0(1+g)^t(D/P_0)}{(1+k)^t} + \frac{E_0(1+g)^N(P/E)_N}{(1+k)^N} \qquad (16.7)$$

In Eq. (*16.7*) $D/P_0 = 1 - b$ is the dividend-payout ratio, N is the holding period in years, and $(P/E)_N$ is the price-earnings ratio expected at time period N. The other terms are defined as before.

SOLVED PROBLEM 16.14

Mr. Carl Ruby is trying to determine the value of Franklin Corporation's common stock. The earnings growth rate over his planned 6-year holding period is estimated to be 10 percent, and the dividend-payout ratio is 60 percent. The ending P/E ratio is expected to be 20, and current earnings per share are \$4. If the required rate of return for this stock is 15 percent, what should be the price of Franklin's stock?

SOLUTION

We have $1 - b = .60$, $N = 6$ years, $g = .10$, $P/E = 20$ times, $E_0 = \$4.00$, and $k = .15$. Inserting these values into Eq. (*16.7*) yields

$$\begin{aligned} P_0 &= \sum_{t=1}^{N} \frac{E_0(1+g)^t(D/P_0)}{(1+k)^t} + \frac{E_0(1+g)^N(P/E)_N}{(1+k)^N} \\ &= \sum_{t=1}^{6} \frac{\$4(1.10)^t(.6)}{(1.15)^t} + \frac{\$4(1.10)^6(20)}{(1+.15)^6} \\ &= \frac{\$2.64}{1.15} + \frac{\$2.904}{(1.15)^2} + \frac{\$3.194}{(1.15)^3} + \frac{\$3.514}{(1.15)^4} + \frac{\$3.865}{(1.15)^5} + \frac{\$4.252}{(1.15)^6} + \frac{\$7.09(20)}{(1.15)^6} \\ &= \$2.296 + \$2.196 + \$2.10 + \$2.01 + \$1.922 + \$1.838 + \$61.272 = \$73.632 \end{aligned}$$

SOLVED PROBLEM 16.15

Mr. Frank Harris is considering purchasing some common stock of the Gibson Corporation. If he purchases the stock he plans to hold it for 3 years. Frank's investment advisor has told him that Gibson's earnings should grow at a rate of 8 percent for the next 3 years with a 50 percent dividend-payout ratio and that the P/E ratio should be 15 in 3 years. Gibson's current earnings per share are \$5. If Mr. Harris purchases the stock for the current price of \$70 per share, what after-tax return should he earn over the 3 years? Assume that Mr. Harris is in a 40 percent tax bracket.

SOLUTION

We have $N = 3$ years, $g = .08$, $1 - b = .50$, $P/E = 15$ times, $E_0 = \$5.00$, $P_0 = \$70$, and the tax rate is $T = .40$. Modifying Eq. (*16.7*) so the taxation of dividends and price appreciation is taken into account, we have

$$P_0 = \sum_{t=1}^{N} \frac{E_0(1+g)^t(D/P_0)(1-T)}{(1+k_{at})^t} + \frac{[P_N - P_0](1-T) + P_0}{(1+k_{at})^N}$$

where k_{at} is the after-tax return, T is the marginal tax rate, $P_N = E_0(1+g)^N(P/E)$, and the term in brackets is price appreciation.

$$\$70 = \sum_{t=1}^{3} \frac{5(1.08)^t(.5)(1-.4)}{(1+k_{at})^t} + \frac{[\$5(1.08)^3(156) - \$70](1-.4) + \$70}{(1+k_{at})^3}$$

$$\$70 = \frac{1.62}{1+k_{at}} + \frac{\$1.75}{(1+k_{at})^2} + \frac{\$1.89}{(1+k_{at})^3} + \frac{\$14.69 + \$70}{(1+k_{at})^3}$$

The solution is found by finding the after-tax return (k_{at}) that will make the present value of the after-tax cash flows equal to the stock's price (\$70). The answer is 8.9017 percent and can be found by trial and error.[1]

[1]Some financial calculators can be used to solve for k_{at}. For example, with the HP-10B, the IRR routine can be used. First, enter −\$70 and push CF_j. (This is cash flow CF_0.) Then, enter cash flow one by entering \$1.62 and pushing CF_j. Next, enter cash flow two by entering \$1.75 and pushing CF_j. Enter the last cash flow, \$86.58, and push CF_j again. To calculate k_{at}, push the shift function and press CST. Very quickly an IRR = k_{at} = 8.9017 percent is calculated. The HP-12C can be used in a similar manner to solve for k_{at}. Any calculator that will solve the IRR for uneven cash flows can be used.

SOLVED PROBLEM 16.16

Georgia Crampton is considering the McKay Company for a possible investment. If Georgia purchases the stock, she plans to hold it for 5 years. McKay's earnings, currently \$3.50 per share, grow at a rate of 9 percent per year. Georgia expects the present cash dividend-payout ratio to remain at 55 percent. If McKay has a current price of \$40, what ending *P/E* ratio will give Georgia a 14 percent before-tax return over the 5-year holding period?

SOLUTION

We have $N = 5$ years, $E_0 = \$3.50$, $g = .09$, $P_0 = \$40$, $1 - b = .55$, and $k = .14$. Solving Eq. (*16.7*) for the *P/E* ratio proceeds as follows:

$$\$40 = \frac{\$3.50(1.09)(.55)}{(1.14)^1} + \frac{\$3.50(1.09)^2(.55)}{(1.14)^2} + \frac{\$3.50(1.09)^3(.55)}{(1.14)^3} + \frac{\$3.50(1.09)^4(.55)}{(1.14)^4}$$

$$+ \frac{\$3.50(1.09)^5(.55)}{(1.14)^5} + \frac{\$3.50(1.09)^5(P/E)_5}{(1.14)^5}$$

$$= \frac{\$2.10}{(1.14)^1} + \frac{\$2.29}{(1.14)^2} + \frac{\$2.49}{(1.14)^3} + \frac{\$2.72}{(1.14)^4} + \frac{\$2.96}{(1.14)^5} + \frac{\$5.96(P/E)_5}{(1.14)^5}$$

$$= \$1.84 + \$1.76 + \$1.68 + \$1.61 + \$1.54 + \$2.8(P/E)_5 = \$8.43 + \$2.8(P/E)_5$$

$$\$2.8(P/E)_5 = \$31.57$$

$$(P/E)_5 = 11.275$$

SOLVED PROBLEM 16.17

Kimberly Jones is thinking about purchasing some common stock of the Edwards Corporation. Edwards has not paid a cash dividend since it started in business 10 years ago. Kimberly expects to hold the stock for 4 years. She has been told by several financial analysts that Edwards will start paying a cash dividend in 3 years that will be 25 percent of its forecasted earnings. Kim has determined that Edward's required return is 16 percent and that an ending *P/E* ratio of 18 is appropriate. If Kim expects earnings, which are currently \$2 per share, to continue to grow at a rate of 15 percent per year, what should she be willing to pay for the stock of the Edwards Corporation?

SOLUTION

We have $N = 4$ years, $1 - b = .25$, $k = .15$, $(P/E)_4 = 18$ times, $g = .15$, and $E_0 = \$2.00$, so we can use Eq. (*16.7*).

$$P_0 = \frac{\$0}{(1.16)^1} + \frac{\$0}{(1.16)^2} + \frac{\$2(1.15)^3(.25)}{(1.16)^3} + \frac{\$2(1.15)^4(.25)}{(1.16)^4} + \frac{\$2(1.15)^4(18)}{(1.16)^4}$$

$$= \frac{\$0}{1.16} + \frac{\$0}{1.3456} + \frac{\$.76}{1.5609} + \frac{\$.875}{1.8106} + \frac{\$62.96}{1.8106}$$

$$= \$0 + \$0 + \$.487 + \$.483 + \$34.773 = \$35.74$$

16.3 VALUE VERSUS PRICE

How does an investor know when a company's common stock is *overvalued* or *undervalued?* Whenever the market price of a company's stock is greater than its present value, the stock is overvalued and is a candidate to be sold. On the other hand, when the appraised value is greater than the market price, the stock is undervalued and a purchase should be considered. If the market price and present value are equal, the stock is priced fairly.

SOLVED PROBLEM 16.18

Jim Evans is considering purchasing the common stock of the Alpine Corporation. Alpine's current market price is \$50 per share. According to Jim's analysis, Alpine has a present value of \$55 per share. What should Jim do?

SOLUTION

Since the appraised value is greater than the market value, the stock is undervalued. Therefore, Jim should purchase the stock.

SOLVED PROBLEM 16.19

Jennifer Miles is seriously thinking about investing in the common stock of the Holmes Company. Holmes has a current market price of $35 per share. Jennifer has estimated that Holmes should be selling for $30 per share. Should Jennifer purchase the stock?

SOLUTION

No, she should not purchase the stock. Since the market price is greater than the appraised value, the stock is overvalued; the stock should be sold. Furthermore, she might consider selling short.

True-False Questions

16.1 With the constant perpetual growth rate valuation model, other things the same, the value derived does not depend upon the assumed holding period.

16.2 If the earnings of the XYZ Company have been growing at a rate of 9 percent per year and if this rate is expected to continue, then in 8 years earnings will increase from their current level of $4 to $7.97.

16.3 There is a direct relationship between the value of a firm's stock and its required rate of return.

16.4 The growth rate of a firm's dividends and a firm's stock value are inversely related.

16.5 One of the assumptions of the underlying finite earnings model is that the stock's required return should be greater than the earnings growth rate.

16.6 With the constant perpetual growth rate model, a stock's price and dividends grow at the same rate.

16.7 With the constant perpetual growth rate model, the dividend yield can not be greater than the stock's required return.

16.8 The constant perpetual growth rate model is invalid if g equals zero.

16.9 An increase in the required return will tend to increase a firm's *P/E* ratio.

16.10 A firm's *P/E* ratio will tend to increase if its earnings growth rate increases.

16.11 A perpetual bond can be valued with the one-stage model.

16.12 The valuation placed on a stock with the one-stage model depends upon the investor's expected holding period.

Multiple Choice Questions

16.1 Which one of the following is not an assumption of the constant perpetual growth valuation model?
(*a*) The required return must be greater than the dividend growth rate.
(*b*) Dividends grow at a constant rate forever.
(*c*) The required rate of return can vary.
(*d*) The firm's risk and its cost of capital remain constant.
(*e*) *a* and *b*.

16.2 The Johnson Corporation's dividends have been growing at a rate of 7 percent per year over the last 10 years, and this rate is expected to continue in the future. Current dividends per share are $3.85, and its required return is 14.5 percent. What is the value of Johnson's stock?
(*a*) $52.48
(*b*) $49.25
(*c*) $54.93
(*d*) $55.75
(*e*) $47.26

16.3 If Johnson's price is $40 per share and its current cash dividend of $3.85 per share is growing at a 7 percent rate per year, determine its required return?
(*a*) 16.2 percent
(*b*) 15.1 percent
(*c*) 16.6 percent
(*d*) 17.3 percent
(*e*) 18.2 percent

16.4 The Gordon Company has been experiencing rapid growth the last few years. Analysts expect the 30 percent growth rate in dividends to continue for the next 4 years. After the above normal growth period ends, dividends should grow at a more normal rate of 6 percent thereafter. Gordon has a current dividend of $2.60 per share. If Gordon has a required return of 17 percent, what is the value of its stock?
(*a*) $45.82
(*b*) $47.25
(*c*) $50.06
(*d*) $51.82
(*e*) $52.90

16.5 The Gordon Company expects a 30 percent growth rate in dividends for the next 4 years. After 4 years, dividends are expected to grow at a rate of 6 percent thereafter. If Gordon has a current dividend of $2.60 per share and a current price of $42, determine its required return.
(*a*) 19.35 percent
(*b*) 20.50 percent
(*c*) 17.77 percent
(*d*) 17.95 percent
(*e*) 18.20 percent

16.6 The Johnson Corporation's dividends are expected to grow at a rate of 7 percent in the future. If Johnson's current dividends per share are $3.85 and its required return is 14.5 percent, determine the price of Johnson's stock 3 years from now, P_3.
(*a*) $60.02
(*b*) $59.25
(*c*) $65.01
(*d*) $55.03
(*e*) $67.29

16.7 The Miller Corporation has current earnings per share of $6. Assume a dividend-payout ratio of 55 percent. Earnings grow at a rate of 8.5 percent per year. If Miller's required rate of return is 15 percent, what is its current value?
(*a*) $51.33
(*b*) $55.08
(*c*) $57.02
(*d*) $52.05
(*e*) $50.75

16.8 The earnings of the Smith Corporation have been growing at a rate of 10 percent per year over the past 5 years, and analysts expect this rate of growth to continue for the next 5 years. Current earnings per share are $4.65. The Smith Corporation has a current dividend-payout ratio of 60 percent, and this should continue in the future. If an investor is interested in purchasing Smith's stock and holding it for 5 years, what is the stock worth? Assume an ending *P/E* ratio of 17 and a required return of 15 percent. [*Hint:* Use Eq. (*16.7*).]
(*a*) $80.02
(*b*) $77.45
(*c*) $75.53
(*d*) $92.01
(*e*) $82.45

16.9 The earnings of the Smith Corporation are expected to grow at a rate of 10 percent for the next 5 years. The Smith Corporation has current earnings per share of $4.65, and its dividend-payout ratio is expected to stay at 60 percent. An ending *P/E* ratio of 17 is expected. If an investor purchases the stock for its current price of $60 and holds it for 5 years, what before-tax return does he expect to earn. [*Hint:* Use Eq. (*16.7*).]
(*a*) 19.20%
(*b*) 20.85%
(*c*) 21.45%
(*d*) 18.65%
(*e*) 19.75%

16.10 The stock of the Wood Corporation has a required return of 16.5 percent. Wood's current price is $55, and its current dividend per share is $1.80. Determine Wood's dividend growth rate.
(*a*) 10.65 percent
(*b*) 11.11 percent
(*c*) 12.81 percent
(*d*) 13.75 percent
(*e*) 14.02 percent

Answers

True-False

16.1. T 16.2. T 16.3. F 16.4. F 16.5. F 16.6. T 16.7. F 16.8. F 16.9. F
16.10. T 16.11. T 16.12. F

Multiple Choice

16.1. c 16.2. c 16.3. d 16.4. d 16.5. a 16.6. e 16.7. b 16.8. c 16.9. b
16.10. c

Chapter 17

Technical Analysis

17.1 THE CONCEPT

Technical analysts believe that important information about future stock price movements can be obtained by studying the historical price movement of stock prices. Financial data are recorded on graph paper and the data are scrutinized in search of repetitive patterns. Technical analysts base their buy and sell decisions on the charts they prepare.

1. Market value is determined by the interaction of supply and demand.
2. Supply and demand are governed by numerous factors, both rational and irrational.
3. Security prices tend to move in trends that persist for an appreciable length of time, despite minor fluctuations in the market.
4. Changes in a trend are caused by shifts in supply and demand.
5. Shifts in supply and demand, no matter why they occur, can be detected sooner or later in charts of market transactions.
6. Some chart patterns tend to repeat themselves.[1]

SOLVED PROBLEM 17.1

What is a fundamental analyst? How does a fundamental analyst differ from a technical analyst?

SOLUTION

A fundamental analyst believes that the true intrinsic value of a security can be ascertained by studying such items as the company's earnings, its products, its management, the company's financial statements, and other fundamental facts. Technical analysts do not accuse fundamentalists of being wrong. However, they believe fundamental analysis takes too long and is difficult to use. Technicians believe they can use various technical tools such as charts to identify underpriced securities.

17.2 TYPES OF CHARTS

Technical analysts use three basic types of charts—bar, line, and point and figure charts (PFC). *Bar charts* have a series of vertical bars representing each day's price movement. Each bar has a range from the day's lowest price to the day's highest price. A small cross on each bar signifies the day's closing price. Figure 17-1 is an example of a bar chart.

A *line chart* is a graph of successive day's closing prices. Figure 17-2 is a line chart for a stock.

Point and figure charts (PFCs) are a third and more complex type of chart. Technical analysts use PFCs to predict not only reversal in price trends for common stocks but to forecast future price movements. By studying PFCs, technicians determine when to buy and sell.

[1] R. D. Edwards and John Magee, Jr., *Technical Analysis of Stock Trends,* 4th ed. (Springfield, Mass.: John Magee, 1958), p. 86.

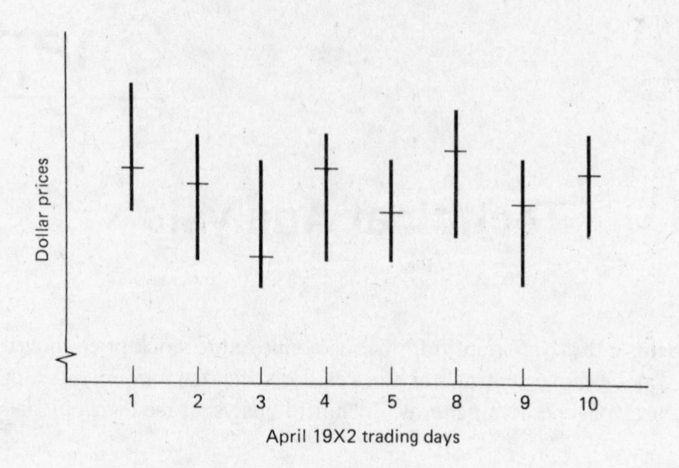

Fig. 17-1 Bar chart for a stock.

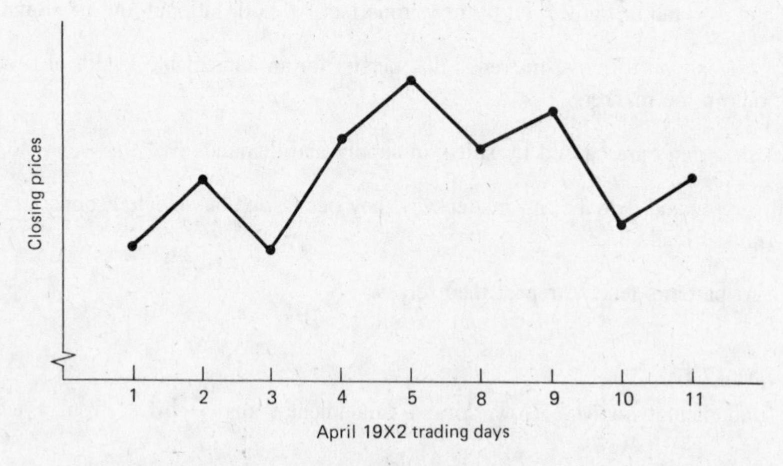

Fig. 17-2 Line chart for a stock.

SOLVED PROBLEM 17.2

Construct (*a*) a line chart based on closing prices and (*b*) a bar chart for the common stock of the Mosher Corporation with the following price information:

February 19X3	Prices		
	High	Low	Closing
2	$50	$45	$46
3	51	46	47
4	49	44	45
5	47	43	44
6	44	39	42
9	47	42	43
10	49	44	45
11	52	47	49

SOLUTION

(*a*) See Fig. 17-3.

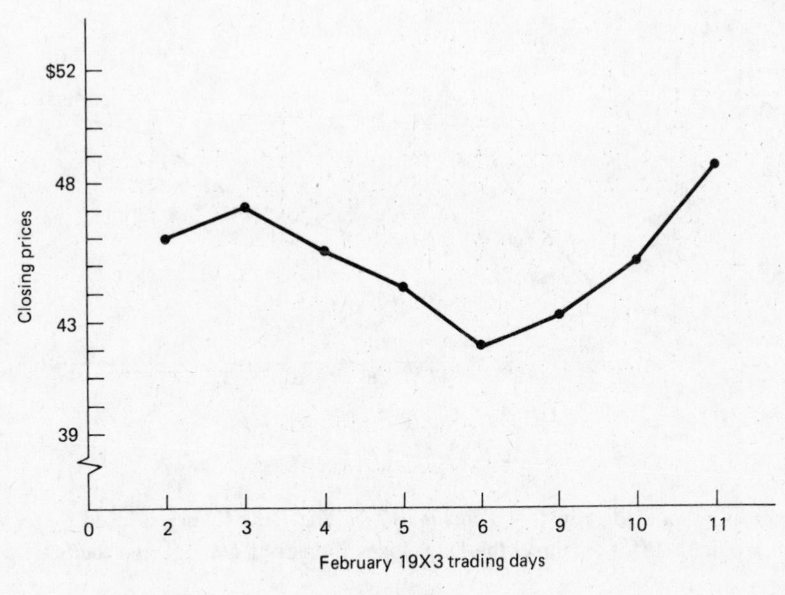

Fig. 17-3

(*b*) See Fig. 17-4.

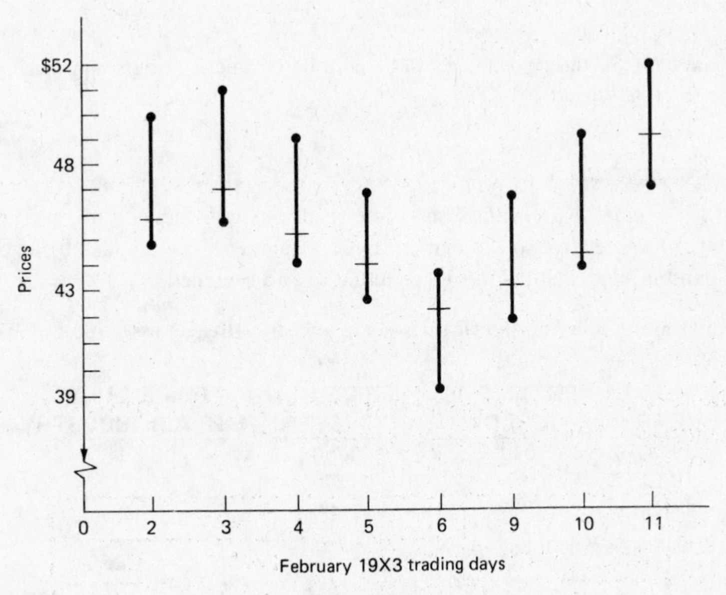

Fig. 17-4

17.3 DOW THEORY

The Dow theory views the movement of market prices as occurring in three categories:

(*a*) *Primary movements:* These are called bull and bear markets. Bull markets are where prices move in an upward manner for several years. Bear markets, on the other hand, are where prices move in a downward manner for several months or a few years.

(*b*) *Secondary movements:* These are up and down movement of stock prices that last for a few months and are called corrections.

(*c*) *Daily movements:* These are meaningless random daily fluctuations.

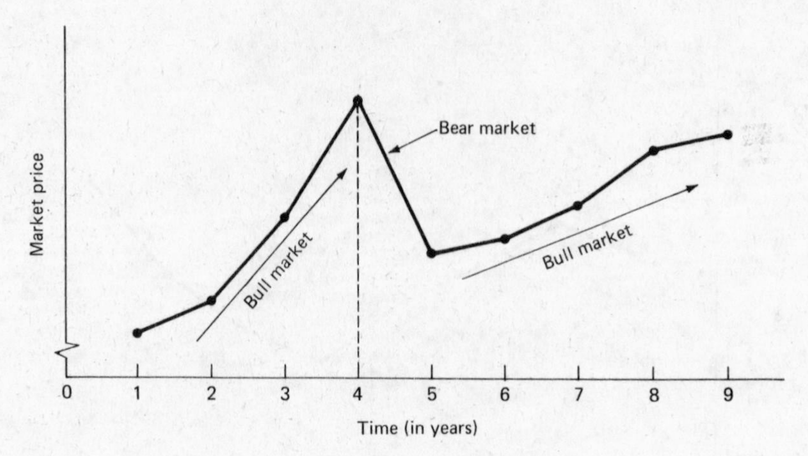

Fig. 17-5 Dow theory.

The Dow theory is graphically illustrated in Fig. 17-5. The Dow theory is used by technical analysts to determine trends in the market (for example, the Dow Jones Industrial Average and the S&P500), or in individual stocks.

SOLVED PROBLEM 17.3

The Dow theory has been subjected to numerous scientific studies which support its validity. True, false, or uncertain. Explain.

SOLUTION

False. While the Dow theory continues to be used by technical analysts, not much scientific evidence has been accumulated for its support.

17.4 RELATIVE STRENGTH

The basic idea behind *relative strength* is that some securities will increase more, relative to the market, in bull markets and decline less, relative to the market, in bear markets. Technicians believe that by investing in those securities that exhibit relative strength higher returns can be earned.

EXAMPLE 17.1 Jim Hankins, a technical analyst, is doing a relative strength assessment of Worldwide Airlines with the following data:

YEAR	PRICE (P_W) OF WORLDWIDE	PRICE (P_M) OF S&P500	PRICE (P_I) OF S&P AIR. INDUSTRY
19X4	$40	$250	$20
19X5	45	270	22
19X6	65	300	25

The relative strength calculations are as follows:

(1) YEAR	(2) $\frac{P_W}{P_I}$	(3) $\frac{P_W}{P_M}$	(4) $\frac{P_I}{P_M}$
19X4	$\frac{\$40}{\$20} = 2.00$	$\frac{\$40}{\$250} = .160$	$\frac{\$20}{\$250} = .080$
19X5	$\frac{\$45}{\$22} = 2.05$	$\frac{\$45}{\$270} = .167$	$\frac{\$22}{\$270} = .081$
19X6	$\frac{\$65}{\$25} = 2.60$	$\frac{\$65}{\$300} = .217$	$\frac{\$25}{\$300} = .083$

As column (2) indicates, Worldwide showed some relative strength in its industry during 19X5, but considerable *industry strength* was shown in 19X6 as the ratio went from 2.05 to 2.60. Similar *market relative strength* was exhibited in column (3). Column (4) indicates that the average firm in the airline industry in 19X5 had relative market strength. However, comparing column (3) and column (4) shows that in 19X6 Worldwide had significantly more relative market strength than the typical airline company.

SOLVED PROBLEM 17.4

The graphs in Fig. 17-6 show relative strength data for the Jones Furniture Company relative to the market and the furniture industry. Does the Jones Corporation appear to be a good investment candidate based on this data?

SOLUTION

From the standpoint of the industry, Jones is showing relative strength. Therefore, Jones would be a good investment candidate for the furniture industry if the past trend continues. However, from the perspective of the overall market, Jones is a poor investment. Jones is weak relative to the market because the furniture industry lacks relative strength.

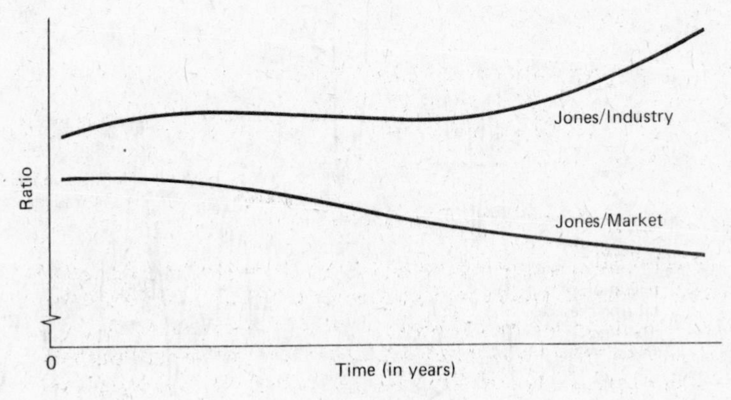

Fig. 17-6

17.5 CONTRARY OPINION

The idea behind *contrary opinion* is that the majority of traders in the market are wrong. So when the crowd does something such as sell, the contrarian should do the opposite and buy. Several contrarian rules are currently used. We will consider two of the more popular ones below.

Odd-Lot Theory

Round lots are transactions in multiples of 100 shares. *Odd-lot* transactions are for less than 100 shares. Odd-lot transactions are supposedly done by amateur investors who are usually wrong—according to the contrarians. Therefore, when the odd-lot purchases are relatively high, stock prices are likely to fall, and, when the odd-lot sales are low, the end of a bear market is supposed to be close at hand.

Theory of Short Sales

Short sales are done by investors who borrow the securities from a broker and sell them. The short sellers hope to profit by replacing the borrowed securities at a lower price than what they sold them for. Contrarians believe that short sellers are usually wrong, so when short sales are high, indicating a bearish attitude about the market, contrarians take a bullish attitude about the market.

Another group of investors take the opposite view of the contrarian short sellers approach. This group believes that short sellers are more sophisticated than the average investor and, when short sales are up, a more bearish situation is indicated for the market.

SOLVED PROBLEM 17.5

What is the New York Stock Exchange (NYSE) short interest ratio, and how is it used?

SOLUTION

The NYSE short interest ratio measures the total amount of short sales as a percent of the total volume of shares traded on the NYSE. A ratio above 1.5 percent is considered bullish and below 1.0 is considered bearish by contrarians.

17.6 MOVING AVERAGE

Moving average technicians calculate a moving average price for a security and use that average as a benchmark to gauge the daily price movements of a security. One of the most commonly used moving averages is the 200-day moving average. The closing prices of a security are averaged for 200 days and then each day the moving average changes as the most recent day is added and the two-hundred-and-first day is deleted. An example of different moving averages for the Dow Jones Industrial Average is given in Fig. 17-7.

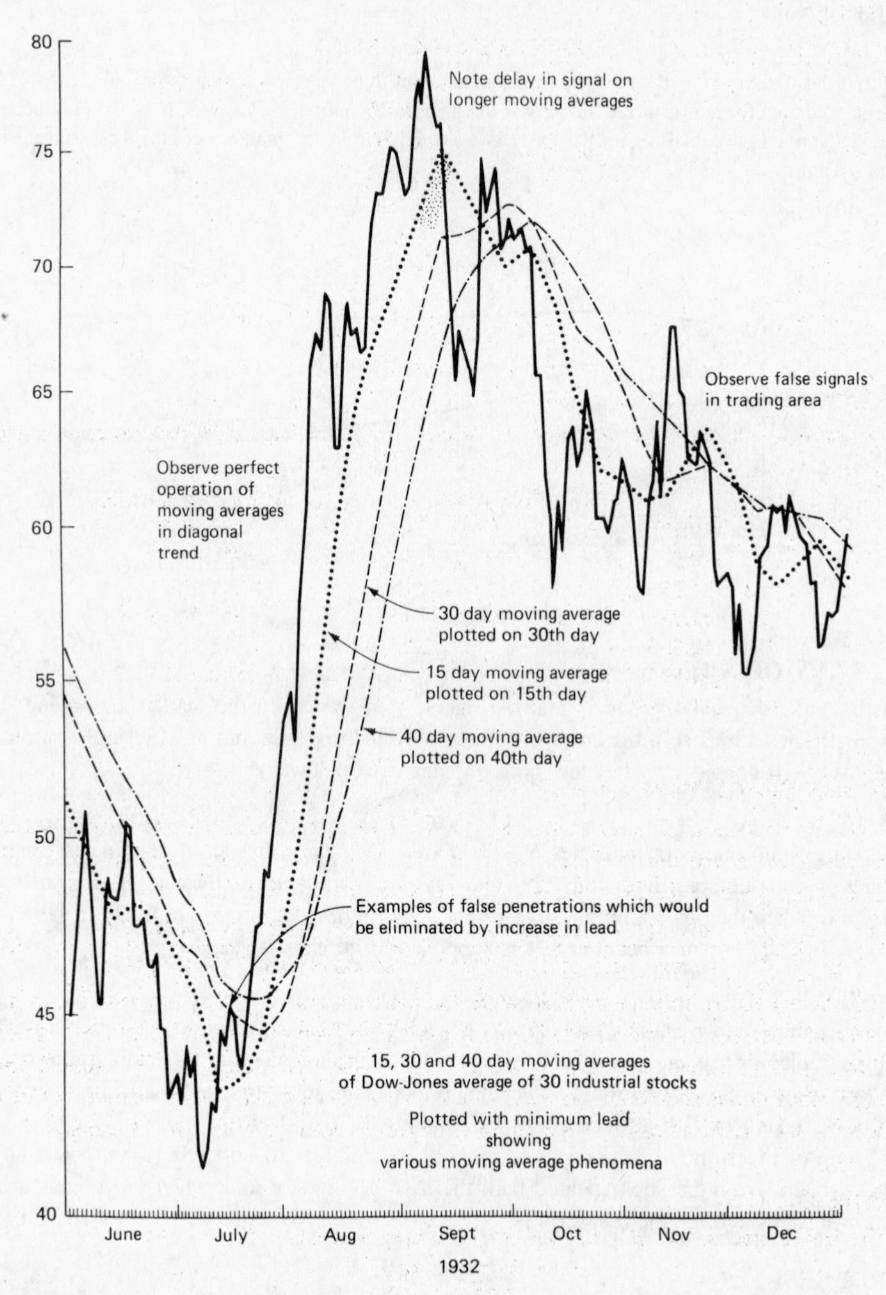

Fig. 17-7 Illustration of different moving averages. (*Source:* H. M. Gartley, *Profits and the Stock Market,* Lambert Gann Publishing, Pomeroy, Wash., 1981.)

Moving average analysis is used to tell a technician when to buy or sell a security. For example, a moving average analyst would recommend buying a stock when (1) the prices of a stock move through a flattened moving average line, (2) the stock's price falls below a moving average line that is rising, and (3) the price of a stock that is above a moving average line falls but turns around and starts up before it ever reaches the moving average line.

SOLVED PROBLEM 17.6

Given the following closing prices for the Hobart Corporation, calculate a 4-day moving average for its stock prices.

DAY	CLOSING PRICES
1	$10.125
2	10.500
3	11.250
4	11.750
5	12.000
6	11.500
7	11.125
8	13.250
9	13.750
10	14.250

SOLUTION

We will start with day 4 and go through day 10 dropping and adding a price each day as we move forward one day at a time:

DAY	COMPUTATIONS		AVERAGE PRICE
4	(10.125 + 10.50 + 11.25 + 11.75)/4	=	$10.90625
5	(10.50 + 11.25 + 11.75 + 12.00)/4	=	$11.375
6	(11.25 + 11.75 + 12.00 + 11.50)/4	=	$11.625
7	(11.75 + 12.00 + 11.50 + 11.125)/4	=	$11.59375
8	(12.00 + 11.50 + 11.125 + 13.250)/4	=	$11.96875
9	(11.50 + 11.125 + 13.25 + 13.75)/4	=	$12.40625
10	(11.125 + 13.25 + 13.75 + 14.25)/4	=	$13.09375

17.7 THE CONFIDENCE INDEX

A confidence index should tell a technician how willing investors are to assume risk. One confidence index is the *Barron's confidence index* (BCI), which is the ratio of the average yield of the 10 highest grade bonds over the average yield of the Dow Jones 40 bond index. In equation form, the BCI is

$$\text{BCI} = \frac{\text{average yield of Barron's 10 highest grade bonds at time } t}{\text{average yield of Dow Jones 40 bonds at time } t \text{ (lesser grade)}}$$

As bond investors become more optimistic about the national economy, they are less risk-averse and some will shift their bond holdings to lower grade bonds. This will bid up prices and lower the yield on low-grade bonds relative to high-grade bonds and thereby increase the confidence index. The BCI should always be less than 1 since high-grade bonds should always yield less than low-grade bonds. Some technicians believe that the confidence index is a leading indicator of the national economy, leading it by 2 to 11 months.

SOLVED PROBLEM 17.7

Over the past 4 weeks, the BCI has had the following values:

WEEK	BCI
1	.70
2	.68
3	.65
4	.61

How might a technician interpret these numbers?

SOLUTION

The BCI tells the technician how investors view the market. In this situation, since the BCI is declining, investors are becoming more pessimistic (or bearish) about the market. Yields on lower-grade bonds are increasing relative to yields on higher-grade bonds. Essentially, the BCI suggests that an investor should not invest in the stock market.

17.8 TRADING VOLUME

Volume technicians believe they can get a better idea whether the market is bullish or bearish by studying its price moves in conjunction with trading volume. If trading volume is high on the days when the market price is moving up, for example, this is considered bullish. On the other hand, a low volume on days when the market is moving up is considered to be less bullish or ambiguous.

17.9 BREADTH OF MARKET

A breadth of market indicator tries to measure the strength of the market's upward or downward movement. Daily newspapers report the number of issues that advance and decline in price each day in the various exchanges such as the NYSE. Daily net advances, which are the number of issues that advance minus the number of issues that decline, are accumulated by technicians. Technicians hope to discern the direction of the underlying market's movement by studying net advances; they try to determine the market's trend.

True-False Questions

17.1 A declining trend in the BCI is an indication of a bullish trend in the stock market.

17.2 According to contrarians, odd-lot transactions are done by professional investors who are usually correct.

17.3 An investor that sells short is bullish on the market.

17.4 A point and figure chart is another name for a bar chart.

17.5 Technicians believe that security prices are primarily determined by supply and demand.

17.6 Tools of the technical analyst are the *P/E* ratio and earnings per share trends.

17.7 According to the Dow theory, primary movements are corrections in stock prices.

17.8 A contrarian approach to investing is doing the opposite of what a large group of investors are doing.

17.9 Technicians would interpret a high level of outstanding short sales as a sign of increased future demand for securities.

17.10 A rising BCI indicates that investors are becoming more pessimistic about the market.

Multiple Choice Questions

Figure 17-8 should be used with the next two questions.

17.1 The graph in Fig. 17-8 shows that B&K Utility has
(*a*) Relative strength in the utility industry
(*b*) Relative weakness in the utility industry
(*c*) Neither strength or weakness in the utility industry
(*d*) Been a leader in the utility industry

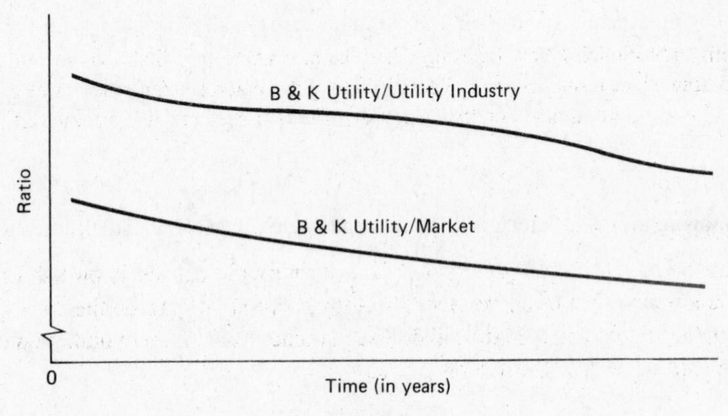

Fig. 17-8

17.2 The above graph shows that B&K Utility has
(*a*) Relative strength in the market
(*b*) Relative weakness in the market
(*c*) Shows less relative weakness in the market than in the utility industry
(*d*) None of the above

17.3 A moving average analyst would recommend selling a stock if
(*a*) A stock's price moves down through the moving average.
(*b*) A stock's price falls through the moving average line after it flattens out.
(*c*) A stock's price rises above a moving average line which is declining.
(*d*) *a* and *b*.
(*e*) *a* and *c*.

17.4 A moving average analyst would recommend buying a stock if
(*a*) A stock's price rises above a moving average line which is declining.
(*b*) The moving average line flattens out and the stock's price rises through the moving average.
(*c*) The price of a stock falls below a moving average line that is rising.
(*d*) *a* and *b*.
(*e*) *b* and *c*.

Use the information given below for the next three questions. The following closing prices are given for the McKay Corporation's stock over an 8-day period:

CLOSING PRICES	DAY
$43	1
44	2
40	3
39	4
45	5
47	6
49	7
50	8

17.5 Using a 5-day moving average, determine the average price for McKay's stock for day 6.
(*a*) $47
(*b*) $43
(*c*) $42.20
(*d*) $44.50
(*e*) $46

17.6 Using a 6-day moving average, determine the average price for McKay's stock for day 8.
(*a*) $42
(*b*) $44
(*c*) $45
(*d*) $46
(*e*) $47

17.7 Using a 4-day moving average, determine the average price for McKay's stock for day 5.
(*a*) $42
(*b*) $41.50
(*c*) $43
(*d*) $44
(*e*) $45

17.8 Some technicians look for a rush of selling that is called a "speculative blowoff" to mark
(*a*) The beginning of a bull market
(*b*) The end of a bear market
(*c*) The end of a bull market
(*d*) None of the above

17.9 Which of the following are contrary opinion indicators?
(*a*) Odd-lot transactions
(*b*) *P/E* ratios
(*c*) Short sales
(*d*) *a* and *c*
(*e*) None of the above

17.10 A rising BCI indicates that
(*a*) Managers of the "smart money" are pessimistic.
(*b*) Managers of the "smart money" are optimistic.
(*c*) The beginning of a bear market.
(*d*) *a* and *c*.
(*e*) None of the above.

Answers

True-False

17.1. F 17.2. F 17.3. F 17.4. F 17.5. T 17.6. F 17.7. F 17.8. T
17.9. T 17.10. F

Multiple Choice

17.1. b 17.2. b 17.3. e 17.4. e 17.5. b 17.6. c 17.7. a 17.8. c
17.9. d 17.10. b

Chapter 18

Efficient Markets Theory

18.1 THE RANDOM WALK THEORY

Do stock price changes move in a random and unpredictable manner? Generally speaking, they do. However, stock prices also tend to move upward at a rate of about 6 percent per year in the long run.

The randomness of stock price changes can be discerned by studying Figs. 18-1 and 18-2. Figure 18-1 is a plot of changes in the prices of the S&P500 over a 52-week period. On the other hand, Fig. 18-2 is generated by throwing dice in a way that makes the process random. The two figures are indeed very similar.

SOLVED PROBLEM 18.1

Since stock price changes apparently follow a random walk, the stock market must operate in an irrational manner. True, false, or uncertain? Explain.

SOLUTION

False. Randomness in stock price changes is what should be expected in a well-functioning stock market. It indicates that market participants act rather quickly to news that is relevant to stock value and that stock prices adjust rather quickly to these information-motivated trades. The more quickly stock prices adjust and reflect information that affects value, the more *efficient* are the market's prices.

18.2 LEVELS OF MARKET EFFICIENCY

Market efficiency refers to the ability of financial assets to quickly adjust and reflect all information that is relevant to value in its price. The subject of market efficiency involves a thorough study of the *efficient market hypothesis.* The efficient market hypothesis has three subhypotheses.

1. Weakly efficient
2. Semistrongly efficient
3. Strongly efficient

We will now take a closer look at each of these subhypotheses.

Weakly Efficient

The *weakly efficient* market hypothesis states that stock prices reflect historical price information and, therefore, an investor cannot "beat the market" by studying historical prices. When we say "beat the market," we mean do better than a stock market index (like the S&P500) that is properly adjusted for risk, transaction costs, and taxes.

Two main types of empirical tests have been performed to determine if the stock market is consistent with the weakly efficient market hypothesis. The first are tests for *serial independence.* Many tests have been performed to see if stock price changes are correlated over time. While a small amount of *autocorrelation* in stock price changes has been found, not enough exists to make their study worthwhile in a monetary sense. Another type are tests of *filter rules.* This is devising mechanical trading strategies using stock prices to beat the market. While numerous mechanical trading rules have been investigated, none appear to help the investor beat the market.

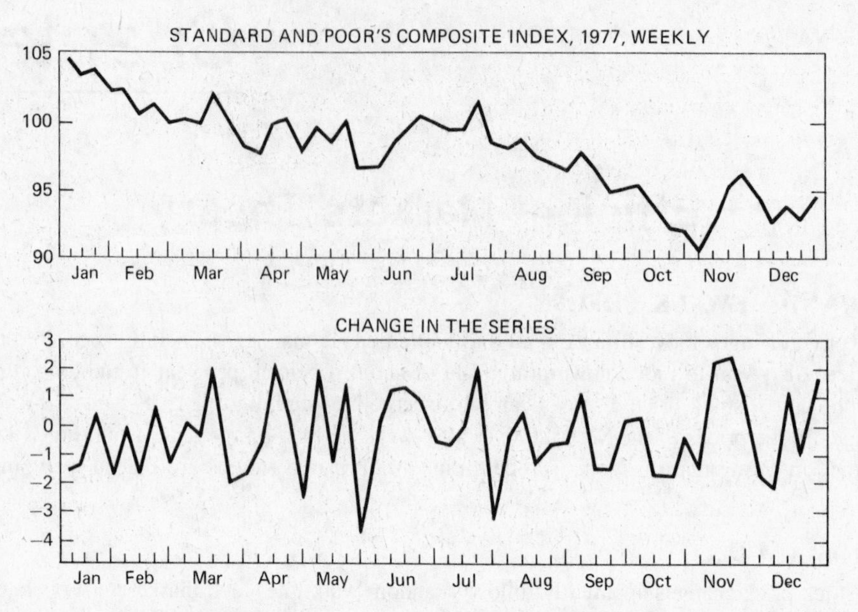

Fig. 18-1 Weekly changes in the S&P500. (*Source:* Neil G. Berkman, "A Primer on Random Walks in the Stock Market," *New England Economic Review,* September/October 1978, pp. 32–50.)

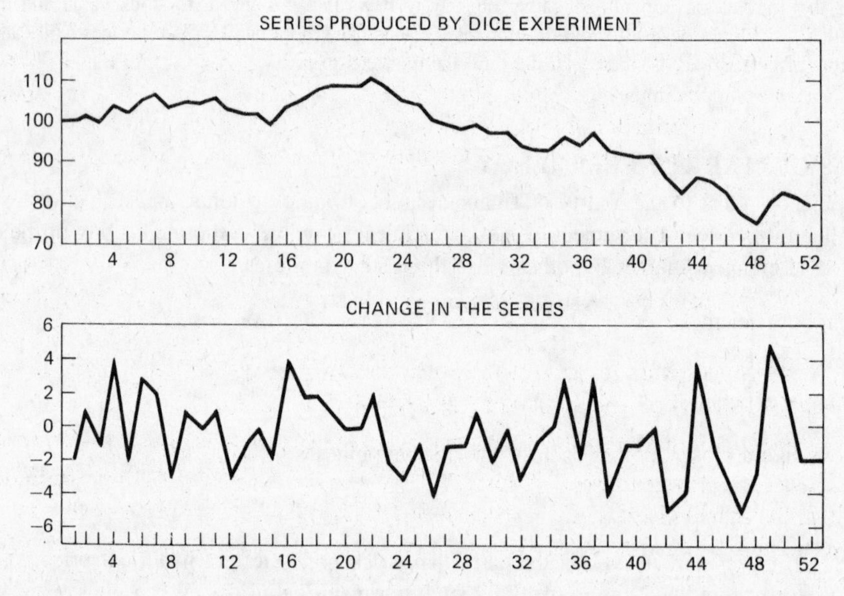

Fig. 18-2 Dice experiment. (*Source:* Neil G. Berkman, "A Primer on Random Walks in the Stock Market," *New England Economic Review,* September/October 1978, pp. 32–50.)

SOLVED PROBLEM 18.2

Since the weakly efficient market hypothesis appears to be strongly supported by the evidence, why does *technical analysis* seem to survive?

SOLUTION

Technical analysis attempts to predict future stock prices by using historical price information and volume data. One reason technical analysis seems to survive is plain luck. The fact that a large number of technical analysis systems exist and they are all vaguely defined means that it would be impossible to test them all. Another reason is that many practicing technical analysts do not read the scientific evidence.

SOLVED PROBLEM 18.3

Which of the following events violate the weakly efficient market hypothesis? Explain.

(*a*) Mr. Evans has been studying the historical price changes of several companies and plotting their movement over time. As a result of his utilization of historical price changes, he has been able to beat the S&P500 over the past 3 years.

(*b*) The historical correlation of the price changes of the Jones Corporation is .60 (a two-quarter lag).

(*c*) Jane Frankle, using a filter rule she developed, has been able to beat the S&P500 by 5 percent per year (on average) the last 20 years. Returns were adjusted for risk, transaction costs, and taxes.

SOLUTION

(*a*) While Mr. Evans may have discovered some useful information, it is not clear that he has beaten the market. For one thing, his portfolio may be more risky than the market and, when properly adjusted for risk, the return on his portfolio may be less than the market. In addition, 3 years does not cover a complete business cycle so it is probably not long enough to properly judge the outcome. Mr. Evans must also properly adjust his return for all the costs—transaction costs, taxes, and his time.

(*b*) Assuming a sample period of at least 30 quarters, this is not consistent with the weakly efficient market hypothesis. With this highly significant serial correlation, a profitable trading rule might be developed.

(*c*) This is not consistent with the weakly efficient market hypothesis. Ms. Frankle appears to be able to beat the market.

Semistrongly Efficient

If financial markets are efficient at the semistrong level, then prices reflect all relevant *public* information. This means that an investor could not beat the market by studying such items as *The Wall Street Journal, Barron's,* and *Moodys.*

Event studies. One of the main ways to test for semistrong efficiency is through event studies. With event studies, we attempt to measure how quickly relevant public information is incorporated into price. For example, the event may be a positive change in earnings. How quickly is the positive information reflected in price? The more quickly the positive information is reflected in price, the more efficient the market.

The methodology used to test for efficiency at the semistrong level with event studies was developed by Fama, Fisher, Jensen, and Roll.[1] The procedure is as follows:

1. A characteristic line for the corporation(s) is(are) calculated. However, a designated period of time before and after the event takes place is eliminated from the calculation. This could be a period of 15 weeks or 30 days before and after the event. (For more details on the characteristic line, see Chap. 23.)
2. Then, an abnormal return is calculated by subtracting the predicted return from the actual return for the designated period of time before and after the event.
3. The abnormal return (AR) is then cumulated over the designated period before and after the event.
4. In the case of positive earnings information in an efficient market, if the information had been unanticipated, the cumulative abnormal return (CAR) should be zero before the event and then shift to a positive level right after the event and remain at that level. On the other hand, if the CAR continues to move upward for several weeks after the positive earnings information is made public, this would be an indication that the market is not perfectly efficient.

EXAMPLE 18.1 Jim Jordan, a financial analyst, is trying to determine if the unannounced increase in cash dividends for the Alpha Corporation is consistent with semistrong market efficiency. Mr. Jordan calculated the following characteristic line for Alpha's stock over a 5-year period of time on a weekly basis up to 5 weeks before the unannounced cash dividend increase:

$$r_{A,t} = 2\% + 1.1r_{m,t}$$

where $r_{A,t}$ is the return for Alpha in time period t and $r_{m,t}$ is the return for the market in time period t. Using the above characteristic line, he calculated the expected returns for the time period under consideration as follows:

$$r_{A,t=-5} = 2\% + 1.1(10\%) = 13\%$$

[1]E. F. Fama, L. Fisher, M. Jensen, and R. Roll, "The Adjustment of Stock Prices to New Information," *International Economic Review,* February 1969, pp. 1–21.

Note that the returns for this example are annualized and that the market returns are taken from Table 18.1. In a similar manner, the characteristic line was applied nine more times to generate Column (1) in Table 18.1.

Table 18.1 Event Study Example

(1) Exp. Ret. Alpha, %	(2) Actual Ret. Alpha, %	(3) Market Ret., %	(4) AR, %	(5) CAR, %	(6) Time (weeks) Relative to Cash Dividend
13	14	10	1	1	−5
−3.5	−4.5	−5	−1	0	−4
15.2	17.2	12	2	2	−3
17.4	15.4	14	−2	0	−2
−4.6	−4.6	−6	0	0	−1
9.7	11.7	7	2	2	0 (Div.)
−2.4	−2.4	−4	0	2	1
8.6	9.6	6	1	3	2
10.8	9.8	8	−1	2	3
−2.4	−2.4	−4	0	2	4
5.3	5.3	3	0	2	5

Column (4), AR, was generated as follows:

$$AR_t = r_{A,t} - E(r_A) = \text{actual return} - \text{expected return}$$

$$AR_{t=-5} = 14\% - 13\% = 1\%$$

The remaining part of Column (4) was generated in a similar manner.

Column (5), CAR, was calculated as follows:

$$CAR_k = \sum_{n=-5}^{k} AR_n = AR_{-5} + AR_{-4} + \cdots + AR_k$$

where k is the ending time period. For example, $CAR_{-3} = 1 + (-1) + 2 = 2$ is how the third value in Column (5) was generated.

In analyzing the results of the CAR given in Column (5), the CAR was 0 until the unannounced cash dividend increase at time 0. After time 0, the CAR went to 2 percent and stayed at that level for the next five periods. This is consistent with semistrong market efficiency.

Numerous event studies that deal with events such as accounting changes and world events have been performed. The majority are consistent with semistrong market efficiency.

SOLVED PROBLEM 18.4

Ed Timms has been studying stock splits and has generated the following information. The data are averages for the 50 stocks that were studied, and the returns are annualized.

EXP. RET., %	ACTUAL RET., %	AR, %	CAR, %	TIME (days)
10	10	0	0	−6
−5	−3	2	2	−5
7	8	1	3	−4
6	7	1	4	−3
4	5	1	5	−2
−6	−5	1	6	−1
8	9	1	7	0
−4	−4	0	7	1
10	12	2	9	2
−3	−2	1	10	3
12	14	2	12	4
14	15	1	13	5
16	16	0	13	6

Are the above results consistent with the semistrong efficient market hypothesis?

SOLUTION

The CARs for the firms not only increase in anticipation of the stock split at time 0, but they continue to increase well after the event (5 days). This type of behavior is not consistent with semistrong market efficiency. If this pattern is consistent (which, in fact, it is not), it would imply that buying stock before they split would be a way to "beat the market."

SOLVED PROBLEM 18.5

Graphically show an unanticipated negative event that is inconsistent with semistrong market efficiency.

SOLUTION

See Fig. 18-3. Rather than adjusting quickly to negative news at time $t = 0$, a few days of learning lag are required for the appropriate downward price adjustment to take place.

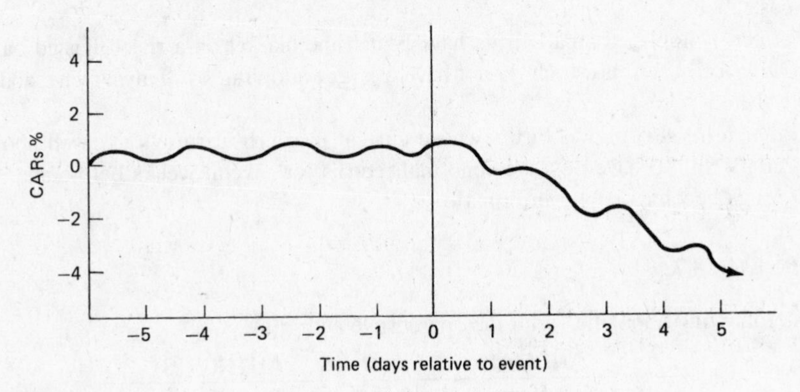

Fig. 18-3

SOLVED PROBLEM 18.6

Explain whether or not the following conditions are consistent with market efficiency at the semistrong level:

(*a*) The PC Investment Company recently developed a powerful computer model for selecting undervalued stocks. Back-testing the model with a universe of 250 stocks resulted in a return, after adjustments for risk, taxes, and transaction costs, that was 7 percent greater that the S&P500.

(*b*) Mary Evans recently started an investment newsletter. The stocks recommended by Mary have beaten the S&P500 by 40 percent the past 3 months.

(*c*) Jerry Simms has been using an investment technique over the past 30 years that concentrates on low *P/E* stocks with good earnings prospects. Jerry's results are quite impressive. After adjusting his annual return for risk, transaction costs, and taxes, he has been able to beat the S&P500 by 10 percent per year.

SOLUTION

(*a*) Even though the PC Investment Company's model has performed well in the past, it may not do that well in the future. Therefore, until the model can prove it can beat the market in the future (an out-of-sample test), it cannot be classified as a market beater.

(*b*) While Mary's results are impressive, there is an excellent chance it was all due to luck. The period of time is too short for a proper evaluation. In addition, returns should be properly adjusted for risk, taxes, and transaction costs.

(*c*) Jerry apparently has developed a technique that has beaten the market at the semistrong level. His returns have been properly adjusted for risk, taxes, and transaction costs.

Strongly Efficient

The strongly efficient market hypothesis states that the market cannot be beaten by using all relevant *public information* and also all *private information*. This is a very strong statement and has been refuted. Evidence has been presented showing that *insiders* have been able to beat the market. However, published evidence has shown that professional money managers have not on the average been able to beat the market.[2]

18.3 ANOMALIES

While a large number of studies support the efficient market hypothesis at the semistrong and weakly efficient levels, there are a growing number of studies which do not. These studies are called *anomalies.* Some of the major anomalies are

(1) *Weekend effect.* Stock returns do not have the same expected return for each day of the week. Typically Monday's return is slightly negative.
(2) *January effect.* Stock returns, especially those of small firms, are usually higher in January than in any other month.
(3) *Low P/E stocks.* Stock with low *P/E* ratios outperform the market, after adjusting for risk, taxes, and transaction costs.
(4) *Small-firm effect.* Stocks of small firms have beaten the market on a risk-adjusted basis.
(5) *Neglected firm effect.* Firms which do not have a large following by analysts have abnormal returns associated with them.
(6) *Unexpected quarterly earnings.* Firms whose current quarterly earnings are well above their expected quarterly earnings tend to have positive abnormal returns for several weeks before and after the large increase in earnings becomes public information.

SOLVED PROBLEM 18.7

Match the following anomalies with the appropriate author(s).

ANOMALY	AUTHOR(S)
1. January effect	A. French
2. Low *P/E* ratio	B. Arbel and Strebel
3. Unexpected quart. earnings	C. Jones and Latane'
4. Weekend effect	D. Basu
5. Small-firm effect	E. Banz
6. Neglected firm effect	F. Keim

SOLUTION

(1) F (2) D (3) C (4) A (5) E (6) B

SOLVED PROBLEM 18.8

The NPV should be 0 for an investment in a financial asset in an efficient market. Why is this true?

SOLUTION

By definition the NPV (net present value) of an investment is the difference between the present value of its expected benefits and its cost. If markets are efficient and prices reflect true value, then the present value of the expected benefits should equal its price and, therefore, the NPV will be 0. To put this another way, when the NPV of an investment is 0, the investment is earning the return it should be earning for its risk level.

True-False Questions

18.1 A useful approach for beating the market is to buy low beta stocks.

18.2 Studies indicate that holding a low *P/E* ratio stock portfolio is a good way to beat the market.

18.3 Studies have proven that a good way to beat the market is to use price and volume information.

[2]M. C. Jensen, "Risk, the Pricing of Capital Assets, and the Evaluation of Investment Portfolios," *Journal of Business,* April 1969, pp. 167–247.

18.4 Insiders should not be able to beat the market if it is efficient at the semistrong level.

18.5 About one-half of the mutual funds have consistently beaten the market.

18.6 The January effect states that during the month of January high *P/E* ratio stocks outperform low *P/E* ratio stocks.

18.7 The weakly efficient market hypothesis states that you cannot beat the market by studying *Value Line*.

18.8 If the market is efficient, investors can have different expected returns for different securities.

18.9 Even if the market were efficient at the semistrong level, some investors would beat the market each year.

18.10 One of the main reasons that financial markets are efficient is the keen competition among investors that search for undervalued securities.

18.11 Significant amounts of nonrandom movements of stock price changes will not be found in semistrong efficient markets.

18.12 If markets are efficient at the semistrong level, then an investor might as well pick a portfolio of common stocks by throwing darts at the financial pages of *The Wall Street Journal*.

Multiple Choice Questions

The four graphs presented in Fig. 18-4 should be used with the next four questions.

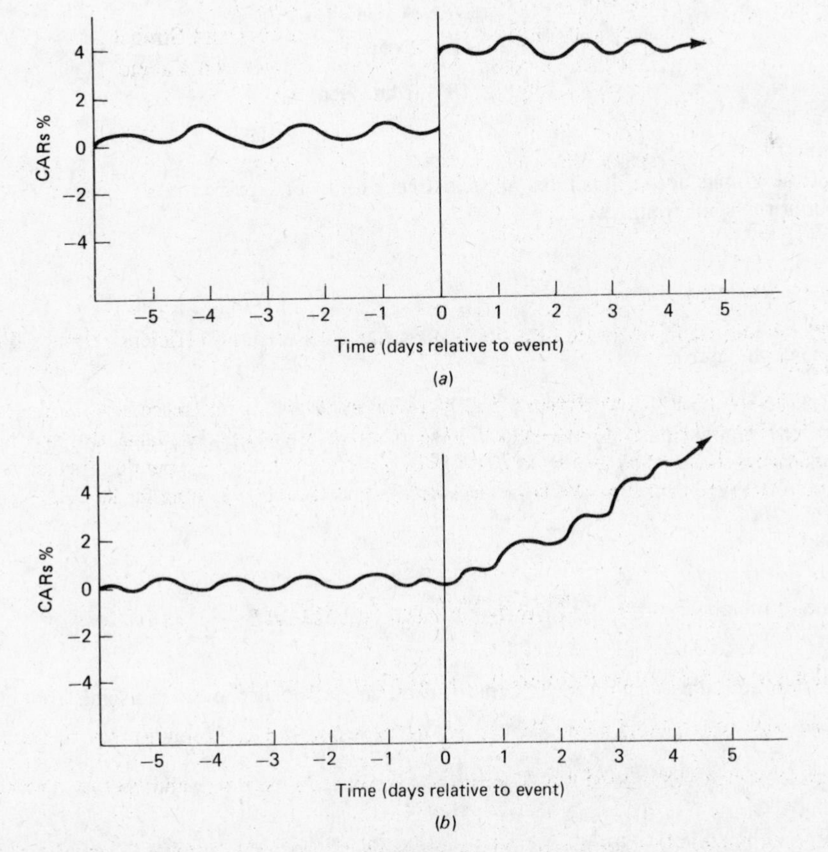

Fig. 18-4

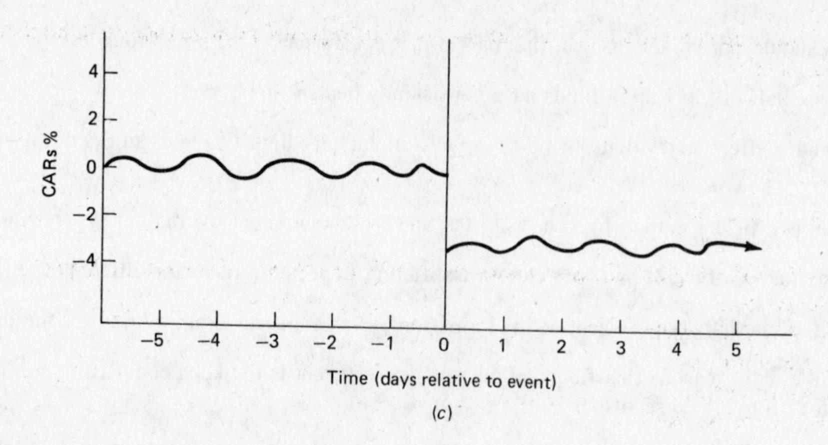

(c)

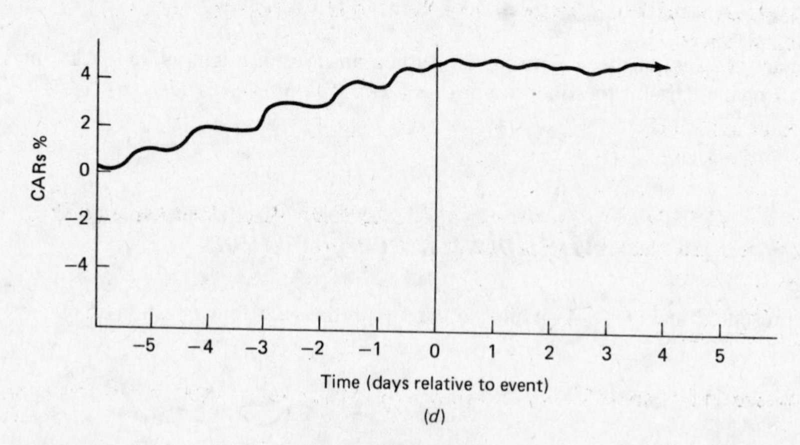

(d)

Fig. 18-4 (continued)

18.1 Which of the graphs above illustrates an adjustment to an unexpected positive event in a market that is inefficient at the semistrong level?
(a) a
(b) b
(c) c
(d) d
(e) None of the above

18.2 Which of the graphs illustrates an adjustment to an unexpected negative event in a semistrong efficient market?
(a) a
(b) b
(c) c
(d) d
(e) None of the above

18.3 Which of the graphs illustrates an adjustment to an anticipated positive event in a semistrong efficient market?
(a) a
(b) b
(c) c
(d) d
(e) None of the above

18.4 Which of the graphs illustrates an adjustment to an unexpected positive event in a market efficient at the semistrong level?
(*a*) *a*
(*b*) *b*
(*c*) *c*
(*d*) *d*
(*e*) None of the above

18.5 Which of the following are consistent with the semistrong theory of market efficiency?
(*a*) January effect
(*b*) Low *P/E* ratio stocks
(*c*) Neglected firms
(*d*) Small-firm effect
(*e*) None of the above

18.6 In a weakly efficient market, you cannot beat the market by studying
(*a*) Historical prices
(*b*) *The Wall Street Journal*
(*c*) *Value Line*
(*d*) Standard and Poors
(*e*) None of the above

18.7 If the market is perfectly efficient, which group listed below should beat the market?
(*a*) Growth-oriented mutual fund managers
(*b*) Corporate insiders
(*c*) Both *a* and *b*
(*d*) None of the above

18.8 Point and figure charts are effective in beating the market under which of the following efficient market hypotheses?
(*a*) Weakly
(*b*) Semistrong
(*c*) Strong-form
(*d*) Both *a* and *b*
(*e*) None of the above

18.9 Which one of the statements below is most consistent with the semistrong efficient market hypothesis?
(*a*) Information contained in annual reports will not be helpful in beating the market.
(*b*) Price and volume information will be helpful in predicting future stock price movements.
(*c*) By reading *The Wall Street Journal,* an investor can beat the market.
(*d*) Both *b* and *c*.
(*e*) None of the above.

18.10 Suppose you find you can beat the market by using information from *Value Line.* This will be consistent with
(*a*) Weak-form inefficiency
(*b*) Semistrong efficiency
(*c*) Semistrong inefficiency
(*d*) Weak-form efficiency
(*e*) None of the above

18.11 In his empirical study of common stocks Basu found
(*a*) Evidence of semistrong efficiency
(*b*) Evidence of weak-form efficiency
(*c*) Evidence against semistrong efficiency
(*d*) Evidence against strong-form efficiency
(*e*) None of the above

18.12 Since studies indicate that stock exchange specialists earn abnormal returns, this is inconsistent with
(*a*) The weakly efficient market hypothesis
(*b*) The semistrong efficient market hypothesis
(*c*) The strong-form efficient market hypothesis
(*d*) None of the above

Answers

True-False

18.1. F 18.2. T 18.3. F 18.4. F 18.5. F 18.6. F 18.7. F 18.8. T
18.9. T 18.10. T 18.11. T 18.12. F

Multiple Choice

18.1. b 18.2. c 18.3. d 18.4. a 18.5. e 18.6. a 18.7. d 18.8. e
18.9. a 18.10. c 18.11. c 18.12. c

Chapter 19

Futures

19.1 COMMODITIES

Futures contracts are traded on several dozen of the commodities that are traded in physical markets. Farm products like wheat, cotton, and soybean oil; metals such as silver and gold; and financial instruments like stock market indexes and foreign currencies have futures contracts traded on them.

19.2 THE FUTURES CONTRACT

Futures contracts are traded in commodity exchanges such as the Chicago Board of Trade, Chicago Mercantile Exchange, and New York Mercantile Exchange. Actual or real commodities are traded in the *cash* (*or physicals*) *markets.* Future contracts that are not due within the current month are called *futures contracts.* Those futures contracts that might be delivered within the current month are called *spot contracts.*

Contracts for futures are standardized. For example, on the Chicago Board of Trade (CBT) a T-bond futures contract calls for one Treasury bond that has a face value of $100,000 and an 8 percent coupon rate, and soybean and corn futures contracts specify 5,000 bushels as the *trading unit.* When trading futures contracts, a trader will tell a *broker* to *short futures* (or sell futures) or take a *long position* (which means purchase futures), and a trader will also give the number of units, maybe a bid or ask price, and the desired delivery month. A trader must either pay *cash* for the contract or pay the *initial margin* requirement of 3 percent to 15 percent when the initial order is placed. Margin traders do not have to pay the balance due until they take delivery. However, most margin traders rarely take delivery because they usually *reverse out* of their contract before its delivery date. For example, they could purchase a futures contract and later sell a similar futures contract so they had no position left.

19.3 HEDGING WITH COMMODITIES

One of the major uses of futures contracts is *hedging.* Hedges are created by combining a long and short position in the same asset to reduce or eliminate *price fluctuation risk.* A *buying hedge* is designed to protect a buyer against a price increase. On the other hand, a *selling hedge* will protect a seller against a falling price.

EXAMPLE 19.1 Jim Ledbetter, a Kansas wheat farmer, expects to harvest 40,000 bushels of wheat in early August. On June 15, the price of wheat is $3.50 per bushel. Jim is concerned that the price of wheat per bushel will fall below $3.50 before his August delivery date. A friend told Jim that he should hedge his position by selling August wheat futures. By selling wheat futures, Jim can lock in the August futures price of $3.45 per bushel. Jim took his friend's advice and sold eight 5,000 bushels of August wheat futures. When August came, the price of wheat had fallen to $3.00 per bushel. However, Jim's hedge covered his losses because what he lost on the cash crop was offset by his gains on the futures contracts minus a small transaction charge. The value of the hedged position was calculated as follows:

$$\text{Revenue from the sale of physical wheat} = \$3.00 \times 40{,}000 = \$120{,}000 \quad \text{revenue}$$

$$\text{Sale of 8 wheat futures contracts} = 8 \times \$3.45 \times 5{,}000 = \$138{,}000 \quad \text{revenue}$$

$$\text{Purchase of 8 wheat futures contracts} = 8 \times \$3 \times 5{,}000 = \$120{,}000$$

$$\text{Gain on futures contracts} = \$18{,}000$$

Jim's net cash flow for August was $138,000 ($120,000 + $18,000), which is $3.45 per bushel of wheat.

Example 19.1 is an illustration of a *perfect hedge.* However, perfect hedges are rare because of the various uncertainties in the hedging process. For example, with farm commodities the quality and the quantity of the products harvested may differ from the ones in the futures contracts, and cash prices and futures prices may not be exactly the same when the futures contracts expire.

Suppose in Example 19.1 that the futures price at the time of expiration of the August wheat futures contracts was $3.05 rather than $3.00, as assumed in the example. When Jim reversed his position by purchasing 8 contracts for $3.05 per bushel his total revenue would have been reduced by $2,000 [(8 × $3 × 5,000) − (8 × $3.05 × 5,000)]. Therefore, the selling hedge would have been less than perfect.

The *basis* for commodity i at a point in time denoted t is

$$\text{Basis}_{it} = \text{futures price}_{it} - \text{spot price}_{it}$$

For a given futures contract, the basis should converge to zero at the delivery date. However, if it does not equal zero when the futures contract expires, a less than perfect hedge will result. The basis in Example 19.1 did converge to zero and this resulted in a perfect hedge. However, at the time of expiration if the basis is positive (negative) then a price loss (gain) will result.

SOLVED PROBLEM 19.1

Tom Evans, a jeweler, normally purchases about 3,000 troy ounces of gold every 6 months. However, Tom is concerned that the price of gold per troy ounce will go from its current price of $450 per ounce to $500 per ounce before his next purchase in 6 months. If 6-month gold futures are currently selling for $460 per troy ounce, what should Tom do to reduce his price fluctuation risk? Each gold futures contract is in units of 100 troy ounces.

SOLUTION

Tom should enter into a *buying hedge,* since he will suffer from an increase in the price of gold. Since each gold contract is for 100 troy ounces, Tom should purchase thirty (3,000/100) 6-month gold futures contracts at $460 per troy ounce. If Tom is correct and the price of gold per troy ounce does increase, the higher price he must pay in the cash market will be offset by his gain on the futures contracts as the basis converges to zero.

SOLVED PROBLEM 19.2

Frank Rayson, a Mississippi delta farmer, expects to harvest 50,000 bushels of soybeans in September. On April 1, the September futures contracts for soybeans is $7.00 per bushel.

(*a*) If Frank would like to lock in the $7.00 per bushel soybeans' price, what should he do?

(*b*) Show Frank's position at harvest time in September if the price of soybeans increases to $8.00 per bushel and the basis is zero. Ignore commission charges and taxes.

SOLUTION

(*a*) Since Frank is concerned with a falling price, he should enter into a *selling hedge.* Frank should sell 10 (50,000/5,000) September contracts for soybeans for $7.00 per bushel.

(*b*)

Revenue from the harvest of soybeans = $8 × 50,000 = $400,000 revenue
Sale of 10 soybeans futures contracts = 10 × 5,000 × $7.00 = $350,000 revenue
Purchase of 10 soybeans futures contracts = 10 × $8 × 5,000 = $400,000 cost

Frank made $50,000 in the cash market because he sold his soybeans for $8.00 rather than $7.00 per bushel but lost $50,000 in the futures market. Frank, in this case, would have been better off if he had not taken the hedge. However, in April Frank could not know in advance what would happen to soybeans in September.

19.4 SPECULATION WITH COMMODITIES

Rather than hedging a long or short position in a commodity, an investor might prefer to engage in price speculation. With hedging, an investor is trying to minimize price risk. However, with speculation, the investor is willing to assume price fluctuation risk in order to have a chance to make a large gain. Gains and losses can be magnified by using margin (that is, leverage can be employed).

EXAMPLE 19.2 Marcus Willians believes that the price of corn will go from its current June price of $3.00 per bushel to $4.00 per bushel in the next 3 months. September corn futures are currently selling for $3.25 per bushel, and Marcus bullishly purchases ten contracts on margin. The initial margin requirement is 15 percent and commission rates for a round trip are $40 per contract. Marcus was overoptimistic. Three months later corn futures prices fell to $2.75 per bushel and Marcus reversed out of his position and made a loss of $25,400.

Purchased 10 September corn futures for $3.25 per bushel = $3.25 × 10 × 5,000
= $162,500

[Margin deposit of 15% = $24,375 (.15 × $162,500) cost.]

Sold 10 September corn futures for $2.75 per bushel = 10 × $2.75 × 5,000
= $137,500 revenue

Gross profit ($137,500 − $162,500) = −$25,000 (loss)
Minus round-trip commission ($40 × 10) = −$400
Net loss = −$25,400

The $25,400 loss is a sizable loss and shows the negative side of leverage. It should be noted that all margin accounts must be *marked to the market* on a daily basis to maintain the margin as prices change. The details of this complication were not considered.

SOLVED PROBLEM 19.3

Refer to Example 19.2 above. What would Marcus have gained or lost if the price of corn had increased to $3.90 per bushel over the 3-month period?

SOLUTION

The purchase cost and initial margin would be the same as in Example 19.2, $162,500 and $24,375, respectively.

Sold 10 September corn futures for $3.90 = 10 × 5,000 × $3.90 = $195,000 revenue
Gross profit ($195,000 − $162,500) = $32,500
Minus round-trip commission = $400
Net profit = $32,100

Marcus benefited from favorable leverage.

19.5 INTEREST-RATE FUTURES

Interest-rate futures exist on such instruments as Treasury bonds, Treasury bills, Treasury notes, and 3-month Eurodollar deposits. Each interest-rate futures contract specifies the type of financial instrument that must be delivered when the futures contract expires. For example, both T-bonds and T-notes come in denominations of $100,000 and both require an 8 percent coupon security be tendered for delivery. However, T-bonds and T-notes can have coupons that differ from 8 percent, if properly adjusted.

EXAMPLE 19.3 Carla Morris is managing a short-term $4 million portfolio of T-bills with a maturity of 91 days and a yield of 8 percent. On September 10, she will roll the portfolio over into new T-bills. Carla is concerned that the yield on T-bills will fall over the next 3 months. Therefore, to maintain the current higher yield, she enters into a long hedge as follows:

(*a*) On June 11, Carla purchased $4 million of physical T-bills for $3,919,112.

$$\left[1.0 - \frac{\text{Days to maturity}}{360} \times \left(\text{T-bill yield}\right)\right] \times (\text{face value}) = \text{price}$$

$$[1.0 - (\tfrac{91}{360} \times .08)] \times \$4{,}000{,}000 = (1 - .020222) \times \$4{,}000{,}000 = \$3{,}919{,}112 \quad \text{cost}$$

(*b*) On June 11 Carla also purchased four $1,000,000 face value September T-bill futures contracts at 8 percent with an International Monetary Market (IMM) value of 92.00 for a $3,920,000 cost. [With T-bill futures, each basis point (.01 percent) is worth $25. Therefore, each contract is selling at a discount of 8 percent, 800 basis points, or $20,000 ($25 × 800). The total is $80,000 (4 × $20,000).]

On September 10, Carla made the following transactions:

(*c*) Carla rolled over (purchased) $4 million worth of T-bills at 7 percent for $3,929,222 {[1 − ($\tfrac{91}{360}$ × .07)] × $4 million = .98230556 × $4 million}.

(*d*) Carla sold (reversed her position in) four September T-bill futures contracts at 7 percent (IMM 93) for $3,930,000 [$4,000,000 − (700 × $25)].

In the cash market, Carla will pay an extra $10,110 ($3,929,222 − $3,919,112) for T-bills in September. However, this is offset in the futures market by a gain of $10,000 ($3,930,000 − $3,920,000).

EXAMPLE 19.4 Mary Lester, the portfolio manager of the 2nd National Bank, is worried because interest rates may rise. If they do, the $1 million in 10 percent coupon 20-year maturity T-bonds with a current value of $849,537 and a yield-to-maturity (YTM) of 12 percent will decline in value. She is concerned because she must liquidate the T-bond portfolio to meet scheduled payment obligations in 6 months. To protect her position, she decides to enter into a short hedge as follows:

(*a*) Current (June 1, 19X2) 20-year 10 percent coupon T-bonds have a market value of $849,537. This is called a *long position* in physicals (or actuals).
(*b*) On June 1, 19X2, she sells ten $100,000 T-bond futures contracts at 84-30 or $84\frac{30}{32}$ each. This is a total value of .849375 × $100,000 × 10 = $849,375. Here Mary has a *short position* in futures.

On December 1, 19X2, interest rates are higher and Mary makes the following transactions:

(*c*) She liquidates her bond portfolio for $761,036 revenue.
(*d*) She purchases (or reverses out of her position) ten December T-bond futures at 76-4 or 76.125 percent of face value. The total cost = .76125 × 10 × $100,000 = $761,250.

In the cash market, the loss on the portfolio was $88,501 ($761,036 − $849,537). In the futures market, a gain of $88,287 ($849,375 − $761,250) was made.

SOLVED PROBLEM 19.4

You are expecting a rise in interest rates over the next 3 months. On December 10, 19X1, T-bill futures contracts for March are selling for 91.25.

(*a*) What should you do to make money?
(*b*) If 3 months later, March T-bill futures are selling for 89.35, what profit or loss did you make, if you sold three contracts in December? Assume a margin requirement of $1,500 per contract is required. Ignore commission charges and maintenance margin costs.

SOLUTION

(*a*) Since you expect interest rates to rise over the next 3 months, you should sell March T-bill contracts short. If you are correct and rates do rise, then you can reverse out of your position by purchasing the same number of contracts you sold and make money.
(*b*) On December 10, 19X1, you sold three $1 million T-bill contracts at 91.25 for a margin cost of $4,500 (3 × $1,500). In March, you purchase three $1 million T-bill contracts for 89.35. You made $4,750 per contract or $14,250 on three contracts. This was determined as follows: 91.25 − 89.35 = 1.9 difference or 190 basis points. Since each basis point is worth $25, 190 × $25 = $4,750 per contract. For three contracts, this is 3 × $4,750 = $14,250.

SOLVED PROBLEM 19.5

What would your gain or loss have been in Solved Problem 19.4*b* above if the price of March T-bill futures had been 92 three months later?

SOLUTION

In this situation, you would lose money: 91.25 − 92 = −.75 or 75 basis points = 75 × $25 = $1,875 loss per contract. Total loss for three contracts is $5,625 ($1,875 × 3).

19.6 STOCK INDEX FUTURES

Stock index futures are futures contracts on stock market indexes. Currently, stock index futures exist on such indexes as the Value Line Composite Average, New York Stock Exchange, S&P500, S&P100, and the Major Market Index. The first three indexes mentioned above have a contract size equal to $500 times the index.

EXAMPLE 19.5 On March 10, 19X3, Jerry Sample, an active stock trader, is bullish about the stock market when the June S&P500 futures is at 250. Jerry purchases one June contract for $125,000 (250 × $500). By June 10, 19X3, the June

S&P500 index has risen to 275 and Jerry decides to sell his contract for $137,500 (275 × $500). Jerry has made a gross profit of $12,500 ($137,500 − $125,000). (*Note:* Jerry could have purchased the initial S&P500 futures contract for only a fraction of its value by purchasing it on margin. His profits would have been reduced by commissions and margin interest costs.)

SOLVED PROBLEM 19.6

Refer to Example 19.5 above. What will be Jerry's profit or loss if the June S&P500 index goes to 225 before the S&P500 futures expire?

SOLUTION

Jerry would lose money. He would sell one June S&P500 futures contract for 225 and obtain $112,500 ($500 × 225). His loss would be $12,500 ($112,500 − $125,000).

SOLVED PROBLEM 19.7

Barry Shorter is managing a $5 million common stock portfolio for the Jones Investment Company. Barry is concerned that the market is going to fall over the next 3 months and, as a result of the market decline, he expects the common stock portfolio that he is managing to fall in value. Barry notes that the 3 month S&P500 index is currently at 200.

(*a*) What should Barry do to hedge his position?

(*b*) If the common stock portfolio falls in value to $4 million over the next 3 months, what would be the ending value of Barry's position if he was fully hedged? Assume the S&P500 index simultaneously falls to 160. Ignore commission and margin costs.

SOLUTION

(*a*) Barry should short hedge to protect the falling value of his stock portfolio. He should sell enough S&P500 futures contracts to cover his common stock portfolio. One contract is equal to $100,000 ($500 × 200). Since he has a $5 million portfolio, he needs 50 ($5 million/$100,000) S&P500 June futures contracts.

(*b*) Barry should sell 50 June S&P500 futures contracts for $5 million (500 × $200 × 50). Three months later, Barry purchases 50 June S&P500 futures contracts for $4 million ($500 × 160 × 50) to reverse his position. His common stock portfolio declined in value by $1 million over the 3-month period. However, he made $1 million in the futures market ($5 million − $4 million). Therefore, he fully hedged his position and had an overall loss of zero on his hedged position.

19.7 FOREIGN CURRENCY FUTURES

Foreign currencies are just another commodity. Foreign currency futures are available on the currency of seven countries. An investor can speculate with foreign currency futures or hedge a foreign exchange position.

EXAMPLE 19.6 Sandra Frets believes that the British pound sterling is going to fall in value relative to the dollar. Sandra plans to act on her belief by selling four 3-month pound futures contracts now and then reversing out of her position in 3 months. Each British pound futures contract comes in units of 62,500 £. Since the current price for the British pound sterling futures contracts is $1.50 per pound, the contracts she sells are worth $375,000 ($1.50 × 4 × 62,500 £). In 3 months, the pound fell to $1.40 and Sandra reversed her position by purchasing four British pound sterling futures contracts for $350,000 ($1.40 × 4 × 62,500 £). She made a gross profit of $25,000 ($375,000 − $350,000), before commission and any margin interest costs.

True-False Questions

19.1 A speculator who believes the price of wheat will increase in the future will purchase wheat futures.

19.2 A bond portfolio manager who is concerned about rising interest rates should take a long position in the interest-rate futures market.

19.3 At the time of expiration, the basis for a futures contract will always be zero.

19.4 The Wilshire index of 5,000 stocks underlies an actively traded futures index.

19.5 Margin requirements can only be met through cash payments.

19.6 Commodity futures contracts have price fluctuation limits that are determined and enforced by the commodity exchange.

19.7 About half the margin buyers of futures contracts take delivery when their contracts expire.

19.8 An *inverted market* takes place when the futures price is greater than the spot price.

19.9 *Index arbitrage* can be done with the S&P500 index and the futures contract on the S&P500 index.

19.10 Evidence accumulated by the U.S. Commodity Futures Trading Commission found that *program trading* destabilized securities markets.

Multiple Choice Questions

Use the following information to answer the next three questions:
You were bullish on corn in May when September corn futures on the Chicago Board of Trade were selling for $3.50 per bushel and so you purchase ten contracts or 50,000 bushels.

19.1 If the margin requirement is 15 percent, how much initial margin money must you deposit with your broker?
(*a*) $25,000
(*b*) $26,250
(*c*) $27,000
(*d*) $28,000
(*e*) $28,500

19.2 Two months after you purchased the ten contracts, the price of September corn futures rose to $3.75 per bushel. If a round-trip commission is $40 per contract, what profit or loss would you make if you reversed out of the contracts?
(*a*) $12,100
(*b*) $11,700
(*c*) $12,500
(*d*) $12,900
(*e*) $13,300

19.3 If the price of September corn futures had fallen to $3.25 in 2 months, what profit or loss would you have made if you closed out the contracts. Assume a round-trip commission is $40.
(*a*) −$12,100
(*b*) −$11,700
(*c*) −$12,900
(*d*) −$13,300
(*e*) −$12,100

Use the following information for the next two questions:
You believe the weather conditions will hurt next year's citrus crop in Florida and cause the price of orange juice to increase. You decided in January to purchase three July frozen concentrated orange juice (FCOJ) futures contracts for $1.50 per pound. Each contract is for 40,000 pounds. The margin requirement is 15 percent and round-trip commission charges are $40 per contract.

19.4 In March, the price of July orange juice futures has risen to $1.75 and you decide to close out your position. What profit or loss will you make if you take a cash position?
(*a*) $2,880
(*b*) $29,880
(*c*) −$30,120
(*d*) $32,300
(*e*) $33,100

19.5 In March, if the price of July orange juice futures have fallen to \$1.35 per pound, what profit or loss will you make if you close out your position?
(*a*) \$14,300
(*b*) −\$15,200
(*c*) −\$17,880
(*d*) −\$18,120
(*e*) \$17,880

Use the following information for the next two questions:
Bud Farrow is the bond portfolio manager for the 1st National Bank. In June Bud is managing a \$5 million portfolio of 8 percent T-bonds that are selling for 84.16 or 84.5 percent of face value. Bud is concerned about rising interest rates and, therefore, sells fifty \$100,000 September T-bond futures contracts short on the CBT for 83.18 or 83.5625 percent of face value.

19.6 In August, 2 months after selling the T-bond futures, Bud decides to reverse out of his position. The bonds have fallen to 80 and the T-bond futures have fallen to 78. What is Bud's gain or loss? Ignore margins and transaction costs.
(*a*) \$125,000
(*b*) −\$75,600
(*c*) \$53,125
(*d*) \$59,125
(*e*) \$65,400

19.7 If Bud decides to close out his position in 2 months, what is his profit or loss, if the bonds are selling at 86 and September T-bond futures are selling at 85? Ignore transaction costs and margins.
(*a*) −\$7,125
(*b*) −\$6,500
(*c*) \$2,225
(*d*) \$3,125
(*e*) \$4,500

Use the following information for the next three questions:
In September, Donna Harper is bullish on the German mark for the next 3 months. Donna purchases one December mark futures contract (125,000 marks) for \$.58 per mark. Assume a 10 percent margin requirement and \$30 round-trip commission costs.

19.8 How much initial margin money must Donna deposit with her broker in order to purchase the contract?
(*a*) \$10,100
(*b*) \$7,250
(*c*) \$5,800
(*d*) \$7,000
(*e*) \$8,000

19.9 In November, Donna decided to sell out her long futures position in marks when the December mark futures are selling for \$.65 per mark. What is her gain or loss including commissions?
(*a*) \$8,720
(*b*) \$6,250
(*c*) −\$4,125
(*d*) \$7,125
(*e*) \$9,300

19.10 If Donna decides to close out her position in mark futures in November when December mark futures are selling for \$.50 per mark, what is her profit of loss including commissions?
(*a*) −\$7,030
(*b*) −\$10,030
(*c*) \$1,130
(*d*) \$2,300
(*e*) −\$3,130

Answers

True-False

19.1. T 19.2. F 19.3. F 19.4. F 19.5. F 19.6. T 19.7. F 19.8. F
19.9. T 19.10. F

Multiple Choice

19.1. b 19.2. a 19.3. c 19.4. b 19.5. d 19.6. c 19.7. d 19.8. b
19.9. a 19.10. b

Chapter 20

Put and Call Options I

20.1 OPTIONS

An *option* is an agreement that gives the holder the right (but not the obligation) to buy or sell specified securities at a given price (called an *exercise price* or *striking price*) during a specified period of time. Two types of options exist. A *call* option gives the holder the right to purchase a designated security (for example, 100 shares of common stock), while a *put* gives the holder the right to sell the security.

SOLVED PROBLEM 20.1

What is the main difference between an American and a European option?

SOLUTION

With an American option, the holder has the right to sell or purchase the security at any time before the option matures. A European option can only be *exercised* on the maturity date.

20.2 CALL OPTIONS

The value of a call option from the prospective of (*a*) a buyer and (*b*) an *uncovered* or *naked* seller (writer) is given in Fig. 20-1. The buyer makes a profit when the price of the underlying asset increases enough to more than cover the cost of the premium beyond point Z in Fig. 20-1*a*. The call writer's gain is the full premium if the price of the underlying asset is equal to or less than the striking price, because it would be unprofitable for the option buyer to exercise. The writer's losses are potentially unlimited if the price of the asset goes above Z in Fig. 20-1*b*.

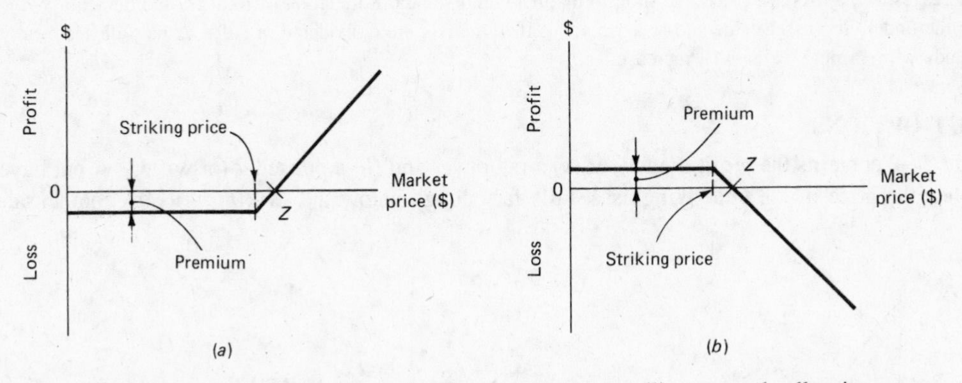

Fig. 20-1 Profit graphs for a call option. (*a*) Call buyer; (*b*) uncovered call writer.

SOLVED PROBLEM 20.2

Jerry House paid a premium of $4 per share for one 6-month call option contract (total of $400 for 100 shares) of the Mahony Corporation. At the time of the purchase, Mahony stock was selling for $56 per share, and the exercise price of the call option was $55.

(*a*) Determine Jerry's profit or loss if the price of Mahony's stock is $54 when the option is exercised.

(*b*) What is Jerry's profit or loss if the price of Mahony's stock is $62 when the option is exercised? Ignore taxes and transaction cost.

SOLUTION

(*a*)

$$\text{Cost of call} = (\$4 \text{ premium}) \times 100 = \$400$$
$$\text{Ending value} = (-\$400 \text{ cost}) + (0 \text{ gain}) = \$400 \text{ loss}$$

The option was worthless because the stock's price is less than the exercise price at maturity.

(*b*)

$$\text{Cost of call} = \$400 \quad \text{same as } (a)$$
$$\text{Ending value} = -\$400 + (\$62 - \$55) \times 100 = -\$400 + \$700 = \$300 \text{ gain}$$

SOLVED PROBLEM 20.3

Melody Pritts currently owns 100 shares of Marler Company stock and she wants to write *covered calls*. If she writes one contract on Marler for a $3 premium with an exercise price of $50, determine her portfolio's overall profit or loss under the following conditions when the option matures. Ignore transaction costs and taxes.

(*a*) The price of the stock falls from its current price of $51 down to $50.
(*b*) The price of the stock rises from its current price of $51 up to $60.

SOLUTION

(a) The call option is worthless to the buyer. However, as the writer Melody keeps the premium of $300 ($3 × 100). She loses $1 per share on her long position in the stock. So, Melody's net gain is $200.

(*b*) Melody keeps the premium of $300. However, she has an opportunity loss of $9 per share on the stock she owned because it will be called away at $50. At maturity the option will have a value of $10 (stock price − exercise price). The option buyer's gain of $9 per share is the writer's opportunity loss.

SOLVED PROBLEM 20.4

Options values or *premiums* on puts and calls are a function of five variables. What are the five variables and how do they affect an options value?

SOLUTION

The five variables are (1) the underlying asset value, (2) the risk-free rate, (3) the standard deviation of the return of the asset, (4) the option's time to maturity, and (5) the option's exercise price. A call option's value will increase with increases in the underlying asset value, risk-free rate, time to maturity, and standard deviation of returns. However, a call's premium will decrease as the striking price increases. A put's value will increase with increases in the exercise price, the time to maturity, and standard deviation of returns, and decrease with increases in the underlying asset value and risk-free rate. If dividends are considered, a call's value will decrease with dividends while a put's value will increase.[1]

20.3 PUT OPTIONS

Figure 20-2 contains the profit graphs for (*a*) a put buyer and (*b*) a put seller (or writer). A put buyer makes money when the price of the underlying asset falls far enough below the striking price to compensate for the

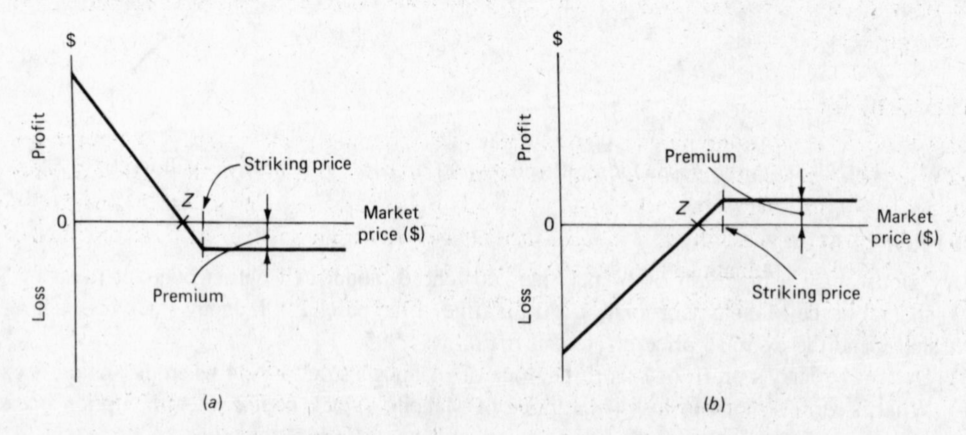

Fig. 20-2 Profit graphs for a put option. (*a*) Put buyer; (*b*) put writer.

[1]A useful reference on this topic is Jarrow and Rudd, *Option Prices* (Homewood, Ill.: Richard D. Irwin, Inc., 1983).

premium paid (point Z represents zero profits in Fig. 20-2). The put buyer's maximum potential losses are limited to the premium. With a put seller (or writer), the potential losses cannot exceed the exercise price minus the premium received. If the price of the underlying asset rises above the striking price, the writer gets to keep the full premium, because the option is unprofitable to exercise.

SOLVED PROBLEM 20.5

Jim Poston is bearish on the stock of the Justus Corporation. Therefore, Jim purchases four put option contracts on Justus stock for a premium of \$3. The option's striking price is \$40 and it has a maturity of 3 months. Justus has a current market price of \$39. If Jim is correct and Justus's price falls to \$30, how much profit will he earn over the 3-month period? Ignore transaction costs and taxes.

SOLUTION

Cost of put = (\$3 per share) × (100 shares per contract) × (4 contracts) = \$1,200

Put's intrinsic value = striking price − ending price = \$40 − \$30 = \$10 per share

Total value at maturity (\$10 per share) × (100 shares) × (4 contracts) = \$4,000

Net gain = \$4,000 − \$1,200 = \$2,800

SOLVED PROBLEM 20.6

Return to Solved Problem 20.5. What is Jim Poston's gain or loss if the ending price of Justus's stock is \$42?

SOLUTION

In this situation, the put will expire worthless and Jim loses his premium of (\$3 per contract) × (100 shares) × (4 contracts) = \$1,200.

20.4 COMBINATIONS

Numerous payoff possibilities exist by combining puts and calls with various exercise prices. Three such possibilities are described below.

Protective Put

When an investor purchases a long position in common stock losses will occur if the price of the stock falls (Fig. 20-3*a*). One way to obtain protection from this loss is to purchase a protective put (Fig. 20-3*b*). A put where the exercise price (k) and current price are equal, an *at-the-money* put, is purchased. Figure 20-3*c* shows the net profit position from using a protective put and compares the use of a protective put with a long position in common stock. If the price of stock increases, the net gain is the change in the asset's price minus the put premium (P_p). A profit is made beyond point Z. If the price of the stock falls, losses are limited to the cost of the premium. Figure 20-3*d* shows the gross payoff from using a protective put. In this situation, the total value of an investor's position will not fall below the exercise price of the put if the cost of the put premium is not considered.

SOLVED PROBLEM 20.7

Jerry Evans is considering purchasing 100 shares of Rome Company's stock at a current price of \$50 per share. However, Jerry is afraid that the price of Rome's stock could fall in the 2 months after he buys it. A current 3-month at-the-money put option for Rome is selling for \$2 premium per share.

(*a*) What profit or loss will Jerry make if he purchases Rome for \$50 per share and the price of Rome's stock falls in 1 month to \$40 per share without a protective put?

(*b*) Determine Jerry's profit or loss if he had purchased the \$2 put.

SOLUTION

(*a*) Cost of stock = \$50 × 100 shares = \$5,000

Ending position = \$40 × 100 − \$5,000 = \$4,000 − \$5,000 = \$1,000 loss

Cost of put = (\$2 per share) × (100 shares) = \$200

(*b*) Since Jerry has the right to put the stock to the seller at an exercise price of \$50, his losses are limited to the cost of the put, \$200 total premium.

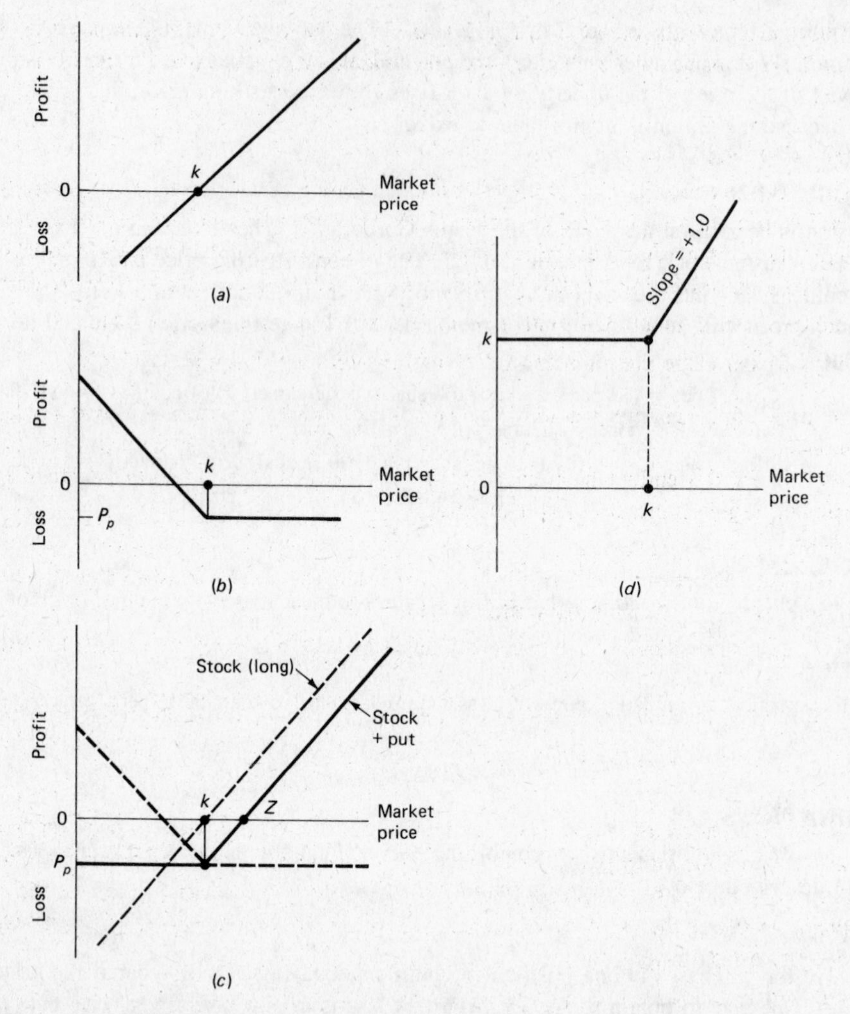

Fig. 20-3 Profit and loss graphs for (*a*) long position in common stock, (*b*) protective put purchase, (*c*) combination of long position in common stock and protective put, and (*d*) payoff from using a protective put.

Straddle

A *straddle* is the simultaneous purchase (or sale) of a put and call with the same exercise price. Profit graphs for a straddle buyer and seller are given in Fig. 20-4. The buyer makes a profit if the price of the stock

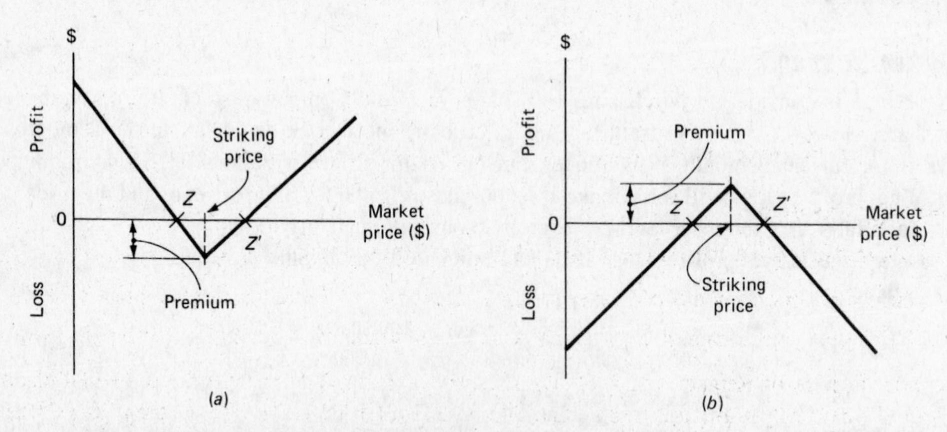

Fig. 20-4 Profit graphs for a straddle option. (*a*) Straddle buyer; (*b*) straddle writer.

either increases beyond Z' or falls below Z in Fig. 20-4*a*. On the other hand, the seller loses if the price of the stock either goes above Z' or below Z in Fig. 20-4*b*. The straddle premium is equal to the sum of the premiums for the put and call.

SOLVED PROBLEM 20.8

Rumors that the Deepocketa Corporation is going to tender a hostile offer for a controlling interest in the Morris Corporation has started the price of Morris's stock moving up. However, if a hostile takeover attempt fails, Morris's stock price will probably fall dramatically. To profit from this Edith Franks has established the following straddle position with the stock of the Morris Corporation:

(1) Purchased one 3-month call with a striking price of $40 for a $2 premium.

(2) Paid a $1 per share premium for a 3-month put with a striking price of $40.

(*a*) Determine Edith's ending position if the takeover offer bids the price of Morris's stock up to $41 in 3 months.

(*b*) Determine Edith's ending position if the takeover fails and the price of the stock falls to $35 in 3 months. Ignore transaction costs and taxes.

SOLUTION

(*a*) Cost of 2 options = ($2 per share) × (100-share call) + ($1 per share) × (100-share put)
= $200 + $100 = $300

Ending position = (−$300 cost of 2 options) + ($1 per share gain on call) × (100 shares)
= $200 net loss

(*b*) Ending position = (−$300 cost of 2 options) + ($5 per share gain on put) × (100 shares)
= −$300 + $500 = $200 gain

Spreads

A spread is a combination of a put and a call that have different exercise prices on the same stock. Figures 20-5*a* and *b* shows the profit graph for a spread buyer and a spread seller, respectively. The market price of the optioned security is *B*. The striking price of the put is *A* and the striking price for the call is *C*. The buyer of the spread profits if the price of the stock falls below *Q* or rises above *Q'*. As always, the option writer's losses are the option buyer's gain.

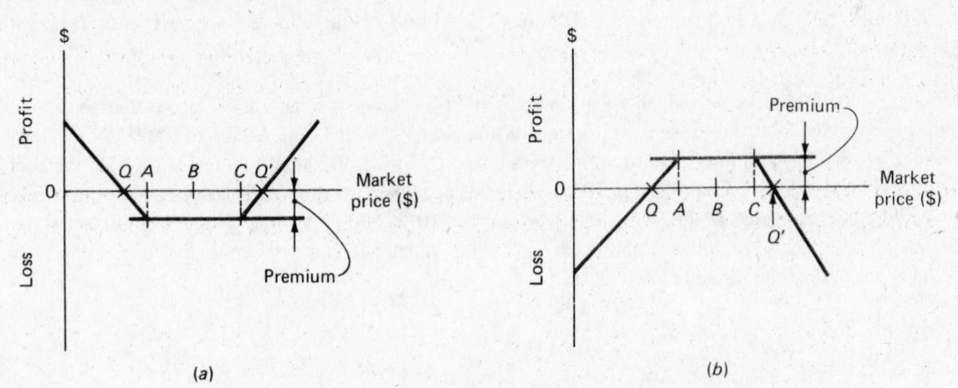

Fig. 20-5 Profit graphs for a spread. (*a*) Spread buyer; (*b*) spread writer.

SOLVED PROBLEM 20.9

Freda Plum established the following spread on the Remco Corporation's stock:

(1) Purchased one 3-month call option with a premium of $3 and an exercise price of $55.

(2) Purchased one 3-month put option with a premium of $.50 and an exercise price of $45.

The current price of Remco is $50. Determine Freda's profit or loss if (*a*) the price of Remco stays at $50 after 3 months, (*b*) the price of Remco falls to $35 after 3 months, and (*c*) the price of Remco rises to $60.

SOLUTION

(*a*) Cost of spread = [($.50 per share) × (100-share put)] + [($3 per share) × (100-share call)]
= $50 + $300 = $350

Ending value = (−$350 cost) + (zero gain) = $350 net loss

(*b*) Since the price of the stock is below the exercise price of the call, the call will not be exercised.

Cost of spread = $350 same as (*a*)

Ending value = −$350 + [($45 − $35) × (100 shares)]
= −$350 + $1,000 = $650 net gain

(*c*) In this situation, the put is worthless since the price of the stock exceeds the put's exercise price. The call is valuable.

Cost of spread = $350 same as (*a*) and (*b*)

Ending value = −$350 + [($60 − $55) × (100 shares)]
= $150

20.5 OPTIONS ON INDEXES

Index options are cash settlement options on stock market indexes. For example, there are options on the S&P500 and 100 indexes, the New York Composite Index, and the Value Line Composite Index. An individual that was bullish on the market could purchase a call option on the S&P500 index, for instance.

EXAMPLE 20.1 Marty Howell is bearish on the S&P100 index. He believes it will fall below its current level of 240. Marty purchases five 3-month put contracts on the S&P100 index with a striking price of 235 for a premium of $3. The cost is (100 shares) × ($3 per share) × (5 contracts) = $1,500 plus commission. A week after the puts are purchased, the S&P100 index falls to 225 causing the put option premium to rise to $14. When Marty sells his puts, his gross profit is ($14 per share) × (100 shares) × (5 contracts) = $7,000. His net profit before taxes and commission was $7,000 − $1,500 = $5,500.

20.6 OPTIONS ON FUTURES

A large number of *futures options* exist. Some of the most popular financial futures options are the ones on T-bills, T-bonds, S&P500 index, and NYSE index. Gold and crude oil are two well-known commodity futures options.

EXAMPLE 20.2 Joe Melton is bearish about the stock market for the next 6 months. One way Joe could possibly make money on this expectation is to purchase a put option on the S&P500 index future. For example, if one put contract is purchased on a 6-month S&P500 index future option with a striking price of 290 and a premium of $3, the contract would cost Joe $3 × 500 = $1,500 plus commission. If the S&P500 index were to drop to 280 during the 6-month period, Joe's put option would have the value of ($290 − $280) × 500 = $10 × 500 = $5,000. His net gain would be $5,000 − ($1,500 cost) = $3,500 minus commission and taxes. Of course, if Joe's forecast is wrong and the S&P500 never dropped below 290, Joe's put option would expire worthless.

True-False Questions

20.1 An *in-the-money* put option occurs when the current price of the underlying asset is less than the striking price.

20.2 An *out-of-the-money* call option is a call where the price of the optioned asset is less than the striking price.

20.3 A put value tends to fall as the time to maturity of the put increases.

20.4 A *covered option* is a written option where the writer owns the underlying asset.

20.5 Selling short and writing a put option are essentially the same thing.

20.6 Call options are purchased by individuals who are bullish on the underlying asset.

20.7 The value of an option tends to increase as the volatility (or risks) of the underlying asset increases.

20.8 If you purchase a put option, you are expecting the value of the underlying asset to increase.

Multiple Choice Questions

			Time to Maturity			
			Call Premium		Put Premium	
Stock	Current Price	Exercise Price	3 Months	6 Months	3 Months	6 Months
Zelda, Inc.	$52	$50	$3	$4.00	$ .35	$1.05
Worthen Corp.	40	45	1	1.25	5.50	6.00
Frosty Corp.	35	30	6	6.30	.45	.65

Use the option information given above to answer the eight questions below. Ignore taxes and transaction costs. Each contract is equal to 100 shares.

20.1 If you purchase one 3-month call contract on Zelda, Inc., what profit or loss will you make at the maturity date if the price of Zelda at that time is $57?
(*a*) $200
(*b*) $400
(*c*) −$460
(*d*) $500
(*e*) $560

20.2 If Worthen Corporation's price is $35 at the maturity of the 6-month option, determine the value of five 6-month put contracts at their maturity date.
(*a*) $2,000
(*b*) $5,700
(*c*) $8,200
(*d*) −$4,000
(*e*) $3,600

20.3 You recently purchased five 3-month call options of the Frosty Corporation. Determine your profit or loss on the investment if the price of Frosty's stock is $32 at maturity.
(*a*) $1,000
(*b*) $1,500
(*c*) −$2,000
(*d*) −$4,000
(*e*) −$500

20.4 If you had purchased five 3-month puts on Frosty, what would your profit or loss position have been at maturity if the stock's price was $32?
(*a*) −$225
(*b*) −$400
(*c*) −$600
(*d*) $400
(*e*) $600

20.5 Mr. Jeff Lander recently wrote five 6-month call options on Worthen Corporation's stock. What is Mr. Lander's profit or loss on the options at maturity if the price of Worthen stock at that time is $43?
(*a*) $625
(*b*) −$600
(*c*) $400
(*d*) $300
(*e*) $200

20.6 If Jeff had written five 6-month put options on Worthen, what would his profit or loss have been at the maturity of the options if the stock price was $43 per share?
(*a*) $1,000
(*b*) $2,000
(*c*) $1,800
(*d*) $1,500
(*e*) −$500

20.7 John Zimmer created a straddle by purchasing a 3-month put and call for the Zelda Corporation. Determine John's profit or loss in 3 months if the price of Zelda's stock is $53.
(*a*) $100
(*b*) $200
(*c*) $250
(*d*) −$60
(*e*) −$35

20.8 Which of the following options are *in the money?*
(*a*) Zelda's 3-month call
(*b*) Worthen's 6-month put
(*c*) Frosty's 6-month put
(*d*) *a* and *b*
(*e*) None of the above

20.9 Whenever an investor is bearish on a stock, buying a put is usually better than selling short because
(*a*) The holder's losses can be no more that the put premium if the stock price rises, but the short seller's losses could be unlimited in this situation.
(*b*) The short sale will become worthless after a short period of time but the put will not become worthless.
(*c*) The short seller must make up for any cash dividends paid by the security the short seller borrowed.
(*d*) *a* and *b*.
(*e*) *a* and *c*.

20.10 Call option premiums for a given asset tend to increase when
(*a*) The price of the underlying asset decreases.
(*b*) The volatility of the underlying asset decreases.
(*c*) The time to maturity of the option increases.
(*d*) *a* and *b*.
(*e*) None of the above.

Answers

True-False

20.1. T 20.2. T 20.3. F 20.4. T 20.5. F 20.6. T 20.7. T 20.8. F

Multiple Choice

20.1. b 20.2. a 20.3. c 20.4. a 20.5. a 20.6. b 20.7. e 20.8. d
20.9. e 20.10. c

Chapter 21

Put and Call Options II

21.1 THE BLACK-SCHOLES FORMULA

The Black-Scholes (B/S) formula of Eq. (*21.1*) can be used to determine the value of a European call option:

$$C_c = SN(D_1) - e^{-RT}kN(D_2) \qquad (21.1)$$

$$D_1 = \frac{\ln(S/k) + (R + .5\sigma^2)T}{\sigma\sqrt{T}} \qquad (21.1a)$$

$$D_2 = D_1 - \sigma\sqrt{T} \qquad (21.1b)$$

where C_c is the cost or premium of the call, S is the price of the underlying optioned asset, k is the exercise (or striking) price, R is the continuously compounded risk-free interest rate, σ^2 is the variance of the underlying asset's returns, T is the time (in fractions of 1 year) to the option's maturity, and $e = 2.7183$. The symbol "ln" represents natural logarithms. The B/S model is based on the following assumptions:

1. Stock returns follow a lognormal distribution.
2. The underlying asset's value and the risk-free rate are constant during the life of the option.
3. There are no transaction costs and taxes.
4. The stock will not pay a dividend during the life of the option.[1]

$N(D_1)$ and $N(D_2)$ will give the probability that a value equal to or less than D_1 or D_2 will take place in a normal probability distribution with a mean of zero and a standard deviation of unity. Table 21.1 can be used to find values for $N(D_1)$ and $N(D_2)$ by substituting values of D_1 and D_2 for X in the term $N(X)$. For example, if D_1 equaled .4, a value of .6554 could be found in Table 21.1 for X equal to .4.

EXAMPLE 21.1 Ed Rhoads wants to earn income by writing a call option on Morgan Corporation's stock. The current price of Morgan is \$40, and Ed wants to write a 3-month call option with a striking price of \$40. Ed plans to use the B/S model to determine the appropriate premium to charge for the call option. Ed has determined that the stock's variance (σ^2) is .25. The riskless rate R is assumed to be 9 percent. Using the B/S model the following call premium value was determined:

$$S = \$40 \qquad k = \$40 \qquad R = 9\% \qquad \sigma^2 = .25 \qquad \text{and} \qquad T = \frac{3 \text{ months}}{12 \text{ months}} = .25$$

We must first determine D_1 and D_2 and then use them to determine C_c.

$$D_1 = \frac{\ln(\$40/\$40) + [.09 + .5(.25)](.25)}{\sqrt{.25}\sqrt{.25}} \qquad (21.1a)$$

$$= \frac{0 + (.215)(.25)}{.25} = .215$$

$$D_2 = .215 - .5\sqrt{.25} = .215 - .25 = -.035 \qquad (21.1b)$$

Rounding to two places and using Table 21.1, $N(D_1) = N(.22) = .5871$ and $N(D_2) = N(-.04) = .4840$.

$$C_c = \$40(.5871) - e^{-(.09)(.25)}\$40(.4840) \qquad (21.1)$$

$$= \$23.484 - (.9778)(\$19.36) = \$23.484 - \$18.9302$$

$$= \$4.554$$

[1] This chapter assumes a knowledge of Chap. 20. For the development of the B/S model, see F. Black and M. Scholes, "The Pricing of Options and Corporate Liabilities," *Journal of Political Economy,* May-June 1973, pp. 637–654.

Table 21.1 Value of $N(X)$ for Given Values of X for a Cumulative Normal Distribution with Zero Mean and Unit Variance

X	0	1	2	3	4	5	6	7	8	9
−3.	.0013	.0010	.0007	.0005	.0003	.0002	.0002	.0001	.0001	.0000
−2.9	.0019	.0018	.0017	.0017	.0016	.0016	.0015	.0015	.0014	.0014
−2.8	.0026	.0025	.0024	.0023	.0023	.0022	.0021	.0021	.0020	.0019
−2.7	.0035	.0034	.0033	.0032	.0031	.0030	.0029	.0028	.0027	.0026
−2.6	.0047	.0045	.0044	.0043	.0041	.0040	.0039	.0038	.0037	.0036
−2.5	.0062	.0060	.0059	.0057	.0055	.0054	.0052	.0051	.0049	.0048
−2.4	.0082	.0080	.0078	.0075	.0073	.0071	.0069	.0068	.0066	.0064
−2.3	.0107	.0104	.0102	.0099	.0096	.0094	.0091	.0089	.0087	.0084
−2.2	.0139	.0136	.0132	.0129	.0126	.0122	.0119	.0116	.0113	.0110
−2.1	.0179	.0174	.0170	.0166	.0162	.0158	.0154	.0150	.0146	.0143
−2.0	.0228	.0222	.0217	.0212	.0207	.0202	.0197	.0192	.0188	.0183
−1.9	.0287	.0281	.0274	.0268	.0262	.0256	.0250	.0244	.0238	.0233
−1.8	.0359	.0352	.0344	.0336	.0329	.0322	.0314	.0307	.0300	.0294
−1.7	.0446	.0436	.0427	.0418	.0409	.0401	.0392	.0384	.0375	.0367
−1.6	.0548	.0537	.0526	.0516	.0505	.0495	.0485	.0475	.0465	.0455
−1.5	.0668	.0655	.0643	.0630	.0618	.0606	.0594	.0582	.0570	.0559
−1.4	.0808	.0793	.0778	.0764	.0749	.0735	.0722	.0708	.0694	.0681
−1.3	.0968	.0951	.0934	.0918	.0901	.0885	.0869	.0853	.0838	.0823
−1.2	.1151	.1131	.1112	.1093	.1075	.1056	.1038	.1020	.1003	.0985
−1.1	.1357	.1335	.1314	.1292	.1271	.1251	.1230	.1210	.1190	.1170
−1.0	.1587	.1562	.1539	.1515	.1492	.1469	.1446	.1423	.1401	.1379
− .9	.1841	.1814	.1788	.1762	.1736	.1711	.1685	.1660	.1635	.1611
− .8	.2119	.2090	.2061	.2033	.2005	.1977	.1949	.1922	.1894	.1867
− .7	.2420	.2389	.2358	.2327	.2297	.2266	.2236	.2206	.2177	.2148
− .6	.2743	.2709	.2676	.2643	.2611	.2578	.2546	.2514	.2483	.2451
− .5	.3085	.3050	.3015	.2981	.2946	.2912	.2877	.2843	.2810	.2776
− .4	.3446	.3409	.3372	.3336	.3300	.3264	.3228	.3192	.3156	.3121
− .3	.3821	.3783	.3745	.3707	.3669	.3632	.3594	.3557	.3520	.3483
− .2	.4207	.4168	.4129	.4090	.4052	.4013	.3974	.3936	.3897	.3859
− .1	.4602	.4562	.4522	.4483	.4443	.4404	.4364	.4325	.4286	.4247
− .0	.5000	.4960	.4920	.4880	.4840	.4801	.4761	.4721	.4681	.4641
.0	.5000	.5040	.5080	.5120	.5160	.5199	.5239	.5279	.5319	.5359
.1	.5398	.5438	.5478	.5517	.5557	.5596	.5636	.5675	.5714	.5753
.2	.5793	.5832	.5871	.5910	.5948	.5987	.6026	.6064	.6103	.6141
.3	.6179	.6217	.6255	.6293	.6331	.6368	.6406	.6443	.6480	.6517
.4	.6554	.6591	.6628	.6664	.6700	.6736	.6772	.6808	.6844	.6879
.5	.6915	.6950	.6985	.7019	.7054	.7088	.7123	.7157	.7190	.7224
.6	.7257	.7291	.7324	.7357	.7389	.7422	.7454	.7486	.7517	.7549
.7	.7580	.7611	.7642	.7673	.7703	.7734	.7764	.7794	.7823	.7852
.8	.7881	.7910	.7939	.7967	.7995	.8023	.8051	.8078	.8106	.8133
.9	.8159	.8186	.8212	.8238	.8264	.8289	.8315	.8340	.8365	.8389
1.0	.8413	.8438	.8461	.8485	.8508	.8531	.8554	.8577	.8599	.8621
1.1	.8643	.8665	.8686	.8708	.8729	.8749	.8770	.8790	.8810	.8830
1.2	.8849	.8869	.8888	.8907	.8925	.8944	.8962	.8980	.8997	.9015
1.3	.9032	.9049	.9066	.9082	.9099	.9115	.9131	.9147	.9162	.9177
1.4	.9192	.9207	.9222	.9236	.9251	.9265	.9278	.9292	.9306	.9319
1.5	.9332	.9345	.9357	.9370	.9382	.9394	.9406	.9418	.9430	.9441
1.6	.9452	.9463	.9474	.9484	.9495	.9505	.9515	.9525	.9535	.9545
1.7	.9554	.9564	.9573	.9582	.9591	.9599	.9608	.9616	.9625	.9633
1.8	.9641	.9648	.9656	.9664	.9671	.9678	.9686	.9693	.9700	.9706
1.9	.9713	.9719	.9726	.9732	.9738	.9744	.9750	.9756	.9762	.9767
2.0	.9772	.9778	.9783	.9788	.9793	.9798	.9803	.9808	.9812	.9817

Table 21.1 *(continued)*

X	0	1	2	3	4	5	6	7	8	9
−3.	.0013	.0010	.0007	.0005	.0003	.0002	.0002	.0001	.0001	.0000
2.1	.9821	.9826	.9830	.9834	.9838	.9842	.9846	.9850	.9854	.9857
2.2	.9861	.9864	.9868	.9871	.9874	.9878	.9881	.9884	.9887	.9890
2.3	.9893	.9896	.9898	.9901	.9904	.9906	.9909	.9911	.9913	.9916
2.4	.9918	.9920	.9922	.9925	.9927	.9929	.9931	.9932	.9934	.9936
2.5	.9938	.9940	.9941	.9943	.9945	.9946	.9948	.9949	.9951	.9952
2.6	.9953	.9955	.9956	.9957	.9959	.9960	.9961	.9962	.9963	.9964
2.7	.9965	.9966	.9967	.9968	.9969	.9970	.9971	.9972	.9973	.9974
2.8	.9974	.9975	.9976	.9977	.9977	.9978	.9979	.9979	.9980	.9981
2.9	.9981	.9982	.9982	.9983	.9984	.9984	.9985	.9985	.9986	.9986
3.	.9987	.9990	.9993	.9995	.9997	.9998	.9998	.9999	.9999	1.0000

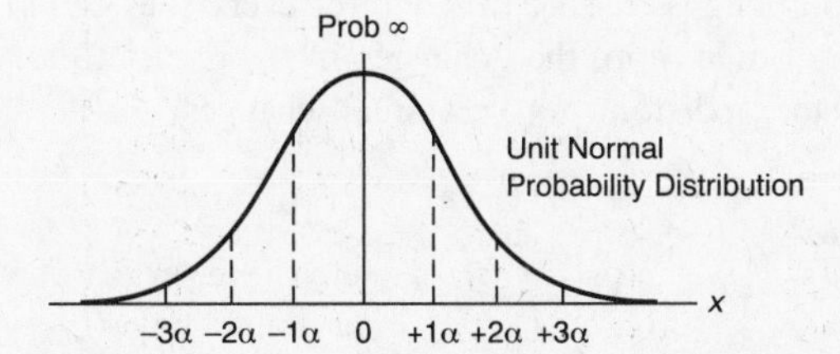

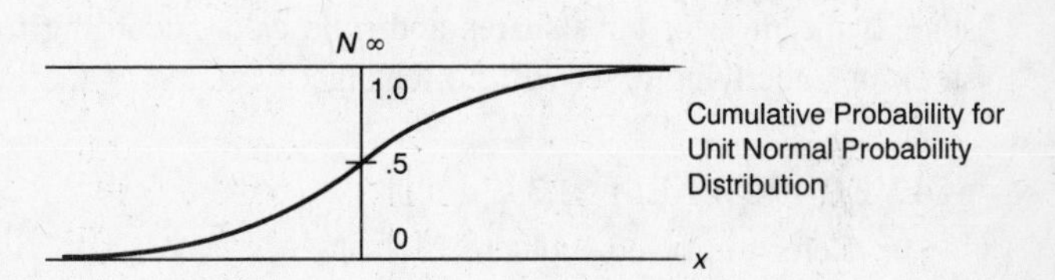

Therefore, Ed should charge a $4.56 premium for the call option on Morgan's stock. A more exact answer, using a microcomputer, is $4.40. The difference is due to rounding.[2]

SOLVED PROBLEM 21.1

Determine the value of a call option with the B/S model for the following inputs:

$$\sigma = .3 \qquad R = .10 \qquad S = \$25 \qquad T = .3 \text{ years} \qquad \text{and} \qquad k = \$28$$

SOLUTION

$$D_1 = \frac{\ln(\$25/\$28) + [.10 + .5(.3)^2](.3)}{.3\sqrt{.3}} \tag{21.1a}$$

$$= \frac{[-.11333 + (.10 + .045)(.3)}{(.3)(.5477)}$$

$$= \frac{-.11333 + .0435}{.16431} = \frac{-.06983}{.16431} = -.4250$$

$$D_2 = -.4250 - (.3)(.5477) \tag{21.1b}$$

$$= -.4250 - .16431 = -.5893$$

$$C_c = \$25N(-.43) - e^{-(.10)(.3)}(\$28)N(-.59) \tag{21.1}$$

$$= \$25(.3336) - (.9704)(\$28)(.2776) = \$8.34 - \$7.54 = \$.80$$

SOLVED PROBLEM 21.2

Determine the standard deviation σ that is implied by the following call option data:

$$T = .25 \text{ years} \qquad S = \$30 \qquad R = .12 \qquad k = \$30 \qquad C_c = \$1.90$$

Use the B/S model.

[2]The B/S model can be precisely and quickly calculated with microcomputers and hand-held calculators. For an HP-12C program, see Richard W. Taylor, "Option Valuation for Alternative Instruments with the Black-Scholes Model: A Pedagogical Note," *Journal of Financial Education,* Fall 1987, pp. 73–77.

SOLUTION

This problem can be solved by trial and error. Find a σ that will make the value of a call equal to \$1.90. Remember that σ and C_c are directly related. The answer is $\sigma = .24$, as shown below:

$$D_1 = \frac{\ln(\$30/\$30) + [.12 + .5(.24)^2](.25)}{.24\sqrt{.25}}$$

$$= \frac{0 + [.12 + (.5)(.0576)](.25)}{.12} = \frac{.0372}{.12} = .31$$

$$D_2 = .31 - .24\sqrt{.25} = .31 - .12 = .19$$

$$C_c = \$30N(.31) + e^{-(.12)(.25)}(\$30)N(.19)$$

$$= \$30(.6217) + (.97045)(\$30)(.5753)$$

$$= \$18.651 - \$16.749 = \$1.902$$

Hedge Ratio

With the B/S model, $N(D_1)$ is the *hedge ratio* or, as it is also called, the option's *delta* for the call option. The hedge ratio indicates the number of units of the asset held long (or purchased) for each call sold. For example, if $N(D_1)$ or delta equals .25, then the investor should hold long one share of stock for every four calls sold. If the investor buys shares and sells calls according to the hedge ratio, then changes in the price of the stock or underlying asset will not change the value of the investor's portfolio for very small changes.

SOLVED PROBLEM 21.3

Refer to Solved Problem 21.1.

(*a*) What is the investor's hedge ratio or delta?

(*b*) What does this value mean?

SOLUTION

(*a*) The hedge ratio is equal to $N(D_1) = .3336$.

(*b*) For every call option sold, .3336 unit of the underlying asset should be held in a long position (that is, owned).

SOLVED PROBLEM 21.4

The following input information exists for the call options on the Roberts Corporation's common stock:

$k = \$30$ $\quad S = \$35$ $\quad \sigma = .52$ $\quad T = .25$ year and $R = .10$

(*a*) Determine the value of a call option with the B/S model.

(*b*) If the current price of a call on the Roberts Corporation's stock is \$6.00, what should an investor do to make money?

SOLUTION

(*a*)

$$D_1 = \frac{\ln(\$35/\$30) + [.10 + .5(.52)^2(.25)]}{.52\sqrt{.25}}$$

$$= \frac{.1542 + (.10 + .1352)(.25)}{.26}$$

$$= \frac{.1542 + .0588}{.26} = .8192$$

$$D_2 = .8192 - .52\sqrt{.25} = .8192 - .26 = .5592$$

$$C_c = \$35N(.82) - e^{-(.10)(.25)}(\$30)N(.56)$$

$$= (\$35)(.7939) + (.9753)(\$30)(.7123)$$

$$= \$27.79 - \$20.84 = \$6.95$$

(*b*) Since the calls are undervalued (\$6.95 > \$6.00), the investor should purchase 1 call for every .7939 share sold short. To put this another way, the investor should purchase 1,000 calls and sell short 794 shares of stock to create a riskless hedge that should be profitable. This will only hold true for very small changes in the price of the stock.

Cash Dividends

Since many stocks pay cash dividends, it is useful to incorporate dividends into the B/S model. One simple way to do this is with a stochastic dividend adjustment. For this to be accomplished, the price of the stock, S, in Eqs. (*21.1*) and (*21.1a*) should be replaced by Se^{-DT}. D is the annual dividend yield and T, as before, is the time until the option matures.

SOLVED PROBLEM 21.5

The Benson Corporation's stock is currently selling for \$45.

(*a*) Determine the call premium on Benson's stock for the following inputs:

$\sigma = .35 \qquad T = .5 \qquad k = \$41 \qquad R = .10$ and zero cash dividends

(*b*) Determine the call premium for Benson's stock if the annual dividend yield (D) is 6 percent.

(*c*) Why do these premiums differ?

SOLUTION

(*a*)

$$D_1 = \frac{\ln(\$45/\$41) + [.10 + .5(.35^2)](.5)}{.35\sqrt{.5}}$$
$$= \frac{.09309 + (.10 + .06125)(.5)}{(.35)(.70711)}$$
$$= \frac{.09309 + .080625}{.24749}$$
$$= \frac{.173715}{.24749} = .70191$$
$$D_2 = .7019 - .35\sqrt{.5} = .7019 - .24749 = .45441$$
$$C_c = \$45N(.70) - e^{-(.10)(.5)}(\$41)N(.45)$$
$$= (\$45)(.758) - (.9512)(\$41)(.6736) = \$34.11 - \$26.27 = \$7.84$$

(*b*) S should be replaced by $Se^{-DT} = \$45e^{-(.06)(.5)} = \$45(.97045) = \$43.67$.

$$D_1 = \frac{\ln(\$43.67/\$41) + [.10 + .5(.35)^2(.5)]}{.35\sqrt{.5}}$$
$$= \frac{.063089 + .080625}{.24749} = \frac{.143714}{.24749} = .5807$$
$$D_2 = .5807 - .24749 = .3332$$
$$C_c = \$43.67N(.58) - e^{-(.10)(.5)}(\$41)N(.33)$$
$$= (\$43.67)(.719) - (.9512)(\$41)(.6293) = \$31.40 - \$24.54 = \$6.86$$

(*c*) The dividend reduces the price of the stock and makes S closer to k. Other things being the same, the closer S is to k, the lower C_c will be.

21.2 USING PUT-CALL PARITY

A put and call on the same underlying asset are related through the following parity formula:

$$P_p + S = C_c + ke^{-RT} \tag{21.2}$$

where P_p is the value of a put's premium.

The put-call parity formula, Eq. (*21.2*), can be used in conjunction with the B/S call model to develop a put pricing model. If the call value determined with the B/S model, Eq. (*21.1*), is substituted in Eq. (*21.2*) and the terms rearranged, the following put valuation formula is developed:

$$P_p = ke^{-RT}[1 - N(D_2)] - S[1 - N(D_I)] \tag{21.3}$$

The put's hedge ratio is $[1 - N(D_1)]$ in Eq. (*21.3*). This tells an investor how many units of the underlying asset should be purchased for each put purchased to form a riskless hedge. For example, if $[1 - N(D_1)]$ equals .35, then .35 unit of the underlying asset should be purchased for each put purchased. As in the B/S call model, the hedge ratio works perfectly only for very small changes in the prices.

SOLVED PROBLEM 21.6

A put and call will expire in 3 months and both have a striking price of $25. The risk-free rate is 10 percent.

(*a*) Determine the price of the put if the call has a price of $4 and the stock has a price of $22.

(*b*) If the put has a price of $5 and the stock price is $20, determine the price of the call.

SOLUTION

(*a*) Use the put-call parity formula, Eq. (*21.2*).

$$P_p + S = C_c + ke^{-RT}$$

$$P_p = ke^{-RT} + C_c - S$$

$$S = \$22 \qquad T = .25 \qquad R = .10 \qquad k = \$25 \qquad C_c = \$4$$

$$P_p = \$25e^{-(.10)(.25)} + \$4 - \$22 = \$24.38 + \$4 - \$22 = \$6.38$$

(*b*) First, rearrange Eq. (*21.2*).

$$C_c = S + P_p - ke^{-RT} = \$20 + \$5 - \$25(.9753) = \$.62$$

SOLVED PROBLEM 21.7

(*a*) Using the information given in Solved Problem 21.4 about the Roberts Corporation, determine the value of a put option on the Roberts Corporation's stock.

(*b*) If the current market value of the put on the Roberts Corporation is $.75, what should an investor do to make money?

SOLUTION

(*a*)

$$P_p = ke^{-RT}[1 - N(D_2)] - S[1 - N(D_1)] \qquad (21.3)$$

$$= \$30e^{-(.10)(.25)}(1 - .7123) - \$35(1 - .7939)$$

Note that $N(D_1)$ and $N(D_2)$ were calculated in the solution to Solved Problem 21.4.

$$P_p = (\$30)(.9753)(.2877) - (\$35)(.2061) = \$8.42 - \$7.21 = \$1.21$$

Since C_c was determined in Solved Problem 21.4, an easier way to solve for the value of the put is to use Eq. (*21.2*):

$$P_p = ke^{-RT} + C_c - S = \$30(.9753) + \$6.95 - \$35 = \$29.259 + \$6.95 - \$35 = \$1.209$$

(*b*) The hedge ratio is 1 − .7939 = .2061. Since the put is undervalued, .2061 share should be purchased for every put purchased. To put this another way, 206 shares should be purchased for every 1,000 puts purchased. This hedge ratio will only hold true for small changes in the price of the stock. If the price changes significantly, the hedge ratio must be recalculated.

SOLVED PROBLEM 21.8

Refer to Solved Problem 21.5 about the Benson Corporation.

(*a*) With the information given in Solved Problem 21.5, determine the value of a put on the Benson Corporation's stock without dividends.

(*b*) Determine the value of a put for Benson's stock if the annual dividend yield (D) is 6 percent.

SOLUTION

(*a*) Use Eq. (*21.2*) as follows:

$$P_p = ke^{-RT} + C_c - S = \$41e^{-(.10)(.5)} + \$7.84 - \$45$$

$$= \$41(.9512) + \$7.84 - \$45 = \$39 - \$37.16 = \$1.84$$

Note that $7.84 was calculated in Solved Problem 21.5(*a*).

(*b*) S should be replaced by $Se^{-DT} = \$45e^{-(.06)(.5)} = \$43.67$ in Eq. (*21.2*).

$$P_p = \$41e^{-(.10)(.5)} + \$6.86 - \$43.67 = \$39 - \$36.81 = \$2.19$$

Note that $6.86 was determined in the solution to Solved Problem 21.5(*b*).

21.3 EQUITY AS A CALL OPTION

Within the option framework, the equity of a corporation can be viewed as a call option on the corporation's assets with the writer of the option being the corporation's debtholder. The striking price of the call option is the face value of a pure discount bond that has the same present value as the corporation's total long-term debt and the maturity of the option is the maturity of the debt.

EXAMPLE 21.2 The Mason Corporation has the following input values: σ (standard deviation of the firm's returns) = .2, S (Mason's total market value) = \$10 million, k (the face value of its pure discount debt) = \$4 million, and T (the time to maturity for its debt) = 7 years. The risk-free rate (R) is 9 percent. The value of Mason's equity within the B/S framework is as follows:

$$D_1 = \frac{\ln (S/k) + (R + .5\sigma^2)T}{\sigma\sqrt{T}}$$

$$= \frac{\ln (\$10M/\$4M) + [.09 + .5(.2)^2]7}{.2\sqrt{7}}$$

$$= \frac{.9163 + .77}{(.2)(2.6458)} = \frac{1.6863}{.52915} = 3.1868$$

$$D_2 = D_1 - \sigma\sqrt{T} = 3.1868 - .52915 = 2.6577$$

$$C_c = SN(D_1) - e^{-RT}kN(D_2)$$

$$= (\$10M)(1.000) - e^{-(.09)(7)}(\$4M)(.9961) = \$10M - (.5326)(\$4M)(.9961) = \$10M - \$2.1221M$$

$$= \$7.8879M = \text{market value of equity}$$

The market value of Mason's debt is \$10M − \$7.8879M = \$2.1121M.

SOLVED PROBLEM 21.9

Refer to Example 21.2 above. Determine the yield-to-maturity (YTM) on Mason's zero coupon debt.

SOLUTION

$$\$2.1221M = \frac{\$4M}{(1 + \text{YTM})^7}$$

$$(1 + \text{YTM})^7 = \frac{\$4M}{\$2.1221M}$$

$$(1 + \text{YTM})^7 = 1.884925$$

Taking the seventh root of both sides of the equation yields

$$1 + \text{YTM} = 1.09478 \qquad \text{YTM} = .09478 \text{ or } 9.478\%$$

SOLVED PROBLEM 21.10

The Osage Corporation has a current market value of \$20 million. Osage has current outstanding debt that consists of \$10 million of pure discount bonds with a maturity of 4 years. The standard deviation of returns for the Osage Corporation is .47. The current risk-free rate (R) is 12 percent.

(*a*) Using the B/S option valuation model, determine the market value of Osage's equity.

(*b*) What is the current market value of Osage's debt?

SOLUTION

(*a*) $$D_1 = \frac{\ln (\$20M/\$10M) + [.12 + .5(.47)^2]4}{.47\sqrt{4}}$$

$$= \frac{.6931 + (.12 + .1105)4}{.94}$$

$$= \frac{.6931 + .922}{.94} = \frac{1.6151}{.94} = 1.7182$$

$$D_2 = 1.7182 - .47\sqrt{4} = 1.7182 - .94 = .7782$$

$$C_c = (\$20M)N(1.72) - e^{-(.12)(4)}(\$10M)N(.78)$$

$$= (\$20M)(.9573) - (.6188)(\$10M)(.7823) = \$19.146M - \$4.8409M = \$14.3051M = \text{equity value}$$

(*b*) The market value of debt is the market value of the firm minus the market value of equity:

$$\text{Debt} = \$20M - \$14.3051M = \$5.6949M$$

True-False Questions

21.1 Within the B/S framework, the market value of a corporation's debt decreases if the overall risk (as measured by the firm's standard deviation of returns) of the firm decreases.

21.2 The put-call parity formula does not hold for an American call.

21.3 If the put option hedge ratio is .4, an investor should sell .4 put for every stock purchased.

21.4 If the call hedge ratio is .6, an investor should sell .6 share for every call purchased.

21.5 The B/S model cannot be used to determine the overall market value of a firm.

21.6 When a firm's cash dividend payment is included in the B/S model, the value of a put decreases.

21.7 A cash dividend on a firm's common stock tends to lower the value of a call option on the firm's equity.

21.8 A riskless hedge should include more options than shares of the optioned stock.

21.9 Option prices that are calculated with the B/S model are not very sensitive to changes in the asset's standard deviation of returns.

21.10 The option values calculated with the binomial model will approach those calculated with the B/S model for a given period of time as we divide the fixed time period into smaller and smaller units.

Multiple Choice Questions

The options on the stock of the Mink Corporation have the following input values:

$S = \$55 \qquad k = \$52 \qquad R = .10 \qquad \sigma = .33 \qquad \text{and} \qquad T = .4$

Assume that no dividends are currently being paid.

By using the information given above, answer questions 1 through 10 with the B/S option model.

21.1 What is the value of a call on the Mink Corporation?
(*a*) $6.50
(*b*) $6.80
(*c*) $7.17
(*d*) $8.05
(*e*) $8.35

21.2 If the call is undervalued, what approach should an investor follow?
(*a*) Buy 1,000 calls, sell short 712 shares of Mink stock.
(*b*) Buy 1,000 calls, sell short 600 shares of Mink stock.
(*c*) Buy 500 shares of Mink, sell 1,000 calls.
(*d*) Buy 714 of Mink, sell 1,000 calls.
(*e*) Buy 600 shares of Mink, sell 1,000 calls.

21.3 Determine the value of a put on Mink's stock.
(*a*) $1.75
(*b*) $2.13
(*c*) $2.65
(*d*) $2.95
(*e*) $3.15

21.4 If the put on Mink's stock is overpriced, what should an investor do?
(*a*) Sell 1,000 puts for every 400 shares sold.
(*b*) Buy 1,000 puts for every 300 shares purchased.
(*c*) Sell 1,000 puts for every 288 shares sold.
(*d*) Sell 1,000 puts for every 350 shares purchased.
(*e*) Buy 1,000 puts for every 400 shares sold.

21.5 Assume the Mink Corporation is paying dividends at the rate of 4 percent per year. Determine the price of a call.
(*a*) \$5.57
(*b*) \$5.85
(*c*) \$6.03
(*d*) \$6.35
(*e*) \$6.74

21.6 Determine the price of a put on Mink's stock with a 4 percent annual dividend.
(*a*) \$2.56
(*b*) \$2.85
(*c*) \$1.95
(*d*) \$2.40
(*e*) \$2.96

21.7 If the price of a Mink call is \$6.41, determine the implied standard deviation of returns without dividends.
(*a*) .37
(*b*) .40
(*c*) .25
(*d*) .35
(*e*) .18

21.8 If R rises to .12, determine the price of a call on Mink's stock if the other inputs do not change. Assume no dividends.
(*a*) \$6.80
(*b*) \$7.25
(*c*) \$7.61
(*d*) \$7.90
(*e*) \$8.10

21.9 If $T = .5$, determine the value of a put on Mink's stock if the other inputs do not change. Assume no dividends.
(*a*) \$1.50
(*b*) \$1.75
(*c*) \$1.91
(d) \$2.51
(*e*) \$2.30

21.10 If $k =$ \$54, determine the value of a call on Mink's stock if the other inputs do not change. Assume no dividends.
(*a*) \$5.86
(*b*) \$6.19
(*c*) \$6.30
(*d*) \$6.42
(*e*) \$6.76

Use the information given below to answer the next four questions.

The Craig Corporation has a total market value of \$20 million. The debt of the corporation, which is composed of pure discount bonds, has a face value of \$8 million with a maturity of 5 years. The firm's standard deviation of returns is .45, and the risk-free rate is 11 percent.

21.11 Determine the market value of Craig's equity.
(*a*) \$14.35M
(*b*) \$14.95M
(*c*) \$15.67M
(*d*) \$16.03M
(*e*) \$16.45M

21.12 What is the market value of Craig's debt?
(*a*) $6.54M
(*b*) $5.59M
(*c*) $4.97M
(*d*) $4.33M
(*e*) $3.96M

21.13 Determine the value of Craig's equity if R rises to 14 percent and the other inputs do not change.
(*a*) $15.65M
(*b*) $16.21M
(*c*) $16.95M
(*d*) $17.56M
(*e*) $18.03M

21.14 Determine the value of Craig's equity if T rises to 8 years and the other inputs do not change.
(*a*) $17.00M
(*b*) $18.02M
(*c*) $18.96M
(*d*) $19.56M
(*e*) $20.07M

Answers

True-False

21.1. F 21.2. T 21.3. F 21.4. T 21.5. T 21.6. F 21.7. T 21.8. T 21.9. F
21.10. T

Multiple Choice

21.1. c 21.2. a 21.3. b 21.4. c 21.5. e 21.6. a 21.7. c 21.8. c 21.9. d
21.10. b 21.11. c 21.12. d 21.13. b 21.14. a

Chapter 22

Portfolio Analysis

22.1 INTRODUCTION

Chapter 13 was concerned with the total risk of an individual asset. Total risk was measured by the standard deviation (or variance) of returns of the asset. In this chapter, we will be interested in explaining the relationship between risk and return for a portfolio of assets. While the return on a portfolio is simply the sum of the individual assets, its risk is not simply the sum of the risk of the single assets. When a portfolio's standard deviation is calculated, attention must be given to the *covariance* of the returns of the assets. Harry Markowitz has shown that portfolios dominate individual assets from a risk and return standpoint. He also showed how the optimal portfolio could be determined.[1]

22.2 COVARIANCE OF RETURNS

The *covariance* is a statistical measure of how the returns of two assets move together. It can be measured with the following ex ante (or expectational) equation:

$$\text{cov}_{ij} = \sum_{s=1}^{N} P_s[r_{is} - E(r_i)][r_{js} - E(r_j)] \tag{22.1}$$

where cov_{ij} is the covariance between assets i and j, r_{is} denotes the rate of return for the i asset for state of nature s, r_{js} is the return for the j asset for state s, $E(r_i)$ and $E(r_j)$ are the expected returns for assets i and j, and P_s is the probability that the state of nature denoted s occurs.

EXAMPLE 22.1 Determine the covariance of returns for assets L and M with the following data:

STATES OF NATURE	PROBABILITY OF OCCURRENCE	ANNUAL RETURNS L	ANNUAL RETURNS M
1	.2	−5%	6%
2	.4	10	−2
3	.3	−4	8
4	.1	7	−9
Total	1.0		

Note that the probabilities across all possible states of nature sum to one.

The covariance formula, Eq. (*22.1*), requires that we determine values for the *expected returns*, $E(r_L)$ and $E(r_M)$. Equation (*22.2*) defines the expected returns:

$$E(r) = \sum_{s=1}^{N} P_s r_s \tag{22.2}$$

$$E(r_L) = (.2)(-5) + (.4)(10) + (.3)(-4) + (.1)(7) = 2.5\%$$

$$E(r_M) = (.2)(6) + (.4)(-2) + (.3)(8) + (.1)(-9) = 1.9\%$$

We will now solve for covariance in table form.

(1) Prob.	(2) r_L	(3) r_M	(4) $r_L - E(r)$	(5) $r_M - E(r)$	(6) = (1)(4)(5)
.2	−5	6	$(-5 - 2.5) = -7.5$	$(6 - 1.9) = 4.1$	−6.15
.4	10	−2	$(10 - 2.5) = 7.5$	$(-2 - 1.9) = -3.9$	−11.70
.3	−4	8	$(-4 - 2.5) = -6.5$	$(8 - 1.9) = 6.1$	−11.895
.1	7	−9	$(7 - 2.5) = 4.5$	$(-9 - 1.9) = -10.9$	−4.905
				$\text{cov}_{LM} = -34.65$	(6)

[1]See Harry Markowitz, "Portfolio Selection," *Journal of Finance*, March 1952, pp. 77–91.

The equation for covariance of returns when historical (or ex post) returns are used is

$$\text{cov}_{ij} = \frac{1}{N}\sum_{t=1}^{N}(r_{it} - \bar{r}_i)(r_{jt} - \bar{r}_j) \tag{22.3}$$

where N is the number of equally likely paired observations, r_{it} and r_{jt} are returns for assets i and j during the period t, and $\bar{r}_i$ and $\bar{r}_j$ are the historical average returns for assets i and j.

22.3 CORRELATION

The correlation is also a measure of the relationship between two assets. The correlation coefficient can take on a value from -1 to $+1$. Correlation and covariance are related by the following equation:

$$\text{cov}_{ij} = \sigma_i \sigma_j \rho_{ij} \tag{22.4}$$

where σ_i and σ_j are the standard deviations of returns for assets i and j, and ρ_{ij} is the correlation coefficient for assets i and j.

EXAMPLE 22.2 Using the information given in Example 22.1, determine the correlation coefficient for assets x and y.

Solving for the correlation coefficient in Eq. (*22.4*) yields

$$\rho_{ij} = \frac{\text{cov}_{ij}}{\sigma_i \sigma_j}$$

Hint: cov_{ij} is given in Example 22.1. However, you must determine σ_i and σ_j.

The following equation for the variance of an asset can be used to determine standard deviation:

$$\sigma_i^2 = \sum_{t=1}^{T} P_i[r_i - E(r)]^2 \tag{22.5}$$

$$\sigma_L^2 = [(.2)(-5 - 2.5)^2 + (.4)(10 - 2.5)^2 + (.3)(-4 - 2.5)^2 + (.1)(7 - 2.5)]^2$$
$$= 11.25 + 22.5 + 12.675 + 2.025 = 48.45$$
$$\sigma_L = \sqrt{48.45} = 6.9606\%$$
$$\sigma_M^2 = [(.2)(6 - 1.9)^2 + (.4)(-2 - 1.9)^2 + (.3)(8 - 1.9)^2 + (.1)(-9 - 1.9)]^2$$
$$= 3.362 + 6.084 + 11.163 + 11.881 = 32.49$$
$$\sigma_M = \sqrt{32.49} = 5.7\%$$
$$\rho_{LM} = \frac{-34.65}{(6.9606)(5.7)} = -.8733$$

SOLVED PROBLEM 22.1

The Jones (J) and Sun (S) Corporations have the following joint probability distribution of returns for next year:

STATE	PROBABILITY	RET. JONES %	RET. SUN %
Boom	.1	14	20
Recession	.2	−5	−2
Normal	.4	10	9
Recovery	.1	9	14
Slow growth	.2	12	18

(*a*) Determine the expected covariance of returns for the Jones and Sun Corporations.

(*b*) What is the correlation of returns between the Jones and Sun Corporations?

SOLUTION

(*a*) First, we must determine the expected return for the Jones and Sun Corporations. Expected return can be determined with the following equation:

$$E(r) = \sum_{s=1}^{N} P_s r_s \tag{22.2}$$

$$E(r_J) = (.1)(14) + (.2)(-5) + (.4)(10) + (.1)(9) + (.2)(12)$$
$$= 1.4 + (-1) + 4 + .9 + 2.4 = 7.7\%$$
$$E(r_S) = (.1)(20) + (.2)(-2) + (.4)(9) + (.1)(14) + (.2)(18)$$
$$= 2 + (-.4) + 3.6 + 1.4 + 3.6 = 10.2\%$$

$$\begin{aligned}
\text{cov}_{JS} &= \sum_{s=1}^{N=5} [r_{Js} - E(r_J)][r_{Ss} - E(r_S)]P_s \\
&= (14 - 7.7)(20 - 10.2)(.1) + (-5 - 7.7)(-2 - 10.2)(.2) + (10 - 7.7)(9 - 10.2)(.4) \\
&\quad + (9 - 7.7)(14 - 10.2)(.1) + (12 - 7.7)(18 - 10.2)(.2) \\
&= 6.174 + 30.988 + (-1.104) + .494 + 6.708 \\
&= 43.26
\end{aligned}$$

$$\rho_{JS} = \frac{\text{cov}_{JS}}{\sigma_J \sigma_S}$$

(*b*) Since we determined covariance in (*a*), we need to calculate σ_J and σ_S.

$$\sigma^2 = \sum_{t=1}^{N=5} P_i[r_i - E(r)]^2$$

$$\begin{aligned}
\sigma_J^2 &= (.1)(14 - 7.7)^2 + (.2)(-5 - 7.7)^2 + (.4)(10 - 7.7)^2 + (.1)(9 - 7.7)^2 + (.2)(12 - 7.7)^2 \\
&= 3.969 + 32.258 + 2.116 + .169 + 3.698 = 42.21
\end{aligned}$$

$$\sigma_J = \sqrt{42.21} = 6.50\%$$

$$\begin{aligned}
\sigma_S^2 &= (.1)(20 - 10.2)^2 + (.2)(-2 - 10.2)^2 + (.4)(9 - 10.2)^2 + (.1)(14 - 10.2)^2 + (.2)(18 - 10.2)^2 \\
&= 9.604 + 29.768 + .576 + 1.444 + 12.168 = 53.56
\end{aligned}$$

$$\sigma_S = \sqrt{53.56} = 7.318\%$$

$$\rho_{JS} = \frac{\text{cov}_{JS}}{\sigma_J \sigma_S} = \frac{43.26}{(6.50)(7.318)} = \frac{43.26}{47.567} = .909454$$

SOLVED PROBLEM 22.2

Stocks *A* and *B* had the following returns over the past 5 years. Determine the covariance and correlation coefficients for the two corporations.

YEAR	RET. *A*%	RET. *B*%
19X1	8	10
19X2	−9	−12
19X3	14	18
19X4	16	20
19X5	20	14

SOLUTION

To calculate cov_{AB}, Eq. (*22.3*) should be used:

$$\text{cov}_{AB} = \frac{1}{N} \sum_{t=1}^{N} (r_{At} - \bar{r}_A)(r_{Bt} - \bar{r}_B) \qquad (22.3)$$

As inputs, we need the arithmetic average returns for stocks *A* and *B*. Average returns can be calculated with the following equation:

$$\bar{r} = \frac{\sum_{t=1}^{N} r_t}{N}$$

$$\bar{r}_A = \frac{8 + (-9) + 14 + 16 + 20}{5} = \frac{49}{5} = 9.8\%$$

$$\bar{r}_B = \frac{10 + (-12) + 18 + 20 + 14}{5} = \frac{50}{5} = 10\%$$

$$\begin{aligned}
\text{cov}_{AB} &= \frac{(8 - 9.8)(10 - 10) + (-9 - 9.8)(-12 - 10) + (14 - 9.8)(18 - 10) + (16 - 9.8)(20 - 10) + (20 - 9.8)(14 - 10)}{5} \\
&= \frac{0 + 413.60 + 33.60 + 62 + 40.8}{5} \\
&= \frac{550}{5} = 110
\end{aligned}$$

To calculate the correlation coefficient, use

$$\rho_{AB} = \frac{\text{cov}_{AB}}{\sigma_A \sigma_B}$$

Since cov_{AB} is calculated above, we need to determine σ_A and σ_B. An asset's standard deviation can be determined with the following equation:

$$\sigma^2 = \frac{\sum_{t=1}^{N} (r_t - \bar{r})^2}{N}$$

$$\sigma_A^2 = \frac{(8 - 9.8)^2 + (-9 - 9.8)^2 + (14 - 9.8)^2 + (16 - 9.8)^2 + (20 - 9.8)^2}{5}$$

$$= \frac{3.24 + 353.44 + 17.64 + 38.44 + 104.04}{5}$$

$$= \frac{516.80}{5} = 103.36$$

$$\sigma_A = \sqrt{103.36} = 10.1666\%$$

$$\sigma_B^2 = \frac{(10 - 10)^2 + (-12 - 10)^2 + (18 - 10)^2 + (20 - 10)^2 + (14 - 10)^2}{5}$$

$$= \frac{0 + 484 + 64 + 100 + 16}{5} = \frac{664}{5} = 132.8$$

$$\sigma_B = \sqrt{132.8} = 11.524\%$$

$$\rho_{AB} = \frac{\text{cov}_{AB}}{\sigma_A \sigma_B} = \frac{110}{(10.1666)(11.524)} = \frac{110}{117.1599} = .93889$$

Sometimes it is useful to calculate the correlation for two assets directly. Equation (*22.6*) is a computationally efficient way to define the correlation:

$$\rho_{AB} = \frac{N\sum AB - \sum A \sum B}{\left\{\left[\left(N\sum A^2\right) - \left(\sum A\right)^2\right]\left[\left(N\sum B^2\right) - \left(\sum B\right)^2\right]\right\}^{.5}} \tag{22.6}$$

To illustrate how to use Eq. (*22.6*), we will calculate the correlation coefficient for assets *A* and *B*. With assets *A* and *B*, $N = 5$.

RET. A	RET. B	A^2	B^2	$A \times B$
8	10	64	100	80
−9	−12	81	144	108
14	18	196	324	252
16	20	256	400	320
20	14	400	196	280
$\Sigma A = 49\%$	$\Sigma B = 50\%$	$\Sigma A^2 = 997$	$\Sigma B^2 = 1{,}164$	$\Sigma AB = 1{,}040$

$$\rho_{AB} = \frac{(5)(1{,}040) - (49)(50)}{\{[(5)(997) - (49)^2][(5)(1{,}164) - (50)^2]\}^{.5}}$$

$$= \frac{2{,}750}{[(4{,}985 - 2{,}401)(5{,}820 - 2{,}500)]^{.5}}$$

$$= \frac{2{,}750}{[(2{,}584)(3{,}320)]^{.5}} = \frac{2{,}750}{(8{,}578{,}880)^{.5}} = \frac{2{,}750}{2{,}928.973}$$

$$= .9389$$

22.4 PORTFOLIO RETURN

The return on a portfolio of assets is simply the weighted average return. A portfolio's return can be calculated with the following equation:

$$r_p = \sum_{t=1}^{N} x_i r_i \tag{22.7}$$

where x_i is the weight for asset *i* and r_i is the return for asset *i*. The weights must sum to 1, $\Sigma x_i = 1$.

EXAMPLE 22.3 Mary Clifford has a portfolio of four common stocks with the following market values and returns:

STOCK	MARKET VALUE	STOCK RET.
X	\$ 10,000	10%
Y	20,000	14
Z	30,000	16
M	40,000	15
	\$100,000	

The return on Mary's portfolio is determined using Eq. (*22.7*):

$$r_p = \left(\frac{\$10{,}000}{\$100{,}000}\right)(10) + \left(\frac{\$20{,}000}{\$100{,}000}\right)(14) + \left(\frac{\$30{,}000}{\$100{,}000}\right)(16) + \left(\frac{\$40{,}000}{\$100{,}000}\right)(15)$$
$$= (.1)(10) + (.2)(14) + (.3)(16) + (.4)(15)$$
$$= (1 + 2.8 + 4.8 + 6.0) = 14.6\%$$

SOLVED PROBLEM 22.3

Jim Earles has a portfolio of five stocks with the following expected market values and returns:

STOCKS	MARKET VALUE	RETURN
Acme	\$ 40,000	8%
Brown	50,000	20
Cole	20,000	15
Dell	100,000	9
Egan	30,000	12
	\$240,000	

Determine Jim's expected portfolio return.

SOLUTION

First, we should determine the relative weights for each asset in the portfolio.

ASSET	WEIGHT
Acme	\$40,000/\$240,000 = .16667
Brown	\$50,000/\$240,000 = .20833
Cole	\$20,000/\$240,000 = .08333
Dell	\$100,000/\$240,000 = .41667
Egan	\$30,000/\$240,000 = .12500

$$r_p = \sum_{i=1}^{N=5} x_i r_i$$
$$= (.16667)(8) + (.20833)(20) + (.08333)(15) + (.41667)(9) + (.125)(12)$$
$$= 1.3334 + 4.167 + 1.25 + 3.75 + 1.5 = 12.00\%$$

22.5 PORTFOLIO STANDARD DEVIATION

The variance of returns for a portfolio of assets can be calculated with the following general formula:

$$\text{var}(r_p) = \sum_{i=1}^{N} x_i^2 \sigma_{ii} + \sum_{i=1}^{N}\sum_{j=1}^{N} x_i x_j \sigma_{ij} \quad \text{for } i = j \tag{22.8}$$

where x_i and x_j are the weights for assets i and j, σ_{ii} is the variance for the ith asset, σ_{ij} is the covariance of assets i and j, and N denotes the number of assets. The $\sqrt{\text{var } r_p}$ is the portfolios' standard deviation of returns (σ_p).

Equation (*22.8*) is reproduced in Table 22.1. The matrix in Table 22.1 represents a weighted sum of the N variance terms plus all the $N^2 - N$ covariance terms. The diagonal of the matrix goes from upper left to lower right and represents the N weighted variance terms of the form $x_i x_i \sigma_{ii} = x_i^2 \sigma_{ii} = x_i^2 \sigma_i^2$. The boxes to the left and right of the diagonal contain each of the $N^2 - N$ weighted covariance terms twice. The covariance terms are symmetric because $x_i x_j \sigma_{ji} = x_j x_i \sigma_{ij}$. This means that there are $\frac{1}{2}(N^2 - N)$ unique covariance terms. Note that σ_{ij} denotes the same thing as cov_{ij}.

EXAMPLE 22.4 Write the portfolio standard deviation formula for the $N = 3$ case. *Hint:* The $N = 3$ case will use the first three rows and columns of Table 22.1. Note that the 3×3 matrix contains nine terms—three variances and six

Table 22.1 Variance-Covariance Matrix

		col. 1		col. 2		col. 3		col. $n-1$		col. n	
var r_p	=	$x_1x_1\sigma_{11}$	+	$x_1x_2\sigma_{12}$	+	$x_1x_3\sigma_{13}$	$+\cdots$	$x_1x_{n-1}\sigma_{1,n-1}$	+	$x_1x_n\sigma_{1n}$	row 1
	+	$x_2x_1\sigma_{21}$	+	$x_2x_2\sigma_{22}$	+	$x_2x_3\sigma_{23}$	$+\cdots$	$x_2x_{n-1}\sigma_{2,n-1}$	+	$x_2x_n\sigma_{2n}$	row 2
	+	$x_3x_1\sigma_{31}$	+	$x_3x_2\sigma_{32}$	+	$x_3x_3\sigma_{33}$	$+\cdots$	$x_3x_{n-1}\sigma_{3,n-1}$	+	$x_3x_n\sigma_{3n}$	row 3
		.		.		.		.		.	
		.		.		.		.		.	
		.		.		.		.		.	
	+	$x_nx_1\sigma_{n1}$	+	$x_nx_2\sigma_{n2}$	+	$x_nx_3\sigma_{n3}$	$+\cdots$	$x_nx_{n-1}\sigma_{n,n-1}$	+	$x_nx_n\sigma_{nn}$	row n

covariances. Since the covariance terms on one side of the diagonal are the mirror image of the covariances on the other side, we have three pairs of covariances. The resulting equation can be expressed more concisely as follows:

$$\sigma_p = \sqrt{\sum_{i=1}^{3} x_i^2\sigma_i^2 + 2x_1x_2\sigma_{12} + 2x_1x_3\sigma_{13} + 2x_2x_3\sigma_{23}}$$

The covariance terms can also be defined the following way:

$$\rho_{12}\sigma_1\sigma_2 = \text{cov}_{12} = \sigma_{12}$$
$$\rho_{13}\sigma_1\sigma_3 = \text{cov}_{13} = \sigma_{13}$$
$$\rho_{23}\sigma_2\sigma_3 = \text{cov}_{23} = \sigma_{23}$$

22.6 TWO-ASSET CASE

A two-asset portfolio ($N = 2$) can be used to illustrate some of the principles of diversification. The variance-covariance matrix from Table 22.1 reduces to Eq. (*22.9*) for $N = 2$:

$$\sigma_p^2 = x_1^2\sigma_1^2 + x_2^2\sigma_2^2 + 2x_1x_2\sigma_{12} \tag{22.9}$$

EXAMPLE 22.5 Using the two asset Eqs. (*22.9*) and (*22.7*) compute the portfolio's risk and return as the assets' correlation coefficient takes on values of -1, 0, .5, and 1.

Portfolio theory suggests that as the correlation coefficient declines risk should decline, but the portfolio's expected return should not vary, if the weights of the assets are held constant. The important point is that if assets are less than perfectly positively correlated (that is, a correlation coefficient below $+1$), diversification can reduce risk. This is shown in Table 22.2 with the following risk and return inputs:

RISK	EXP. RET.	CORRELATION CANDIDATES
$\sigma_A = 15\%$	$E(r_A) = 10\%$	$\rho_{AB} = 1, 0, .5, \text{and } -1$
$\sigma_B = 30\%$	$E(r_B) = 20\%$	

Table 22.2 Portfolio Risk and Return for Two Assets

Weights %		Port.	Portfolio Standard Deviation			
X	Y	Ret.%	$\rho_{XY} = 1$	$\rho_{XY} = .5$	$\rho_{XY} = 0$	$\rho_{XY} = -1$
100	0	10.0	15.000	15.000	15.000	15.000
90	10	11.0	16.500	15.223	13.829	10.500
80	20	12.0	18.000	15.875	13.416	6.000
70	30	13.0	19.500	16.904	13.829	1.500
60	40	14.0	21.000	18.248	15.000	3.000
50	50	15.0	22.500	19.843	16.771	7.500
40	60	16.0	24.000	21.633	18.974	12.000
30	70	17.0	25.500	23.574	21.497	16.500
20	80	18.0	27.000	25.632	24.187	21.000
10	90	19.0	28.500	27.780	27.042	21.500
0	100	20.0	30.000	30.000	30.000	30.000

SOLVED PROBLEM 22.4

Table 22.2 shows that the return and risk for a portfolio composed of 20 percent A and 80 percent B is 18 percent and 25.632 percent, respectively, when the correlation between A and B is .5. How were these numbers derived?

SOLUTION

$$r_p = x_A r_A + x_A r_A \tag{22.7}$$
$$= .2(10\%) + .8(20\%) = 2\% + 16\% = 18\%$$

Using the square root of Eq. (22.9),

$$\sigma_p = \sqrt{x_A^2\sigma_A^2 + x_B^2\sigma_B^2 + 2x_A x_B \rho_{AB}\sigma_A\sigma_B}$$
$$= \sqrt{(.2)^2(15)^2 + (.8)^2(30)^2 + 2(.2)(.8)(.5)(15)(30)}$$
$$= \sqrt{(.04)(225) + (.64)(900) + 72} = \sqrt{9 + 576 + 72}$$
$$= \sqrt{657} = 25.632\%$$

Figure 22-1 graphs the risk and return possibilities for the two-asset portfolio given in Example 22.5. The solid lines are the portfolio possibilities when short sales are not allowed. The dashed lines illustrate the results when short sales are allowed.

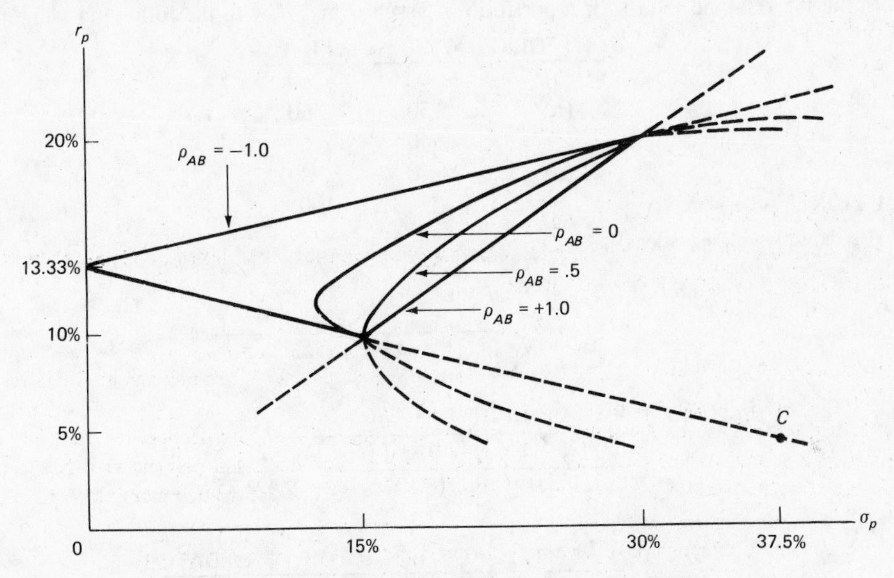

Fig. 22-1 Markowitz diversification with short selling.

SOLVED PROBLEM 22.5

(*a*) Refer to Fig. 22-1. Point C shows an expected return and risk of 5 percent and 37.5 percent, respectively. How were these numbers calculated?

(*b*) Determine the risk for a portfolio composed of assets A and B if the correlation coefficient is .5 and the return is 5 percent.

SOLUTION

(*a*) These numbers can be determined by using Eqs. (22.7) and (22.9). In order to earn 5 percent, a portfolio composed of assets A and B must have appropriate weights. These weights can be determined by setting Eq. (22.7) equal to 5 percent (for the $N = 2$ case) and solving for the weights:

$$5\% = X_1(10\%) + (1 - X_1)(20\%)$$

where X_1 is the weight for A. Since the two assets must sum to 1, $(1 - X_1)$ is the weight for B.

$$5\% = 10\%X_1 + 20\% - 20\%X_1$$
$$-15\% = -10\%X_1$$
$$X_1 = \frac{15\%}{10\%} = 1.5$$
$$1 - X = 1 - 1.5 = -.5 \qquad \text{the weight for } B$$

The negative weight for security B means that B was sold short and the proceeds used to purchase security A. The weights are $X_A = 1.5$ and $X_B = -.5$. Point C is on the graph where $\rho_{AB} = -1$. σ_A and σ_B are the risk of A and B, 15 percent and 30 percent.

$$\begin{aligned}\sigma_p &= \sqrt{x_A^2\sigma_A^2 + x_B^2\sigma_B^2 + 2x_Ax_B\rho_{AB}\sigma_A\sigma_B} \\ &= \sqrt{(1.5)^2(15)^2 + (-.5)^2(30)^2 + 2(1.5)(-.5)(-1)(15)(30)} \\ &= \sqrt{506.25 + 225 + 675} = \sqrt{1{,}406.25} = 37.5\%\end{aligned}$$

(*b*) The weights are the same as in (*a*)—A and B are 1.5 and $-.5$, respectively.

$$\begin{aligned}\sigma_p &= \sqrt{(1.5)^2(15)^2 + (-.5)^2(30)^2 + 2(1.5)(-.5)(.5)(15)(30)} \\ &= \sqrt{506.25 + 225 - 337.50} = \sqrt{393.75} = 19.84\%\end{aligned}$$

SOLVED PROBLEM 22.6

Two assets J and K, have the following risk and return characteristics:

$$\sigma_J = 25\% \qquad E(r_J) = 18\% \qquad \rho_{JK} = -.2$$
$$\sigma_K = 20\% \qquad E(r_K) = 14\%$$

Determine the risk and return for a portfolio of assets J and K with the following weights:

PORTFOLIO	WT. *J* %	WT. *K* %
(*a*)	90	10
(*b*)	50	50
(*c*)	40	60
(*d*)	20	80

SOLUTION

Use the following equations:

$$E(r_p) = \sum_{i=1}^{N} x_iE(r_i)$$
$$\sigma_p = \sqrt{x_A^2\sigma_A^2 + x_B^2\sigma_B^2 + 2x_Ax_B\rho_{AB}\sigma_A\sigma_B}$$

(*a*)

$$\begin{aligned}E(r_p) &= (.90)(18) + (.10)(14) = 17.6\% \\ \sigma_p &= \sqrt{(.9)^2(25)^2 + (.1)^2(20)^2 + 2(.9)(.1)(-.2)(25)(20)} \\ &= \sqrt{(.81)(625) + (.01)(400) - 18} = \sqrt{492.25} = 22.187\%\end{aligned}$$

(*b*)

$$\begin{aligned}E(r_p) &= (.5)(18) + (.5)(14) = 16\% \\ \sigma_p &= \sqrt{(.5)^2(25)^2 + (.5)^2(20)^2 + 2(.5)(.5)(-.2)(25)(20)} \\ &= \sqrt{(.25)(625) + (.25)(400) - 50} = \sqrt{206.25} = 14.361\%\end{aligned}$$

(*c*)

$$\begin{aligned}E(r_p) &= (.4)(18) + (.6)(14) = 15.6\% \\ \sigma_p &= \sqrt{(.4)^2(25)^2 + (.6)^2(20)^2 + 2(.4)(.6)(-.2)(25)(20)} \\ &= \sqrt{(.16)(625) + (.36)(400) - 48} = \sqrt{196} = 14\%\end{aligned}$$

(*d*)

$$\begin{aligned}E(r_p) &= (.2)(18) + (.8)(14) = 14.8\% \\ \sigma_p &= \sqrt{(.2)^2(25)^2 + (.8)^2(20)^2 + 2(.2)(.8)(-.2)(25)(20)} \\ &= \sqrt{(.04)(625) + (.64)(400) - 32} = \sqrt{249} = 15.78\%\end{aligned}$$

SOLVED PROBLEM 22.7

Determine the risk and return for an equally weighted (that is, $\frac{1}{3} + \frac{1}{3} + \frac{1}{3}$) portfolio of assets X, Y, and Z with the following inputs:

$$E(r_X) = 15\% \qquad E(r_Y) = 17\% \qquad E(r_Z) = 20\%$$
$$\sigma_X = 18\% \qquad \sigma_Y = 20\% \qquad \sigma_Z = 25\%$$
$$\rho_{XY} = .5 \qquad \rho_{YZ} = .2 \qquad \rho_{XZ} = -.5$$

SOLUTION

$$E(r_p) = x_X r_X + x_Y r_Y + x_Z r_Z = (.333)(15) + (.333)(17) + (.333)(20) = 17.321\%$$

$$\sigma_p = \sqrt{x_X^2\sigma_X^2 + x_Y^2\sigma_Y^2 + x_Z^2\sigma_Z^2 + 2x_X x_Y \rho_{XY}\sigma_X\sigma_Y + 2x_Y x_Z \rho_{YZ}\sigma_Y\sigma_Z + 2x_X x_Z \rho_{XZ}\sigma_X\sigma_Z}$$

$$= \sqrt{(.333)^2(18)^2 + (.333)^2(20)^2 + (.333)^2(25)^2 + 2(.333)(.333)(.5)(18)(20) + 2(.333)(.333)(.2)(20)(25) + 2(.333)(.333)(-.5)(18)(25)}$$

$$= \sqrt{(.1111)(324) + (.1111)(400) + (.1111)(625) + 39.924 + 22.18 - 49.905}$$

$$= \sqrt{162.1111} = 12.73\%$$

SOLVED PROBLEM 22.8

The Burr (B) and Poe (P) Corporations have the following expected risk and return inputs for next year:

$$E(r_B) = 18\% \qquad E(r_P) = 22\%$$

$$\sigma_B = 22\% \qquad \sigma_P = 30\%$$

$$\rho_{BP} = .4$$

The portfolio risk (standard deviation) for a portfolio of 50 percent in each asset is 21.8632 percent. Determine the correlation coefficient that will be necessary to reduce the level of portfolio risk by 25 percent. What is the expected return of the equally weighted portfolio?

SOLUTION

A 25 percent reduction in risk is (.25)(21.8632%) = 5.4658%. Therefore, the new level of risk will be 21.8632% − 5.4658% = 16.3974%.

$$\sigma_P = \sqrt{x_B^2\sigma_B^2 + x_P^2\sigma_P^2 + 2x_B x_P \rho_{BP}\sigma_B\sigma_P}$$

$$16.3974 = \sqrt{(.5)^2(22)^2 + (.5)^2(30)^2 + 2(.5)(.5)(22)(30)\rho_{BP}}$$

$$= \sqrt{121 + 225 + 330\rho_{BP}}$$

$$(16.3974)^2 = 121 + 225 + 330\rho_{BP}$$

$$268.8747 = 346 + 330\rho_{BP}$$

$$-77.1253 = 330\rho_{BP}$$

$$\rho_{BP} = -.2337$$

$$E(r_p) = (.5)(18) + (.5)(22\%) = 20\%$$

SOLVED PROBLEM 22.9

Prove that for a two-asset portfolio composed of assets a and b, the minimum risk portfolio requires an investment in asset a equal to

$$x_a = \frac{\sigma_b^2 - \rho_{ab}\sigma_a\sigma_b}{\sigma_a^2 + \sigma_b^2 - 2\rho_{ab}\sigma_a\sigma_b}$$

where x_a is the percent invested in asset a.

SOLUTION

Since $\Sigma^2 x = 1$, we can say $x_b = 1 - x_a$ and write

$$\text{var } r_p = x_a^2\sigma_a^2 + (1 - x_a)^2\sigma_b^2 + 2x_a(1 - x_a)\sigma_a\sigma_b\rho_{ab} = 0 \tag{1}$$

$$= x_a^2\sigma_a^2 + (1 - 2x_a + x_a^2)\sigma_b^2 + (2x_a - 2x_a^2)\sigma_a\sigma_b\rho_{ab} = 0 \tag{1a}$$

$$= x_a^2\sigma_a^2 + \sigma_b^2 - 2x_a\sigma_b^2 + \sigma_b^2 x_a^2 + 2x_a\sigma_a\sigma_b\rho_{ab} - 2x_a^2\sigma_a\sigma_b\rho_{ab} = 0 \tag{1b}$$

$$\frac{d(\text{var } r_p)}{dx_a} = 2x_a\sigma_a^2 - 2\sigma_b^2 + 2x_a\sigma_b^2 + 2\sigma_a\sigma_b\rho_{ab} - 4x_a\rho_{ab}\sigma_a\sigma_b = 0 \quad \text{(divide by 2)} \tag{2}$$

$$= x_a\sigma_a^2 - \sigma_b^2 + x_a\sigma_b^2 + \sigma_a\sigma_b\rho_{ab} - 2x_a\rho_{ab}\sigma_a\sigma_b = 0 \tag{3}$$

$$= x_a(\sigma_a^2 + \sigma_b^2 - 2\rho_{ab}\sigma_a\sigma_b) + \rho_{ab}\sigma_a\sigma_b - \sigma_b^2 = 0 \tag{4}$$

$$x_a(\sigma_a^2 + \sigma_b^2 - 2\rho_{ab}\sigma_a\sigma_b) = 0 - \rho_{ab}\sigma_a\sigma_b + \sigma_b^2 \tag{5}$$

$$x_a = \frac{\sigma_b^2 - \rho_{ab}\sigma_a\sigma_b}{\sigma_a^2 + \sigma_b^2 - 2\rho_{ab}\sigma_a\sigma_b} \tag{22.10}$$

SOLVED PROBLEM 22.10

Using the results of Solved Problem 22.9, develop a minimum risk investment equation for two assets when the correlation coefficient between the two assets are 0 and −1.

SOLUTION

From Solved Problem 22.9, the minimum risk variance (or standard deviation) is Eq. (*22.10*). When $\rho_{ab} = 0$, the equation for x_a reduces to Eq. (*22.11*):

$$x_a = \frac{\sigma_b^2}{\sigma_a^2 + \sigma_b^2} \tag{22.11}$$

If $\rho_{ab} = -1$, then

$$x_a = \frac{\sigma_b^2 + \sigma_a\sigma_b}{\sigma_a^2 + \sigma_b^2 + 2\sigma_a\sigma_b} = \frac{\sigma_b(\sigma_b + \sigma_a)}{(\sigma_b + \sigma_a)^2} = \frac{\sigma_b}{\sigma_b + \sigma_a} \tag{22.12}$$

SOLVED PROBLEM 22.11

The Roe and Toab Corporations, denoted *R* and *T*, have the following risk and return statistics:

$$E(r_R) = 20\% \qquad E(r_T) = 25\%$$

$$\sigma_R = 30\% \qquad \sigma_T = 40\%$$

$$\rho_{RT} = -1$$

Determine the minimum risk portfolio for *R* and *T*.

SOLUTION

From Eq. (*22.12*) developed in Solved Problem 22.10, we know

$$x_R = \frac{\sigma_T}{\sigma_T + \sigma_R} = \frac{40}{40 + 30} = \frac{40}{70} = .5714 = 57.14\%$$

Therefore, x_T equals 1 − .5714 = .4286 or 42.86%.

SOLVED PROBLEM 22.12

The Spaulding (*S*) and Johnson (*J*) Corporations have the following risk and return statistics:

$$E(r_J) = 14\% \qquad E(r_S) = 16\%$$

$$\sigma_J = 22\% \qquad \sigma_S = 25\%$$

$$\rho_{JS} = .5$$

Determine the minimum risk portfolio.

SOLUTION

Using Eq. (*22.10*) developed in Solved Problem 22.9,

$$x_a = \frac{\sigma_b^2 - \rho_{ab}\sigma_a\sigma_b}{\sigma_a^2 + \sigma_b^2 - 2\rho_{ab}\sigma_a\sigma_b}$$

Letting $J = a$ and $S = b$ results in

$$x_a = \frac{(25)^2 - (.5)(22)(25)}{(22)^2 + (25)^2 - 2(.5)(22)(25)} = \frac{625 - 275}{484 + 625 - 550} = \frac{350}{559}$$

$$= .6261 \quad \text{or} \quad 62.61\% \qquad (\text{for } J)$$

$$\text{Percent in } S = 1 - .6261 = .3739 \quad \text{or} \quad 37.39\%$$

22.7 EFFICIENT FRONTIER (EF)

If we consider the infinite number of portfolios that could be formed from two or more securities and plotted these portfolios' expected return and risk, we would create a graph like the one in Fig. 22-2. The efficient frontier is represented by the heavy dark line from *E* to *F* in Fig. 22-2. Porfolios along curve *EF* dominate all other investment possibilities. Portfolio *F*, the highest return portfolio, is the only one that is likely a one-asset portfolio. The curvature of the efficient frontier depends upon the correlation of the asset's returns. The efficient frontier curve is convex toward the *E*(*r*) axis because all assets have correlation coefficients that are less that positive unity and greater than negative unity.

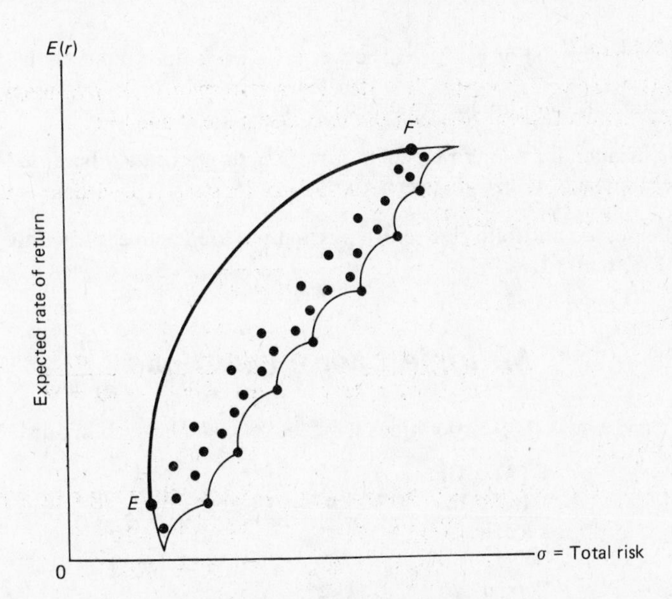

Fig. 22-2 Efficient frontier.

22.8 OPTIMUM PORTFOLIO

Markowitz portfolio analysis makes the following assumptions:

1. The investor seeks to maximize the expected utility of total wealth.
2. All investors have the same expected single period investment horizon.
3. Investors are risk-averse.
4. Investors base their investment decisions on the expected return and standard deviation of returns from a possible investment.
5. Perfect markets are assumed (e.g., no taxes and no transaction costs).

Given the above assumptions, an investor will want to hold a portfolio somewhere along the efficient frontier (that is, along *EF* in Fig. 22-2). The exact location depends on the investor's risk-return preferences. A set of indifference curves for each investor will show his or her risk-return tradeoff. Those investors with more risk-aversion require more compensation for assuming risk and will choose a portfolio along the lower end of the efficient frontier close to *E* in Fig. 22-2. The portfolio chosen will be optimal because no other portfolio along the efficient frontier can dominate another in terms of risk and return.

True-False Questions

22.1 All possible portfolios of assets lie along the efficient frontier.

22.2 In the two-asset model, if the correlation coefficient between the assets is -1, then any combination of the two assets will result in a portfolio risk of zero, as long as the weights of the two assets sum to 1.

22.3 Those investors with a greater preference for risk will choose a portfolio along the upper part of the efficient frontier.

22.4 With two zero correlated assets, portfolio risk can be reduced to zero if the proper weights are determined for the two assets.

22.5 Investing in a portfolio that lies off of the efficient frontier is not what Markowitz suggested.

22.6 The Markowitz efficient frontier forms a convex risk-return tradeoff function.

22.7 With two assets, as the correlation coefficient between the two assets is reduced, the portfolio's risk is reduced.

22.8 A 50-asset portfolio has 1,225 unique covariance terms.

22.9 Markowitz diversification is an improvement over random diversification because Markowitz diversification considers the covariance of returns between assets.

22.10 In the two-asset case, the portfolio risk-return possibilities are nonlinear when the correlation between the asset returns is less than +1.

Multiple Choice Questions

22.1 The Harvey (H) and Lewis (L) Corporations have the following probability distribution of returns:

STATE OF NATURE	PROBABILITY	r_H	r_L
Recession	.1	10	20
Boom	.2	−12	−30
Normal	.2	−7	−20
Slow growth	.1	20	40
Recovery	.4	30	35

Determine the expected covariance of returns for the Harvey and Lewis Corporations for next year.
(*a*) 600
(*b*) 508
(*c*) 400
(*d*) −300
(*e*) 550

22.2 Refer to Problem 22.1. Determine the correlation of returns between the Harvey and Lewis Corporations.
(*a*) .9692
(*b*) .9331
(*c*) .9422
(*d*) .8993
(*e*) .9011

22.3 The Edwards and Harvey Corporations had the following ex post returns:

YEAR	EDWARDS RET.	HARVEY RET.
19X1	20%	30%
19X2	−10	−20
19X3	15	18
19X4	17	10
19X5	19	5

Determine the covariance of returns for the Edwards and Harvey Corporations.
(*a*) 220.32
(*b*) −420.11
(*c*) 145.22
(*d*) 270.36
(*e*) 162.08

22.4 Refer to Problem 22.3. Determine the correlation coefficient for the Edwards and Harvey Corporations.
(*a*) .540
(*b*) .869
(*c*) .923
(*d*) .758
(*e*) .697

22.5 Two Corporations, Zappa (Z) and Quincy (Q), have the following risk and return statistics:

$$\sigma_Z = 18\% \qquad \sigma_Q = 30\%$$
$$E(r_Z) = 14\% \qquad (r_Q) = 19\%$$
$$\rho_{ZQ} = .28$$

Determine the risk of a portfolio of 25 percent Z and 75 percent Q.
(*a*) 18.25 percent
(*b*) 30.15 percent
(*c*) 24.15 percent
(*d*) 21.75 percent
(*e*) 27.13 percent

22.6 Refer to Problem 22.5. Determine the risk of a portfolio of 50 percent Z and 50 percent Q.
(*a*) 19.5 percent
(*b*) 21.7 percent
(*c*) 17.8 percent
(*d*) 23.0 percent
(*e*) 25.4 percent

22.7 Two assets, 1 and 2, have the following risk and return statistics:

$$E(r_1) = 17\% \qquad E(r_2) = 21\%$$
$$\sigma_1 = 22\% \qquad \sigma_2 = 27\%$$
$$\rho_{12} = 0$$

Determine the minimum risk combination for a portfolio of assets for 1 and 2.
(*a*) $X_1 = 25$ percent and 75 percent $= X_2$
(*b*) $X_1 = 60.1$ percent and 39.9 percent $= X_2$
(*c*) $X_1 = 35$ percent and 65 percent $= X_2$
(*d*) $X_1 = 27.1$ percent and 72.9 percent $= X_2$
(*e*) $X_1 = 40.1$ percent and 59.9 percent $= X_2$

22.8 Two assets, 3 and 4, have the following risk and return inputs:

$$E(r_3) = 14\% \qquad E(r_4) = 22\%$$
$$\sigma_3 = 19\% \qquad \sigma_4 = 32\%$$
$$\rho_{34} = -1$$

Determine the minimum risk portfolio for a portfolio containing assets 3 and 4.
(*a*) Percent in 3 = 62.75 percent; percent in 4 = 37.25 percent
(*b*) Percent in 3 = 55.67 percent; percent in 4 = 44.33 percent
(*c*) Percent in 3 = 25.10 percent; percent in 4 = 74.90 percent
(*d*) Percent in 3 = 35.20 percent; percent in 4 = 64.80 percent
(*e*) Percent in 3 = 40.00 percent; percent in 4 = 60.00 percent

22.9 The assets X, Y, and Z have the following risk and return statistics:

$$E(r_X) = 18\% \qquad E(r_Y) = 22\% \qquad E(r_Z) = 26\%$$
$$\sigma_X = 25\% \qquad \sigma_Y = 30\% \qquad \sigma_Z = 40\%$$
$$\rho_{XY} = .4 \qquad \rho_{YZ} = -.3 \qquad \rho_{XZ} = .65$$

Determine the risk of a portfolio of 25 percent X, 50 percent Y, and 25 percent Z.
(*a*) 19.225 percent
(*b*) 18.632 percent
(*c*) 17.111 percent
(*d*) 20.744 percent
(*e*) 22.868 percent

22.10 Refer to Problem 22.9. What is the expected return of the 25-50-25 portfolio containing X, Y, and Z?
(*a*) 17.25 percent
(*b*) 22.00 percent
(*c*) 16.34 percent
(*d*) 19.76 percent
(*e*) 18.72 percent

Answers

True-False

22.1. F 22.2. F 22.3. T 22.4. F 22.5. T 22.6. T 22.7. T 22.8. T 22.9. T
22.10. T

Multiple Choice

22.1. b 22.2. a 22.3. e 22.4. b 22.5. c 22.6. a 22.7. b 22.8. a 22.9. d
22.10. b

Chapter 23

Capital Market Theory

23.1 CAPITAL MARKET LINE (CML)

The assumptions underlying capital market theory are as follows:

1. Investors are Markowitz efficient diversifiers who delineate and seek to attain the efficient frontier. (The assumptions listed at the end of Chap. 22 apply.)
2. Money can be borrowed and lent at the risk-free interest rate, denoted R. Stated differently, $\text{var}(R) = 0$.
3. Investors have homogeneous expectations (idealized uncertainty).
4. Investments are infinitely divisible.
5. No taxes or transaction costs exist.
6. No inflation exists.
7. Capital markets are in equilibrium.

When we introduce a risk-free asset into Markowitz portfolio analysis, given the above assumptions, the efficient frontier is changed from a curve to a straight line. This new efficient frontier is called a *capital market line* (*CML*) and is illustrated in Fig. 23-1. The CML starts with the risk-free asset R and is tangent to the risky portfolio m on the Markowitz efficient frontier. Note that portfolio m is now the only risky portfolio desired.

To the left of m, investors on the CML will hold both the risk-free asset and the risky portfolio. Since these investors are holding part of their investment in R, they are lending at the rate of R. Just the opposite is true to the right of m. In this case investors are borrowing at R and investing more in m—they are utilizing leverage. Portfolio m is called the *market portfolio* and contains all assets.

The expected return on a CML portfolio composed of R and m is

$$E(r_p) = x_R R + x_m E(r_m)$$

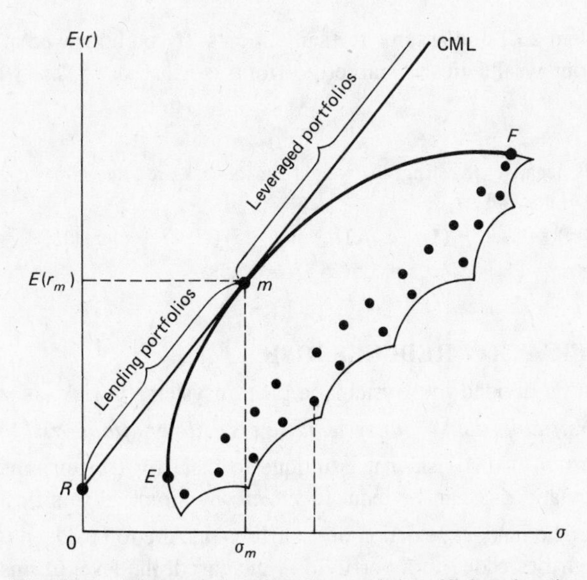

Fig. 23-1 The capital market line and the efficient frontier.

or since

$$x_R + x_m = 1 \qquad \text{and} \qquad x_m = 1 - x_R$$

$$E(r_p) = x_R R + (1 - x_R)E(r_m) \tag{23.1}$$

x_R is the proportion of an investor's wealth invested in R, and $E(r_m)$ is the expected return on the market portfolio.

The risk of a portfolio composed of R and m is measured with the following quadratic equation:

$$\sigma_p = \sqrt{x_R^2\sigma_R^2 + (1 - x_R)^2\sigma_m^2 + 2x_R(1 - x_R)\rho_{Rm}\sigma_R\sigma_m}$$

However, since $\sigma_R = 0$, then $\rho_{Rm} = 0$, and the risk formula collapses to the following linear form:

$$\sigma_p = (1 - x_R)\sigma_m = x_m\sigma_m \tag{23.2}$$

where σ_p is the standard deviation of the portfolio's returns and σ_m is the standard deviation of the market portfolio's returns.

SOLVED PROBLEM 23.1

Suppose the standard deviation of the market portfolio is 20 percent, its expected return is 14 percent, and the risk-free asset is 9 percent. What return can an investor expect to earn on an investment of 50 percent of his wealth in the risk-free asset and 50 percent of his wealth in the market portfolio? What is the 50-50 portfolio's risk?

SOLUTION

$$E(r_p) = x_R R + (1 - x_R)E(r_m) = (.5)(9\%) + (.5)(14\%) = 11.5\%$$
$$\sigma_p = (1 - x_R)\sigma_m = (.5)(20\%) = 10\%$$

SOLVED PROBLEM 23.2

Suppose you are interested in investing 60 percent of your wealth in the market portfolio and 40 percent in the risk-free asset. What is the expected risk and return of the 60-40 lending portfolio? Assume the market portfolio has an expected return of 15 percent and a standard deviation of 25 percent. The risk-free rate is $R = 10\%$.

SOLUTION

$$E(r_p) = x_R R + (1 - x_R)E(r_m) = (.4)(10\%) + (.6)(15\%) = 13\%$$
$$\sigma_p = (1 - x_R)\sigma_m = (.6)(25\%) = 15\%$$

SOLVED PROBLEM 23.3

Refer to Solved Problem 23.1 and assume the same inputs. If you borrowed at risk so that x_R is $-.5$ and invested 1.5 times your wealth in the market portfolio, so that $x_m = 1.5$, what will be your expected risk and return?

SOLUTION

Since borrowing is negative investing, the weight for the risk-free rate is negative and x_m exceeds 1.0 so that the weights sum to 1.0. Thus, we have

$$E(r_p) = x_R R + (1 - x_R)E(r_m) = (-.5)(10\%) + (1.5)(15\%) = 17.5\%$$
$$\sigma_p = (1 - x_R)\sigma_m = 1.5(25\%) = 37.5\%$$

23.2 SIMPLE DIVERSIFICATION REDUCES RISK

An asset's total risk can be divided into systematic plus unsystematic risk, as shown below:

Systematic risk (undiversifiable risk) + *unsystematic risk (diversifiable risk)* = total risk = var(r)

Unsystematic risk is that portion of the risk that is unique to the firm (for example, risk due to strikes and management errors). Unsystematic risk can be reduced to zero by simple diversification.

Simple diversification is the random selection of securities that are to be added to a portfolio. As the number of randomly selected securities added to a portfolio is increased, the level of unsystematic risk approaches zero. However, market-related systematic risk cannot be reduced by simple diversification. This risk is com-

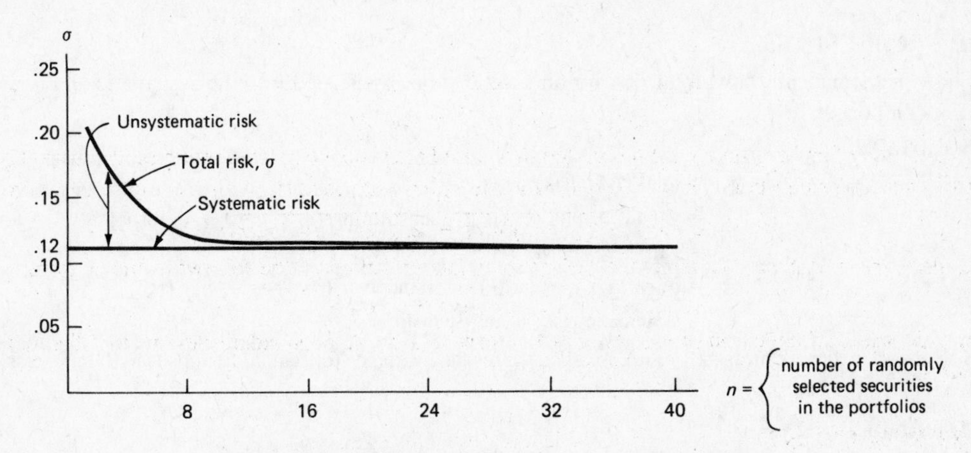

Fig. 23-2 Portfolio size, total risk, and systematic risk.

mon to all securities. Figure 23-2 illustrates how total risk approaches systematic risk as the number of securities in a portfolio increases.

23.3 CHARACTERISTIC LINE

Systematic risk can be measured statistically by using ordinary least squares (OLS) simple linear regression analysis. A financial model called the *characteristic line* is used to measure both systematic and unsystematic risk. The equation for the characteristic line (or regression line) is

$$r_{it} = a_i + b_i r_{mt} + e_{it} \tag{23.3}$$

where a_i = the intercept for the ith asset
b_i = the slope b for the ith asset, a measure of undiversifiable risk
e_{it} = the random error around the regression line for security i during time period t

Equation (*23.3*) shows the relationship of one security with the market and is sometimes called a *market model* for one security. OLS regressions are formulated so that the error terms (e_{it}) will average out to zero. As a result, the characteristic line is normally written (without the time subscripts) as

$$r_i = a_i + b_i r_m \tag{23.4}$$

The term a_i is called an *alpha coefficient* for security i. It measures the ith asset's rate of return when the market return $r_m = 0$. The term b_i is called the *beta coefficient;* it measures the slope of the characteristic line. Beta is defined mathematically as

$$b_i = \frac{\text{cov}\,(r_i, r_m)}{\text{var}(r_m)} = \frac{\text{units of rise}}{\text{units of run}} = \text{slope of regression line}$$

where cov (r_i, r_m) = the covariance of returns of the ith asset with the market
var (r_m) = the variance of the returns of the market index

SOLVED PROBLEM 23.4

Using the characteristic line model's beta, define an aggressive asset. What is a defensive asset?

SOLUTION

The beta coefficient is an index of systematic risk. Betas can be used for an ordinal ranking of the systematic risk of assets, but not for a direct comparison with total risk or systematic risk. An asset with $b > 1$ is an *aggressive* asset because it is more volatile than the market portfolio. For example, if an asset has a beta of 2 and the market (e.g., as represented by the S&P500) goes up by 10 percent, this asset will increase in return by 20 percent on average. With a *defensive asset,* beta is <1, and the response of the asset will be less than that of the market.

SOLVED PROBLEM 23.5

Show mathematically how total risk for an asset can be partitioned into the systematic and unsystematic risk components.

SOLUTION

$$\begin{aligned}
\text{var}(r_i) &= \text{total risk of the asset} \\
&= \text{var}(a_i + b_i r_m + e) \qquad [\text{substituting } (a_i + b_i r_m + e) \text{ for } r_i] \\
&= \text{var}(b_i r_m) + \text{var}(e) \qquad [\text{since var}(a_i) = 0] \\
&= b_i^2 \text{ var}(r_m) + \text{var}(e) \qquad [\text{since var}(b_i r_m) = b_i^2 \text{ var}(r_m)] \\
&= \text{systematic risk} + \text{unsystematic risk}
\end{aligned}$$

The unsystematic risk measure, var (e), is called the residual variance (or standard error squared) in regression terms.

SOLVED PROBLEM 23.6

The annual rates of return for the Jarvis Corporation and the market are given below:

YEAR	RET. JARVIS	RET. MARKET
19X1	−5%	−6%
19X2	14	16
19X3	10	12
19X4	12	14
19X5	17	20

(*a*) Determine the beta coefficient for Jarvis.

(*b*) What percent of the total risk for Jarvis is systematic?

SOLUTION

(*a*) The same beta coefficient can be calculated with the following computationally efficient equation:

$$b = \frac{N\sum_i X_i Y_i - \sum_i X_i \sum_i Y_i}{N\sum_i X_i^2 - \left(\sum_i X_i\right)^2} \tag{23.5}$$

where N is the number of observations, X_i is the return for security X_i, and Y_i is the return for security Y_i.

Equation (*23.5*) can be applied to Jarvis and the market return as follows:

YEAR	r_J	r_m	r_J^2	$r_J r_m$
19X1	−5	−6	36	30
19X2	14	16	256	224
19X3	10	12	144	120
19X4	12	14	196	168
19X5	17	20	400	340
	$\Sigma = 48$	$\Sigma = 56$	$\Sigma = 1{,}032$	$\Sigma = 882$

[*Note:* The independent (or explanatory) variable is usually called X, so $X = r_m =$ the market return. The dependent variable is $Y = r_i =$ the individual stock return.]

With $N = 5$,

$$b = \frac{(5)(882) - (56)(48)}{(5)(1{,}032) - (56)^2} = \frac{4{,}410 - 2{,}688}{5{,}160 - 3{,}136} = \frac{1{,}722}{2{,}024} = .85079$$

The beta coefficient for Jarvis is .85079.

(*b*) The correlation coefficient squared (ρ^2) will tell you what percent of total risk is systematic. The following equation can be used to calculate ρ:

$$\rho_{XY} = \frac{N\sum XY - \sum X \sum Y}{\left\{\left[\left(N\sum X^2\right) - \left(\sum X\right)^2\right]\left[\left(N\sum Y^2\right) - \left(\sum Y\right)^2\right]\right\}^{.5}} \tag{22.6}$$

The above equation was discussed in Chap. 22. Note that Eq. (*23.5*), given in (*a*), includes most of the values needed to calculate ρ. The exception is the Y^2 term.

Y^2
25
196
100
144
289
754

With Y^2 and the other inputs from part (*a*), ρ can be calculated as follows:

$$\rho_{XY} = \frac{(5)(882) - (56)(48)}{\{[(5)(1{,}032) - (56)^2][(5)(754) - (48)^2]\}^{.5}}$$

$$= \frac{4{,}410 - 2{,}688}{[(5{,}160 - 3{,}136)(3{,}770 - 2{,}304)]^{.5}}$$

$$= \frac{1{,}722}{[(2{,}024)(1{,}466)]^{.5}} = \frac{1{,}722}{(2{,}967{,}184)^{.5}}$$

$$= \frac{1{,}722}{1{,}722.5516} = .99968$$

$$\rho^2_{XY} = (.99968)^2 = .99936 \quad \text{or} \quad 99.94\% \text{ is systematic}$$

SOLVED PROBLEM 23.7

The quarterly returns for the Morgan Fund and the S&P500 are given below:

YEAR/QUART.	MORGAN FUND RET. %	S&P500 RET. %
1985/Q3	−2.2	−4.1
1985/Q4	18.0	17.2
1986/Q1	11.0	14.0
1986/Q2	3.2	5.9
1986/Q3	−9.7	−6.9
1986/Q4	4.3	5.6
1987/Q1	25.2	21.3
1987/Q2	3.3	5.0

Determine the beta coefficient for Morgan.

SOLUTION

$$b = \frac{N\sum XY - \sum X \sum Y}{N\sum X^2 - \left(\sum X\right)^2} \qquad (23.5)$$

where X is the return for the S&P500 and Y is the return for Morgan.

Y	X	X^2	XY
−2.2	−4.1	16.81	9.02
18	17.2	295.84	309.60
11	14	196.00	154.00
3.2	5.9	34.81	18.88
−9.7	−6.9	47.61	66.93
4.3	5.6	31.36	24.08
25.2	21.3	453.69	536.76
3.3	5	25.00	16.50
$\Sigma = 53.1$	$\Sigma = 58$	$\Sigma = 1{,}101.12$	$\Sigma = 1{,}135.77$

$$b = \frac{(8)(1{,}135.77) - (58)(53.1)}{(8)(1{,}101.12) - (58)^2}$$

$$= \frac{9{,}086.16 - 3{,}079.80}{8{,}808.96 - 3{,}364.00} = \frac{6{,}006.36}{5{,}444.96} = 1.1031$$

SOLVED PROBLEM 23.8

Listed below are the characteristic lines for three mutual funds:

Fund 1:

$$r_1 = -.5\% + 1.25r_m \qquad \rho = .8$$

Fund 2:

$$r_2 = 1.25\% + .95r_m \qquad \rho = .75$$

Fund 3:

$$r_3 = .75\% + 1.35r_m \qquad \rho = .7$$

(*a*) Which fund has the most systematic risk?

(*b*) What percent of each fund's risk is systematic? Unsystematic?

SOLUTION

(*a*) Fund 3's beta of 1.35 is the highest of the three, so it has the most systematic risk. Beta is a measure of systematic risk and is the slope of the characteristic line. It measures the response of the asset's return to a change in the market return.

(*b*) The correlation coefficient squared (ρ^2) measures the amount of total risk that is systematic. Therefore, 1 − systematic proportion = unsystematic risk proportion. Fund 1: $(.8)^2 = .64$ or 64 percent of the total risk is systematic. And $1 - .64 = .36$ or 36 percent is unsystematic risk. Fund 2: $(.75)^2 = .5625$ or 56.25 percent is the systematic proportion. Thus, $1 - .5625$ or 43.75 percent is unsystematic risk. Fund 3: $(.7)^2 = .49$ or 49 percent is systematic risk. And $1 - .49 = .51$ or 51 percent is unsystematic risk.

23.4 CAPITAL ASSET PRICING MODEL (CAPM)

The relevant risk for an individual asset is systematic risk (or market-related risk) because nonmarket risk can be eliminated by diversification. The relationship between an asset's return and its systematic risk can be expressed by the CAPM, which is also called the *security market line (SML)*. The equation for the CAPM is

$$E(r_i) = R + [E(r_m) - R]b_i \tag{23.6}$$

where $E(r_i)$ is the expected return for an asset, R is the risk-free rate (usually assumed to be a short-term T-bill rate), $E(r_m)$ equals the expected market return (usually assumed to be the S&P500), and b_i denotes the asset's beta.

The CAPM is an equilibrium model for measuring the risk-return tradeoff for all assets including both inefficient and efficient portfolios. A graph of the CAPM is given in Fig. 23-3.

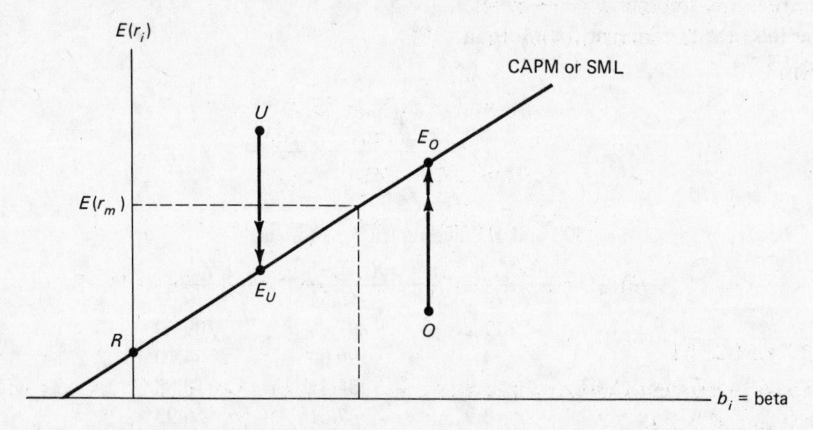

Fig. 23-3 The CAPM or security market line (SML).

Figure 23-3 depicts two assets, *U* and *O*, that are not in equilibrium on the CAPM. Asset *U* is undervalued and, therefore, a very desirable asset to own. *U*'s price will rise in the market as more investors purchase it. However, as *U*'s price goes up, its return falls. When *U*'s return falls to the return consistent with its beta on the SML, equilibrium is attained. With *O*, just the opposite takes place. Investors will attempt to sell *O*, since it is overvalued, and, therefore, put downward pressure on *O*'s price. When the return on asset *O* increases to the rate that is consistent with the beta risk level given by the SML, equilibrium will be achieved and downward price pressure will cease.

SOLVED PROBLEM 23.9

Assume $R = 8\%$, $E(r_m) = 14\%$, and $b = 1.25$ for the ith security.

(a) Determine the expected return for security i.

(b) What happens to $E(r_i)$ of the security if $E(r_m)$ increases to 16 percent? Assume the other inputs do not change.

(c) What happens to $E(r_i)$ if beta falls to .75 and everything else stays the same?

SOLUTION

(a)
$$E(r_i) = R + [E(r_m) - R]b_i = 8\% + (14\% - 8\%)1.25$$
$$= 8\% + (6\%)1.25 = 15.5\%$$

(b)
$$E(r_i) = 8\% + (16\% - 8\%)1.25 = 8\% + (8\%)(1.25) = 18\%$$

(c)
$$E(r_i) = 8\% + (14\% - 8\%).75 = 12.5\%$$

SOLVED PROBLEM 23.10

The BMC Corporation's dividends per share have grown at a rate of 6 percent per year for the past few years. If this rate continues in the future, determine the value of BMC stock. Assume BMC's current dividend per share (D_0) is \$3.50, $R = 9\%$, $E(r_m) = 16\%$, and $b_{\text{BMC}} = 1.3$.

SOLUTION

The value (or price, P) of a share of common stock can be determined with the following equation:

$$P = \frac{D_0(1 + g)}{k - g} \qquad (16.3)$$

where g is the annual dividend growth rate and k is the stock's required return. (For more details about this stock valuation, see Chap. 16.)

$$k = E(r_i) = R + [E(r_m) - R]b_i$$
$$= 9\% + (16\% - 9\%)1.3 = 18.1\%$$
$$P = \frac{\$3.50(1.06)}{.181 - .06} = \frac{\$3.71}{.121} = \$30.66$$

SOLVED PROBLEM 23.11

Assume that $R = 10\%$, $E(r_m) = 16\%$, and the return on stock C is 18 percent.

(a) Determine the implicit beta for stock C.

(b) What is stock C's return if its beta is .75?

SOLUTION

(a)
$$E(r_i) = R + [E(r_m) - R]b_i \qquad (i = C)$$
$$18\% = 10\% + (16\% - 10\%)b_C$$
$$18\% = 10\% + 6\%b_C$$
$$b_C = \frac{8\%}{6\%} = 1.333$$

(b)
$$E(r_C) = 10\% + (16\% - 10\%).75 = 10\% + 4.5\% = 14.5\%$$

SOLVED PROBLEM 23.12

The Jefferson Investment Company manages a stock fund consisting of five stocks with the following market values and betas:

STOCK	MARKET VALUE	BETA
Zell	\$100,000	1.10
Carr	50,000	1.20
Arms	75,000	.75
Dole	125,000	.80
Ord	150,000	1.40
Total	\$500,000	

If R is 7 percent and $E(r)$ is 14 percent, what is the portfolio's expected return?

SOLUTION

$$W_Z = \frac{\$100{,}000}{\$500{,}000} = .2$$

$$W_C = \frac{\$50{,}000}{\$500{,}000} = .1$$

$$W_A = \frac{\$75{,}000}{\$500{,}000} = .15$$

$$W_D = \frac{\$125{,}000}{\$500{,}000} = .25$$

$$W_O = \frac{\$150{,}000}{\$500{,}000} = \underline{.30}$$

$$\text{Total} = 1.00$$

In order to calculate the fund's expected return with the SML, we need the fund's beta. This can be determined with the following equation:

$$b_p = \sum_{t=1}^{N} x_i b_i$$

where x_i is the weight for the ith security and b_i is the beta coefficient for the ith security.

$$b_p = (.2)(1.1) + (.1)(1.2) + (.15)(.75) + (.25)(.8) + (.3)(1.4)$$
$$= .22 + .12 + .1125 + .20 + .42 = 1.0725$$
$$E(r_p) = R + [E(r_m) - R]b_p = 7\% + (14\% - 7\%)1.0725$$
$$= 7\% + (7\%)1.0725 = 14.5075\%$$

SOLVED PROBLEM 23.13

Assume $R = 9\%$ and $E(r_m) = 15\%$. The expected returns and betas are given below for three stocks:

STOCK	EXPECTED RETURN	EXPECTED BETA
Hall	14%	1.20
Izzo	15%	.75
Jenn	20%	1.50

Which stock(s) are undervalued? Overvalued?

SOLUTION

First, we should determine the return for each stock that is consistent with equilibrium using the CAPM.

$$E(r_i) = R + [E(r_m) - R]b_i$$
$$= 9\% + (15\% - 9\%)b_i$$
$$E(r_H) = 9\% + (6\%)1.2 = 16.2\% \quad \text{(overvalued)}$$
$$E(r_I) = 9\% + (6\%).75 = 13.5\% \quad \text{(undervalued)}$$
$$E(r_J) = 9\% + (6\%)1.5 = 18\% \quad \text{(undervalued)}$$

Stock's I and J are undervalued because their equilibrium return is less than their expected return. On the other hand, stock H is overvalued because its expected return is less than its equilibrium return.

SOLVED PROBLEM 23.14

Mr. Ed Moss is considering investing in the stock of the Shemp Corporation. Ed expects Shemp to earn a return of 16 percent. Shemp's beta is 1.4, R is 8 percent, and $E(r_m)$ is 14 percent. Should Ed invest in the Shemp Corporation?

SOLUTION

The CAPM suggests that Shemp's equilibrium return is 16.4 percent.

$$E(r_S) = R + [E(r_m) - R]b_S$$
$$= 8\% + (14\% - 8\%)1.4 = 8\% + (6\%)1.4 = 16.4\%$$

Since Shemp's equilibrium return exceeds its expected return, he should not make the purchase. Shemp's stock is overvalued and its price should fall.

SOLVED PROBLEM 23.15

Refer to Solved Problem 23-14. What should Ed do if Shemp's beta is 1.2? Assume the other inputs do not change.

SOLUTION

With the change in beta, Shemp's equilibrium return is 15.2 percent.

$$E(r_S) = R + [E(r_m) - R]b_S$$
$$= 8\% + (14\% - 8\%)1.2 = 15.2\%$$

Since the expected return for Shemp is now greater than the equilibrium return, Shemp is a good investment. Shemp's price should increase.

True-False Questions

23.1 The CAPM contains only efficient portfolios and securities.

23.2 Securities whose returns are above the CAPM should be sold while securities whose returns are below the CAPM should be purchased.

23.3 All portfolios on the Markowitz efficient frontier are on the CML, if we ignore borrowing and lending.

23.4 The CAPM and the CML have positive but different linear risk-return tradeoffs.

23.5 Portfolios of securities contain less unsystematic risk than individual securities.

23.6 Systematic risk can usually be reduced by random diversification.

23.7 The CAPM assumes that individual investors are compensated for assuming unsystematic risk.

23.8 The characteristic line and the CAPM are essentially the same.

23.9 Along the CML, leveraged portfolios have more unsystematic risk than unleveraged portfolios.

23.10 Where an individual should invest along the CML is based on his or her personal risk-return tradeoff.

Multiple Choice Questions

The quarterly returns for the mutual funds and S&P500 listed below will be used with the next six questions.

DATE	RET. WINDSOR FUND	RET. GROWTH FUND	RET. S&P500
1985/Q1	7.4%	7.9%	9.2%
1985/Q2	8.5	9.5	7.3
1985/Q3	−3.4	−6.6	−4.1
1985/Q4	13.7	21.3	17.2
1986/Q1	14.5	17.5	14.0
1986/Q2	3.2	11.6	5.9
1986/Q3	−.9	−14.7	−6.9
1986/Q4	2.6	6.7	5.6

23.1 Determine the correlation of returns for Windsor Fund and the S&P500.

(*a*) .9267
(*b*) .9003
(*c*) .9346
(*d*) .8911
(*e*) .8532

23.2 Determine the correlation of returns for Growth Fund and the S&P500.
(*a*) .9744
(*b*) .8914
(*c*) .9536
(*d*) .9312
(*e*) .9015

23.3 Determine the beta coefficient for the Windsor Fund.
(*a*) 1.02
(*b*) .88
(*c*) .75
(*d*) .74
(*e*) 1.35

23.4 Determine the beta coefficient for the Growth Fund.
(*a*) 1.25
(*b*) 1.63
(*c*) 1.52
(*d*) 1.42
(*e*) 1.35

23.5 How much of the total risk (%) of Windsor Fund is systematic?
(*a*) 92 percent
(*b*) 89 percent
(*c*) 84 percent
(*d*) 79 percent
(*e*) 87 percent

23.6 How much of the total risk (%) of the Growth Fund is systematic risk?
(*a*) 85 percent
(*b*) 95 percent
(*c*) 98 percent
(*d*) 90 percent
(*e*) 88 percent

23.7 The Clark Corporation expects its dividends per share to continue to grow at an annual rate of 7 percent in the foreseeable future. Clark's current dividend per share is $2.75. If $R = 10\%$, $E(r_m) = 15\%$, and $b_c = .85$, determine the value of Clark's stock.
(*a*) $36.70
(*b*) $43.40
(*c*) $40.59
(*d*) $41.79
(*e*) $44.23

23.8 Assume $R = 9.5\%$, $E(r_m) = 14.2\%$, and the return on stock ZBZ is 16 percent. Determine the beta for stock ZBZ.
(*a*) 1.197
(*b*) 1.383
(*c*) 1.417
(*d*) 1.523
(*e*) 1.343

23.9 Refer to Problem 23.8. What will be the return for ZBZ's stock if its beta is 1.25?
(*a*) 16.251 percent
(*b*) 17.452 percent
(*c*) 14.752 percent
(*d*) 15.375 percent
(*e*) 18.221 percent

23.10 The Alton Investment Company has a stock fund with the following four stocks and corresponding betas:

STOCK	MARKET VALUE	BETA
Zello	$ 20,000	.75
Reed	40,000	1.05
Rose	100,000	1.15
Cobb	90,000	1.25

If we assume that $R = 6\%$ and $E(r_m) = 12\%$, determine the portfolio's expected return.

(*a*) 12.828 percent
(*b*) 11.719 percent
(*c*) 14.621 percent
(*d*) 10.971 percent
(*e*) 15.005 percent

Answers

True-False

23.1. F 23.2. F 23.3. F 23.4. T 23.5. T 23.6. F 23.7. F 23.8. F
23.9. F 23.10. T

Multiple Choice

23.1. c 23.2. a 23.3. d 23.4. d 23.5. e 23.6. b 23.7. c 23.8. b
23.9. d 23.10. a

Chapter 24

Arbitrage Pricing Theory (APT)

24.1 THE LAW OF ONE PRICE

The foundation for APT is the *law of one price*. The law of one price states that two identical goods should sell at the same price. If they sold at differing prices anyone could engage in *arbitrage* by simultaneously buying at the low price and selling at the high price and make a riskless profit. Arbitrage also applies to financial assets. If two financial assets have the same risk, they should have the same expected return. If they do not have the same expected return, a riskless profit could be earned by simultaneously issuing (or selling short) at the low return and buying the high-return asset. Arbitrage causes prices to be revised as suggested by the law of one price.

24.2 ARBITRAGE PRICING FOR ONE RISK FACTOR

The *arbitrage pricing line* for one risk factor can be written as

$$E(r_i) = \lambda_0 + \lambda_1 b_i \tag{24.1}$$

where $E(r_i)$ is the expected return on security i, λ_0 is the return for a zero beta portfolio, b_i is the sensitivity of the ith asset to the risk factor, and λ_1 is the factor's risk premium.

The one-factor model, Eq. (*24.1*), is equivalent to the capital asset pricing model (CAPM) presented in Chap. 23: λ_0 is equal to the risk-free rate (R). However, the assumptions of the two models differ. Both models assume investors (1) prefer more wealth to less, (2) are risk-averse, (3) have homogeneous expectations, and (4) that capital markets are perfect. However, the APT, unlike the CAPM, does not assume (1) a one-period horizon, (2) returns are normally distributed, (3) a particular type of utility function, (4) a market portfolio, or (5) that the investor can borrow or lend at the risk-free rate. The one assumption unique to the APT is that unrestricted short selling exists. This utopian situation is available to only a few (such as investment bankers and stock exchange specialists) in today's financial markets.

EXAMPLE 24.1 Assume that the one-factor APT model applies. Determine the equilibrium arbitrage pricing line that is consistent with the following two equilibrium-priced portfolios:

EQUILIBRIUM PORTFOLIO	$E(r)$	b_P
A	15%	1.5
B	10%	.5

The equilibrium equation is in the form

$$E(r_p) = \lambda_0 + \lambda_1 b_p \tag{24.2}$$

λ_0 and λ_1 must take on values that will make the risk-return relationship between portfolio *A* and *B* linear. The solution can be found by simultaneously solving the following two equations for λ_0 and λ_1:

$$15\% = \lambda_0 + \lambda_1(1.5) \qquad \text{(portfolio } A\text{)} \tag{24.2a}$$

$$10\% = \lambda_0 + \lambda_1(.5) \qquad \text{(portfolio } B\text{)} \tag{24.2b}$$

To find a simultaneous solution, we first subtract Eq. (*24.2b*) from Eq. (*24.2a*); we obtain

$$\lambda_1 = 5\%$$

Substituting for λ_1 in Eq. (*24.2b*) yields

$$10\% = \lambda_0 + 5\%(.5) = \lambda_0 + 2.5\%$$

$$\lambda_0 = 7.5\%$$

Therefore, the equilibrium APT equation is

$$E(r_p) = 7.5\% + b_p(5\%) \tag{24.2c}$$

EXAMPLE 24.2 Assume we are in the world of Example 24.1. Suppose that asset C existed as follows:

E(r)* FOR ASSET *C	**BETA FOR *C***
$15\% = E(r_C)$	$1.2 = b_C$

With the above situation, arbitrage profit could be made because the expected return for asset C is higher than the equilibrium return suggested by Eq. (*24.2c*). Riskless profit could be obtained by selling short a portfolio composed of A and B with the same level of risk as asset C. Algebraically, this portfolio's risk is represented as follows:

$$b_C = x_A(b_A) + (1 - x_A)(b_B) \qquad \text{where } x_A + x_B = 1.0$$
$$1.2 = x_A(1.5) + (1 - x_A)(.5) \qquad (x_A \text{ is the proportion of A})$$
$$1.2 = 1.5x_A + .5 - .5x_A$$
$$x_A = .7$$

Therefore, the amount of portfolio B is $.3 = 1 - x_A$. A new portfolio called D will be created that will be 70 percent invested in A and 30 percent in B. Portfolio D will have a beta of 1.2, the same as C. The expected return on portfolio D, which is the same as asset C, is

$$r_D = .7(r_A) + .3(r_B)$$
$$= .7(15\%) + .3(10\%) = 13.5\%$$

If we sell portfolio D short for \$100 and use the funds from the short sale to purchase portfolio C, a pure arbitrage profit of \$1.50 will be made at the end of the period. These results are summarized below:

PORTFOLIO	**INITIAL OUTFLOW**	**ENDING CASH FLOW**	**PORTFOLIO BETA**
D (short)	+\$100	−\$113.50	−1.2
C (long)	−\$100	+\$115.00	+1.2
	0	+\$1.50	0

As indicated above, the shrewd investor who recognized this opportunity would make a riskless profit of \$1.50 with a zero commitment of funds. This is *arbitrage*. More investors will recognize this situation. The price of portfolio D will rise and its return will fall until the equilibrium return of 13.5 percent is reached.

SOLVED PROBLEM 24.1

Continue assuming the world outlined in Examples 24.1 and 24.2. Will this arbitrage cause any price changes?

SOLUTION

Yes; generally speaking, arbitrage causes price revisions. The expected return of portfolio D will be driven down further and further as long as the short selling (or issuing of a security like D) continues to be profitable.

$$\frac{\text{Expected income (assumed constant)}}{\text{Purchase price of } D\uparrow} = E(\overset{\downarrow}{r_D})$$

$$\frac{\text{Sum of the expected incomes from } A \text{ and } B}{\text{Pur. price of } D[.7(\text{price of } A) + .3(\text{price of } B)\uparrow]} = E(\overset{\downarrow}{r_D})$$

The two equivalent equations above imply that the prices of assets A and B (which are what comprises portfolio D) will be driven down by the short selling of portfolio D.

SOLVED PROBLEM 24.2

Continue assuming the world outlined in Examples 24.1 and 24.2. Will this arbitrage go on and continue to be profitable forever?

SOLUTION

No; arbitrage ceases when it is no longer profitable to perform. The arbitrage and associated short selling of portfolio D (and therefore its component assets A and B) will continue until the expected return of portfolio D— and $E(r_A)$ and $E(r_B)$—are driven up to a level that is appropriate for their risk class. When the market price of portfolio D (and assets A and B) fall and their expected returns rise to these equilibrium levels, the arbitrage will no longer be profitable and the price revisions will cease.

SOLVED PROBLEM 24.3

(*a*) Determine the equilibrium factor pricing equation implied by the following two equilibrium portfolios:

EQUILIBRIUM PORTFOLIOS	$E(r)$	ONE-FACTOR BETA
Gold	14%	1.3
Hensley Fund	12%	1.1

(b) What are the arbitrage opportunities if stock in the Quest Fund may be purchased?

PORTFOLIO	$E(r)$	ONE-FACTOR BETA
Quest	14%	1.15

SOLUTION

(*a*) The general form of the equilibrium equation is

$$E(r_p) = \lambda_0 + \lambda_1 b_p \tag{24.2}$$

Substituting in the values from equilibrium portfolios G and H gives

$$14\% = \lambda_0 + \lambda_1(1.3) \quad \text{(portfolio } G) \tag{24.3a}$$

$$12\% = \lambda_0 + \lambda_1(1.1) \quad \text{(portfolio } H) \tag{24.3b}$$

If we subtract Eq. (*24.3b*) from Eq. (*24.3a*), we obtain $.2\lambda_1 = 2\%$. Multiplying this equation by 5 yields $\lambda_1 = 10\%$.

Substituting for λ_1 in Eq. (*24.3b*) yields

$$12\% = \lambda_0 + 1.1(10\%)$$

$$\lambda_0 = 1\%$$

Therefore, the equilibrium APT equation that encompasses both G and H is

$$E(r_p) = 1\% + b_p(10\%)$$

(*b*) We want to create a new portfolio called Zeta with a beta of 1.15 (the same as Quest). Zeta will be composed of portfolios of gold bullion and Hensley shares. This is determined algebraically as follows:

$$b_Z = (x_G)(1.3) + (x_H)(1.1) \qquad \text{where } x_G + x_H = 1.0$$

$$1.15 = x_G(1.3) + (1 - x_G)(1.1)$$

$$1.15 = 1.3x_G + 1.1 - 1.1x_G$$

$$.05 = .2x_G$$

$$x_G = \frac{.05}{.2} = .25 \quad \text{or} \quad 25\%$$

Therefore, the weight for H is $75\% = 1 - x_G$.

Portfolio Z that is composed of a 25 percent investment in G and 75 percent in H has a beta of 1.15, the same as portfolio Q. The expected return on Z is

$$r_Z = .25(r_G) + .75(r_H) \qquad \text{where } x_G + x_H = 1.0$$

$$= .25(14\%) + .75(12\%)$$

$$= 3.5\% + 9\% = 12.5\%$$

If we sell portfolio Z short to raise cash of \$1,000 and use the funds to purchase portfolio Q, an arbitrage profit will be made at the end of the period. The results are summarized below:

PORTFOLIO	INITIAL CASH FLOW	ENDING CASH FLOW	PORTFOLIO BETA
Z (short)	+\$1,000	−\$1,250	−1.15
Q (long)	−\$1,000	+\$1,400	+1.15
Arbitrage (hedged)	0	+\$150.00	0

The investor that recognizes this situation will make a riskless profit of \$150 with zero commitment of funds.

SOLVED PROBLEM 24.4

Jim Edwards is considering purchasing an asset and holding it for 1 year. If the expected ending cash flow is \$2,000, what should he pay for the asset? Assume the following one-factor APT applies:

$$E(r_i) = 6\% + 7\% b_i$$

The asset being considered by Jim has a factor beta of 1.4.

SOLUTION

First, we need to determine the asset's return with the APT model given.

$$E(r_i) = 6\% + 7\%(1.4) = 15.8\%$$

Using the 15.8 percent expected return as a discount rate allows us to find the present value of the expected cash flow.

$$\text{Expected value} = \frac{1}{1 + E(r_i)} = \frac{\$2{,}000}{1.158} = \$1{,}727.12$$

The price Jim should pay for the asset is $1,727.12.

SOLVED PROBLEM 24.5

Melissa Tate is considering purchasing a financial asset and holding it for 4 years. If the asset has the following expected cash flows, what should she pay for the asset?

YEAR	CASH FLOW
1	$100
2	200
3	400
4	500

The financial asset has a factor beta of 1.25. Assume the following one-factor APT model applies:

$$E(r_i) = 5\% + 8\% b_i$$

SOLUTION

First, the return should be determined as follows:

$$E(r_i) = 5\% + 8\%(1.25) = 15\%$$

The price of the asset should be determined using the 15 percent rate determined above.

$$\text{Price} = \frac{\$100}{(1.15)^1} + \frac{\$200}{(1.15)^2} + \frac{\$400}{(1.15)^3} + \frac{\$500}{(1.15)^4}$$
$$= \$86.96 + \$151.23 + \$263.01 + \$285.88 = \$787.08$$

24.3 TWO-FACTOR ARBITRAGE PRICING

This section assumes the following two-factor model describes returns:

$$E(r_i) = \lambda_0 + \lambda_1 b_{i1} + \lambda_2 b_{i2} \qquad (24.3)$$

where λ_2 is the risk premium associated with risk factor 2 and b_{i2} is the factor beta coefficient for factor 2, and factors 1 and 2 are uncorrelated. Remember, as with the CAPM, only systematic risk has pricing implications.

Assume the following three equilibrium-priced assets exist:

PORTFOLIO	EXP. RETURN %	b_{i1}	b_{i2}
Quary Stone Corp.	16	1.0	.8
Zerb, Inc.	12	.6	.5
Telemarc, Inc.	18	.9	1.1

What is the equilibrium two-factor APT model for these three portfolios? In order to determine the equilibrium equation, we must solve the following three equations simultaneously for λ_0, λ_1, and λ_2:

$$E(r_Q) = 16\% = \lambda_0 + \lambda_1(1.0) + \lambda_2(.8) \qquad (24.4a)$$
$$E(r_Z) = 12\% = \lambda_0 + \lambda_1(.6) + \lambda_2(.5) \qquad (24.4b)$$
$$E(r_T) = 18\% = \lambda_0 + \lambda_1(.9) + \lambda_2(1.1) \qquad (24.4c)$$

These three equations were created by substituting the $E(r)$ and factor beta values for the three portfolios into Eq. (24.3).

The simultaneous solution to these three equations can be found algebraically as follows. Subtract Eq. (24.4b) from Eq. (24.4a):

$$4\% = 4\lambda_1 + .3\lambda_2 \qquad (24.4d)$$

Subtract Eq. (24.4b) from Eq. (24.4c):

$$6\% = .3\lambda_1 + .6\lambda_2 \qquad (24.4e)$$

Multiply Eq. (*24.4d*) by 2 to obtain Eq. (*24.4f*):

$$8\% = .8\lambda_1 + .6\lambda_2 \tag{24.4f}$$

Subtract Eq. (*24.4e*) from Eq. (*24.4f*) and rearrange to get:

$$\lambda_1 = \frac{2}{.5} = 4\%$$

Substituting λ_1 in Eq. (*24.4f*) yields

$$8\% = 3.2\% + .6\lambda_2 = .8(4\%) + .6\lambda_2$$

$$.6\lambda_2 = 4.8\% \longrightarrow \frac{4.8\%}{.6} = 8\%$$

Substituting the calculated values for λ_1 and λ_2 in Eq. (*24.4a*) yields

$$16\% = \lambda_0 + 4\% + .8(8\%) = \lambda_0 + 4\% + 6.4\%$$

$$\lambda_0 = 16\% - 10.4\% = 5.6\%$$

Therefore, the equilibrium equation is

$$E(r_i) = 5.6\% + (4\%)b_{i1} + (8\%)b_{i2} \tag{24.4g}$$

The above equations can be stated in matrix form as Eqs. (*24.4h*) and (*24.4i*) below:

$$\begin{vmatrix} 16 \\ 12 \\ 18 \end{vmatrix} = \begin{vmatrix} 1.0 & 1.0 & .8 \\ 1.0 & .6 & .5 \\ 1.0 & .9 & 1.1 \end{vmatrix} \begin{vmatrix} \lambda_0 \\ \lambda_1 \\ \lambda_2 \end{vmatrix} \tag{24.4h}$$

$$r \quad = \quad C \quad \lambda \tag{24.4i}$$

The vector of unknowns λ is evaluated by first finding the inverse of the coefficient matrix, C^{-1}. Second, premultiplying the inverse of matrix C times the vector r yields the values of the vector of unknowns λ as shown below in Eqs. (*24.4j*) and (*24.4k*)[1]

$$\begin{vmatrix} -1.400 & 2.533 & -1.333 \\ 4.000 & -2.000 & -2.000 \\ -2.000 & -0.666 & 2.666 \end{vmatrix} \begin{vmatrix} 16 \\ 12 \\ 18 \end{vmatrix} = \begin{vmatrix} 5.600 \\ 4.000 \\ 8.000 \end{vmatrix} = \begin{vmatrix} \lambda_0 \\ \lambda_1 \\ \lambda_2 \end{vmatrix} \tag{24.4j}$$

$$C^{-1} \quad r \quad = \quad \lambda \quad = \quad \lambda \tag{24.4k}$$

EXAMPLE 24.3 Suppose a disequilibrium asset called Walter Transportation, Inc., is not in the equilibrium specified by Eq. (*24.4g*). What should an investor do to make money?

PORTFOLIO	$E(r)$	b_{W1}	b_{WZ}
Walter, Inc.	17%	.8	.65

This can be accomplished by creating a weighted average portfolio called Chi that is composed of Quary and Zerb. The algebraic solution is as follows.

Let x_Q equal the weight for Quary and x_Z equal the weight for Zerb.

$$x_Q + x_Z = 1 \tag{24.5a}$$

$$1x_Q + .6x_Z = .8 = b_{C,1} = b_{W,1} \tag{24.5b}$$

$$.8x_Q + .5x_Z = .65 = b_{C,2} = b_{W,2} \tag{24.5c}$$

The beta coefficients for portfolio Chi (C) must be equal to the beta coefficients for Walter (W). Chi's weights are:

$$x_Q = 1 - x_Z \tag{24.5d}$$

Substituting x_Q from Eq. (*24.5d*) in Eq. (*24.5b*) yields the value for weight x_2.

$$1 - x_Z + .6x_Z = .8$$

$$.4x_Z = .2$$

$$x_Z = .5$$

Therefore, x_Q must also equal .5, since x_Q and x_Z must sum to 1. For x_Q and x_Z to be a solution to the three simultaneous equations, they must be consistent with Eq. (*24.5c*). When the values for x_Q and x_Z are substituted in Eq. (*24.5c*), the solution is consistent with $b_{C,2} = .65$.

[1]Matrix solutions are available on several calculators. For example, the HP41CV or CX has software available for solving simultaneous equations in matrix form (*Advantage Solutions Pac*). In addition, several HP scientific calculators could be used (e.g., the HP15C and HP28S). The TI-81 also has matrix capabilities. LOTUS 1-2-3 (version 2 or higher) has matrix capabilities that can also be used to invert a matrix.

The expected return on portfolio Chi is equal to the following:

$$E(r_C) = (.5)E(r_Q) + (.5)E(r_Z)$$
$$= (.5)(16\%) + (.5)(12\%) = 8\% + 6\% = 14\%$$

The makeup of a riskless hedge (or arbitrage portfolio) can now be stated.

PORTFOLIO	INITIAL CASH FLOW	ENDING CASH FLOW	b_{i1}	b_{i2}
Chi (short)	+$100	−$114	−.8	−.65
Walter (long)	−$100	+$117	.8	.65
Arbitrage (hedged)	0	+$3.00	0	0

It is assumed that $100 worth of portfolio Chi is sold short and the proceeds are used to purchase Walter, Inc. The activity of selling portfolio Chi short and purchasing Walter, Inc., will eventually bring portfolio Chi into equilibrium where it will earn an annual return of 14 percent. The combined portfolios are risk-free, require zero capital, and earn an arbitrage profit of $3 per $100 of arbitrage.

SOLVED PROBLEM 24.6

Suppose the following two-factor model describes security returns:

$$E(r_i) = \lambda_0 + \lambda_1 b_{i1} + \lambda_2 b_{i2}$$

The following three portfolios are observed:

PORTFOLIO	E(r)	b_{i1}	b_{i2}
Delta	17%	1	.8
Gamma	15%	.7	1
Kappa	12%	.6	.5

Determine the two-factor equilibrium equation for the three portfolios.

SOLUTION

First, an algebraic solution will be obtained for the following three simultaneous equations:

$$E(r_D) = 17\% = \lambda_0(1.0) + \lambda_1(1.0) + \lambda_2(.8) \tag{24.6a}$$
$$E(r_G) = 15\% = \lambda_0(1.0) + \lambda_1(.7) + \lambda_2(1.0) \tag{24.6b}$$
$$E(r_K) = 12\% = \lambda_0(1.0) + \lambda_1(.6) + \lambda_2(.5) \tag{24.6c}$$

Subtract Eq. (*24.6b*) from Eq. (*24.6a*):

$$2\% = .3\lambda_1 - .2\lambda_2 \tag{24.6d}$$

Multiply Eq. (*24.6d*) by 10:

$$20\% = 3\lambda_1 - 2\lambda_2 \tag{24.6e}$$

Subtract Eq. (*24.6c*) from Eq. (*24.6b*):

$$3\% = .1\lambda_1 + .5\lambda_2 \tag{24.6f}$$

Multiply Eq. (*24.6f*) by 4:

$$12\% = .4\lambda_1 + 2\lambda_2 \tag{24.6g}$$

Add Eqs. (*24.6e*) and (*24.6g*) to obtain

$$32\% = 3.4\lambda_1$$
$$\lambda_1 = \frac{32}{3.4} = 9.4118\%$$

Substitute the value of λ_1 in Eq. (*24.6g*) to yield

$$12\% = .4(9.4118) + 2\lambda_2$$
$$12\% = 3.7647 + 2\lambda_2$$
$$\lambda_2 = \frac{8.2353}{2} = 4.1176\%$$

Substitute the values for λ_1 and λ_2 into Eq. (*24.6a*) to find the riskless rate (or intercept term):

$$17\% = \lambda_0 + 9.4118 + (.8)(4.1176)$$
$$17\% = \lambda_0 + 9.4118 + 3.2941$$
$$\lambda_0 = 4.2941\%$$

A matrix algebra solution is as follows:

$$\begin{vmatrix} 17 \\ 15 \\ 12 \end{vmatrix} = \begin{vmatrix} 1 & 1 & .8 \\ 1 & .7 & 1 \\ 1 & .6 & .5 \end{vmatrix} \begin{vmatrix} \lambda_0 \\ \lambda_1 \\ \lambda_2 \end{vmatrix}$$

$$r = C \quad \lambda$$

$$\begin{vmatrix} -1.4706 & -.1176 & 2.5882 \\ 2.9412 & -1.7647 & -1.1765 \\ -.5882 & 2.3529 & -1.7647 \end{vmatrix} \begin{vmatrix} 17 \\ 15 \\ 12 \end{vmatrix} = \begin{vmatrix} 4.2941 \\ 9.4118 \\ 4.1176 \end{vmatrix} = \begin{vmatrix} \lambda_0 \\ \lambda_1 \\ \lambda_2 \end{vmatrix}$$

$$C^{-1} \quad r = \lambda = \lambda$$

For some additional information on the use of matrix algebra, see the footnote in the first part of this section of the chapter (Section 24.3).

SOLVED PROBLEM 24.7

Refer to Solved Problem 24.6 above. Suppose the stock of the Rho Corporation was in disequilibrium.

STOCK	***E(r)***	b_{R1}	b_{R2}
Rho Corp.	16%	.8	.7

Can you make a riskless profit?

SOLUTION

Yes. Create a portfolio called Tau from portfolios Delta, Gamma, and Kappa that has the same beta risk for each of the two coefficients as Rho. We will first algebraically solve the following three equations simultaneously:

$$x_D + x_G + x_K = 1 \tag{24.7a}$$

$$1x_D + .7x_G + .6x_K = .8 = b_{R,1} \tag{24.7b}$$

$$.8x_D + 1 + x_G + .5x_K = .7 = b_{R,2} \tag{24.7c}$$

where x_D is the percent invested in portfolio Delta, x_G is the percent invested in portfolio Gamma, and x_K is the percent invested in portfolio Kappa. In Eqs. (*24.7b*) and (*24.7c*), we are constraining the three portfolios so that the portfolio created, Tau, has the same beta coefficients as portfolio Rho.

Subtract Eq. (*24.7b*) from Eq. (*24.7a*):

$$.3x_G + .4x_K = .2 \tag{24.7d}$$

Multiply Eq. (*24.7c*) by 1.25 to get Eq. (*24.7e*):

$$1x_D + 1.25x_G + .625x_K = .875 \tag{24.7e}$$

Subtract Eq. (*24.7e*) from Eq. (*24.7a*):

$$-.25x_G + .375x_K = .125 \tag{24.7f}$$

Multiply Eq. (*24.7d*) by 5:

$$1.5x_G + 2x_K = 1 \tag{24.7g}$$

Multiply Eq. (*24.7f*) by 6:

$$-1.5x_G + 2.25x_K = .75 \tag{24.7h}$$

Add Eqs. (*24.7g*) and (*24.7h*):

$$4.25x_K = 1.75$$

which implies

$$x_K = \frac{1.75}{4.25} = .4118$$

Substitute x_K in Eq. (*24.7g*):

$$1.5x_G + .8236 = 1$$

$$1.5x_G = .1764$$

$$x_G = \frac{.1764}{1.5} = .1176$$

Substitute x_G and x_K in (*24.7a*):

$$x_D + .1176 + .4118 = 1$$

$$x_D = .4706$$

A matrix algebra formulation follows.

$$\begin{vmatrix} 1 & 1 & 1 \\ 1 & .7 & .6 \\ .8 & 1 & .5 \end{vmatrix} = \begin{vmatrix} 1 \\ .8 \\ .7 \end{vmatrix} \begin{vmatrix} x_D \\ x_G \\ x_K \end{vmatrix}$$

$$C = r \quad x$$

$$\begin{vmatrix} -1.4706 & 2.9441 & -.5882 \\ -.1176 & -1.7647 & 2.3529 \\ 2.5882 & -1.1765 & -1.7647 \end{vmatrix} \begin{vmatrix} 1 \\ .8 \\ .7 \end{vmatrix} = \begin{vmatrix} .4706 \\ .1176 \\ .4118 \end{vmatrix} = \begin{vmatrix} x_D \\ x_G \\ x_K \end{vmatrix}$$

$$C^{-1} \quad r = x = x$$

For more information on the matrix algebra approach, see the footnote in the first part of this section of the chapter (Section 24.3).

The return on portfolio Tau is

$$x_1 r_D + x_2 r_G + x_3 r_K = r_T$$

$$.4706(17\%) + .1176(15\%) + .4118(12\%) = r_T$$

$$r_T = 8\% + 1.764\% + 4.942\% = 14.71\%$$

The results of the riskless hedge are given below.

PORTFOLIO	INITIAL CASH FLOW	ENDING CASH FLOW	b_{i1}	b_{i2}
Tau (short)	+$100	−$114.71	−.8	−.7
Rho (long)	−$100	+$116.00	.8	.7
Arbitrage	0	+$1.29	0	0

SOLVED PROBLEM 24.8

Determine the required (or equilibrim) return for the following three securities:

SECURITY	b_{i1}	b_{i2}
Alpha	1.2	1
Eta	−.5	.75
Iota	.75	1.30

Assume the following two-factor model applies:

$$E(r_i) = 4\% + 3\% b_{i1} + 5\% b_{i2}$$

SOLUTION

$$E(r_A) = 4\% + 3\%(1.2) + 5\%(1) = 12.6\%$$

$$E(r_E) = 4\% + 3\%(-.5) + 5\%(.75) = 6.25\%$$

$$E(r_I) = 4\% + 3\%(.75) + 5\%(1.3) = 12.75\%$$

SOLVED PROBLEM 24.9

Determine the present value of the following cash flows:

YEAR	CASH FLOW
1	−$100
2	300
3	400
4	−500
5	700

Assume the following two-factor model applies:

$$E(r_i) = 3\% + 2\% b_{i1} + 5\% b_{i2}$$

The relevant factor betas are

$$b_{i1} = -.75 \qquad b_{i2} = 1.5$$

SOLUTION

First, determine the required return.

$$E(r_i) = 3\% + -.75(2\%) + 1.5(5\%) = 9\%$$

$$\text{Present value of cash flow} = \frac{-\$100}{(1.09)^1} + \frac{\$300}{(1.09)^2} + \frac{\$400}{(1.09)^3} + \frac{-\$500}{(1.09)^4} + \frac{\$700}{(1.09)^5}$$

$$= -\$91.7431 + \$252.504 + \$308.8734 - \$354.2126 + \$454.952 = \$570.3737$$

SOLVED PROBLEM 24.10

The Carson Company's earnings and dividends have been growing at a rate of 7 percent the past several years, and this rate of growth is expected to continue in the foreseeable future. If Carson's current dividend per share is \$3, what is its current value (or equilibrium price)? Assume the following two-factor model applies and that b_{i1} and b_{i2} for the Carson Company are .6 and 1.4, respectively.

$$E(r_i) = 5\% + 2\%b_{i1} + 6\%b_{i2}$$

SOLUTION

The constant-growth Gordon dividend model should be used. (For more information on the Gordon model, see Chap. 16.)

$$P_0 = \frac{D_0(1+g)}{k-g} \tag{16.3}$$

where P is current price, D is current dividend per share, $k = E(r)$ is the stock's required return or expected return, and g is the constant annual growth rate for dividends.

$$k = E(r_i) = 5\% + 2\%(.6) + 6\%(1.4)$$
$$= 5\% + 1.2\% + 8.4\% = 14.6\%$$
$$P_0 = \frac{\$3(1.07)}{.146 - .07} = \frac{\$3.21}{.076} = \$42.24$$

24.4 MULTIFACTOR ARBITRAGE PRICING

The APT model can be extended to k risk factors as follows:

$$E(r_i) = \lambda_0 + \lambda_1 b_{i1} + \lambda_2 b_{i2} + \cdots + \lambda_k b_{ik} \tag{24.4}$$

The APT does not tell us how many factors we should have or what they might be. This is something that must be determined through empirical research. One study reported the following four risk factors:[2]

(1) Unanticipated changes in inflation

(2) Unanticipated changes in industrial production

(3) Unanticipated changes in risk premiums (difference between low-grade and high-grade bonds)

(4) Unanticipated changes in the slope of the yield curve

Other researchers have reported more and different risk factors.

SOLVED PROBLEM 24.11

Assume the risk-free rate is $7\% = R = \lambda_0$. The market prices of risk for the following three factors are expected to exist for next year:

$\lambda_1 = 1.8$ for interest-rate risk

$\lambda_2 = 1.25$ for purchasing power risk

$\lambda_3 = .5$ for default risk

Preferred stock issued by the Zelda Corporation has the following beta sensitivity index to undiversifiable risk:

$$b_{Z1} = 1.2 \qquad b_{Z2} = 1.5 \qquad b_{Z3} = -.75$$

(*a*) Determine the expected rate of return for Zelda's preferred stock with the APT model.

(*b*) If Zelda's preferred stock is to be held for 1 year with an expected ending cash flow of \$300, what is the asset worth?

[2] See Roll and Ross, "The Arbitrage Pricing Theory Approach to Strategic Portfolio Planning," *Financial Analysts Journal*, May-June 1984, pp. 14–26.

SOLUTION

(*a*)

$$E(r_i) = R + \lambda_1 b_{i1} + \lambda_2 b_{i2} + \lambda_3 b_{i3}$$

$$E(r_Z) = 7\% + (1.8\%)(1.2) + (1.25\%)(1.5) + (.5\%)(-.75)$$

$$= 7\% + 2.16\% + 1.875\% + (-.375\%) = 10.66\%$$

(*b*)

$$\text{Value} = \frac{\$300}{1 + E(r_Z)} = \frac{\$300}{1.1066} = \$271.10$$

True-False Questions

24.1 Diversifiable risk plays an important factor pricing role in the APT.

24.2 The slope coefficient for a one-factor arbitrage pricing line is the expected return on a zero beta portfolio.

24.3 An underpriced asset will lie above the arbitrage pricing line.

24.4 *The law of one price* implies that investors can profit from mispriced assets.

24.5 The CAPM can be viewed as an APT model with one factor.

24.6 An empirical study by Roll and Ross identified the S&P500 as a significant risk factor for the APT model.

24.7 Factor analysis has been one of the primary statistical tools used to determine the relevant factors for the APT.

24.8 Unlike the CAPM, the APT does not depend upon the assumption of a unique market portfolio that is desired by all investors.

24.9 In order to derive the APT, a normal probability distribution of returns must be assumed.

Multiple Choice Questions

The following information should be used with the next four questions:

Assume the following three portfolios exist:

PORTFOLIO	$E(r)$	b_p
Delta	14%	.8
Epsilon	11%	.5
Kappa	15%	.7

The one-factor APT applies.

24.1 Determine the values for λ_0 and λ_1 that are consistent with portfolios Delta and Epsilon.
(*a*) $\lambda_0 = 5\%;\ \lambda_1 = 7\%$
(*b*) $\lambda_o = 6\%;\ \lambda_1 = 8\%$
(*c*) $\lambda_0 = 6\%;\ \lambda_1 = 10\%$
(*d*) $\lambda_0 = 7\%;\ \lambda_1 = 10\%$
(*e*) $\lambda_0 = 4\%;\ \lambda_1 = 7\%$

24.2 Determine the equilibrium return for the Kappa portfolio, using the answers for τ_0 and τ_1 from Question 24.1.
(*a*) 10 percent
(*b*) 12 percent
(*c*) 13 percent
(*d*) 15 percent
(*e*) 16 percent

24.3 To earn an arbitrage profit determine the amount (percent) that should be invested in the Delta and Epsilon portfolios.
(*a*) Delta = 80% and Epsilon = 20%
(*b*) Delta = 40% and Epsilon = 60%
(*c*) Delta = 42% and Epsilon = 58%
(*d*) Delta = 67% and Epsilon = 33%
(*e*) Delta = 25% and Epsilon = 75%

24.4 Determine the amount of pure arbitrage profit that could be made by selling short the portfolio composed of Delta and Epsilon for $100 and purchasing portfolio Kappa.
(*a*) $5
(*b*) $2
(*c*) $10
(*d*) $7
(*e*) $12

The following information applies to the next three questions. A two-factor APT model applies as follows:

$$E(r_i) = \lambda_0 + b_{i1}\lambda_1 + b_{i2}\lambda_2$$

where $\lambda_0 = 7\%$, $\lambda_1 = 4\%$, and $\lambda_2 = 3\%$.

24.5 The stock of the Griner Corporation has the following risk factor coefficients:

$$b_{G1} = -.5 \qquad b_{G2} = 1.5$$

Determine Griner's equilibrium rate of return.
(a) 9.00 percent
(b) 9.50 percent
(c) 10.25 percent
(d) 10.75 percent
(e) 11.25 percent

24.6 Determine the present value of the following cash flows with the two-factor APT model:

YEAR	CASH FLOWS
1	$300
2	−$200
3	$800

Assume the following beta coefficients for the factors:

$$b_{i1} = 1.25 \qquad b_{i2} = .75$$

(*a*) $525.25
(*b*) $605.15
(*c*) $615.45
(*d*) $705.16
(*e*) $645.80

24.7 The Sloan Corporation has been experiencing dividend growth of 7 percent the last few years, and this annual rate of growth is expected to continue in the future. Sloan's dividend last year was $3.25. Determine the value (or price) of Sloan's stock. The following beta coefficients apply to Sloan's stock:

$$b_{S1} = .75 \qquad b_{S2} = 1.30$$

(*a*) $39.75
(*b*) $47.26
(*c*) $38.22
(*d*) $50.40
(*e*) $45.18

24.8 Which of the following assumptions does the APT and CAPM *not* have in common?
(*a*) Homogeneous expectations.
(*b*) Capital markets are perfect.
(*c*) One-period planning horizon.
(*d*) Investors prefer more wealth to less wealth.
(*e*) None of the above.

24.9 Overpriced assets can reach their equilibrium return by
(*a*) Having their expected rate of return reduced
(*b*) Having their expected rate of return increased
(*c*) Having their price increased
(*d*) Both *b* and *c*
(*e*) None of the above

24.10 An arbitrage portfolio that is consistent with the APT
(*a*) Requires no funds to create
(*b*) Has no risk
(*c*) Has no systematic risk but some nonsystematic risk
(*d*) Both *a* and *b*
(*e*) None of the above

Answers

True-False

24.1. F 24.2. F 24.3. T 24.4. T 24.5. T 24.6. F 24.7. T 24.8. T 24.9. F

Multiple Choice

24.1. c 24.2. c 24.3. d 24.4. b 24.5. b 24.6. e 24.7. d 24.8. c 24.9. b
24.10. d

Chapter 25

Portfolio Performance Evaluation

25.1 MUTUAL FUNDS

Investment companies come in two forms. The *open-end* investment company, or as it is usually called, a *mutual fund,* is the most common type of investment fund. *Closed-end* funds, the second type of investment company, are not as popular as the open-end funds. Unlike the open-end funds, closed-end funds cannot sell more shares after the initial public offering.

There are 2,700 open-end mutual funds in the United States with more than 54 million investors—individuals, companies, and other organizations.[1] Stock and bond mutual funds can be classified into various categories such as growth funds, balanced funds, and income funds. Mutual funds offer the small investor the ability to diversify for a modest management fee.

SOLVED PROBLEM 25.1

Open-end mutual funds are usually classified as either *no-load* or *load* funds. What do these two terms mean?

SOLUTION

No-load funds are bought and sold by mail without a sales commission. On the other hand, *load* funds are sold with a sales commission. *Load* funds have sales commissions of about 3 to 8.5 percent.

SOLVED PROBLEM 25.2

Most mutual funds usually do better than the market (for example, the S&P500). True, false, or uncertain. Explain.

SOLUTION

False. Most of the empirical evidence to date indicates that most mutual funds do not beat the market, after adjustments are made in their returns for transaction costs and risk.

Net Asset Value per Share

A mutual fund's *net asset value per share (NAV)* is equal to the total market value of all the mutual fund's holdings minus liabilities divided by the fund's total number of outstanding shares on a particular day. For example, if the Haverty Fund has \$48.2 million in assets and \$200,000 in liabilities with 5 million outstanding shares, then its NAV = (\$48.2 million − \$.2 million)/5 million = \$9.60. Investors can redeem their shares in a mutual fund on a particular day at that day's NAV.

SOLVED PROBLEM 25.3

The Baltic Growth Fund has a total amount of assets equal to \$60.1 million. Its liabilities are \$100,000 and the number of outstanding shares are equal to 7 million. What is Baltic's NAV?

SOLUTION

$$\text{NAV} = \frac{\text{assets} - \text{liabilities}}{\text{number of shares}}$$

$$= \frac{\$60.1\text{ million} - \$100{,}000}{7\text{ million}} = \frac{\$60\text{ million}}{7\text{ million}} = \$8.57$$

[1]Investment Company Institute, *Mutual Fund Fact Book,* 1989.

One-Period Rate of Return

A mutual fund's one-period rate of return can be calculated with the following equation:

$$r_t = \frac{c_t + d_t + (\text{NAV}_t - \text{NAV}_{t-1})}{\text{NAV}_{t-1}} \tag{25.1}$$

where r_t is the fund's return for time period t, c_t is the capital gains disbursement during time period t, d_t is cash dividend or interest disbursement during time period t, NAV_t is the fund's net asset value per share at the end of time period t, and $(\text{NAV}_t - \text{NAV}_{t-1})$ is the change in the fund's net asset value per share from the beginning of time period t until the end of time period t [or, equivalently, the beginning of period $(t - 1)$] as the result of capital gains and cash dividends that were not distributed to the owners during time period t.

SOLVED PROBLEM 25.4

The information for Growth Fund A and Growth Fund B is given below:

Growth Fund A

End of Year	Ending NAV	Capital Gains Distribution	Cash Dividend Distribution
19X3	$45	$1.25	$.25
19X2	40	1.50	.15
19X1	38	1.10	.10

Growth Fund B

End of Year	Ending NAV	Capital Gains Distribution	Cash Dividend Distribution
19X3	$50	$3.00	$.45
19X2	42	2.50	.40
19X1	40	1.75	.35

Which fund had the higher rate of return in year 19X3?

SOLUTION

Equation (*25.1*) should be used.

$$r_t = \frac{c_t + d_t + (\text{NAV}_t - \text{NAV}_{t-1})}{\text{NAV}_{t-1}} \tag{25.1}$$

For Growth Fund A,

$$r_{19X3} = \frac{\$1.25 + \$.25 + (\$45 - \$40)}{\$40}$$

$$= \frac{\$1.50 + \$5}{\$40} = \frac{\$6.50}{\$40} = 16.25\%$$

For Growth Fund B,

$$r_{19X3} = \frac{\$3 + \$.45 + (\$50 - \$42)}{\$42}$$

$$= \frac{\$3.45 + \$8}{\$42} = \frac{\$11.45}{\$42} = 27.26\%$$

Growth Fund B had the higher return.

SOLVED PROBLEM 25.5

Refer to Solved Problem 25.4 above. What after-tax return would an investor in a tax bracket of 33 percent (federal, state, and local) earn on Growth Fund B in 19X3? In addition, assume a capital gains tax rate of 30 percent.

SOLUTION

Equation (*25.1*) can be used but c_t and d_t must be put on an after-tax basis. In other words, c_t and d_t should be multiplied by $(1 - T)$, where T in this context is 33 percent for ordinary income and 30 percent for capital gains. In addition, $(\text{NAV}_t - \text{NAV}_{t-1})$ should also be multiplied by $(1 - T)$.

For Fund B,

$$c_{19X3}(1 - T) = \$3(1 - .30) = \$2.10$$

$$d_{19X3}(1 - T) = \$.45(1 - .33) = \$.30$$

$$r_{19X3} = \frac{\$2.10 + \$.30 + (\$50 - \$42)(1 - .30)}{\$42}$$

$$= \frac{\$2.40 + \$5.60}{\$42} = \frac{\$8.00}{\$42} = 19.05\%$$

25.2 GEOMETRIC MEAN RETURN

There are two important aspects of any investment that must be evaluated over the investment's holding period—the return and the risk. The multiperiod (or compounded) rate of return is called the geometric mean return. The geometric mean rate of return for an investment can be calculated with the following equation:

$$\text{GMR} = \sqrt[T]{(1 + r_1)(1 + r_2)\cdots(1 + r_T)} - 1 \qquad (25.2)$$

where GMR is the geometric mean return, r_1 is the return for time period 1, r_2 is the return for time period 2, r_T is the return for time period T, and T is the total number of time periods.

EXAMPLE 25.1 The annual returns over the past 5 years are given below for the Dempsey Corporation:

YEAR	RETURN
19X1	10%
19X2	12
19X3	15
19X4	13
19X5	16

The geometric mean rate of return for the Dempsey Corporation over the past 5 years is determined with Eq. (*25.2*) as follows:

$$\text{GMR} = \sqrt[5]{(1.10)(1.12)(1.15)(1.13)(1.16)} - 1$$

$$= \sqrt[5]{1.8571414} - 1 = 1.131798 - 1 = 13.18\%$$

SOLVED PROBLEM 25.6

The Choate Corporation has had the following returns for the past 4 years:

YEAR	RETURN
19X1	14%
19X2	−5
19X3	7
19X4	9

Determine Choate's (*a*) geometric and (*b*) arithmetic mean rates of return. (*c*) Which return is larger?

SOLUTION

(*a*) The geometric mean rate of return can be determined with Eq. (*25.2*) as follows:

$$\text{GMR} = \sqrt[4]{(1.14)[1 + (-.05)](1.07)(1.09)} - 1$$

$$= \sqrt[4]{(1.14)(.95)(1.07)(1.09)} - 1$$

$$= \sqrt[4]{1.2631} - 1 = 1.0601 - 1 = 6.01\%$$

(*b*) The arithmetic mean can be determined as follows:

$$\text{Arithmetic mean} = \frac{\text{sum of returns}}{\text{total number of returns}}$$

$$= \frac{14 + (-5) + 7 + 9}{4} = \frac{25}{4} = 6.25\%$$

(*c*) The arithmetic mean return will always exceed the geometric mean return unless there is no variation in the returns over the time period.

SOLVED PROBLEM 25.7

Clyde Sexton made a $2,000 investment that was worth $2,500 after 1 year but dropped in value to $2,000 after 2 years. Determine (*a*) Clyde's arithmetic and (*b*) geometric mean rates of return for the investment. (*c*) Which return is correct?

SOLUTION

Clyde's investment had the following single-period rates of return for 2 years:

YEAR	RETURN
1	25% ($2,500/$2,000 − 1 = 1.25 − 1 = .25)
2	−20 ($2,000/$2,500 − 1 = .8 − 1 = −.20)

(*a*)
$$\text{Arithmetic mean} = \frac{\text{sum of returns}}{\text{total number}}$$
$$= \frac{25 + (-20)}{2} = \frac{5}{2} = 2.5\%$$

(*b*)
$$\text{GMR} = \sqrt{(1.25)(.8)} - 1 = \sqrt{1} - 1 = 0$$

(*c*) Since Clyde's initial investment was $2,000 and his ending investment 2 years later was $2,000, his true return was obviously zero percent. The geometric mean return is the correct answer for multiperiod rates of return.

25.3 SHARPE'S PERFORMANCE MEASURE

When considering a portfolio's performance it is important to consider both returns and risk. One performance measure that has been developed to evaluate a portfolio's performance, considering both return and risk simultaneously, is the Sharpe index of portfolio performance. It is defined by Eq. (*25.3*) below:

$$S_p = \frac{\text{risk premium}}{\text{total risk}} = \frac{\bar{r}_p - R}{\sigma_p} \qquad (25.3)$$

where S_p = Sharpe's index of portfolio performance for portfolio p
$\bar{r}_p$ = average return for portfolio p
σ_p = standard deviation of returns for portfolio $p = \sqrt{\text{var}(r)}$
R = riskless rate of interest, var $(R) = 0$

SOLVED PROBLEM 25.8

The rate of return and risk for three growth-oriented mutual funds were calculated over the most recent 5 years and are listed below:

GROWTH FUND	RETURN	RISK (STD. DEV.)
Jones (J)	15%	16%
Packer (P)	13	18
Franklin (F)	12	11

Rank each fund by Sharpe's index of portfolio performance if the risk-free rate is 7 percent.

SOLUTION

$$S_P = \frac{\bar{r}_p - R}{\sigma_p} \qquad (25.3)$$

$$S_J = \frac{15\% - 7\%}{16\%} = \frac{8\%}{16\%} = .5 \quad \text{(first)}$$

$$S_P = \frac{13\% - 7\%}{18\%} = \frac{6\%}{18\%} = .333 \quad \text{(third)}$$

$$S_F = \frac{12\% - 7\%}{11\%} = \frac{5\%}{11\%} = .455 \quad \text{(second)}$$

25.4 TREYNOR'S PERFORMANCE MEASURE

Another index of portfolio performance that is similar to the Sharpe index is the Treynor performance index. The Treynor index, however, is concerned with systematic (or beta) risk while the Sharpe index is concerned with total risk as measured by a portfolio's standard deviation of returns (σ). The Treynor index is defined as follows:

$$T_p = \frac{\text{risk premium}}{\text{portfolio's beta coefficient}} = \frac{\bar{r}_p - R}{b_p} \tag{25.4}$$

where T_p = Treynor's index of performance for portfolio p
$\bar{r}_p$ = the average return for portfolio p
R = the risk-free rate of interest, var $(R) = 0$
b_p = the beta for the portfolio

SOLVED PROBLEM 25.9

Rank the three funds below with the Treynor performance index. Refer to Solved Problem 25.8 for the other inputs needed to make the calculation.

GROWTH FUND	FUND'S BETA
Jones (J)	1.15
Packer (P)	1.25
Franklin (F)	.90

SOLUTION

$$T_p = \frac{\bar{r}_p - R}{b_p} \tag{25.4}$$

$$T_J = \frac{15 - 7}{1.15} = \frac{8}{1.15} = 6.96 \quad \text{(first)}$$

$$T_P = \frac{13 - 7}{1.25} = \frac{6}{1.25} = 4.8 \quad \text{(third)}$$

$$T_F = \frac{12 - 7}{.9} = \frac{5}{.9} = 5.55 \quad \text{(second)}$$

25.5 JENSEN'S PERFORMANCE MEASURE

Michael Jensen has also developed a method for evaluating a portfolio's or asset's performance. The Jensen measure is computed with regression Eq. (*25.5*):

$$r_{i,t} - R_t = A_i + B_i(r_{m,t} - R_t) + u_{i,t} \tag{25.5}$$

where $(r_{i,t} - R_t) = r_{p,t}$ = the risk premium for asset i in time period t
R_t = the risk-free rate in time period t
$r_{m,t}$ = the return on the market for time period t
B_i = the beta coefficient for asset i
A_i = Jensen's performance measure (also called the alpha regression intercept term)
r_i = the return on asset i for time period t
$u_{i,t}$ = error term for asset i in time period t

With the Jensen measure A, an ordinary least-squares regression is calculated in risk-premium form for an asset's returns and the market's returns. If A is positive, the asset did better than the market (for example, the S&P500) on a risk-adjusted basis during the time period of the study. On the other hand, if A turns out to be negative, then the asset did worse than the market on a risk-adjusted basis over the time period of the study. An A of zero indicates that the asset earned an equilibrium rate of return that is appropriate for its level of risk over the time period of the study.

The alpha calculated with ordinary least-squares regression can be interpreted from a statistical standpoint since it is a sample statistic subject to sampling error. Statistically speaking, the alpha coefficient may not be statistically significant. In fact, many of the alphas calculated for individual common stocks are not statistically significant; these are interpreted to be values of zero.

When Jensen's alpha is used for ranking the performance of an asset, an investor should be careful because the Jensen measure may give a misleading performance ranking unless it is properly adjusted. To properly adjust the Jensen measure for ranking purposes, each asset's alpha should be divided by its beta coefficient. For example, if two assets called D and E are being ranked, the A_D/B_D and A_E/B_E should be used.

SOLVED PROBLEM 25.10

The Wiley Fund, T-bills, and the S&P500 have had the following returns over the past 5 years:

TIME	WILEY FUND RETURNS %	T-BILLS RETURNS %	S&P500 RETURNS %
19X0	7	5	5
19X1	−5	9	−4
19X2	13	7	10
19X3	11	6	9
19X4	15	8	12

Determine Wiley Fund's alpha and beta coefficients for the 5-year period of time.

SOLUTION

Ordinary least-squares regression should be used. The regression model to be determined is as follows:

$$(r_{i,t} - R_t) = A_i + B_i(r_{m,t} - R_t) + u_{i,t} \tag{25.5}$$

$(r_{i,t} - R_t)$ is the Y variable and $(r_{m,t} - R_t)$ is the X variable for the regression in risk-premium form.

The following equation should be computed:

$$\overline{Y} = A + B\overline{X}$$

where $\overline{Y}$ is the mean of the dependent variable, $\overline{X}$ is the mean of the independent variable, A is the alpha coefficient, and B is the beta coefficient.

$\overline{Y} = \Sigma Y/N$ and $\overline{X} = \Sigma X/N$, where N is the number of observations. Beta can be determined with Eq. (*23.5*) from Chap. 23:

$$B = \frac{N\sum XY - \sum X \sum Y}{N\sum X^2 - \left(\sum X\right)^2} \tag{23.5}$$

YEAR	S&P500 RETURNS $r_{m,t}$	WILEY FUND RETURNS $r_{i,t}$	T-BILL RETURNS R_t	X $(r_{m,t} - R_t)$	Y $(r_{i,t} - R_t)$	$X \times Y$	X^2
19X0	5%	7%	5%	0%	2%	0	0
19X1	−4	−5	9	−13	−14	182	169
19X3	10	13	7	3	6	18	9
19X4	9	11	6	3	5	15	9
19X5	12	15	8	4	7	28	16
				$\Sigma X = -3$	$\Sigma Y = 6$	$\Sigma XY = 243$	$\Sigma X^2 = 203$

$$B = \frac{5(243) - (-3)(6)}{5(203) - (-3)^2} = \frac{1{,}215 + 18}{1{,}015 - 9} = \frac{1{,}233}{1{,}006} = 1.226$$

$$\overline{Y} = \tfrac{6}{5} = 1.2 \qquad \overline{X} = -\tfrac{3}{5} = -.6$$

$$\overline{Y} = A + B\overline{X} \qquad A = \overline{Y} - B\overline{X}$$

$$A = 1.2 - (1.226)(-.6) = 1.2 + .7356 = 1.936$$

Because alpha is positive ($A = 1.936$), the Wiley Fund outperformed the market on a risk-adjusted basis over this period of time.

SOLVED PROBLEM 25.11

Jensen's alpha and the beta coefficients for four stocks are given below:

STOCKS	ALPHA	BETA
Craft Corporation	1.00%	.9
Lewis Corporation	1.25	1.25
Berry Corporation	1.07	1.15
Hawkings Corporation	1.15	.85

Rank the four stocks using the Jensen performance measure.

SOLUTION

Each stock's alpha should be divided by its beta, as shown below:

$$\text{Craft's value} = \frac{1\%}{.9} = 1.111\% \quad \text{(second)}$$

$$\text{Lewis' value} = \frac{1.25\%}{1.25} = 1\% \quad \text{(third)}$$

$$\text{Berry's value} = \frac{1.07\%}{1.15} = .93\% \quad \text{(fourth)}$$

$$\text{Hawkings' value} = \frac{1.15\%}{.85} = 1.35\% \quad \text{(first)}$$

Positive values for Jensen's alpha imply the asset is underpriced and therefore a desirable investment. Each of the above assets outperformed the market on a risk-adjusted basis.

25.6 COMPARISON OF PERFORMANCE MEASURES

The Sharpe portfolio performance measure is based on the capital market line (CML) and total risk, which makes it more suitable for evaluating portfolios rather than individual assets. On the other hand, both the Jensen and Treynor performance measures are based on the capital asset pricing model (CAPM) and are more flexible because by using systematic risk (beta) they can be used to evaluate the performance of both portfolios and individual assets.[2] All three performance measures tend to rank a group of diversified portfolios similarly.

True-False Questions

25.1 Most growth-oriented mutual funds tend to do better than the S&P500 on a risk-adjusted basis.

25.2 The Sharpe performance measure is better than the Treynor performance measure for evaluating the performance of individual common stocks.

25.3 The internal rate of return is another name for the geometric mean rate of return.

25.4 The geometric mean rate of return for an asset will always be greater than its arithmetic mean rate of return.

25.5 Most empirical studies of mutual funds report that the funds did not consistently do better than the market average.

25.6 Federal law requires an open-ended mutual fund to distribute 50 percent or more of its cash dividends and its interest income each year in order to be exempt from federal income taxes.

25.7 One good way for small investors to diversify their holdings is to purchase mutual funds.

25.8 After its initial offering, a closed-end mutual fund cannot sell more shares.

25.9 Studies have shown that no-load mutual funds outperform load mutual funds.

25.10 Studies have shown that mutual fund managers are good market timers.

[2]For more information on the CML and CAPM, see Chap. 23.

Multiple Choice Questions

25.1 The Weston Corporation has had the following returns over the past 5 years: 15 percent, −5 percent, −3 percent, 18 percent, and 17 percent. Determine the geometric mean rate of return for the Weston Corporation's stock over the past 5 years.
(*a*) 5.93 percent
(*b*) 6.09 percent
(*c*) 7.05 percent
(*d*) 7.91 percent
(*e*) 8.15 percent

25.2 The Rose Corporation's returns over the past 6 years are as follows:

YEAR	RETURNS %
19X1	10
19X2	−3
19X3	12
19X4	−7
19X5	9
19X6	12

Determine the geometric mean rate of return for the Rose Corporation for the 6-year period.
(*a*) 4.01 percent
(*b*) 4.93 percent
(*c*) 5.22 percent
(*d*) 6.07 percent
(*e*) 6.75 percent

Use the following information for the next six questions. *Note:* See Chap. 13 for an example on how to calculate an asset's standard deviation of returns. In addition, the riskless rate is the average of the five annual T-bill returns.

TIME	KESLER FUND'S RETURNS %	VOGUE FUND'S RETURNS %	S&P500's RETURNS %	T-BILL'S RETURNS %
19X0	15	10	11	6
19X1	−6	−2	−5	5
19X2	17	13	12	7
19X3	18	9	11	6
19X4	22	11	13	7

25.3 Determine the Sharpe performance index for the Kesler Fund for the 5-year period.
(*a*) .71
(*b*) .68
(*c*) .91
(*d*) 1.05
(*e*) 1.10

25.4 Determine the Sharpe performance index for the Vogue Fund for the 5-year period.
(*a*) .48
(*b*) .38
(*c*) .78
(*d*) .92
(*e*) 1.05

25.5 Determine the Jensen performance measure (alpha) for the Kesler Fund over the 5-year period. Calculate *A*, not *A*/*B*.
(*a*) 3.72
(*b*) 2.69
(*c*) 1.76
(*d*) 2.01
(*e*) 3.76

25.6 Calculate the Jensen performance measure for the Vogue Fund for the 5-year period. Calculate *A*, not *A*/*B*.
(*a*) .35
(*b*) .42
(*c*) .18
(*d*) .39
(*e*) .76

25.7 What is the Treynor performance measure for the Kesler Fund for the 5-year period?
(*a*) 3.02
(*b*) 3.19
(*c*) 4.02
(*d*) 4.70
(*e*) 5.09

25.8 What is the Treynor performance measure for the Vogue Fund for the 5-year period?
(*a*) 1.69
(*b*) 2.73
(*c*) 2.92
(*d*) 3.12
(*e*) 3.61

Use the following information for the next two questions:

PORTFOLIO	RETURN %	PORTFOLIO BETA	RISK (σ) %
A	12	1.2	15
B	14	1.1	12
C	16	1.4	18

Assume the T-bill rate is 7 percent.

25.9 Rank the portfolios according to the Treynor performance measure in descending order.
(*a*) A, B, C
(*b*) C, B, A
(*c*) B, A, C
(*d*) C, A, B
(*e*) B, C, A

25.10 Rank the portfolios according to the Sharpe performance measure in descending order.
(*a*) A, B, C
(*b*) C, B, A
(*c*) B, A, C
(*d*) C, A, B
(*e*) B, C, A

Answers

True-False

25.1. F 25.2. F 25.3. F 25.4. F 25.5. T 25.6. F 25.7. T 25.8. T
25.9. F 25.10. F

Multiple Choice

25.1. d 25.2. c 25.3. a 25.4. b 25.5. a 25.6. d 25.7. d 25.8. b
25.9. b 25.10. e

Chapter 26

International Investing

26.1 INTERNATIONAL DIVERSIFICATION

As previously illustrated in Fig. 23-2, the simplest kind of random diversification typically reduces risk substantially. Furthermore, as Fig. 26-1 indicates, it is possible to reduce risk below the level in domestic markets by diversifying internationally.

Table 26.1 shows a correlation matrix of returns for the stock indexes of various countries. These correlations are in most cases lower than the correlation between large portfolios of domestic stocks. The lower international correlation of stock returns encourages multinational investing because it allows an investor to reduce risk even further.

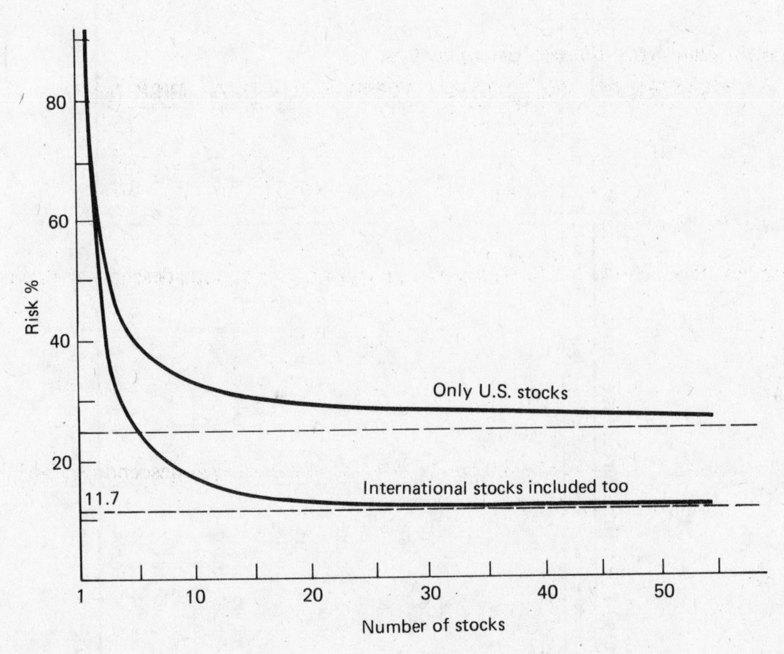

Fig. 26-1 International diversification. (*Source:* Bruno H. Solnik, "Why Not Diversify Internationally Rather than Domestically?" *Financial Analysts Journal,* July-August 1974, pp. 50–51.)

SOLVED PROBLEM 26.1

Why are the international correlation coefficients lower than the correlation between domestic stocks?

SOLUTION

Countries have different political systems, different customs, different regulations governing trade and business, and cultural differences. In addition, some countries are experiencing internal conflicts. Furthermore, some countries may have high inflation while other countries may be experiencing low inflation, or some may be having a booming economy, while others may be experiencing a recession. All these factors tend to cause the correlation of security returns between countries to be lower than the correlation of returns between securities (or groups of securities) in the domestic economy.

Table 26.1 Correlation Coefficients of Monthly Percentage Changes in Major Stock Indexes (local currencies, June 1981–September 1987)

	Australia	Austria	Belgium	Canada	Denmark	France	Germany	Hong Kong	Ireland	Italy	Japan	Malaysia	Mexico	Netherlands	New Zealand	Norway	Singapore	South Africa	Spain	Sweden	Switzerland	UK
Austria	0.219																					
Belgium	0.190	0.222																				
Canada	0.568	0.250	0.215																			
Denmark	0.217	−0.062	0.219	0.301																		
France	0.180	0.263	0.355	0.351	0.241																	
Germany	0.145	0.406	0.315	0.194	0.215	0.327																
Hong Kong	0.321	0.174	0.129	0.236	0.120	0.201	0.304															
Ireland	0.349	0.202	0.361	0.490	0.387	0.374	0.067	0.320														
Italy	0.209	0.224	0.307	0.321	0.150	0.459	0.257	0.216	0.275													
Japan	0.182	−0.025	0.223	0.294	0.186	0.361	0.147	0.137	0.183	0.241												
Malaysia	0.329	−0.013	0.096	0.274	0.151	−0.134	−0.020	0.159	0.082	−0.119	0.109											
Mexico	0.220	0.018	0.104	0.114	−0.174	−0.009	0.002	0.149	0.113	0.114	−0.021	0.231										
Netherlands	0.294	0.232	0.344	0.545	0.341	0.344	0.511	0.395	0.373	0.344	0.333	0.151	0.038									
New Zealand	0.389	0.290	0.275	0.230	0.148	0.247	0.318	0.352	0.314	0.142	−0.111	0.136	0.231	0.230								
Norway	0.355	0.009	0.233	0.381	0.324	0.231	0.173	0.356	0.306	0.042	0.156	0.262	0.050	0.405	0.201							
Singapore	0.374	0.030	0.133	0.320	0.133	−0.085	0.037	0.219	0.102	−0.038	0.066	0.891	0.202	0.196	0.212	0.280						
South Africa	0.279	0.159	0.143	0.385	−0.113	0.267	0.007	−0.095	0.024	0.093	0.225	−0.013	0.260	0.058	0.038	0.156	−0.056					
Spain	0.147	0.018	0.050	0.190	0.019	0.255	0.147	0.193	0.175	0.290	0.248	−0.071	0.059	0.170	0.095	0.075	0.056	−0.088				
Sweden	0.327	0.161	0.158	0.376	0.131	0.159	0.227	0.196	0.122	0.330	0.115	0.103	0.000	0.324	0.136	0.237	0.180	0.070	0.181			
Switzerland	0.334	0.401	0.276	0.551	0.283	0.307	0.675	0.379	0.290	0.287	0.130	0.099	0.026	0.570	0.397	0.331	0.157	0.112	0.192	0.334		
United Kingdom	0.377	0.073	0.381	0.590	0.218	0.332	0.263	0.431	0.467	0.328	0.354	0.193	0.068	0.534	0.014	0.313	0.250	0.168	0.209	0.339	0.435	
United States	0.328	0.138	0.250	0.720	0.351	0.390	0.209	0.114	0.380	0.224	0.326	0.347	0.063	0.473	0.083	0.356	0.377	0.218	0.214	0.279	0.500	0.513

Source: Richard Roll, "The International Crash of October, 1987, "*Financial Analysts Journal,* September/October 1988, Table II, pp. 20–21.

SOLVED PROBLEM 26.2

Jim Stallings, a resident of Alpha, is considering investing half of his funds in the domestic equities of Alpha and the other half in either the equities of country Beta or the country Gamma. Beta's equity market index has a correlation of .5 with Alpha's equity index, while Gamma's equities have a correlation of .3 with Alpha's equities. The expected risk and return of the equities in Alpha, Beta, and Gamma are the same: $E(r_A) = E(r_B) = E(r_G) = 12\%$. $\sigma_A^2 = \sigma_B^2 = \sigma_G^2 =$ variance of returns $= (12\%)^2$. Given the above information, in which country should Jim invest the other half of his money.

SOLUTION

Since the expected return will be the same regardless of which country is selected, the country that is least correlated with Alpha, which is Gamma, should be selected to achieve the lowest level of risk. This can be proven by calculating the portfolio's standard deviation with Eq. (*22.9*):

$$\sigma_p = \sqrt{x_1^2\sigma_1^2 + x_2^2\sigma_2^2 + 2x_1x_2\rho_{12}\sigma_1\sigma_2} \qquad (22.9)$$

where x_1 and x_2 are the weights for countries 1 and 2, σ_1 and σ_2 are the standard deviation of returns for countries 1 and 2, ρ_{12} is the correlation coefficient for countries 1 and 2, and σ_p is the portfolio's standard deviation of returns.

$$\sigma_{AB} = \sqrt{(.5)^2(12)^2 + (.5)^2(12)^2 + 2(.5)(.5)(.5)(12)(12)}$$
$$= \sqrt{36 + 36 + 36} = \sqrt{108} = 10.39\%$$
$$\sigma_{AG} = \sqrt{(.5)^2(12)^2 + (.5)^2(12)^2 + 2(.5)(.5)(.3)(12)(12)}$$
$$= \sqrt{36 + 36 + 21.6} = \sqrt{93.6} = 9.67\%$$

26.2 FOREIGN EXCHANGE RISK

While international investing can reduce risk below domestic levels, one important risk factor was not considered—*foreign exchange risk.* When investing in another country the investor must convert domestic currency into a foreign currency. Then, when the foreign investment is terminated, the process must be reversed. In essence, two investments are made. One investment is in the foreign security and the other is in that foreign country's currency.

EXAMPLE 26.1 Melissa James plans to purchase $1,000 worth of German stock and hold it for 1 year. The current exchange rate is 1 dollar for 1 Deutsche mark (DM). Therefore, Melissa can purchase stock worth DM1,000.

A 10 percent annual rate of return was earned from the German stock, and the exchange rate at the end of the year was $.90/DM1. Melissa's return from a U.S. perspective was as follows: First, convert her German investment into U.S. dollars. This is 1,000 × 1.1 = DM1,100 (ending investment with 10 percent growth) × $.90 = $990. Her end-of-year return was $990/$1,000 − 1 = .99 − 1 = −.01 or −1%. Melissa lost money even though she earned a positive 10 percent return from her German investment. Her loss on foreign currency investment more than offset her gain from the German security. Another way to view this is as follows:

(1) The gain on her German investment = DM1,100/DM1,000 − 1 = 1.10 − 1 = .10 or 10%.

(2) The loss on her currency investment = $.90/$1.00 − 1 = .9 − 1 = −.10 or −10%.

Her net return can be calculated with the following equation:

$$r_n = (1 + r_d)(1 + r_c) - 1 \qquad (26.1)$$

$$\text{Net return} = (1 + \text{foreign security's return})(1 + \text{currency return}) - 1$$

Investors can do something about exchange risk. An investor could lock in a fixed return by purchasing the appropriate forward contract on the foreign currency. For the hedge to work properly, however, the investor needs to know exactly how much foreign currency to sell in the forward market.

EXAMPLE 26.2 Mary Evans is planning to purchase a gilt, a British government bond, with an annual yield-to-maturity of 9 percent. Currently, the exchange rate is $1.80 per pound sterling, and the 1-year forward exchange rate is $1.90 per pound. If Mary hedges her position, what annual return can she lock in with the British bills (ignoring transaction costs)?

Mary makes two investments, one in a British government bond and the other in the British pound. The British bill will earn a riskless 9 percent. Her currency investment will yield 5.56 percent.

$$\frac{\$1.90/1£}{\$1.80/1£} - 1 = \frac{\$1.90}{\$1.80} - 1 = 1.056 - 1 = .0556 = 5.56\%$$

The combined net return that is locked in, using Eq. (*26.1*), is

$$\begin{aligned} r_n &= (1 + r_d)(1 + r_c) - 1 \\ &= (1.09)(1.0556) - 1 \\ &= 1.1506 - 1 = .1506 \quad \text{or} \quad 15.06\% \end{aligned}$$

This type of hedge will work because Mary knows exactly how many pounds sterling she will have from the riskless British government bond at the end of the year. If her investment had been in the risky British equity market, she would have been uncertain about the investment's outcome and, as a result, uncertain about the number of pounds she would have at the end of the year.

SOLVED PROBLEM 26.3

Suppose a U.S. investor purchased $10,000 British gilts with a guaranteed annual return of 9 percent in 1 year. The current exchange rate is $1.50/£1, and the 1-year forward rate is $1.48/£1.

(*a*) What return would be earned by the U.S. investor at year end if the exchange rate is $1.25/£1?

(*b*) Show how this investment could have been hedged.

SOLUTION

(*a*) The $10,000 is equal to $10,000/($1.50/pound) = £6,666.67. The ending amount is £6,666.67 × (1.09) = £7,266.67. Converting this to dollars equals £7,266.67 × $1.25/£1 = $9,083.34. Therefore, the ending return is $9,083.34/$10,000 − 1 = .9083 − 1 = −.092 or −9.2%. The loss takes place because of the fall in the dollar relative to pounds. That is, the U.S. investor obtains fewer dollars per pound when converting from pounds to dollars at the end of the investment period.

(*b*) To hedge, lock in £7,266.67 at the forward rate of $1.48 per pound or £7,266.67 × $1.48/£1 = $10,754.67. Therefore, the annual rate locked in is $10,754.67/$10,000 − 1 = 1.0755 − 1 = .0755 or 7.55%.

SOLVED PROBLEM 26.4

Assume the exchange rate is $.75/DM1 at the beginning of the year and $.90/DM1 at the end of the year. Over this one-year period, the West German equity market increased by 18 percent. What is the net return to a U.S. investor in the West German equity market over this 1-year period?

SOLUTION

$$r_n = (1 + r_d)(1 + r_c) - 1 \qquad (26.1)$$

$$r_d = .18$$

$$r_c = \frac{\$.90/\text{DM}1}{\$.75/\text{DM}1} - 1 = \frac{\$.90}{\$.75} - 1 = 1.2 - 1 = .2$$

$$r_n = (1.18)(1.2) - 1 = 1.416 - 1 = .416 \quad \text{or} \quad 41.6\%$$

SOLVED PROBLEM 26.5

Refer to Solved Problem 26.4. What return would the U.S. investor have earned if the exchange rate at the end of the year was $.50/DM1?

SOLUTION

$$r_n = (1 + r_d)(1 + r_c) - 1 \qquad (26.1)$$

$$r_d = .18$$

$$r_c = \frac{\$.50/\text{DM}1}{\$.75/\text{DM}1} - 1 = \frac{\$.50}{\$.75} - 1 = .6666 - 1 = -.333$$

$$r_n = (1 + .18)(1 - .333) - 1 = (1.18)(.666) = .786 - 1 = -.214 \quad \text{or} \quad -21.4\%$$

SOLVED PROBLEM 26.6

The rate of inflation is expected to be 9 percent next year while in Germany the inflation rate is expected to be 6 percent. The current interest rate in Germany is 8 percent on 1-year federal government bonds. If markets are in equilibrium, what should the German bill rate be in the United States?

SOLUTION

In equilibrium, expected differences in inflation rates between countries will equal the expected differences between interest rates.

$$\frac{E(I_{US} - I_G)}{1 + I_G} = \frac{r_{US} - r_G}{1 + r_G}$$

where I_{US} is the expected rate of inflation in the United States, I_G is the expected inflation rate in Germany, r_{US} is the current 1-year interest rate in the United States, and r_G is the current 1-year interest rate in Germany.

$$\frac{.09 - .06}{1 + .06} = \frac{r_{US} - .08}{1 + .08}$$

$$(1.08)(.03) = (r_{US} - .08)(1.06)$$

$$.0324 = 1.06r_{US} - .0848$$

$$r_{US} = \frac{.1172}{1.06} = .11057 \quad \text{or} \quad 11.057\%$$

SOLVED PROBLEM 26.7

Suppose Al Kramer plans to invest in Martin, Ltd., a British corporation that is currently selling for £50 per share. Al has $112,500 to invest at the current exchange rate of $2.25/£1.

(*a*) How many shares can Al purchase?

(*b*) What is his net return if the price of Martin, Ltd., at the end of the year is £60 and the exchange rate at that time is $2.00/£1.

SOLUTION

(*a*) First, dollars should be converted to pounds. $112,500/($2.25/£) = £50,000. Then, divide total pounds by the price of the stock: £50,000/£50 = 1,000 shares.

(*b*) Equation (*26.1*) can be used to determine the net return:

$$r_n = (1 + r_d)(1 + r_c) - 1 \qquad (26.1)$$

$$r_d = \frac{£60}{£50} - 1 = 1.2 - 1 = .2$$

$$r_c = \frac{\$2.00/£1}{\$2.25/£1} - 1 = \frac{\$2.00}{\$2.25} - 1 = .8889 - 1 = -.111$$

$$r_n = (1.20)(1 - .1111) - 1 = (1.2)(.8889) - 1 = 1.06668 - 1 = .06668 \quad \text{or} \quad 6.67\%$$

SOLVED PROBLEM 26.8

Refer to Solved Problem 26.7. Determine Al's return in (*b*) if the ending price of the stock is £45 and the ending rate of exchange is $2.50/£1.

SOLUTION

$$r_n = (1 + r_d)(1 + r_c) - 1 \qquad (26.1)$$

$$r_d = \frac{£45}{£50} - 1 = .9 - 1 = .1$$

$$r_c = \frac{\$2.50}{\$2.25} - 1 = 1.1111 - 1 = .1111$$

$$r_n = [1 + (-.10)](1 + .1111) - 1 = (.9)(1.1111) - 1 = .99999 - 1 = -0.000010 \quad \text{or} \quad 0\%$$

SOLVED PROBLEM 26.9

If the current exchange rate is $.75/DM1, the 1-year forward rate is $.85/DM1, and the interest rate is 10 percent on 1-year German bills, what rate can be locked in by investing in German bills?

SOLUTION

$$r_n = (1 + r_d)(1 + r_c) - 1 \qquad (26.1)$$

$$r_d = 10\% \quad \text{or} \quad .1$$

$$r_c = \frac{\$.85/\text{DM}1}{\$.75/\text{DM}1} - 1 = \frac{\$.85}{\$.75} - 1 = 1.1333 - 1 = .1333 \quad \text{or} \quad 13.33\%$$

$$r_n = (1 + .1)(1 + .1333) - 1 = (1.1)(1.1333) - 1 = 1.2466 - 1 = .2466 \quad \text{or} \quad 24.66\%$$

SOLVED PROBLEM 26.10

Consider the following annual rates of return and foreign exchange rates:

YEAR	UNITED STATES	BRITAIN	BEG. OF YEAR EXCHANGE RATE
19X1	12%	7%	\$2.50/£1
19X2	−7	15	2.00/£1
19X3	11	−5	1.75/£1
19X4	10	9	2.00/£1
19X5	7	11	1.60/£1
19X6			1.50/£1

(*a*) Determine the arithmetic mean rate of return in each market from the perspective of an investor of U.S. dollars.

b) Determine the arithmetic mean rate of return in each market from the perspective of a British pound investor.

SOLUTION

The arithmetic mean return ($\bar{r}$) can be determined with the following equation:

$$\bar{r} = \frac{\sum_{t=1}^{T} r_t}{T}$$

where r_t is the return in time period t and T is the total number of annual returns.

(*a*) From the U.S. perspective, the U.S. returns may be used. The mean rate of return is [12% + (−7%) + 11% + 10% + 7%]/5 = 33%/5 = 6.6% = $\bar{r}$.

In order to determine the return in Britain from a U.S. investor's perspective, we should use Eq. (*26.1*):

$$r_n = (1 + r_d)(1 + r_c) - 1$$

The return (r_c) from investing in the British pound sterling over the 5-year period must be determined as follows:

19X1: $$\frac{\$2.0}{\$2.5} - 1 = .8 - 1 = -.2$$

19X2: $$\frac{\$1.75}{\$2.0} - 1 = .875 - 1 = -.125$$

19X3: $$\frac{\$2.0}{\$1.75} - 1 = 1.143 - 1 = .143$$

19X4: $$\frac{1.6}{\$2.0} - 1 = .8 - 1 = -.2$$

19X5: $$\frac{\$1.5}{\$1.6} - 1 = .9375 - 1 = -.0625$$

Equation (*26.1*) suggests the following:

19X1: $$r_n = (1 + .07)[1 + (-.2)] - 1 = (1.07)(.8) - 1$$
$$= .856 - 1 = -.144 \text{ or } -14.4\%$$

19X2: $$r_n = (1 + .15)[1 + (-.125)] - 1 = (1.15)(.875) - 1$$
$$= 1.00625 - 1 = .00625 \quad \text{or} \quad .625\%$$

19X3: $$r_n = [1 + (-.05)](1 + .143) - 1 = (.95)(1.143) - 1$$
$$= 1.0859 - 1 = .0859 \quad \text{or} \quad 8.59\%$$

19X4: $$r_n = (1 + .09)[1 + (-.2)] - 1 = (1.09)(.8) - 1$$
$$= .872 - 1 = -.128 \quad \text{or} \quad -12.8\%$$

19X5: $$r_n = (1 + .11)[1 + (-.0625)] - 1 = (1.11)(.9375) - 1$$
$$= 1.0406 - 1 = .0406 \quad \text{or} \quad 4.06\%$$

The arithmetic mean return of investing in Britain from a U.S. perspective is [−14.4% + 6.25% + 8.59% + (−.12.8%) + 4.06%]/5 = −8.3%/5 = −1.66%.

(*b*) The arithmetic mean return in Britain is [7% + 15% + (−5%) + 9% + 11%]/5 = 37%/5 = 7.4%. In order to determine the return in the United States from the standpoint of Britain, we need to look at the dollar in terms of the pound as follows:

19X1: £1/$2.50 = .4 pound per dollar
19X2: £1/$2.00 = .5 pound per dollar
19X3: £1/$1.75 = .5714 pound per dollar
19X4: £1/$2.00 = .5 pound per dollar
19X5: £1/$1.60 = .625 pound per dollar
19X6: £1/$1.50 = .6666 pound per dollar

The currency return from investing in the dollar should first be determined.

19X1: £.5/£.4 − 1 = 1.25 − 1 = .25 = r_c
19X2: £.5714/£.5 − 1 = 1.1428 − 1 = .1428 = r_c
19X3: £.5/£.5714 − 1 = .875 − 1 = −.125 = r_c
19X4: £.625/£.5 − 1 = 1.25 − 1 = .25 = r_c
19X5: £.6666/£.625 − 1 = 1.06656 − 1 = .06656 = r_c

Equation (*26.1*) suggests the following:

19X1: $r_n = (1 + .12)(1 + .25) - 1 = (1.12)(1.25) - 1$
$= 1.4 - 1 = .40$ or 40%

19X2: $r_n = [1 + (-.07)](1 + .1428) = (.93)(1.1428) - 1$
$= 1.0628 - 1 = .0628$ or 6.28%

19X3: $r_n = (1 + .11)[1 + (-.125)] - 1 = (1.11)(.875) - 1$
$= .97125 - 1 = -.02875$ or −2.875%

19X4: $r_n = (1 + .10)(1 + .25) - 1 = (1.1)(1.25) - 1$
$= 1.375 - 1 = .375$ or 37.5%

19X5: $r_n = (1 + .07)(1 + .06656) - 1 = (1.07)(1.06656) - 1$
$= 1.1412 - 1 = .1412$ or 14.12%

The arithmetic mean return from investing in the United States from the standpoint of Britain is [40% + 6.28% + (−2.875%) + 37.5% + 14.12%]/5 = 95.025%/5 = 19.005% = $\bar{r}$.

True-False Questions

26.1 International investing offers the individual investor the potential to reduce risk below the level in the domestic market.

26.2 Exchange rate risk can always be eliminated by hedging in the forward foreign exchange market.

26.3 An efficient frontier that is constructed with international equities usually dominates one constructed only with domestic equity securities.

26.4 The correlation coefficient between international equity market indexes is usually lower that the correlation coefficient between different domestic market indexes.

26.5 While exchange rate risk is a problem when investing in international equities, it is not a problem with international bonds.

26.6 The majority of international equity indexes have betas greater than one when their returns are regressed with the returns of the S&P500 index.

26.7 If an investor buys a British security, the investor's return will be the same whether the investment is made in dollars or pounds sterling.

26.8 If you invest in a Mexican corporation and earn a 12 percent rate of return on your Mexican investment, this return will be enhanced from a U.S. perspective if the dollar increases in value relative to the peso. *Hint:* The dollar went from $.05 per peso to $.04 per peso.

26.9 An American investing in Germany would be happy if the dollar appreciated in value relative to the mark, but a German investing in the United States would not.

26.10 Even though a U.S. and British investor may experience identical returns from an investment in France, from the perspective of their particular currencies, their returns will most likely differ.

Multiple Choice Questions

26.1 Bruno's investment in an Italian security was worth 2,000,000 lira 1 year ago when 1 dollar was worth 1,000 lira and 2,200,000 lira today when 1 dollar is worth 666.67 lira. What is the annual return on Bruno's dollar investment in Italy?
(*a*) 40 percent
(*b*) 65 percent
(*c*) 30 percent
(*d*) 72 percent
(*e*) 51 percent

26.2 ADRs (American Depository Receipts) are
(*a*) Issued at rates that compare favorably with the rates charged for ordinary domestic transactions
(*b*) Created when a U.S. bank with foreign offices purchases securities in a foreign corporation for its domestic clients
(*c*) Used to purchase and sell foreign securities at twice the rate charged for domestic purchases and sales
(*d*) *a* and *b*
(*e*) *a* and *c*

26.3 An American named Rolf had a 20 percent net return (r_n) last year on a dollar investment in Switzerland. However, if Rolf experienced an unfavorable change in the exchange rate of 5 percent (r_c), what was his return on the investment in Swiss francs (that is, before it was translated into dollars)? *Hint:* Determine r_d.
(*a*) 15.7 percent
(*b*) 18.2 percent
(*c*) 26.3 percent
(*d*) 25 percent
(*e*) 20 percent

26.4 Assume the exchange rate was $1.50/£1 at the beginning of the year and $1.70/£1 at the end of the year. Over this 1-year period, the British equity market increased by 16 percent. What is the net return to an American who invests dollars in the British stock market over this 1-year period?
(*a*) 27.2 percent
(*b*) 31.5 percent
(*c*) 18.9 percent
(*d*) 24.1 percent
(*e*) 33.2 percent

26.5 The rate of inflation is expected to be 7 percent next year in the United States while in Britain it is expected to be 12 percent. The current federal government bill rate in Britain is 14 percent. If the markets are in equilibrium, what should the T-bill rate be in the United States.
(*a*) 8.2 percent
(*b*) 9.4 percent
(*c*) 8.5 percent
(*d*) 8.9 percent
(*e*) 7.2 percent

26.6 Susan Flowers in the United States plans to purchase a 1-year British gilt with a current yield of 8.7 percent and hold it until maturity. The current exchange rate is $2.20 per pound, and the 1-year forward rate is $2.35 per pound. If she invests U.S. dollars, what return can Susan lock in for 1 year?
(*a*) 11.2 percent
(*b*) 14.3 percent
(*c*) 15.7 percent
(*d*) 17.2 percent
(*e*) 16.1 percent

The following information should be used with the next two questions:

Suppose George Givens plans to pay dollars for the stock of Braun, Inc., a German company that is selling for DM40 per share. George has $28,000 to spend on Braun. The current exchange rate is $.70/DM1.

26.7 How many share of Braun, Inc., can George purchase?
(*a*) 1,000
(*b*) 592
(*c*) 960
(*d*) 1,500
(*e*) 1,100

26.8 What will George's net return be at the end of the year if the stock has a price of DM50 and the exchange rate is $.65/DM1?
(*a*) 14.7 percent
(*b*) 14.9 percent
(*c*) 15.4 percent
(*d*) 15.6 percent
(*e*) 16.1 percent

The following information should be used with the next two questions:

Jim Seals, a dollar investor, plans to diversify his equity portfolio with an investment in foreign equities. Two countries are being considered, Britain and France. The expected return and risk (standard deviation) for the three countries' equity markets are as follows:

	Return	Risk (s.d.)
France	12%	16%
Britain	14%	20%
United States	16%	22%

Assume the following correlation matrix is expected to exist:

	United States	Britain	France
United States	1		
Britain	.56	1	
France	.41	.62	1

26.9 If Jim decided to invest 50 percent of his funds in the U.S. equity market and 50 percent in Britain's equity market, what level of risk would be expected? *Hint:* Chapter 22 on portfolio analysis should be consulted for the appropriate formula, Eq. (*22.9*).
(*a*) 17.2 percent
(*b*) 18.6 percent
(*c*) 19.4 percent
(*d*) 20.1 percent
(*e*) 20.5 percent

26.10 If Jim decided to invest 40 percent of his funds in the U.S. equity market, 40 percent in the British equity market, and 20 percent in the French equity market, what risk level should he expect over a 1-year period? *Hint:* Chapter 22 contains the formula that should be used with this problem. See Example 22.3.
(*a*) 15.4 percent
(*b*) 16.2 percent
(*c*) 16.9 percent
(*d*) 17.3 percent
(*e*) 17.7 percent

Answers

True-False

26.1. T 26.2. F 26.3. T 26.4. T 26.5. F 26.6. F 26.7. F 26.8. F
26.9. F 26.10. T

Multiple Choice

26.1. b 26.2. d 26.3. c 26.4. b 26.5. d 26.6. e 26.7. a 26.8. e
26.9. b 26.10. c

Appendix A

Present Value of $1

Period	1%	2%	3%	4%	5%	6%	7%	8%	9%	10%	12%	14%	15%	16%	18%	20%	24%	28%	32%	36%
1	.9901	.9804	.9709	.9615	.9524	.9434	.9346	.9259	.9174	.9091	.8929	.8772	.8696	.8621	.8475	.8333	.8065	.7813	.7576	.7353
2	.9803	.9612	.9426	.9246	.9070	.8900	.8734	.8573	.8417	.8264	.7972	.7695	.7561	.7432	.7182	.6944	.6504	.6104	.5739	.5407
3	.9706	.9423	.9151	.8890	.8638	.8396	.8163	.7938	.7722	.7513	.7118	.6750	.6575	.6407	.6086	.5787	.5245	.4768	.4348	.3975
4	.9610	.9238	.8885	.8548	.8227	.7921	.7629	.7350	.7084	.6830	.6355	.5921	.5718	.5523	.5158	.4823	.4230	.3725	.3294	.2923
5	.9515	.9057	.8626	.8219	.7835	.7473	.7130	.6806	.6499	.6209	.5674	.5194	.4972	.4761	.4371	.4019	.3411	.2910	.2495	.2149
6	.9420	.8880	.8375	.7903	.7462	.7050	.6663	.6302	.5963	.5645	.5066	.4556	.4323	.4104	.3704	.3349	.2751	.2274	.1890	.1580
7	.9327	.8706	.8131	.7599	.7107	.6651	.6227	.5835	.5470	.5132	.4523	.3996	.3759	.3538	.3139	.2791	.2218	.1776	.1432	.1162
8	.9235	.8535	.7894	.7307	.6768	.6274	.5820	.5403	.5019	.4665	.4039	.3506	.3269	.3050	.2660	.2326	.1789	.1388	.1085	.0854
9	.9143	.8368	.7664	.7026	.6446	.5919	.5439	.5002	.4604	.4241	.3606	.3075	.2843	.2630	.2255	.1938	.1443	.1084	.0822	.0628
10	.9053	.8203	.7441	.6756	.6139	.5584	.5083	.4632	.4224	.3855	.3220	.2697	.2472	.2267	.1911	.1615	.1164	.0847	.0623	.0462
11	.8963	.8043	.7224	.6496	.5847	.5268	.4751	.4289	.3875	.3505	.2875	.2366	.2149	.1954	.1619	.1346	.0938	.0662	.0472	.0340
12	.8874	.7885	.7014	.6246	.5568	.4970	.4440	.3971	.3555	.3186	.2567	.2076	.1869	.1685	.1372	.1122	.0757	.0517	.0357	.0250
13	.8787	.7730	.6810	.6006	.5303	.4688	.4150	.3677	.3262	.2897	.2292	.1821	.1625	.1452	.1163	.0935	.0610	.0404	.0271	.0184
14	.8700	.7579	.6611	.5775	.5051	.4423	.3878	.3405	.2992	.2633	.2046	.1597	.1413	.1252	.0985	.0779	.0492	.0316	.0205	.0135
15	.8613	.7430	.6419	.5553	.4810	.4173	.3624	.3152	.2745	.2394	.1827	.1401	.1229	.1079	.0835	.0649	.0397	.0247	.0155	.0099
16	.8528	.7284	.6232	.5339	.4581	.3936	.3387	.2919	.2519	.2176	.1631	.1229	.1069	.0930	.0708	.0541	.0320	.0193	.0118	.0073
17	.8444	.7142	.6050	.5134	.4363	.3714	.3166	.2703	.2311	.1978	.1456	.1078	.0929	.0802	.0600	.0451	.0258	.0150	.0089	.0054
18	.8360	.7002	.5874	.4936	.4155	.3503	.2959	.2502	.2120	.1799	.1300	.0946	.0808	.0691	.0508	.0376	.0208	.0118	.0068	.0038
19	.8277	.6864	.5703	.4746	.3957	.3305	.2765	.2317	.1945	.1635	.1161	.0829	.0703	.0596	.0431	.0313	.0168	.0092	.0051	.0029
20	.8195	.6730	.5537	.4564	.3769	.3118	.2584	.2145	.1784	.1486	.1037	.0728	.0611	.0514	.0365	.0261	.0135	.0072	.0039	.0021
25	.7798	.6095	.4776	.3751	.2953	.2330	.1842	.1460	.1160	.0923	.0588	.0378	.0304	.0245	.0160	.0105	.0046	.0021	.0010	.0005
30	.7419	.5521	.4120	.3083	.2314	.1741	.1314	.0994	.0754	.0573	.0334	.0196	.0151	.0116	.0070	.0042	.0016	.0006	.0002	.0001
40	.6717	.4529	.3066	.2083	.1420	.0972	.0668	.0460	.0318	.0221	.0107	.0053	.0037	.0026	.0013	.0007	.0002	.0001	*	*
50	.6080	.3715	.2281	.1407	.0872	.0543	.0339	.0213	.0132	.0085	.0035	.0014	.0009	.0006	.0003	.0001	*	*	*	*
60	.5504	.3048	.1697	.0951	.0535	.0303	.0173	.0099	.0057	.0033	.0011	.0004	.0002	.0001	*	*	*	*	*	*

*The factor is zero to four decimal points.

Appendix B

Future Value of $1

Period	1%	2%	3%	4%	5%	6%	7%	8%	9%	10%	12%	14%	15%	16%	18%	20%	24%	28%	32%	36%
1	1.0100	1.0200	1.0300	1.0400	1.0500	1.0600	1.0700	1.0800	1.0900	1.1000	1.1200	1.1400	1.1500	1.1600	1.1800	1.2000	1.2400	1.2800	1.3200	1.3600
2	1.0201	1.0404	1.0609	1.0816	1.1025	1.1236	1.1449	1.1664	1.1881	1.2100	1.2544	1.2996	1.3225	1.3456	1.3924	1.4400	1.5376	1.6384	1.7424	1.8496
3	1.0303	1.0612	1.0927	1.1249	1.1576	1.1910	1.2250	1.2597	1.2950	1.3310	1.4049	1.4815	1.5209	1.5609	1.6430	1.7280	1.9066	2.0972	2.3000	2.5155
4	1.0406	1.0824	1.1255	1.1699	1.2155	1.2625	1.3108	1.3605	1.4116	1.4641	1.5735	1.6890	1.7490	1.8106	1.9388	2.0736	2.3642	2.6844	3.0360	3.4210
5	1.0510	1.1041	1.1593	1.2167	1.2763	1.3382	1.4026	1.4693	1.5386	1.6105	1.7623	1.9254	2.0114	2.1003	2.2878	2.4883	2.9316	3.4360	4.0075	4.6526
6	1.0615	1.1262	1.1941	1.2653	1.3401	1.4185	1.5007	1.5869	1.6771	1.7716	1.9738	2.1950	2.3131	2.4364	2.6996	2.9860	3.6352	4.3980	5.2899	6.3275
7	1.0721	1.1487	1.2299	1.3159	1.4071	1.5036	1.6058	1.7138	1.8280	1.9487	2.2107	2.5023	2.6600	2.8262	3.1855	3.5832	4.5077	5.6295	6.9826	8.6054
8	1.0829	1.1717	1.2668	1.3686	1.4775	1.5938	1.7182	1.8509	1.9926	21.436	2.4760	2.8526	3.0590	3.2784	3.7589	4.2998	5.5895	7.2058	9.2170	11.703
9	1.0937	1.1951	1.3048	1.4233	1.5513	1.6895	1.8385	1.9990	2.1719	2.3579	2.7731	3.2519	3.5179	3.8030	4.4355	5.1598	6.9310	9.2234	12.166	15.916
10	1.1046	1.2190	1.3439	1.4802	1.6289	1.7908	1.9672	2.1589	2.3674	2.5937	3.1058	3.7072	4.0456	4.4114	5.2338	6.1917	8.5944	11.805	16.059	21.646
11	1.1157	1.2434	1.3842	1.5395	1.7103	1.8983	2.1049	2.3316	2.5804	2.8531	3.4785	4.2262	4.6524	5.1173	6.1759	7.4301	10.657	15.111	21.198	29.439
12	1.1268	1.2682	1.4258	1.6010	1.7959	2.0122	2.2522	2.5182	2.8127	3.1384	3.8960	4.8179	5.3502	5.9360	7.2876	8.9161	13.214	19.342	27.982	40.037
13	1.1381	1.2936	1.4685	1.6651	1.8856	2.1329	2.4098	2.7196	3.0658	3.4523	4.3635	5.4924	6.1528	6.8858	8.5994	10.699	16.386	24.748	36.937	54.451
14	1.1495	1.3195	1.5126	1.7317	1.9799	2.2609	2.5785	2.9372	3.3417	3.7975	4.8871	6.2613	7.0757	7.9875	10.147	12.839	20.319	31.691	48.756	74.053
15	1.1610	1.3459	1.5580	1.8009	2.0789	2.3966	2.7590	3.1722	3.6425	4.1772	5.4736	7.1379	8.1371	9.2655	11.973	15.407	25.195	40.564	53.358	100.71
16	1.1726	1.3728	1.6047	1.8730	2.1829	2.5404	2.9522	3.4259	3.9703	4.5950	6.1304	8.1372	9.3576	10.748	14.129	18.488	31.242	51.923	84.953	136.96
17	1.1843	1.4002	1.6528	1.9479	2.2920	2.6928	3.1588	3.7000	4.3276	5.0545	6.8660	9.2765	10.761	12.467	16.672	22.186	38.740	66.461	112.13	186.27
18	1.1961	1.4282	1.7024	2.0258	2.4066	2.8543	3.3799	3.9960	4.7171	5.5599	7.6900	10.575	12.375	14.462	19.673	26.623	48.038	85.070	148.02	253.33
19	1.2081	1.4568	1.7535	2.1068	2.5270	3.0256	3.6165	4.3157	5.1417	6.1159	8.6129	12.055	14.231	16.776	23.214	31.948	59.567	108.89	195.39	344.53
20	1.2202	1.4859	1.8061	2.1911	2.6533	3.2071	3.8697	4.6610	5.6044	6.7275	9.6463	13.743	16.366	19.460	27.393	38.337	73.864	139.37	257.91	468.57
21	1.2324	1.5157	1.8603	2.2788	2.7860	3.3996	4.1406	5.0338	6.1088	7.4002	10.803	15.667	18.821	22.574	32.323	46.005	91.591	178.40	340.44	637.26
22	1.2447	1.5460	1.9161	2.3699	2.9253	3.6035	4.4304	5.4365	6.6586	8.1403	12.100	17.861	21.644	26.186	38.142	55.206	113.57	228.35	449.39	866.67
23	1.2572	1.5769	1.9736	2.4647	3.0715	3.8197	4.7405	5.8715	7.2579	8.9543	13.552	20.361	24.891	30.376	45.007	66.247	140.83	292.30	593.19	1178.6
24	1.2697	1.6084	2.0328	2.5633	3.2251	4.0489	5.0724	6.3412	7.9111	9.8497	15.178	23.212	28.625	35.236	53.108	79.496	174.63	374.14	783.02	1602.9
25	1.2824	1.6406	2.0938	2.6658	3.3864	4.2919	5.4274	6.8485	8.6231	10.834	17.000	26.461	32.918	40.874	62.668	95.396	216.54	478.90	1033.5	2180.0
26	1.2953	1.6734	2.1566	2.7725	3.5557	4.5494	5.8074	7.3964	9.3992	11.918	19.040	30.166	37.856	47.414	73.948	114.47	268.51	612.99	1364.3	2964.9
27	1.3082	1.7069	2.2213	2.8834	3.7335	4.8223	6.2139	7.9881	10.245	13.110	21.324	34.389	43.535	55.000	87.259	137.37	332.95	784.63	1800.9	4032.2
28	1.3213	1.7410	2.2879	2.9987	3.9201	5.1117	6.6488	8.6271	11.167	14.421	23.883	39.204	50.065	63.800	102.96	164.84	412.86	1004.3	2377.2	5483.8
29	1.3345	1.7758	2.3566	3.1187	4.1161	5.4184	7.1143	9.3173	12.172	15.863	26.749	44.693	57.575	74.008	121.50	197.81	511.95	1285.5	3137.9	7458.0
30	1.3478	1.8114	2.4273	3.2434	4.3219	5.7435	7.6123	10.062	13.267	17.449	29.959	50.950	66.211	85.849	143.37	237.37	634.81	1645.5	4142.0	10143.
40	1.4889	2.2080	3.2620	4.8010	7.0400	10.285	14.974	21.724	31.409	45.259	93.050	188.88	267.86	378.72	750.37	1469.7	5455.9	19426	66520	*
50	1.6446	2.6916	4.3839	7.1067	11.467	18.420	29.457	46.901	74.357	117.39	289.00	700.23	1083.6	1670.7	3927.3	9100.4	46890	*	*	*
60	1.8167	3.2810	5.8916	10.519	18.679	32.987	57.946	101.25	176.03	304.48	897.59	2595.9	4383.9	7370.1	20555	56347	*	*	*	*

*FVIF > 99.999

Appendix C

Present Value of an Annuity of $1

Number of Payments	1%	2%	3%	4%	5%	6%	7%	8%	9%	10%	12%	14%	15%	16%	18%	20%	24%	28%	32%
1	0.9901	0.9804	0.9709	0.9615	0.9524	0.9434	0.9346	0.9259	0.9174	0.9091	0.8929	0.8772	0.8696	0.8621	0.8475	0.8333	0.8065	0.7813	0.7576
2	1.9704	1.9415	1.9135	1.8861	1.8594	1.8334	1.8080	1.7833	1.7591	1.7355	1.6901	1.6467	1.6257	1.6052	1.5656	1.5278	1.4568	1.3916	1.3315
3	2.9410	2.8839	2.8286	2.7751	2.7232	2.6730	2.6243	2.5771	2.5313	2.4869	2.4018	2.3216	2.2832	2.2459	2.1743	2.1065	1.9813	1.8684	1.7663
4	3.9020	3.8077	3.7171	3.6299	3.5460	3.4651	3.3872	3.3121	3.2397	3.1699	3.0373	2.9137	2.8550	2.7982	2.6901	2.5887	2.4043	2.2410	2.0957
5	4.8534	4.7135	4.5797	4.4518	4.3295	4.2124	4.1002	3.9927	3.8897	3.7908	3.6048	3.4331	3.3522	3.2743	3.1272	2.9906	2.7454	2.5230	2.3452
6	5.7955	5.6014	5.4172	5.2421	5.0757	4.9173	4.7665	4.6229	4.4859	4.3553	4.1114	3.8887	3.7845	3.6847	3.4976	3.3255	3.0205	2.7594	2.5342
7	6.7282	6.4720	6.2303	6.0021	5.7864	5.5824	5.3893	5.2064	5.0330	4.8684	4.5638	4.2883	4.1604	4.0386	3.8115	3.6046	3.2423	2.9370	2.6775
8	7.6517	7.3255	7.0197	6.7327	6.4632	6.2098	5.9713	5.7466	5.5348	5.3349	4.9676	4.6389	4.4873	4.3436	4.0776	3.8372	3.4212	3.0758	2.7860
9	8.5660	8.1622	7.7861	7.4353	7.1078	6.8017	6.5152	6.2469	5.9952	5.7590	5.3282	4.9464	4.7716	4.6065	4.3030	4.0310	3.5655	3.1842	2.8681
10	9.4713	8.9826	8.5302	8.1109	7.7217	7.3601	7.0236	6.7101	6.4177	6.1446	5.6502	5.2161	5.0188	4.8332	4.4941	4.1925	3.6819	3.2689	2.9304
11	10.3676	9.7858	9.2526	8.7605	8.3064	7.8869	7.4987	7.1390	6.8052	6.4951	5.9377	5.4527	5.2337	5.0286	4.6560	4.3271	3.7757	3.3351	2.9776
12	11.2551	10.5753	9.9540	9.3851	8.8633	8.3838	7.9427	7.5361	7.1607	6.8137	6.1944	5.6603	5.4206	5.1971	4.7932	4.4392	3.8514	3.3868	3.0133
13	12.1337	11.3484	10.6350	9.9856	9.3936	8.8527	8.3577	7.9038	7.4889	7.1034	6.4235	5.8424	5.5831	5.3423	4.9095	4.5327	3.9124	3.4272	3.0404
14	13.0037	12.1062	11.2961	10.5631	9.8986	9.2950	8.7455	8.2442	7.7862	7.3667	6.6282	6.0021	5.7245	5.4675	5.0081	4.6106	3.9616	3.4587	3.0609
15	13.8651	12.8493	11.9379	11.1184	10.3797	9.7122	9.1079	8.5595	8.0607	7.6061	6.8109	6.1422	5.8474	5.5755	5.0916	4.6755	4.0013	3.4834	3.0764
16	14.7179	13.5777	12.5611	11.6523	10.8378	10.1059	9.4466	8.8514	8.3126	7.8237	6.9740	6.2651	5.9542	5.6685	5.1724	4.7296	4.0333	3.5026	3.0882
17	15.5623	14.2919	13.1661	12.1657	11.2741	10.4773	9.7632	9.1216	8.5436	8.0216	7.1196	6.3729	6.0472	5.7487	5.2223	4.7746	4.0591	3.5177	3.0971
18	16.3983	14.9920	13.7535	12.6593	11.6896	10.8276	10.0591	9.3719	8.7556	8.2014	7.2497	6.4674	6.1280	5.8178	5.2732	4.8122	4.0799	3.5294	3.1039
19	17.2260	15.6785	14.3238	13.1339	12.0853	11.1581	10.3356	9.6036	8.9501	8.3649	7.3658	6.5504	6.1982	5.8775	5.3162	4.8435	4.0967	3.5386	3.1090
20	18.0456	16.3514	14.8775	13.5903	12.4622	11.4699	10.5940	9.8181	9.1285	8.5436	7.4694	6.6231	6.2593	5.9288	5.3527	4.8696	4.1103	3.5458	3.1129
25	22.0232	19.5235	17.4131	15.6221	14.0939	12.7834	11.6536	10.6748	9.8226	9.0770	7.8431	6.8729	6.4641	6.0971	5.4669	4.9476	4.1474	3.5640	3.1220
30	25.8077	22.3965	19.6004	17.2920	15.3725	13.7648	12.4090	11.2578	10.2737	9.4269	8.0552	7.0072	6.5660	6.1772	5.5168	4.9789	4.1601	3.5693	3.1242
40	32.8347	27.3555	23.1148	19.7928	17.1591	15.0463	13.3317	11.9246	10.7574	9.7791	8.2438	7.1050	6.6418	6.2335	5.5482	4.9966	4.1659	3.5712	3.1250
50	39.1961	31.4236	25.7298	21.4822	18.2559	15.7619	13.8007	12.2335	10.9617	9.9148	8.3045	7.1327	6.6605	6.2463	5.5541	4.9995	4.1666	3.5714	3.1250
60	44.9550	34.7609	27.8756	22.6235	18.9293	16.1614	14.0392	12.3766	11.0480	9.9672	8.3240	7.1401	6.6651	6.2492	5.5553	4.9999	4.1667	3.5714	3.1250

Appendix D

Future Value of an Annuity of $1

Number of Periods	1%	2%	3%	4%	5%	6%	7%	8%	9%	10%	12%	14%	15%	16%	18%	20%	24%	28%	32%	36%
1	1.0000	1.0000	1.0000	1.0000	1.0000	1.0000	1.0000	1.0000	1.0000	1.0000	1.0000	1.0000	1.0000	1.0000	1.0000	1.0000	1.0000	1.0000	1.0000	1.0000
2	2.0100	2.0200	2.0300	2.0400	2.0500	2.0600	2.0700	2.0800	2.0900	2.1000	2.1200	2.1400	2.1500	2.1600	2.1800	2.2000	2.2400	2.2800	2.3200	2.3600
3	3.0301	3.0604	3.0909	3.1216	3.1525	3.1836	3.2149	3.2464	3.2781	3.3100	3.3744	3.4396	3.4725	3.5056	3.5724	3.6400	3.7776	3.9184	4.0624	4.2096
4	4.0604	4.1216	4.1836	4.2465	4.3101	4.3746	4.4399	4.5061	4.5731	4.6410	4.7793	4.9211	4.9934	5.0665	5.2154	5.3680	5.6842	6.0156	6.3624	6.7251
5	5.1010	5.2040	5.3091	5.4163	5.5256	5.6371	5.7507	5.8666	5.9847	6.1051	6.3528	6.6101	6.7424	6.8771	7.1542	7.4416	8.0484	8.6999	9.3983	10.146
6	6.1520	6.3081	6.4684	6.6330	6.8019	6.9753	7.1533	7.3359	7.5233	7.7156	8.1152	8.5355	8.7537	8.9775	9.4420	9.9299	10.980	12.135	13.405	14.798
7	7.2135	7.4343	7.6625	7.8983	8.1420	8.3938	8.6540	8.9228	9.2004	9.4872	10.089	10.730	11.066	11.413	12.141	12.915	14.615	16.533	18.695	21.126
8	8.2857	8.5830	8.8923	9.2142	9.5491	9.8975	10.259	10.636	11.028	11.435	12.299	13.232	13.726	14.240	15.327	16.499	19.122	22.163	25.678	29.731
9	9.3685	9.7546	10.159	10.582	11.026	11.491	11.978	12.487	13.021	13.579	14.775	16.085	16.785	17.518	19.085	20.798	24.712	29.369	34.895	41.435
10	10.462	10.949	11.463	12.006	12.577	13.180	13.816	14.486	15.192	15.937	17.548	19.337	20.303	21.321	23.521	25.958	31.643	38.592	47.061	57.351
11	11.566	12.168	12.807	13.486	14.206	14.971	15.783	16.645	17.560	18.531	20.654	23.044	24.349	25.732	28.755	32.150	40.237	50.398	63.121	78.998
12	12.682	13.412	14.192	15.025	15.917	16.869	17.888	18.977	20.140	21.384	24.133	27.270	29.001	30.850	34.931	39.580	50.894	65.510	84.320	108.43
13	13.809	14.680	15.617	16.626	17.713	18.882	20.140	21.495	22.953	24.522	28.029	32.088	34.351	36.786	42.218	48.496	64.109	84.852	112.30	148.47
14	14.947	15.973	17.086	18.291	19.598	21.015	22.550	24.214	26.019	27.975	32.392	37.581	40.504	43.672	50.818	59.195	80.496	109.61	149.23	202.92
15	16.096	17.293	18.598	20.023	21.578	23.276	25.129	27.152	29.360	31.772	37.279	43.842	47.580	51.659	60.965	72.035	100.81	141.30	197.99	276.97
16	17.257	18.639	20.156	21.824	23.657	25.672	27.888	30.324	33.003	35.949	42.753	50.980	55.717	60.925	72.939	87.442	126.01	181.86	262.35	377.69
17	18.430	20.012	21.761	23.697	25.840	28.212	30.840	33.750	36.973	40.544	48.883	59.117	65.075	71.673	87.068	105.93	157.25	233.79	347.30	514.66
18	19.614	21.412	23.414	25.645	28.132	30.905	33.999	37.450	41.301	45.599	55.749	68.394	75.836	84.140	103.74	128.11	195.99	300.25	459.44	700.93
19	20.810	22.840	25.116	27.761	30.539	33.760	37.379	41.446	46.018	51.159	63.439	78.969	88.211	98.603	123.41	154.74	244.03	385.32	607.47	954.27
20	22.019	24.297	26.870	29.778	33.066	36.785	40.995	45.762	51.160	57.275	72.052	91.024	102.44	115.37	146.62	186.68	303.60	494.21	802.86	1298.8
21	23.239	25.783	28.676	31.969	35.719	39.992	44.865	50.442	56.764	64.002	81.698	104.76	118.81	134.84	174.02	225.02	377.46	633.59	1060.7	1767.3
22	24.471	27.299	30.536	34.248	38.505	43.392	49.005	55.456	62.873	71.402	92.502	120.43	137.63	157.41	206.34	271.03	469.05	811.99	1401.2	2404.6
23	25.716	28.845	32.452	36.617	41.430	46.995	53.436	60.893	69.531	79.543	104.60	138.29	159.27	183.60	244.48	326.23	582.62	1040.3	1850.6	3271.3
24	26.973	30.421	34.426	39.082	44.502	50.815	58.176	66.764	76.789	88.497	118.15	158.65	184.16	213.97	289.49	392.48	723.46	1332.6	2443.8	4449.9
25	28.243	32.030	36.459	41.645	47.727	54.864	63.249	73.105	84.700	98.347	133.33	181.87	212.79	249.21	342.60	471.98	898.09	1706.8	3226.8	6052.9
26	29.525	33.670	38.553	44.311	51.113	59.156	68.676	79.954	93.323	109.18	150.33	208.33	245.71	290.08	405.27	567.37	1114.6	2185.7	4260.4	8233.0
27	30.820	35.344	40.709	47.084	54.669	63.705	74.483	87.350	102.72	121.09	169.37	238.49	283.56	337.50	479.22	681.85	1383.1	2798.7	5624.7	11197.9
28	32.129	37.051	42.930	49.967	58.402	68.528	80.697	95.338	112.96	134.20	190.69	272.88	327.10	392.50	566.48	819.22	1716.0	3583.3	7425.6	15230.2
29	32.450	38.792	45.218	52.966	62.322	73.689	87.346	103.96	124.13	148.63	214.58	312.09	377.16	456.30	669.44	984.06	2128.9	4587.6	9802.9	20714.1
30	34.784	40.568	47.576	56.084	66.438	79.058	94.460	113.28	136.30	164.49	241.33	356.78	434.74	530.31	790.94	1181.8	2640.9	5873.2	12940	28172.2
40	48.886	60.402	75.401	95.025	120.79	154.76	199.63	259.05	337.88	442.59	767.09	1342.0	1779.0	2360.7	4163.2	7343.8	22728	63977	*	*
50	64.463	84.579	112.79	152.66	209.34	290.33	406.52	573.76	815.08	1163.9	2400.0	4994.5	7217.7	10435	21813	45497	*	*	*	*
60	81.669	114.05	163.05	237.90	353.58	533.12	813.52	1253.2	1944.7	3034.8	7471.6	18535	29219	46057	*	*	*	*	*	*

*FVIFA > 99.999

Index